CORPORATE FINANCIAL REPORTING
Public or Private Control?

By Robert Chatov

- Why are the standards of corporate financial reporting—empowered to the Securities and Exchange Commission—now controlled by a private accounting group?
- How have the accounting profession and the financial-industrial sector made use of this power?
- How have alternative accounting techniques encouraged speculation, made meaningless the SEC's financial disclosure policy, and facilitated the continuing concentration of industrial assets?
- What aspects of the U.S. institutional structure have guaranteed this failure of the regulatory process?

This fascinating—and sometimes alarming—account is concerned with why and how a public authority is being privately administered. Focusing on the deliberate manipulation of corporate financial reporting rules resulting from the surrender of part of the SEC's regulatory power to the private sector, author Robert Chatov provides a new perspective on corporate-financial affairs of the last forty years.

Corporate Financial Reporting investigates the question of financial reporting methods against the background of the modern conglomerate merger movement, and the interaction of the self-regulating accounting profession with the SEC. Using legal, historical, economic, and sociological analysis, the author examines this problem comprehensively, not as a simple power

CORPORATE FINANCIAL REPORTING

Public or Private Control?

Robert Chatov

play, but as a system event, a social process working itself out in the financial arena over a long period of time. This approach offers insights that guide Chatov's recommendations for structural changes in the present system of financial reporting.

This book provides a uniquely critical view of the pivotal role of the accounting profession within the U.S. financial system. Accounting procedures are too often invisible phenomena with an enormous impact on the economy and on U.S. public policy. *Corporate Financial Reporting* reveals some of the unseen forces that have shaped our present economic condition, and it imparts a sense of urgency to the question, *"public or private control?"*

About the Author
ROBERT CHATOV is Assistant Professor in the Department of Environmental Analysis and Policy at the School of Management, State University of New York at Buffalo. He did graduate study at Northwestern University in economic history, and received his law degree from Wayne State University in 1957 and his Ph.D. from the Graduate School of Business Administration, University of California at Berkeley, in 1973. Chatov has been a member of the state bar of Michigan since 1958. From 1951 to 1968, he held positions in the Product and Marketing staffs of the Ford Motor Company.

THE FREE PRESS

Publishing Co., Inc.

NEW YORK

er Macmillan Publishers

LONDON

The Free Press
A Division of Macmillan Publishing Co., Inc.
866 Third Avenue, New York, N.Y. 10022

Collier–Macmillan Canada Ltd.

Library of Congress Catalog Card Number: 74–15368

Printed in the United States of America

printing number
1 2 3 4 5 6 7 8 9 10

Library of Congress Cataloging in Publication Data

Chatov, Robert.
  Corporate financial reporting.

  Bibliography: p.
  Includes index.
  1. Accounting--History--United States. 2. United States. Securities and Exchange Commission. 3. Financial statements--United States. I. Title.
HF5616.U5C47   658.1'512   74-15368
ISBN 0-02-905410-9

To the Memory of My Father

Abraham Chatov

and for My Mother

Esther Chatov

contents

dards Authority within the Private Sector / Why the SEC
Failure? / The FASB and the Transfer of Power to the
Corporate Sector / Specialization, Industrialization, and
the Growth of Power

preface

Whether or not we prefer it, government regulation is pervasive and likely to become more so because of the need to coordinate an industrial society inexorably growing more specialized and complex. A key regulatory device employed during the last century is the independent regulatory agency (IRA). Disillusion with the operation of these regulatory units is widespread, and on the increase. A significant cause for the present dissatisfaction with IRAs is the growing realization that their impacts extend far beyond the immediate influence on their regulatees—for example, that trucks returning empty waste fuel and that, as this study demonstrates, abrogation of responsibility to set rules of corporate financial reporting promotes increased concentration of industrial assets, hence, power. The present controversy over IRAs dramatizes the contrast between the expectations and realities of their behavior, and also demonstrates our limited understanding of these units.

Theories about IRA behavior cover a spectrum running from protection of the public interest on the one hand, to Marxian conspiracy notions on the other, with "capture" and "cartel" theories somewhere between. There is some basis for all of these approaches, but no single one provides a satisfactory model for all IRA behavior. This situation is unfortunate, because a reliable theory of IRA behavior is desperately needed if their operations are to be made both effective and tolerable. But before that can happen, more research and analysis are required.

This study has two objectives. It is an attempt to add to the knowledge of independent regulatory agency behavior by focusing on a particular agency—the Securities and Exchange Commission (SEC)—in its interaction with other groups within the financial-industrial sector. Primary stress is upon the SEC's relation with the American Institute of Certified Public Accountants (AICPA), the nation's most influential organization of professional accountants, and the AICPA's attempts to develop rules for corporate financial reporting. The second objective is directed toward public policy analysis, and is intended to explain how the by-product of the relation of the SEC with its fellow financial-industrial sector units made a colossal impact upon financial markets and so furthered the continuing process of American industrial concentration. This book, then, is both an analysis of organizations and organizational interaction, and an investigation of public policy formation, implementation, and effects.

The study began in 1969 when I took an extended (later permanent) leave from Ford Motor Company, where I worked since 1951, and entered the doctoral program at the University of California, Berkeley, Graduate School of Business Administration. It was a refreshing change except for an assault upon reason, which made me an innocent inhaler of tear gas on the campus within two months of leaving the quiet Central Marketing Staff in Dearborn. Still, doing doctoral work at Berkeley gave opportunity to investigate another apparent assault upon reason: the conglomerate merger movement. The speculative aspects of the conglomerate merger movement were marvelous to contemplate.

After a long, upward ride during the 1960s, the stock market dropped precipitously in 1969. Former high-flying stocks fell into disrepute as their earnings evaporated more quickly than they had grown during the previous years of frenzied market speculation. And why had not the excessive speculative activity attracted the attention of one or more concerned IRAs?

Why had the antitrust agencies not acted? As a lawyer I knew the Justice Department and the Federal Trade Commission (FTC) had legislative license to look into possible anticompetitive activity, but investigation showed that the antitrust agencies had dealt themselves out of the picture. The Justice Department was convinced that the antitrust provision most likely to contain the conglomerate craze, Section 7 of the Clayton Antitrust Act (forbidding mergers likely to result in a substantial lessening of competition) could not touch conglomerate mergers. This perspective was held during the Johnson administration, when the antitrust chief was Donald F. Turner, Harvard Law professor and economist. Richard W. McLaren, the antitrust chief under the Nixon administration, was willing to try Section 7 on a new theory featuring a variant of potential market reciprocity based on asset power, but he was squelched by Attorney General John Mitchell for reasons that are still murky.

In any event, it became evident that the conglomerate merger movement was an accounting-financial event, and the implicated agency was the Securities and Exchange Commission. The primary device used to further the worst speculative aspects of the conglomerate merger movement was an accounting technique: the pooling of interests method of accounting for a business combination. The SEC had the authority to limit or halt the use of this device, but had not done so. Instead, the SEC looked to a private group to act—the AICPA, which had a body to pass on matters pertaining to accounting "principles," the Accounting Principles Board (APB). The APB, however, was not doing anything about the conglomerate merger movement either.

How had a private body gotten a public authority in the first place? Obviously, the conglomerate merger movement was a *very complex event*, the key to which was the dominant institutional arrangements in the financial-industrial sector. The investigation became a major part of my doctoral work, and was completed in November, 1973.

I was delighted that The Free Press, through editor-in-chief Charles E. Smith, thought the topic important enough and the analysis good enough to want to publish a revised manuscript based on my study, from which substantial changes have been made. The description of the early years of the accounting profession has been shortened. Much of the background on the 1920s, the crash, and its aftermath has been condensed. Many quotations have been eliminated, attentuated, or placed in notes following chapters. Some views expressed in the dissertation have been revised, and new material has been added, including a chapter on the prospects for the new private sector group now in charge of corporate financial reporting rules, and another on a suggested revision of the entire present structure of the development and interpretation of those financial regulations.

The problem analyzed in this book is very serious, although some of the incidents described have their humorous sides as well. There are bizarre reversals of role, reckless comments made by certain principals and surprising twists evident at many stages. Nevertheless, the problem is of desperate importance to many.

I hope that few will be offended by observations they will find here. The accountants, "in my opinion" a likable but thin-skinned group, are most likely to be angered. I am sorry if they are. No insult is intended. I have an advantage in this study because I am *not* an accountant and therefore can look at the events of the past forty or so years with less commitment to a particular perspective than one whose professional group is closely involved. Those associated with the SEC and thus heir to a tradition of subordination to the private sector will also forgive, I hope, any judgments that may appear too harsh.

My approach is socio-historical, imbued with a legal and economic perspective. I was interested in the total regulatory process, the operation of social and political controls, and the second and third impacts of a dramatic event in its own right. I hope the book sparks the kind of vigorous debate involving the general public the subject deserves but has not thus far generated.

I have tried to eliminate jargon—sociological, legal, and otherwise—from the book. I think I have succeeded, but I apologize for occasional slips. Because so many different groups and organizations are involved whose identification demands initials, I have provided a key for ready reference following this Preface. The notations in the text explain my reference immediately, without necessitating a glance elsewhere. For example, the notation (Landis, 1935a:18) indicates that the source of the statement was something written by James M. Landis, in 1935, item a, on page 18. A full reference appears in the bibliography. I mention this because the style of reference used is common in some academic journals, but not yet general in semi-technical books. Notes, where used, are included at the end of each chapter.

Chapters 1–3 discuss the importance of the power to control the development of rules for corporate financial reporting, how this function was handled before the creation of the SEC, and how regulation was placed upon a reluctant financial-industrial sector in 1933. Chapter 4 describes the development of professional accounting societies, and how they came to play an important role in the battle over revision of the Securities Act of 1933 that culminated in the Securities Exchange Act of 1934, described in chapters 5 and 6. In the 7th and 8th chapters I have detailed the process by which the SEC abandoned its powers over the development of corporate financial reporting standards by 1938. Chapters 9–11 discuss the results of the SEC abandonment of power to the private sector prior to World War II, and how the patterns established in those crucial years became institutionalized thereafter. Chapters 12–14 deal with the private sector's failures to formulate corporate financial standards, culminating in the debacle of the AICPA's Accounting Principles Board because of its performance during the conglomerate merger movement. Chapter 15 is devoted to an analysis of the most recent private sector group to administer financial reporting rules, the Financial Accounting Standards Board (FASB). Chapter 16 summarizes and concludes on the history of SEC-private sector interaction in a sociological interpretation of that event. Chapters 17 and 18, as mentioned on page xiii, discuss the merits of private versus public control of corporate financial reporting, and offer what I believe to be a more satisfactory alternative than the present arrangement.

Some thanks are in order. My gratitude is extended first to my patient and suffering (at times I so hoped) Ph.D. Committee at the University of California, Berkeley, who offered their guidance but not dictates, and who waded through more than 500 pages of material promptly and without whimper: Professor Dow Votaw, chairman of the committee, head of the Department of Social, Political, and Legal Environment of Business, and Professor Maurice Moonitz, of the Accounting Department, both of the Graduate School of Business Administration; Professor Richard M. Buxbaum, Boalt School of Law; and University Professor Neil J. Smelser, Department of Sociology—all first-rate people and scholars. Thanks are also due to Professors Philip Selznick and Philippe Nonet of the Center for the Study of Law and Society, University of California, Berkeley, for providing me with travel funds to pursue personal interviews.

Professor Lee E. Preston, my department head at the School of Management, State University of New York at Buffalo, was generous beyond the call of duty or friendship in providing me the atmosphere in which to complete the study and the book. Two particularly heroic typists deserve special mention: Mrs. Jo Galdon and Mrs. Irene Forster, both of whom displayed great cunning in deciphering my manuscripts at little loss in speed and accuracy. Several people had also read the dissertation earlier and offered comments, and so I thank Mr. Leonard Spacek, former Chairman of Arthur Andersen & Co., and some colleagues at the School of Management, State University of New York at Buffalo: Professor Robert Hagerman, who offered vig-

orous objection and constructive criticism; and Professor Ron
Huefner, who kindly reviewed some technical parts and offered important suggestions, as did Professor Meir Schneller. Others who
looked at a summary and offered comments or encouragement or
both include SEC Commissioner A. A. Sommer, Justice William O.
Douglas, and Alan E. Throop, Esq. Justice Douglas clarified some
points about the early operations of the SEC and the 3–2 split on the
Commission. Interviews were granted by Carman Blough, Benjamin
V. Cohen, Reed Storey, Mr. Throop, and one gentleman from among
the practitioners, who, after reading the summary, requested I not
mention his name because some of his friends would never understand. I respect his wishes, and hereby thank him also. My wife Phia
was appropriately prodding, patient, impatient, and supporting while
I waded through both dissertation and book, and honor and love
are due her for not resenting all the time given to the manuscripts.
Finally, my thanks to my son Justin, who arrived on January 1, 1973,
and who kept his colic and protests within reasonable limits, providing the pleasure of his company when further concentration was
impossible and future efforts demanded an immediate recess. Of
course, I accept exclusive responsibility for any faults or errors in
the book.

                                                              ROBERT CHATOV

Corporate Financial Reporting

key to abbreviations

AAA	American Association of Accountants (the academic branch, previously known as the AAUIA)
AAPA	American Association of Public Accountants (later the AIA)
AIA	American Institute of Accountants ("the Institute")
AICPA	The American Institute of Certified Public Accountants (successor to the AIA, also referred to as "the Institute")
APB	Accounting Principles Board
AR	*Accounting Review*
ARB	Accounting Research Bulletins (issued by the APB)
ARS	Accounting Research Study (issued by the APB)
ASCPA	American Society of Certified Public Accountants
ASR	Accounting Series Release (issued by the SEC)
CAP	Committee on Accounting Procedure
CASB	Cost Accounting Standards Board
CPA	*Certified Public Accountant*
FAF	Financial Accounting Foundation
FASAC	Financial Accounting Standards Advisory Committee
FASB	Financial Accounting Standards Board
FEI	Financial Executives Institute (formerly the Controllers Inst.)
FRB	Federal Reserve Board of Governors, or "The Fed"
FRS	Federal Reserve System
FTC	Federal Trade Commission
GAAPs	Generally accepted accounting principles
IBA	Investment Bankers Association
IRA	Independent regulatory agency
JA	*Journal of Accountancy*
NAA	National Association of Accountants (formerly the Nat'l Assn. of Cost Accountants, NACA)
NYCPAs	New York State Society of CPAs
NYSE	New York Stock Exchange
RFC	Reconstruction Finance Corporation
RMA	Robert Morris Associates
SEC	Securities and Exchange Commission
TFAF	The Financial Analysts Federation

The stakes are very high

The Contrast Between SEC Powers and SEC Behavior

When a new independent regulatory agency created by the United States Government transfers its most important authority back to the private groups it is supposed to control, it is an event deserving respectful attention. That is precisely what the Securities and Exchange Commission (SEC) did within three years of its initial operation. Founded in 1934, presumably to cure some of the ills believed to have precipitated the nation's worst financial disaster—begun with the stock crash of 1929—the SEC between 1936 and 1938 gave up its public mandate to develop corporate financial reporting standards to the private sector, which has retained that authority ever since. The event does not commend the SEC very highly, but it does demonstrate the resilience of the financial-industrial sector.

Federal control was placed over the securities exchanges and the corporations whose shares were traded on them by the Securities Act of 1933 and by the Securities Exchange Act of 1934. The 1934 act creating the SEC specified several objectives, among which were to provide investors with reliable information, to prevent stock price manipulation, and to discourage ruinous financial speculations that could hurt the economy.[1] To accomplish these objectives, the SEC was given power to determine the form, content, and accounting

1

rules governing the corporate financial reports to be filed with it.[2] These powers were adequate for the securities acts' objectives. But the SEC has utilized only a small part of its powers and so failed its mission. Instead, the powers that could be exercised by the SEC are administered by certain private sector groups whose primary aims are different from those of the securities acts. With each passing year, the public powers are more firmly entrenched within these private groups, becoming the accepted way of doing things. It is time that this arrangement be questioned and examined because the stakes involved for the nation at large, as well as for the immediate participants, are high. *Very* high.

The failure of the SEC became completely apparent because of its incapacity to curtail the accounting abuses that facilitated the conglomerate merger movement of the 1960s. An accounting technique called pooling of the interests was adopted by the practicing accountants of the American Institute of Certified Public Accountants (AICPA) and sanctioned by the SEC. Pooling of interests allowed a firm that was the product of a merger with another company to show per share earnings greater than those of either firm before the merger. Merger, rather than economic efficiency, became the route toward earnings growth for many companies that became the "glamour" darlings of the market. The accountants of the AICPA, presumably in charge of developing "generally accepted accounting principles" (GAAPs), were aware of what was happening—they had invented the device—but were unwilling or unable to halt abuses of the practice. Throughout this entire period, the SEC stood by ineptly, figuratively shuffling from foot to foot, all the while muttering vague, ritual threats about "doing something" or about "stepping in" if the accountants "failed to act."

The scenario describing the transfer of authority from the SEC to the accountants had all the qualities of a low farce. Indeed, it would have been funny had it not been for its second- and third-level economic, social, and political effects. Speculation was still permitted to run unchecked, and the collapse of the stock market in 1969 was probably in some measure due to the fact that the golden edge of the conglomerate stocks finally rubbed off. Small investors withdrew from the market in numbers sufficient to affect the business of a substantial amount of stock-brokerage firms, many of which failed in the market slide following 1969. A significant group of glamorous conglomerates of the 1960s, like LTV, Boise-Cascade, and Gulf and Western, found themselves transformed into overleveraged firms of the 1970s, scrambling to divest themselves of the acquisitions they had so happily pursued short years before.

There were social costs as well. Executives and their families were uprooted as managements were folded into each other or the managers of the acquired firm were fired after a brief period of time. Numerous small firms previously located outside major metropolitan areas found their headquarters transferred to centers like New York, Chicago, and Los Angeles, the local area losing an important, autonomous citizen. Although the physical operation remained, the civic dedication of local management was lost. And the presumed offset of the added efficiency of sophisticated management, which had been affirmed by conglomerators using the magic catchword "synergism" —that is, getting more than the sum of the individual parts—proved to be as much of an illusion as the earnings produced by the pooling of interests technique.

As if these effects were not enough, the conglomerate merger movement had a further economic-political impact by accelerating the concentration of industrial *assets* to levels unattained in any previous merger movements. This type of concentration is considerably different from what economists refer to as "market" concentration, which refers to the number or percent of companies holding given shares of a defined market. Whether the conglomerate merger movement increased market concentration is a debated point; it should not have done so. The antitrust decisions of the United States Supreme Court in the early 1960s definitively extended Section 7 of the Clayton Act to mergers likely to result in substantially decreased competition, thereby forcing acquisitions into noncompatible markets. Some anticompetitive effects may have taken place anyhow, because of the possibility of reciprocal arrangements being made among the disparate elements of a far-reaching conglomerate, but whether or not this happened remains conjectural.[3]

What is not conjectural is that the control of industrial assets now lies in fewer hands because the major portion of these assets are concentrated in fewer groups. Supreme Court antitrust interpretations say that size in and of itself is not illegal. But it is questionable whether increasingly large enclaves of monetary resources and power are desirable in a democracy already characterized by numerous politically influential interest groups. How one feels about power concentration depends, of course, on the observer's view of what an ideal political body ought to be, and, perhaps, on how much of the power one controls and of what benefit it is personally.

The Pivotal Importance of Financial Standards
Rule Making Authority

For members of the financial-industrial sector, the value of controlling the authority to determine corporate financial reporting standards is difficult to overestimate. To the uninitiated this authority may appear esoteric, unimportant, or unfathomable, but in reality the development of rules for financial reporting represents a pivotal function in the control, amassing, and redistribution of wealth in the United States. Not only have methods of accounting for business combinations provided the manipulative, technical device for the conglomerate merger movement, but accounting treatment, favorably applied, has provided a key to control corporate profits and valuation. Permission to use alternative accounting methods has offered opportunities to tailor accounting treatment to the needs of individual firms. The less stringent the required accounting treatment, the greater the flexibility in reporting corporate accounts. And the greater the discretion available to the accountant, the greater the value of his services to the client. Accounting practitioners, therefore, have always vigorously opposed inflexible accounting requirements, though they have taken care to couch their opposition in terms of violations of assumed legitimate professional prerogatives and the "unsoundness" of strict accounting rules.

Both accountants and their corporate clients worked hard and successfully to keep the SEC from exercising financial accounting controls. Between 1938 and 1972, the AICPA had de facto authority over generally accepted accounting principles, but the desire of its members to avoid limitations on their freedom to choose among accounting alternatives guaranteed that the AICPA would do a mediocre job at best in its attempt to develop effective principles. After the AICPA failure became completely evident, authority for the development of accounting principles, now institutionalized in the private sector, did not revert to the SEC. Instead, the authority was assumed by a new group composed of representatives from self-selected private organizations.

Corporate financial reporting standards presently are administered by a three-tiered organization drawn almost exclusively from accounting practitioners, industrial corporations, financial analysts, and accounting "educators." At the time of the organization's initial announcement, its structure and composition looked like this:[4]

Financial Accounting Foundation(FAF)

Nine trustees:
     5 accounting practitioners
     3 from the corporate-financial sector
     1 accounting educator
who:
     (1) appoint members of the Financial Accounting Stan-
           dards Board (FASB), and
     (2) raise money for its support.

Financial Accounting Standards Board (FASB)

Seven members:
     4 accounting practitioners
     3 others "well versed in problems of financial reporting."
        Presently includes people drawn from the corporate finan-
        cial executives, accounting educators, and the Federal
        Government Accountants Association.
who:
     (1) establish standards of financial accounting and present
           them as a guide to users and issuers of financial state-
           ments and CPAs, and
     (2) appoint task forces to study specific problems.

Financial Accounting Standards Advisory Council (FASAC)

Twenty seven members:
     6 from public-accounting firms
     5 from corporations
     8 from the financial sector
     3 from academe
     2 from law firms
     2 from government
     1 ex-chief SEC accountant
who:
     (1) are named by the FAF, and
     (2) consist of persons with skills valuable to the FASB.

Accountants now quite clearly share authority for setting financial standards with people from the financial and corporate sectors. Representation of people with present or past government affiliation is minimal, consisting of only one person on the FASB and two persons on the FASAC. Oddly enough, this entire private organization was created with the specific approval of the SEC.

The existence of the three-tiered, private financial standards group is a tribute to the often bizarre manner in which federal independent regulatory agencies malfunction. The private sector groups which subsequently dominated the financial standards organization held "hearings" prior to its formation, but there was no broad public debate over the plan. It was reported in the financial press, though little attention seems to have been paid to the event by Congress. The issue of whether the FAF-FASB-FASAC organization could legitimately exercise public functions appears never to have come up. What is probably one of the most amazing episodes in the administration of U.S. public policy took place in an unquestioning atmosphere.

The sanctioning by the SEC of private sector administration of accounting rulemaking can be regarded as a significant failure of the independent regulatory agency system. The initial transfer of authority to the accounting practitioners between 1936 and 1938 was certainly unfortunate, and probably improper. Was congressional permission of the recent arrangement between the SEC, the AICPA, and others an oversight? Was the arrangement deliberately ignored because the interests involved were too powerful to handle? Or was it just simply lack of comprehension by Congress of the issues involved? Why was the authority for promulgating rules of financial reporting, an authority with the potential of having an enormous economic impact, given to a private group whose administration of that responsibility was complicated not only by a conflict of interests and vulnerability to strenuous client pressures on the part of the accounting practitioners, but also included the clients themselves?

Major conflict of interest problems arise when accounting principles are developed by the very group that engages in the day-to-day business of administering those principles (especially now that accounting firms also offer management-consulting services) and whose interpretation of those principles directly influences the profits and stock value of the client corporation. A crude comparison can be made with the justice of the peace system, which is equally suspect because of the predictable results of permitting the administrator of justice to have a financial stake in the outcome. The interests of the administrators of financial reporting standards and the operation of that system have been and will continue to be highly correlated, at least in the absence of unexpected stupidity, which is too much to ask for inasmuch as the people involved constitute as keen a collection of talent as found in the United States. Chicanery or malevolence is not a prerequisite for congruence of interests and decisions; ideology, with its self-deluding possibilities, will do as well, if not better.

The issue, very simply, is self regulation, with all of its hazards, versus some form of government regulation or legislation, with all of *its* hazards. The present situation has placed massive responsibility for corporate financial reporting standards with the self-selected three-tiered private group, and kept the SEC in a subsidiary position. Ought the system to be maintained that way? The question needs close study for a variety of reasons that center on performance and legitimacy :

- The private sector groups may not have a legitimate right to control corporate financial reporting standards. Did the SEC make an actual delegation of authority as sweeping as the mandate assumed by the private sector, and did the SEC have the right to delegate that authority?
- Because the private sector groups now responsible for setting financial standards are similar in composition to those previously controlling GAAP authority, it is likely that their operations will be a continuation of the unsatisfactory administration of those standards.
- Reversion of financial standards authority to the private sector was not the result of a conscious public policy; it happened, but has never been seriously questioned. It is too essential a function to be administered by a group without official, defined responsibility to the larger society. The Congress has administrative responsibility over the SEC; it has none over the FAF, FASB, and FASAC groups.
- Even if the private sector should administer financial standards, the question remains, which private sector organizations ought to be included? The exclusion of many private institutions from participation in the FAF, FASB, and FASAC organizations demands reflection; only a self-selected, limited part of the private sector presently controls financial standards. But other groups, for example, like the American Economic Association, have a legitimate professional interest in administering financial standards. Among government components, the Commerce Department, the Council of Economic Advisers, as well as the Office of Management and Budget, all have vital interests involved in

corporate financial reporting standards. The list of interested and affected professional, academic, and government bodies is not infinite, but it is long. The present incumbents should be required to defend their roles.

· The function of setting and administering corporate financial reporting standards is esoteric, done far from the attention of the public, with only those trained in the area able to understand the results of the process. The function is too important to be so removed from general understanding and scrutiny; it deserves broad publicity.

· Corporate profit data is used frequently for economic analysis and as the basis for making government decisions. It is almost certain that major biases exist in reported profit data, which undermine their uses for either analyses or decisions. Comparing the profits of one corporation with another or one industry's profits with another's is probably meaningless because of the wide variety of financial reporting standards and alternatives applied. If that is true, and biases in corporate data occur because of the manner in which a corporation's accounting rules are formulated, then there is an overriding public interest in reviewing the developmental process of corporate financial reporting standards.

· Some scholars argue that the data made available for investors through the interaction of the SEC and the private sector have been useless for investment purposes. This allegation deserves consideration. If true, the system certainly requires a thorough overhaul.

· The inability of the SEC to repress major speculative waves demands that the present process of accounting control be revaluated to determine the degree to which the transfer of financial standards authority to the private sector contributed to that failure.

· SEC performance has broad implications for government regulatory operations. The SEC has long had the reputation of being the "jewel" of the independent regulatory agency system. If the SEC performance is ineffective, it may indicate the IRA concept is hopeless and ought to be abandoned for another type of government control mechanism.

· The present system of accounting, which probably maximizes the purposes of one group—that is, the corporate-financial group—is probably marginal for the larger social system. If the present system has too many biases and ought to be revised, what are the best alternatives and from which points of view?

The process of developing existing corporate financial standards came about without design. Perhaps it was an accident. Perhaps also it was inevitable. The present system may be the best or only available alternative, given the level of accounting art, the lack of government objectives, and the political power of those who possess the rule-making authority over corporate financial standards. Nevertheless, the issue demands examination. Many view the present arrangement as constituting a private usurpation of public authority, one that ought to be justified by those responsible for it.

Private Control of Public Functions

It is usual in the United States that private groups control important public functions. Private sector operation of the economy is a persistent American ideal. Opposition to government controls is always strong. Whenever a major function is taken over by the public from the private sector, the latter struggles tenaciously before surrendering possession. On the basis of past experience in government control, those arguing for it can demonstrate little gained efficiency or equity to justify their position, and those who want to retain private sector control are quick to point this out. Independent regulatory agencies, like the SEC, Interstate Commerce Commission (ICC), and Federal Trade Commission (FTC), operate either as cartel agents or as crippled sanction mechanisms that enjoy, at best, only periodic moments of control. Grand congressional welfare plans have had little effect; efforts to "fine tune" the economy have had mediocre results. The cost overruns of the military, for example, are frequently horrendous.

There is, indeed, much wrong with government controls, and there are schools of thought that make a career of pushing the point. But expanding economies with increasingly complex and specialized operations require coordination. Where private, ad hoc mechanisms break down, government controls must be instituted.

The development of corporate financial standards in the United States is only one instance of the private administration of functions that have a strong public interest. The pitfalls of permitting the private industrial sector to determine alone both product and output was dramatically illustrated in the 1973 oil crisis when the government realized it had no reliable planning data on the oil industry. A less obvious but important private exercise of a public function is profes-

sional licensing. Attorneys, accountants, physicians, physical thera-
pists, and pharmacists, among others, establish their own acceptance
standards; these determinations are officially sanctioned by the states.
This procedure has certain advantages and disadvantages. The state
escapes the expense of administering professional standards, but the
price it pays is restricted entry into the self-regulated fields; its sanctioning of professional monopolies tends to restrict its control and
raise prices. Some private upgrading of professional standards does
occur, but no one can assert for certain whether the standards would
be lower, higher, or the same under government supervision. The
problem with self-regulating groups is that they lack scrutiny by a
public institution politically powerful enough and sufficiently independent to act in a vigorous adversary capacity. The inevitable cry
of the self-regulated body against public pressure is governmental
"harassment," governmental "failure to cooperate" with the industry
or profession, governmental inability "to understand" its problems.
Some of these protests are mere charades; others are very real. Struggles between the private and public sectors have been bitter, and the
history of the SEC in its encounter with the accountants and other
members of the financial-industrial sector is certainly representative
of these struggles, particularly in its early years.

Dramatic public-private encounters take place when a seques-
tered but key function of the private sector is given to a public group
for administration, and, as in the case of the SEC and the accountants,
where the public administration of that function is partially mandatory, partially optional. The private sector, unreconciled to the loss
of the treasured function, tries to regain it as the new commissioners
of the untested regulatory agency attempt to define the limits of their
authority, which are usually subject to a broad set of constraints.
Again in the case of the SEC, not only the accountants but other
members of the financial community and industrial sector were also
deeply involved and concerned. For all participants in the private sector, the stakes were high, though perhaps highest for the accountants.

The primary focus of this study is on the accounting profession,
upon the practitioners especially. They spearheaded the attack on the
SEC's powers in the years immediately following passage of the
Securities Exchange Act of 1934. They threatened, cajoled, and
balked the SEC over the issue of authority for developing generally
accepted accounting principles. Once they succeeded in obtaining it,
they administered that function exclusively for a generation until
forced to share it with other private groups in the early 1970s. They

remain a potent force, probably holding more prestige and power than any other group involved in corporate financial standards.

Accounting practitioners are highly sensitive about several subjects. For one, about their dependence on clients. For another, about their antagonism toward the SEC. For a third, about their ad hoc approach to the creation of generally accepted accounting principles. Fourth, about their dismal performance during the conglomerate merger movement. And fifth, about the potential conflict of interest between their auditing activities and their consulting services. Their touchiness is augmented by their inclination to take themselves with ultra-seriousness, demonstrated by a lack of humor as once noted by former SEC Chairman James M. Landis. They are not a forgiving group. For them, the stakes involve more than just client fees. Caught between responsibility to clients and their needs on the one hand, and civil liability to third parties and government requirements on the other, the accounting practitioners are in a position where it is difficult to maintain and demonstrate independence. They have always been faced with the need to define their primary responsibility in the face of the impracticability of trying to adopt a middle course. As a professional group, they are relative newcomers. Their newness places them at a disadvantage relative to their clients, particularly because accounting is an ancillary outgrowth of big business. Nevertheless, they have, through the AICPA, managed to contain the SEC throughout most of the latter's history.

No villains are depicted in this book; on the contrary, some, depending on their perspective of the events following 1933, will find heroes. What is described, however, is a vast system at work involving many thousands of people spread over three generations, a system that involves the control of the nation's economic and financial life. Vying for that control are representatives of the public and the private sectors. The struggle is dynamic. Powers change and shift. Some future options are conditioned by past events, while others are closed off.

The fight to control financial reporting conventions was and is a human event. It is a fight involving some of the most powerful forces in the nation: the corporate and financial interests and the highest levels of government. For the most part this struggle, or "arrangement" if one chooses to look at it that way, has gone unnoticed because of the technical nature of the subject (except for certain dramatic incidents like the Pecora investigation of banking and securities practices and the conglomerate merger movement). It does, after all, take considerable skill and interest to unravel financial statements and their significance.

Few instances of surprising behavior are revealed in this analysis. Those with great interests to protect, try to do so. Thus, the accountants and other members of the financial community attempt to keep the SEC from exercising its authority. The corporate sector pressures the accountants for a greater voice in the development of accounting principles. The SEC is anxious to avoid constant acrimony with the accountants. The accounting practitioners manage to keep the academic accountants "in their place." The academic accountants display less interest in actual accounting problems than in theoretical aspects of the same problem. The security analysts put pressure on the corporate sector for more information, and the corporate sector tries to release as little of it as it can.

Although all participants pursued their own interests, as they saw them, the entire event cannot be explained in such simple terms. Why, for example, did the present system of corporate financial reporting evolve as it did, rather than in some other way? What does this system mean for the future and for future alternatives? These are among the questions this book attempts to answer as it deals with the period of vicious encounters between America's private and public sectors in the tumultuous and changing atmosphere of the 1930s.

Notes

1.   Section 2 of the Securities Exchange Act of 1934 contained a lengthy statement on the "necessity for Regulation. . . ." See Appendix B for the specific provisions of Section 2.

2.   The sweeping financial reporting control authorities granted to the FTC and its successor, the SEC, largely were contained in the following provisions: Securities Act of 1933, Section 19; Securities and Exchange Act of 1934, Section 13. See Appendix B for specific provisions.

3.   See Chapter 13 for details.

4.   Drawn from the Financial Accounting Foundation Certificate of Incorporation and By-Laws, and the Financial Accounting Standards Board Rules of Procedure. See also Appendix A for details on membership composition of the original FASB and associated groups. Full references are in the bibliography.

Life without the Securities and Exchange Commission

The Stock Market Boom of the Late 1920s

The stock market boom was a swelling madness by 1928, an upward series of waves sucking into it investors who had never before purchased stocks. Even the market-easing backwash of each surge seemed to eddy out, touch and infect more people with the fantasy of near-instant riches. The speculative orgy probably started in mid-1924, an initial phase that ran until the setback of 1926. The boom picked up in 1927, aided by the Federal Reserve Board's increase in funds and lowered rediscount rate designed to aid distressed foreign currency. Herbert Hoover's election in 1928 only accentuated the movement by promising a continuation of laissez-faire economic policies. By 1929, the Fed was letting the boom go its own way.[1]

The Fed was caught in an uncomfortable position. The economy was in some trouble. The industrial area was showing weakness. Agriculture had been distressed all during the 1920s. To cool the stock market boom would require restricting the money supply, which in turn would likely slow the economy even further, which was something the Fed wanted to avoid. Also, technically, the Fed was in a poor position. Lacking securities, the Federal Reserve System could not soak up bank funds by selling in the open market, nor was it willing to dampen credit by severely raising interest rates. Nor did it attempt to restrain margin trading, then operating at the 10 percent level.

So the Fed steered a middle course, neither increasing funds to aid the weakening economy nor restricting funds to suppress market speculation. Thus the boom continued, overcoming even a lack of securities. The lack of securities, however, was a technical problem that the inventiveness of the financial and corporate sectors could solve easily. Solve it they did, thereby adding to the speculation—and, incidentally, pushing along the concentration of U.S. industry just a bit further. Two new devices were added to the set of equities eager purchasers could obtain: holding companies and investment trusts. These were something new, and they affected subsequent New Deal regulatory legislation. They deserve examination.

HOLDING COMPANIES

The 1897–1903 merger movement was typified by horizontal integration—mergers, for example, in steel, tobacco, and nickel. Consolidations of the 1920s operated along vertical as well as horizontal lines, but the holding companies characterized the merger movement of the twenties. Holding companies were used most frequently to centralize utility company management and control.

Huge corporate pyramids resulted when holding companies had shares in one or more layers of other holding companies, with an operating company somewhere at the base. The resulting structure was extremely unstable. Efficient operation was difficult. Financial plans were complex and revealed nothing about the finances of subsidiaries. Concentration of control was achieved through extensive borrowing. The complex organization made regulation difficult; some legal liabilities could be escaped and the agglomeration of firms permitted certain companies—banks, for instance—to carry on business otherwise forbidden. The failure to publish consolidated financial statements was one of the keys to the problem. (Mason, 1933: 465–467).

Criticism of the public utility holding companies of the twenties and early thirties resembles attacks on their spiritual conglomerate cousins some forty years later—namely, violation of sound intercorporate relationships; the draining of profitable subsidiaries of cash or credit; an "almost maniacal urge to show earnings, no matter from what source"; and defiance of conservative financing and accounting practices. Principles of valuation were bent to maximize current income, and public accountants were coerced into accepting valuation theories that violated their "plainest duties to the public." Holding company managements were arrogant, they shrouded their transactions with secrecy, and they were quick to demand that the government stay out of business whenever federal control was suggested. As the *Accounting Review* saw it, publicity of corporate affairs and responsible directors were needed (Editorial, *AR*, December, 1932: 303–305).

The overextended empires of the utility holding companies collapsed after the stock market crash. The cause was not lower earnings by the operating company, but "extravagant financial misrepresentation" (Dewing, 1953: 2:994). Three types of mismanagement were common. First, excessive prices were paid for good *and* bad operating companies as management competed for the properties. High prices made reasonable returns impossible. By 1928, hopelessly inflated values prevailed throughout the country for independent operating utilities (Ibid., p. 995).

Secondly, public utility holding companies included business activities, such as controlling natural gas properties (less significant at the time than presently) and retail ice companies, that had little relation to traditional utility operations. These unrelated enterprises were usually promoted by a banker who planned to profit from the increased value of the common stock, much of which he retained (Ibid., p. 996). The shareholder in this hybrid public utility company had no information suggesting his investment was based more on the earnings of an ice company than upon the electric utility company in which he thought he was investing. Accountants' certificates under these circumstances correctly reported the *consolidated* earnings, but because they did not disclose individual income sources the investor was completely deceived about the venture's risk. Firms relying on ice properties for earnings to pay bond interest and preferred share requirements characteristically failed during the depression. In any reorganization, the bond holders usually divided their interest evenly between the utility company's bonds and stock, discarding the ice company. The common and preferred shareholders, of course, got nothing (Ibid., fn. pp. 996–998).

Thirdly, several large utility holding companies were involved in unrelated fields about which their management knew nothing. These unrelated enterprises frequently had operating losses, thus draining the earnings and credit of the holding company (Ibid., p. 998).

INVESTMENT TRUSTS

The investment trust company was the most important financial technique of the late twenties adapted specifically to satisfy the demand for common stocks. Practically unknown in the United States before World War I, investment trusts originated in Great Britain in the 1870s, grew rapidly, but suffered setbacks in the nineties due to management frauds. At the close of the 1920s, even a serious underestimate of trusts and invested capital looked impressive to a contemporary writer, Walter Stegman—from 15 trusts with a $15 million capital in 1923 to 199 trusts with $400 million in capital in June, 1929. By then, investment bankers were heavily involved in new investment trust promotion and management (Stegman, 1929: 362). But the investment trusts were far more numerous and financially important than Stegman realized. There were about 160 beginning in 1927 and 300 at year's end; 186 more were organized in 1928 and 265 in 1929. Before the crash their estimated assets of securities in other companies were $8 billion (Hacker, 1970: 293).

Investment trusts gave small investors a chance to hold shares indirectly in a wide group of actively traded corporations. Total outstanding securities on the stock market were increased without any increase in total corporate assets. Investment trusts invested the excess of cash received minus purchased securities either in the call market or real estate. The promoters of trusts also profited. Investment trusts seldom disclosed holdings. The New York Stock Exchange permitted listing of trust companies in 1929, provided, however, an inventory of their holdings was submitted at the time they listed and each year thereafter—a requirement sufficient to keep most of them away from the NYSE.

Almost always, trust-sponsoring concerns included investment bankers, commercial banks, brokerage firms, securities dealers, and other investment trusts. Promoters received fees based on a percent of capital or trust earnings. Stock exchange firms sponsoring trusts received commissions on purchase and sale of trust securities, and the investment bankers involved were actually manufacturing securities they could then market, usually at premiums. Sponsors or promoters got stock or warrant allotments at the offering price, which they sold immediately at a profit that could be split with marketing dealers.

The use of leverage by the investment trust companies added to their vulnerability—and made the market more volatile. Increases in trust holdings were reflected primarily by an increase in the investment company common, which might be as low as one-third of its capital. Leverage created additional investment trusts whose primary assets were the common stocks of other investment trusts—a tactic that geometrically expanded values based on the original trust. The entire process, of course, worked the other way as well, and was a major deflationary force during the crash. Probably all the principal Wall Street investment houses were involved. It was an example, as John Galbraith put it, of "gargantuan insanity" (Galbraith, 1954:51–69).

Among the funds coming into the market that kept adding to the boom were the loans made to securities houses to cover margin purchases—that is, call or broker's loans. These totaled $1 billion in the early 1920s, $3.5 billion at the end of 1927, and $8 billion at the end of 1929. The funds were supplied by individuals and commercial banks and from foreign short term money attracted by high rates. The loans of interest brokers climbed from 5 percent to 12 percent in 1928 and to 20 percent in May, 1929. New securities issued by investment bankers and affiliates of commercial banks attracted money, too, and investment trust managers also entered the call market (Hacker, 1970: 293).

Accountants and the Crash

Caught in the midst of the speculative carnival—and very much involved in the preparation of financial statements circulated to gull investors—were the practicing and academic accountants. Were they alert to the growing danger of market collapse? Did they warn of financial excesses, spurious figures, and misleading statements? And after the crash took place, were they quick to reassess their responsibilities in light of the debacle? The answers to these questions, which need be asked to appraise the subsequent protestations of the accounting profession against government interference, offer a sad indictment.

Accounting and financial techniques were playing a critical role in the progress of the stock market boom, which was nothing new for either United States or European speculative movements. The famous "South Sea Bubble" of the early eighteenth century was partly based upon the expectations and reports of excessive earnings. In the nineteenth century, misleading asset statements and fanciful earnings projections helped American promoters attract generations of eager European investors (and fleece many of them) and supported overcapitalized industrial consolidations of the first U.S. merger movement.

What made the 1920s' stock market madness different was that for the first time in the history of U.S. financial speculations accountants were on hand as a recognized, organized, and presumably responsible professional body. They vigorously proclaimed their public responsibilities and functions. As it turned out, what they really meant was that their legal responsibility was to their client only, that their "public responsibility" was moral, not legal. Their influence over clients was considerably less than they liked to admit (Auld, 1929: 363). Liability to third persons stemming from representations made in auditors' certificates was a major concern that received attention at the time, from accountants (Fernald, 1929: 1–9), who nevertheless ignored the flimsy financial data supporting much of the stock market optimism during the 1920s. The most important critic of the time was non-accountant William Z. Ripley, professor of political economy at Harvard University.

Ripley's Attack on Wall Street

Ripley's attack first appeared in the *Atlantic Monthly* in three installments in 1926 (Ripley: 1926). The following year he published a book called *Main Street and Wall Street* containing the three Atlantic articles plus additional material (Ripley, 1927). The articles and the book received widespread attention, including a condescending reaction from George O. May, senior partner of Price Waterhouse, at the 1926 annual meeting of the American Institute of Accountants. Ripley's critique achieved no substantive reforms prior to the 1929 stock market crash. But it became influential in the reform movement following the election of Franklin Delano Roosevelt in 1932.

Main Street and Wall Street is a spiritual continuation of the Progressive movement of the early twentieth century. The first part of the book contains a 1911 Woodrow Wilson excerpt arguing for individualization of corporate responsibility and favoring a law establishing the premise that one "has no more right to do wrong as a member of a corporation than as an individual" (Ibid., p. 15). Ripley proposed to increase the liability of the corporate wrongdoer, make him identifiable and accountable, and thus improve the ethics and integrity of the financial community, albeit through coercion. He believed corporate-charter shopping among states and the seeking of minimum requirements for disclosure of operations and financial accounts to be abuses that led to legislative corruption. It evidenced an "unholy alliance" between corporations and states. Management, he asserted, was absorbing the rights of shareholders, including denial of preemptive rights, assuming exclusive rights to issue and dispose of new securities as it saw fit, selling corporate assets "without let or hinderance," and attempting to exempt itself from liability for personal interests adverse to those of the corporation (Ibid., pp. 29–38). Directors attempting to invoke legal devices that would enable them to escape legal liability was not new, but in the previous five years had been "elaborated" by contractual provision and statutory authority (Ibid., p. 55). The holding company, permitted first by New Jersey in the late 1880s and followed quickly by other "charter-mongering states," also attracted Ripley's adverse comment. But the stockholders of holding companies were willing victims of corporate directors, "permitting themselves to be honeyfugled or dragooned into exchanging securities of one corporation for another . . ." (Ibid., p. 97).

Ripley saw a wide range of abuses in the American financial sector, including lack of cumulative voting, the absence of effective government regulation, nonstandardized corporate accounting practices, and excessive trading on the equity (leverage) that permitted massive holding companies with minimum ownership interest. Corporate audits, he argued, should be required from independent parties as required in Britain, and corporate accounts needed publicity. Balance sheet and income statements were inadequate. "Enigmatic accounting" obscured distinctions between capital and income; current statements were needed. Goodwill was described as the "outward expression of inward unsubstantiality," and he observed that corporate surplus depended on the valuation techniques selected. Prophetically, Ripley argued that the need for corporate publicity was urgent.

Accountants' Comments before the Crash

Ripley identified many of the abuses that were to receive specific government remedial treatment in the following decade. His impact in the 1920s, however, was only in stimulating discussion as far as reform was concerned. But there was one important side effect. His efforts prompted the AIA to make an overture late in 1926 to the NYSE for cooperation in setting standards for financial reports for listed companies. The AIA was rebuffed, but G. O. May was hired by the NYSE as a private advisor.

The *Accounting Review*, the journal of the academic accountants (American Association of Accountants), carried no review of Ripley's book between 1927 and 1930. References to and discussion of the book were sparse in the *Journal of Accountancy,* the official journal of the American Institute of Accountants (AIA). By and large, both publications ignored Ripley. Not one full-fledged article appeared in either the *Journal* or the *Review* between 1926 and 1930 discussing the dangers of the current speculation or the inadequacy of financial information. Because Ripley's field was economics, not accounting, the accountants felt free to ignore him. Clearly, he was not one of the club. Though his book did get some grudging notice well after the crash, at the time of its publication it was viewed by accountants as semipopular literature (Mason, 1933: 467; Taylor, 1941: 192).

There is a striking absence of articles by accountants in the late 1920s analyzing the financial techniques then employed that were contributing negative, cumulative effects to the stock market. Was it lack of concern or the editorial policy of accounting journals? Perhaps the most typical view of the period is found in a *JA* editorial: ". . . in the realm of finance there can be no serious question that prosperity to an extraordinary extent exists" (June, 1929: 447). Nevertheless, serious reservations appear in the same editorial about capital impairment caused by laws permitting no-par stock. The lack of alarm expressed in these periodicals is significant. Articles questioned whether statutory audits or government regulation or both were desirable (Ibid., February, 1929: 134–135; Springer, 1929: 138); they analyzed new demands on the accountant and a shifting emphasis to the income statement and earnings performance compared with previous balance sheet emphasis (Daines, 1929: 94–110); they noted the expanded uses of accounting by government, business and nonprofit institutions (Rorem, 1928: 261–268); and they included the plea of the academic to the practicing accountant to pay more attention to theory—in fact, to develop theory as part of their practice (Hatfield, 1927: 267–279). Even after the crash and the economy went into a continuing decline, it took time for the immensity of the disaster to sink in, for accountants to appreciate how inadequate their technical equipment was and how those inadequacies contributed to the disaster.

The Market Breaks

Optimism reigned throughout summer, 1929; predictors of a market break were called pessimists. Those much involved in the market, like bankers, forecast continued boom times. The financial press leaders were realists, however. Poors, Standard Statistics Company, and the *Commercial and Financial Chronicle* were very skeptical, as was the *New York Times* (Allen, 1931: 227–232; Galbraith, 1954: 69–79).

"The Big Bull Market had become a national mania," wrote Frederick Lewis Allen, and on September 3, 1929, it hit its peak, although a majority expected a continued advance (Allen, 1931: 223–226). On the fifth there was a break resulting from comments made by investment adviser Roger Babson, who predicted a market decline. The effects of his opinion quickly evaporated, and a rally followed the next day. Yet the market continued to slide down throughout September, and by Saturday, October 19, it was weak. Declines occurred on the twenty-first and the twenty-third. On October 24, a turning point was reached in United States social, economic, and political history.

October 24, 1929, would thereafter be known as "Black Thursday." By "11 o'clock the market had degenerated into a wild, mad scramble to sell" (Galbraith, 1954: 104). Even so, a pool pulled the market together, confidence was restored at least momentarily, prices turned upward, and at the end of the day the *Times* industrials were off only 12 points. October 28, however, was the major break; 9.5 million shares traded amid great losses. Tuesday, October 29, was a disaster; almost 16.5 million shares sold. Thereafter, the market declined, engulfing the commodity markets. The January–March, 1930, recovery spell ended in April. In June another large drop occurred, and the market then continued to slide toward a new low in the summer of 1932. By that time the economy was in serious distress, and having dire effects on Wall Street and the banking institutions. In April of 1932 the Senate Committee on Banking and Currency under the guidance of Ferdinand Pecora began a series of investigations that focused on the widespread manipulations.

The depression became violently worse, abetted by several factors. Income distribution was bad. The management of some corporations was unscrupulous and holding companies and investment trusts were wobbly. The banking system was vulnerable. The foreign trade balance was in default. Economic analysis was poor. After an initial attempt by the government to increase spendable income, subsequent monetary policy became deflationary. Security value declines adversely affected the wealthy, and restricted their spending and investment. Weak corporate structures were affected by the crash, and the collapse of holding and investment companies helped ruin the capital market. Unemployment increased. While European economies were beginning to recover from their own recession, monetary mismanagement in the United States pulled the entire Western economic community into a state of economic torpor (Friedman and Schwartz, 1963: 676–700; Galbraith, 1954: 179–193).

Accountants' Comments after the Crash

The traumatic set of revelations of Wall Street improprieties and outright fraud during the 1920s prompted the appearance of an article in the *Accounting Review* in June, 1930, about the insiders' opportunity to defraud investors. What proportion of the income stream went to corporate insiders? the author asked. Citing Ripley and Columbia law profesor Adolph A. Berle, he described how insiders could feasibly manipulate accounts, mainly by tampering with the valuation of assets and liabilities. The conclusion was that insiders could, within the law, appropriate considerable sums without rendering any service to society, but no remedies were recommended (Nerlove, 1930: 153–156).

Some 1932 articles were prophetic. The American Society of Certified Public Accountants (ASCPA) had a program to keep track of activities within the federal government that could affect them. The 1932 report of the ASCPA Committee on Federal Legislation mentioned, for instance, the presence of members at the House Ways and Means Committee hearing in January, 1932 (CPA, 1932: 97). The ASCPA also offered its help to the new Reconstruction Finance Corporation (RFC), pleading that otherwise the RFC would have to build a large "central force" or borrow assistance from other government agencies. The government ought to take advantage of existing private agencies available to help with investigations, the society argued (Springer, 1932: 132–133). The institutionalization of accounting concepts in the law was discussed by Berle, ex-child prodigy and later New Deal adviser, in April, 1932. Although a large group of legal decisions existed where the subject was accounting, Berle said, a greater amount of work on accounting concepts remained to be done (Berle and Fisher, 1932: 573–622).

Items perhaps designed to provide diversion from the worsening situation also appeared. One, for example, described the evolution of accounting procedures through the Middle Ages, and another offered a review of famous failures and infamous swindles (Brown, 1932: 411–415; McAlister, 1932: 521–525). The American Association of Accountants (AAA) formed a Council of Accounting Research; obviously, accountancy required support and guidance from the teachers as well as from the professional practitioners. The academics adopted a public policy that called for "actual research work—vigorous, intelligent study of important problems by individuals with sound training, broad experience, and the capacity for independent thinking" (Greer, 1932: 592–593; 626). At about the same time articles, or rather personal short observations on the depression, began to appear, indicating anxiety on the part of accountants. One entitled his article, "Accountancy on Trial" (Peisch, 1932: 706–707). It signified the movement of accountants into a pivotal role in the impending struggle between the private and public sectors for control of corporate financial reporting standards. Nothing would ever be quite the same for them again.

The old, pre-involvement era for accountants unofficially ended with the death on October 10, 1932, of George Wilkinson, a partner of Price Waterhouse, in his day one of the nation's leading accountants. In November, 1932, a Democratic triumph placed Roosevelt in the White House, and he immediately began planning for financial reforms and regulation. Roosevelt took office in March, 1933, and the speed with which some of those plans were implemented disconcerted the nation's financial sector. Indeed, that sector would thereafter spend much of its energy attempting to prevent the government from exercising the powers it assumed in the first three months of the Roosevelt administration.

Notes

1.   There is much literature describing the circumstances leading up to the crash. Diverse, perceptive, and entertaining treatments have been given by John Kenneth Galbraith in *The Great Crash* (1954) and by Milton Friedman and Anna J. Schwartz in *A Monetary History of the United States* (1963). Frederick Lewis Allen's *Only Yesterday* (1931) gives much of the flavor of those times, and remains eminently readable. Full references are given in the bibliography.

3

Enter the dragon: regulation comes to the financial sector

The New Deal

The demand for reform became irresistible by 1932, and the New Deal under Franklin D. Roosevelt promised to supply that reform. The New Deal had certain similarities with the Progressive movement that developed before World War I, but it was a "drastic new departure" in American reformism (Hofstadter, 1955: 303). New Deal problems were different from Progressive problems, in content, in scale, and in the spirit with which they were approached. Some progressives were hysterically opposed to what they saw as the New Deal's irreconcilable variations from progressivism, but they correctly understood that something new was happening in U.S. politics and economics. The economic situation by early 1933 was desperate. All social and economic classes were demoralized. Millions were unemployed. Investment was insufficient to replace used-up capital, and the banking system was in near collapse.

The reformist mentality assumed that America was an essentially healthy society that needed democratizing. It was not oriented like the conservatives, simply toward reviving a prostrate economy. Hoover, an amateur politician whose election to the Presidency in 1928 was his first try for elected office, represented traditional, moral, Protestant ethic politics, and his doctrinaire allegiance to those inherited principles prevented his adjusting to the collapse. Conservatives like Hoover were not prepared for 1929 and its aftermath.

Roosevelt's economics were primitive, but he was flexible. He was also a seasoned political professional—"thoroughly at home in the realities of machine politics and a master of the machine techniques of accommodation." Experimentation and improvisation were going to be necessary, and he was the man to try anything that might work (Ibid., pp. 304–307).

The revolution that was occurring in public opinion meant Washington was going to be responsible for recovery. Unforeseen in the early 1930s, the permanent intervention of the government in the economic affairs of the nation—its new fiscal role—was now recognized as a necessity. Government spending was designed to keep the economy going, and the resulting unbalanced budgets were initially an imperative response. The depression had brought with it a distrust of big business leadership, even though great corporations remained an accepted part of American reality. Understandably enough, big-business men as a group came to detest the New Deal, but in retrospect, it is difficult to see the Roosevelt administration as seriously anti-big business.

One of the New Deal's early programs was the National Recovery Act (NRA), a complicated system of governmental codes designed to restore industrial price, and hence profit, levels. The Justice Department's new antitrust activity under Thurman Arnold was not geared primarily for stringent prosecutions of organized business power but for protecting consumer interests (Ibid., pp. 302–316). And, finally, new securities regulations were also designed to make the existing economic structure operate effectively rather than to restructure the American financial system.

The popular mandate given the New Deal provided a strong support base for the passage of its programs. Roosevelt also had the backing of a substantial part of the business community and his initial moves—the closing and reopening of banks, the proposed cutback of government spending, and the repeal of Prohibition, strengthened his support in certain conservative quarters. The NRA, which required close business-government interaction, also employed ideas strongly advocated by business leaders. In any event, the moral and political authority of business leadership in the early months of the New Deal was temporarily quiescent, unable to oppose the new administration's first efforts. Nonetheless, while business self-confidence was low, it was not completely submissive to the government. The Wall Street institutions, particularly the bankers, were very resistant to any changes in the old status quo. In this respect, the history of the Reconstruction Finance Corporation is particularly instructive.

The RFC was established during the Hoover administration. Jesse H. Jones, an able and unsentimental Texas businessman and banker, had been brought to the RFC by Hoover in 1932 as a Democrat to serve on the bipartisan board. Jones opposed the RFC's cautious lending policies. He wanted the RFC to be an inflationary agent; Hoover and Secretary of the Treasury Mills, on the other hand, saw the RFC as a primarily psychological weapon. After Roosevelt appointed Jones RFC chairman, however, the corporation took on Jones's vigorous character. Lawyer Thomas G. Corcoran, then serving occasionally as special counsel to the RFC, noted Jones's extraordinary energy, shrewdness, and competence, and believed that only those qualities "could have withstood the Wall Street drive to dominate government lending" (Schlesinger, 1958: 433).

The idea Jones had was that loans simply were not enough to save the banks; they needed capital, and capital could be supplied only if the government were permitted to purchase the banks' preferred stock. This permission the banks obstinately refused to allow, because they were desperately fearful of government control. The federal deposit insurance plan, however, finally broke the resistance of the banks because they needed a certificate of solvency from the Treasury to qualify for insurance. By the end of 1933, the banks were beginning to accept government aid (Ibid., pp. 423–430). The episode nonetheless underlines the crucial and intransigent opposition of the bankers and the financial community to the New Deal administration.

FINANCIAL SECTOR RESISTANCE TO THE NEW DEAL

The passage of time and the death of participants in an historic event, however traumatic, remove its emotional content and make it difficult for those who come afterward to understand fully the enormous intensity of feeling that the event generated. The atmosphere surrounding passage of the securities acts in the early thirties was charged with emotion, and the hostilities the acts provoked materially shaped and helped define the roles played today by the financial institutions and the SEC. The key to understanding that atmosphere lies in comprehending the change in fortune and status that had come to the financial institutions, particularly the bankers, in a very short time.

From their lofty position as national civic and political consultants, the bankers had been humiliated at the Pecora hearings and had come to be regarded by much of the nation as little better than criminals. Understandably, the bankers were unwilling to accept their new image, and fought to keep things as they once were. Hold on and wait, they insisted; self-corrections were always inherent in the nation's economy and problems work themselves out; the nation would soon be on the way to recovery. The formula had always worked before, and so why would it not be effective again? Then things would return to the way they had always been. What seems to have been unappreciated by the financial sector at the time was that as a response to increasing industrialization the American financial system had already changed extensively in the twenty or so years before the crash. Before World War I it was still possible for the private financial sector to more or less manage the economy through artful manipulations by powerful business leaders. J. P. Morgan, for instance, had put together a pool that helped out the Treasury Department when it ran short of gold in 1895 (Chamberlain, 1963: 164). But that had been more than a generation ago. Even in 1907 the private banking system had not been able to prevent a panic. After that, government regulations began to make significant alterations among the private financial institutions.

Prior Efforts to Regulate the Securities Markets

The regulation of securities markets became a serious matter in the 1910s. Disillusionment with state regulatory efforts and a desire for consistent securities marketing standards were important motivations toward national regulation. Initial suggestions for federal legislation before World War I were made by various groups, including the Investment Bankers Association (IBA) which was organized in 1912. No effective attempts to regulate securities occurred while the United States was involved in the war, though Congress temporarily established the Capital Issues Committee. Composed of the Treasury, Federal Reserve, and private bankers, it was given a degree of approval authority over all public and private financing, but it had no specific enforcement powers. State regulatory attempts and private efforts by the IBA had some positive results for a time, but fraudulent or poorly financed schemes increased, and by 1919 the opportunity for more comprehensive federal legislation appeared favorable.

After-the-fact prosecutions were the usual method for policing securities violations. Should the federal government have the authority to restrain the issue of fraudulent or misleading securities? The IBA said the government should not, although its committee on legislation did recommend such governmental authority. From 1919 to 1921, the IBA helped prevent adoption of any federal regulatory legislation. A bill written by Huston Thompson of the FTC, among others, never left the House Judiciary Committee; opposed by the bankers, it provided for securities registration, Treasury administration of securities regulations, detailed corporate income statements and balance sheets for all securities issues, and extension of personal liability. The IBA instead backed a toothless measure, which it abandoned after Treasury opposition to it developed. Thereafter, the IBA failed to support any federal securities legislation, advocating that the field be left to the states and to self-regulation by the financial sector.

During the 1920s the IBA forced some modifications in state regulations, tried to discipline the securities industry, and promoted uniform state regulation. In New York, the association opposed registration or licensing laws, but it did endorse the 1921 Martin Act which permitted the state attorney general to investigate fraudulent practices, issue subpoenas, and seek injunctions. Under the act, however, there was little chance of discovering in advance who was likely to issue fraudulent securities because no registration statute was on the books. Well after the stock market crash, in 1932, the IBA continued to defend the Martin Act against amendments requiring securities registration.

The New York Stock Exchange also opposed the licensing of dealers, regulation of exchange ticker service, and examination of an investment firm's financial records. Registration and disclosure were thus avoided by the IBA, the NYSE, and their corporate clients. The IBA also followed the same tack in other states.[1]

Self-regulation was the accepted way to control the securities markets in the 1920s. Formal regulatory powers were not broadly assumed as public functions, although continuing, but ineffectual, pressure was exerted to implement them. Of course, inadequate financial information was a disadvantage to IBA member houses, too, but their agitation in the states for better data went unsatisfied by the corporations (Parrish, 1970: 5–24).

The New York Stock Exchange's potential for requiring disclosure of corporate financial data and preventing market abuses
was greater than the IBA's. By 1926–1927 stocks had become more
numerous and of greater total value than bonds, but the NYSE's
staff was too small to examine the new listings effectively. Less than
one-half of the listed corporations on the NYSE filed quarterly earning statements. Most corporations excluded gross income, and sales
and depreciation policy from their statements. Inventory valuation
methods were unstated, inventory goods unidentified, and earned
and capital surplus were combined, as were reserves. In 1929, the
NYSE tried to improve disclosure policy and regulation and managed
to eliminate some offensive accounting practices from new listing
applications (Parrish, 1970: 40–41). These new requirements reflected G. O. May's influence. But unfortunately, the new requirements did not affect the majority of listed companies. Failure of the
IBA and the NYSE to control either the quality of the securities
distributed or to provide adequate investor information was probably a major contributing factor to the boom conditions of the late
1920s.

FINANCIAL SECTOR SOPHISTICATION IN THE 1920s

The stock market crash in 1929 has obscured some substantial
innovations that the financial sector did achieve at that time. Although the system ultimately failed, certain functions within it
operated well. Much needed stabilization had been brought to banking and finance through the Federal Reserve System (FRS), created
in 1913. The FRS established a loose, regionalized control over the
money market, and, potentially, had the power to influence business
conditions for good or ill, depending upon its policies. The most important private financial institutions were the commercial, savings,
and investment banks, the stock and bond houses and jobbers, the
stock exchanges, and the ancillary professional groups that served
them, mainly the attorneys and accountants of the large, New York-
based firms. The corporations were the main users of funds and the
principal sellers of securities, and they were integrally associated
with the American financial system. Unlike many other sectors
of the U.S. business community, however—like utilities, railroads,
banks, communications, food and drug companies—important segments of the financial sector had managed to avoid federal regulation. The Federal Reserve System was the only regulatory agency

that was a direct part of the private financial system, although the government was also represented in that system by the Treasury, the Internal Revenue Service, the Department of Commerce, the FTC, and the Justice Department. The private financial sector had managed to provide industry with risk and investment capital, offer investors the chance to place funds where they liked, minimize federal intervention in its affairs, assume leading roles in the direction of the nation and its economic affairs, and develop, through all of this, a system of complex, sophisticated institutions that were highly integrated with one another. The cohesiveness of the financial sector was perhaps its prime asset when the time came for its representatives to resist the New Deal, though the financiers, and the bankers in particular, would first have to endure the agony of public pillory.

The Senate Banking and Currency Committee Hearings on Stock Exchange Practices

Initiated in the belief that public exposure might check speculative manipulation, the hearings of the Senate Banking and Currency Committee began in April, 1932. After the November election, Ferdinand Pecora, more than ten years Assistant District Attorney of New York County, was hired by the committee as its chief counsel, and he brought with him financial journalist John T. Flynn and corporate lawyer Max Lowenthal. Senator Duncan Fletcher of Florida assumed the chairmanship of the committee, presided over the hearings, and gave Pecora his "unwavering support" (Schlesinger, 1958: 434–435).

Pecora was exceptionally able, and could absorb huge masses of information. The most prestigious people in the financial community were brought before the committee: Charles Mitchell, A. H. Wiggin, Clarence Dillon, Winthrop Aldrich, Thomas W. Lamont, George and Richard Whitney, and the younger J. P. Morgan. The investigation which ran into 1934, revealed widespread malpractice, the dissemination of deliberate misinformation, and rampant speculative activity involving highly questionable ethics on the part of both financial community leaders and small operators. Among the revelations were "avoidance of personal taxes" by Morgan Company partners, the existence of the Morgan "preferred list"—friends to whom Morgan would occasionally sell stock at below market prices, presumably to establish future "credit" with the favored.[2]

Coldly Pecora made his witnesses recollect the gilded path—the stupendous bonuses they had received and the taxes they had avoided, the stock market pools they had rigged, the holding companies they had launched, the bad investments they had palmed off on a trusting nation. From their reluctant testimony emerged the portrait of a world of insiders where for years businessmen had greedily stuffed their own pockets at the expense of the innocent dumb American citizen (Ibid., p. 437).

Several conclusions were drawn from the Senate investigation. Complete disclosure of financial information would remedy securities misrepresentation. Commercial banks ought to give up their stock-jobbing business. Private banks should not be allowed to both float securities and accept deposits. A model reform law was available in the British Companies Act. Roosevelt had called for financial regulation during his 1932 campaign, and he found helpful support from opponents of bigness like Harvard law professor Felix Frankfurter and rural progressives like Congressman Sam Rayburn of Texas (Ibid., pp. 434–440).

The 1933 Securities Act

The Senate hearings put the nation into a mood to support legislation regulating the securities markets and its institutions, and the initial legislation went through comparatively quickly. Nevertheless, regulation of the nation's financial sector was a momentous event, with serious ramifications.

FALSE STARTS

Roosevelt's special assistant Raymond Moley asked Samuel Untermeyer, former chief counsel of the pre-World War I Pujo Committee, which had examined the securities markets, to work on a possible stock exchange securities bill. Untermeyer's early 1933 bill proposed using the Post Office Department as the regulatory agency, apparently a modification of his 1914 proposal (Ibid., p. 440). Roosevelt then turned to the Department of Commerce head, Daniel C. Roper, who assigned two aides, Walter Miller and Ollie M. Butler, to work on the bill, and added former FTC Chairman Huston Thompson on March 13, 1933 (Parrish, 1970: 44–45).

Roosevelt, Moley, Roper, and economist Charles Taussig examined the Thompson (Miller-Butler) bill on March 19. Roosevelt was unsatisfied with the draftsmanship and excessive responsibilities imposed, and asked Thompson and Untermeyer to collaborate. The attempt at collaboration failed. Roosevelt then split the assignment. Thompson was to draft a bill regulating the issue of new stocks and bonds; Untermeyer was to draft a bill regulating the exchanges (Schlesinger, 1958: 440). Roosevelt accepted Thompson's bill after revisions. Congressional leaders then saw it, and on March 21 Roosevelt told the press that securities legislation was coming soon. The President's March 29 special message to Congress called for a law accenting the fiduciary responsibility of people who manage the money of others. In a much quoted section of the message, Roosevelt said: "What we seek is a return to a clearer understanding of the ancient truth that those who manage banks, corporations, and other agencies handling or using other people's money are trustees acting for others" (Flexner, 1934: 241).

The bill, however, encountered significant opposition in the House and was considered hopeless by Representative Sam Rayburn who told Moley that a new bill was needed (Schlesinger, 1958: 441). The Thompson bill called for disclosure and forbid interstate securities unless previously registered with the FTC. The British Companies Act and many state laws were precedents for this kind of law, which was preventive rather than punitive. Registration exemption would not be granted to corporations previously listed on a stock exchange or with state public utility commissions. Registration of new securities was critical, and under the bill the registration statement was to be signed by the corporation's executive officers and directors. Considerable corporate information was also required, including capitalization, voting and dividend rights, funded debt, a balance sheet, an income statement, underwriting syndicate identification, offering price, net amount returnable to capital investment, the stock issue's purposes, and identification of commissions and remunerations. All securities sold in interstate commerce were to have a prospectus with information similar to the registration statement's.

Two aspects of the act aroused powerful opposition. The first was the provision for individual liability. Purchasers were presumed to have relied upon representations in registration statements. If any statement was false in any material way, purchasers of securities from original issuers or others could rescind the transaction and recover from either the vendor who knew of the falsity or from persons signing the statement. Damages could also be obtained from signers of the statement containing the falsity, or from those authorizing the statement.

The bill's second flaw, according to opponents, was that it imposed absolute liability upon corporate directors. Some thought business would be paralyzed; others considered it impractical. And the investment bankers were horrified (Parrish, 1970: 53). The IBA preferred the common law of the British Companies Act, which would protect those associated with the issue of securities from liability if they had exercised diligence—that is, if there were reasonable grounds to believe the statements made were true. In addition, the FTC was to have the power to prevent issuance of a security if fraud, legal violations, or improper business practices were being conducted.[3]

The Thompson bill was attacked in both the House Interstate Commerce Committee and the Senate Banking and Currency Committee. FTC registration prevention powers seemed too vague, particularly to Rayburn; elimination of the revocation section was demanded by the IBA; and to critics from Congress and Wall Street the legislative draftsmanship was amateurish—all of which prompted Rayburn to ask Moley for help (Parrish, 1970: 48–57; Schlesinger, 1958: 440–441).

ENTER THE FRANKFURTER TEAM

Moley called Felix Frankfurter of the Harvard Law School on April 5, 1933, and on the seventh he arrived in Washington with James McCauley Landis, a professor of law at Harvard, and Benjamin V. Cohen, a lawyer then practicing in New York. Corcoran was already in Washington and working for the RFC; he would be joining them in the evenings to assist in the preparation of the securities legislation.

The three young men, Cohen (39), Landis (34), and Corcoran (33), and their mentor Professor Frankfurter, represented an absolutely outstanding combination of legal talent, intellectual ability, and physical energy. Their individual and collective accomplishments made a distinctive stamp on the New Deal. Landis topped his class at Harvard Law School and was a law clerk of Justice Louis Brandeis. Although he lacked extensive administrative experience, his theoretical tools, flexibility, and intelligence were superb. Cohen, "a man of deep and sensitive idealism" (Schlesinger, 1958: 441), had a reputation for brilliance and legal skill in interpreting corporate financial statements. He held degrees in law and economics, and was known as a "lawyer's lawyer" in New York City. Corcoran had been an outstanding law student at Harvard, had co-authored law review articles with Frankfurter while there, and had served as Justice Oliver Wendell Holmes's law clerk. Thereafter, he joined a New York law firm, Cotton & Franklin, in 1927, specializing in corporate reorganizations. In 1932 Corcoran went with the RFC on Frankfurter's recommendation. Cohen, Corcoran, and Landis "were valuable legal analysts. Cosmopolitan, mature, comfortable with business problems, they could think in terms of administrative framework rather than just legislative prescription" (Parrish, 1970: 61).

Frankfurter wanted a bill modeled on the British Companies Act requiring full disclosure but no general power to disapprove securities issuance. Landis and Cohen proposed going beyond that by adding the stop-order device when disclosure was insufficient, and by requiring greater disclosure provisions (Schlesinger, 1958: 442). Cohen and Landis developed a draft bill over the weekend and presented it to the House committee on April 10. Rayburn, impressed, requested them to continue working on it with two House legislative advisers (Schlesinger, 1958: Parrish, 1970: 63; Landis, 1959: 29–38).

The new bill dealt with the interrelationship of finance, business, professional, and interest groups by recommending separation of functions and responsibility. The Cohen-Landis-Corcoran bill did not ignore accountants, engineers, appraisers, lawyers, and other experts. The April 10 draft diminished liabilities but made them more specific. A mandatory 30-day delay between the filing of a registration statement and the issuance of a security was specified, during which the FTC could require modifications of the statement or issue a stop order suspending the registration if it believed untrue statements had been made or material facts omitted.

A second draft, slowed by internal conflicts, was made between April 10 and April 20. Landis and Cohen clashed with the House Legislative Council—and with each other. Landis believed in more general administrative mandates than did Cohen; Cohen also advocated flexible administration, but he wanted detailed information schedules included in the bill's text. Differences between the two were ironed out by Frankfurter, Rayburn, and Moley. The April 21 subcommittee print of the bill contained Cohen's schedule of 32 items, a significant increase over the 9 classes mentioned in Thompson's bill. The Cohen-Landis proposal also gave the FTC full power to define accounting and trade terms and to prescribe the preparation methods for the accounts (Parrish, 1970: 65).

Thompson's bill was still alive, having been endorsed by the Senate, and Frankfurter & Co. turned their attention to attacking it as inadequate. The Cohen-Landis bill was introduced in the House on May 3 and passed on May 5. In its final form, the bill's civil liabilities standards in Section 11 stated that civil suits for recision or damages could be instituted by investors where the registration statement contained untrue statements or omitted material facts. Professionals signing the registration statement could be sued, plus all associated underwriters and dealers. The corporation was unconditionally liable. Liability could be avoided by others, providing they sustained one of the two burdens of proof with respect to the registration statement: first, that the statement was made on the authority of an expert and that there was, after reasonable investigation, reasonable grounds to believe that the statements therein were true and no material facts had been omitted; second, with respect to statements purported to be made on the authority of an expert, that the expert had reasonable grounds to believe, and did believe, that the statements were true, that no material facts had been omitted, and that the registration statement fairly represented the expert's statement or was a fair copy of or exact copy from his report of valuation (Parrish, 1970: 67).

The standard of care defined in the statute was that required of a fiduciary, which was much more rigorous than that required under the common law or under the British statutes. Purchasers did not have to prove reliance upon the registration statement or the prospectus of an inducement to purchase. The bill put the burden of proof on the issuers of the securities, not the plaintiff. This shift, of course, represented a major reversal of the traditional common law rules of procedure.

The bill, naturally, did not receive the enthusiasm of everyone. Special interests, sponsored by individual congressmen, forced certain changes in it. Exemptions under the act were extended to municipal funding projects, railroad securities, building and loan associations, state chartered banks, and homestead and savings and loan associations.

Wall Street lawyers attacked the bill's liability provisions, about which the IBA was also unhappy. On the other hand, some house committee members thought the liability section too lenient. Moley insisted the Committee hear the New York lawyers privately before sending the bill to the full House. In spite of the lawyers' opposition to the liability and waiting-period sections, however, no modifications were made (Parrish, 1970: 68). The Cohen-Landis draft was rapidly approved by the House. House-Senate conferees got authority to set the legislation's final form, and the House bill won over the Senate-approved Thompson bill; the only major alteration made was a reduction in waiting period from 30 to 20 days. The conference report was passed by the House on May 22, by the Senate on May 23, and signed by President Roosevelt on May 27, 1933.

Assurances were made by the bill's spokesmen that security dealers, corporation executives, accountants, lawyers, and persons involved in marketing securities were safe if ordinary business obligations were handled with reasonable competence. A new standard of accountability and professionalization was now anticipated. Cohen believed some of the better financial institutions in New York were becoming reconciled to the measure. Nevertheless, the business and financial community "saw only an immediate, terrifying, defeat." Old legal doctrines were destroyed and respected, traditional business practices were prohibited, they thought. Temporarily vanquished, many in the private financial sector determined to resist further changes and to use all their legislative influence and administrative pressure to save what they could (Parrish, 1970: 71). The fight would be bitter and would leave permanent wounds.

Notes

1.   Throughout the 1920s, the IBA continued its efforts to exert greater influence upon state securities legislation and administration, particularly where the state insisted upon registration of either securities or individual dealers. In Michigan, for example, the IBA persuaded the state agency to exempt securities from registration requirements if they were listed on the New York Stock Exchange. These efforts were supported by other groups. A revised model act by the National Conference of Commissioners on Uniform State Laws, which received the approval of the American Bar Association, provided that securities listed on the New York, Chicago, and Boston stock exchanges, the Chicago Board of Trade, the New York Curb Exchange, and any other recognized and responsible stock exchange, be completely exempt from registration. Additional loopholes provided for other possible exemptions. IBA-sponsored state regulation permitting the nonregistration of corporations whose stocks were listed on recognized exchanges ended after the 1929 stock market crash.

Michael Parrish's excellent *Securities Regulation and The New Deal,* from which much of the information in this chapter is drawn, provides a lucid and detailed description of attempts in the 1920s to regulate securities.

2.   The "preferred list" included Owen D. Young, Newton D. Baker, John J. Raskob, William G. McAdoo, General Pershing, Charles A. Lindbergh, future Justice of the Supreme Court Owen J. Roberts, William H. Woodin (a subsequent Roosevelt cabinet appointee), Calvin Coolidge, Norman H. Davis, John W. Davis, and Bernard Baruch (Schlesinger, 1958: 436).

3.   Section 6 of Thompson's bill allowed the Federal Trade Commission to revoke a security's registration if it appeared that any provisions of the act were violated; or if the issuers had engaged in or were about to engage in fraudulent transactions or dishonest behavior, or were not conducting their business in accordance with the law, or their affairs were in an unsound condition or insolvent, or that the business itself was not based upon sound principles (Parrish, 1970: 50).

chapter

4

Between the acts:
accountants at center stage

The Accounting Practitioners Assume a Major Role

It was apparent that the federal government had intervened in the private economy in a highly significant way. The NRA accepted business as a partner, but the Securities Act of 1933 was coercive and the financial community knew it. To members of that community, the implication of irresponsibility was unmistakable and extremely unpleasant. Accustomed to respect rather than attack, the financiers and bankers were shocked by the act. Even worse was the denial to them of access to the determination of public policy, and that evoked the bitterest possible reaction from Wall Street.

On the other hand, some thought the Securities Act was not tough enough. People like Berle and William O. Douglas, then a professor at the Yale Law School, believed that despite the act's apparent severity its objectives were too limited in terms of reconstructing the financial system or instituting a program of economic control (Schlesinger, 1958: 444–445).

Opposition to the Securities Act surfaced soon after its passage, intensified in the latter part of 1933, and was exacerbated by the introduction of the proposed Securities Exchange Act in February, 1934. An important phase of the battle was fought in March and April of 1934. Between May 27, 1933, and June 6, 1934, when the second act was signed, the financial community waged a relentless, effective fight for modification of the original act and for softening some provisions of the proposed exchange act.

The accountants played a crucial role between June, 1933, and June, 1934. Compared with their relative exclusion from the deliberations prior to passage of the Securities Act, their new involvement was incredible. Before the acts, accountants were weak auxiliaries in the financial system. Subsequently, they were the fulcrum in the critical battle over the determination of financial standards. How did they acquire this power?

As comparative newcomers to the financial system, the accountants at the turn of the century were playing the characteristic part of the outsiders trying to get inside. Technical improvements in accounting had occurred rapidly, a response to the increasing specialization of industry and the distribution of products that had taken place after the 1880s. The differentiation of functions had become the result of more sophisticated manufacturing processes. Double entry bookkeeping had been around for centuries, but the development of cost accounting was sparked by aggressive entrepreneurs like Albert Fink, who thereby created new roles for the accountants (Krooss and Gilbert, 1972: 157).

British Influence on U.S. Accounting

Accounting was professionalized in Britain by the mid-nineteenth century, a time when U.S. accounting was still unorganized and technically crude. British accountants were integrated into industry and government through legislation that required their services for specified corporate auditing and reporting. A model set of accounting articles were included in the 1844, 1856, and 1862 British Companies Acts; in 1900 compulsory reporting requirements became permanent fixtures. Government interest in controlling corporations gave British accountants considerable independence, permitting a quasi-judicial attitude toward their duties.

The early development of U.S. accounting was clearly an attempt to adopt British practices. U.S. accounting relied heavily on British personnel, organization and technique. The various British Companies Acts were frequently cited, and American professional accounting societies and proposed apprenticeship programs were inspired by British models.

In the 1880s English firms established U.S. subsidiaries—for example, Barrow, Wade, Guthrie & Co. and Price Waterhouse & Co., the latter sending Arthur Lowes Dickinson and May to the United States where each became a senior partner of the American firm. The British model was looked to even when local conditions made inappropriate full adoption of their methods, such as apprenticeship (Sterrett, 1905: 10). American accountants may have admired British techniques, but they resented the invader's profitable practices, and their attitude complicated early efforts to form a single, national accounting association. Efforts by important practitioners to install the British apprenticeship system created considerable professional acrimony, helping precipitate two episodes of splitting and subsequent reconsolidation of national practitioner accounting societies. Furthermore, British practice depended upon practical experience and apprenticeship. This dependence supported an anti-intellectual tradition among American practicing accountants toward accounting academics, an attitude that still prevails and helps explain the appropriation of authority for the development of accounting principles almost exclusively by the accounting practitioners. Finally, British tradition excluded government from supervising accountants' qualifications and certification. This tradition was emulated in the United States and materially contributed to the accountants' success in maintaining autonomy *vis-à-vis* the SEC.

Government Legislation and Accounting Growth

The demand for accounting services in the United States increased early in the century in response to two trends: American industrialization and the passage of Progressive Era legislation. The new laws, especially those pertaining to banking and income tax, promoted U.S. accounting just as the British Companies Acts had advanced British accounting. The different thrust of the laws in the United States, however, permitted much less structured accountant–government relations. In Britain the relevant laws concentrated on uniform systems of accounting and auditing standards. In America the early emphasis was upon corporate disclosure, not uniformity and auditing. Practitioners in the United States resisted the development of uniform systems of accounts for unregulated corporations, a feeling shared even by expatriate British accountants. In the absence of uniform accounting systems sanctioned by the government, burgeoning corporate practice improved accounting "technique," but it also encouraged the optional treatment of accounts, which made accountants more, rather than less, dependent upon their clients.

Accounting legislation, an inevitable consequence of growing industrialization, created a demand for people skilled in accounting and financial controls. But the regulation's direction and style left maximum influence with the regulated groups, and represented a continuing bargaining process (Wiebe, 1967: 194–195). American accounting was still crude when the Interstate Commerce Commission (ICC) was created in 1887. The national accounting organization was just being organized, and its help was not requested when the ICC established uniform systems of accounts for railroads.

The first big corporate merger movement in the United States took place between 1897–1903, and the financial panic of 1907 revealed the inadequacy of publicly available corporate financial information. It also revealed outright fraud by some industrial and insurance company managers. Corporate and banking failures increased the demand for remedial legislation which, when it came, created new and sizable demands for accounting services. The creation of the Bureau of Corporations within the new Department of Commerce and Labor in 1903 brought business and government officially into permanent contact, an event that received a great deal of attention at the time (Hofstadter, 1955: 247; Wiebe, 1967: 199). The 1905 Pure Food and Drug Act became the "headquarters for still another experiment in bureaucratic reform" (Wiebe, 1967: 191). Government control over railroads was furthered by the 1906 Hepburn Act, which gave the ICC rate-making powers, and the 1910 Mann-Elkins Act permitted the ICC to initiate rate proceedings and calculate fair earnings on physical property valuation (Hays, 1957: 57).

Reform legislation related to three aspects of the financial sector—income taxes, banking, and antitrust laws—was passed in 1914 (Wiebe, 1967: 219). Each had a definitive effect upon the accounting profession. The income-tax law, appended to the Underwood-Simmons Tariff Act, had been made possible in 1913 by the Sixteenth Amendment to the Constitution. The Federal Reserve Act finally established reasonable cohesion in the banking system, and the Federal Trade Commission Act, passed along with its companion measure the Clayton Antitrust Act, established a commission with a rather vague mandate to oversee corporate activity.

After 1914 accountants were essential, and they came into national prominence by setting the techniques to be used in handling legal reporting requirements. The accountants made the most of the opportunity, though ideologically they were often given to deprecating the new laws, the creators of the new laws, and government attempts to develop administrative machinery (Montgomery, 1939: 120–121). The income tax laws of 1909 and 1913 offered accountants an almost limitless prospect for financial gain. With lawyers initially avoiding the field, accountants became necessary in the preparation of individual and corporate returns (Editorial, *JA* October, 1909: 307, and November, 1909: 373; Edwards, 1960: 93; Carey, 1969: 70).

The Federal Reserve Act also increased the demand for accounting services. Many banks wanted CPA attested statements from corporate borrowers, and the Federal Reserve Banks needed essential financial information from corporations whose rediscounted paper was presented to them (Carey, 1969: 62–63). Although corporate financial statements by accountants were not required at first, they were soon being prepared by independent auditors. New securities evolving from the formation of mergers, holding companies, and investment trusts also promoted the services of accountants. Many of the largest firms employed independent auditors to review or develop their financial statements.

Government regulation and industrial and financial activity in the early twentieth century also forced the accounting practitioners into encounters with the government. From these they invariably emerged with expanded functions and power. The professional accounting societies, well established by 1917, served the practitioners well in their brushes with the government.

Professional Accounting Societies

American accountants at the turn of the century faced a dilemma. A single national society was desirable. But standards of competence that would cover everyone calling themselves accountants would be too low, and if entrance standards were too high, most public accountants would be excluded. The choice between forming a national organization to which most accountants would belong and raising professional standards lay behind the successive organizational splits and mergers that characterized the field of accountancy in the 40 years that followed passage of the first CPA law in New York in 1897. Only after 1936 did the practicing accountants achieve a single dominant national organization.

The American Association of Public Accountants—1887–1916

The American Association of Public Accountants (AAPA) was formed in New York in 1887. British traditions were reflected by designations of the 31 founding members: 24 fellows (subscribers with three years of practice) and 7 associates (those who were to pass an exam later). Membership in the AAPA grew slowly, partially because the organization had a decidedly "New York" flavor (Carey, 1969: 38; Edwards, 1960: 57; Wilkinson, 1928a: 261–285).

The Federation of Societies of Public Accountants in the U.S.A. —1902–1905

A competing "national" group formed in Philadelphia in 1902, and it included some influential spokesmen for the future practitioner: R. H. Montgomery, Arthur Lowes Dickinson, Wilkinson, and Charles Waldo Haskins. The new group was called the Federation of Societies of Public Accountants in the United States of America, better known as the Federation. The Federation may have been formed to force liberalizing concessions from the AAPA, which neglected outside members. If so, the strategy was successful (Montgomery, 1939: 65; Edwards, 1960: 84–85; Carey, 1969: 50).

AAPA and Federation Merger—1905

The Federation's formation brought to three the number of large accounting societies in the United States, the AAPA and New York State Society of CPAs (NYCPA) being the other two. Competition among the three caused dissatisfaction, and in 1904 Wilkinson brought them together to effect a merger. The attendees included Dickinson, May, Joseph E. Sterrett, William M. Lybrand, Montgomery, John B. Niven, Elijah Watt Sells, and Walter A. Staub. A committee was appointed to study the possibility of a merger of the national organizations, the AAPA, and the Federation, and in 1905 the two groups were joined with the AAPA the surviving unit. The absorbed Federation had formed a league of state societies, and this group gave the new AAPA a broader geographical base. The influx of new members, including those from 15 state societies was significant. Membership in the new AAPA required membership in a state society, if one existed.

The objectives of the reorganized AAPA were to improve CPA laws and professional standards and to achieve a centralized national organization, and these aims were partially accomplished. But the problem of adjusting the standards of a national organization to those of the various state CPA groups forced a limited return on the part of the AAPA to a policy of selective membership, with the same divisive results it encountered before the creation of the Federation. The superior attitude of the leading New York accountants continued to irritate the situation, although several ex-Federation members did hold influential positions, among them Wilkinson, Sterrett, and Montgomery. It was clear that revisions in membership requirements and organizational objectives would be needed (Carey, 1969: 49–52, 108–113; Edwards, 1960: 86–87, 114–115; Montgomery, 1939: 64–66).

ORGANIZATION PROBLEMS FOR THE PRACTITIONERS

The new AAPA membership requirements adopted in 1906 dramatized a continuing dilemma: selective or universal admission standards. The first route would result in a highly qualified, prestigious body without full national representation; the other path would provide a national organization at the sacrifice of professional standards. The 1906 standards followed the spirit of the merger and allowed easy membership: fellows had to be in practice three years before application and need not be CPAs; associates could apply with less than three years of practice. Examinations for membership were not required. Applications were to be made through affiliated state groups where they existed (Carey, 1969: 110), thus eliminating AAPA control over membership—a festering source of dissatisfaction to some.

Professional exclusivity was achieved through the state CPA associations. Between 1896 and 1920 all states adopted CPA laws, and by 1927 the major U.S. dependencies had also done so (Wilkinson, 1928b: 297–301). State CPA laws characteristically accepted existing practitioners and established education, examination, and experience requirements for newcomers. Local monopolies were usually created through nonrecognition of other state CPAs. The New York CPAs, for instance, voted overwhelmingly in 1905 to keep all accounting business in the state exclusively theirs (Editorial, *JA*, January, 1906: 239–245). Montgomery, a Pennsylvania CPA at the time, was particularly offended and condemned the action (Montgomery, 1906: 246–247). But non-New York CPAs were not prevented from heading New York accounting firms, and even in the 1920s, many senior partners of those firms were not New York CPAs (Montgomery, 1939:

258–260). Some state societies sought monopolies for CPAs by excluding newcomers and restricting the practice of accounting to CPAs, but these efforts were declared unconstitutional in the 1920s. The inability of an accountant to join a state CPA organization automatically prevented his membership in the AAPA, which brought into question the national association's mission. Was the AAPA to be a national qualifying group or just a national CPA organization? (Carey, 1969: 116–117).

THE INSTITUTE OF ACCOUNTANTS IN THE UNITED STATES OF AMERICA— 1916 (AMERICAN INSTITUTE OF ACCOUNTANTS)

Lack of disciplinary authority by the AAPA and its slow membership growth prompted the association to assume qualifying authority over the profession in 1916. Membership requirements were raised significantly [1] and ties with the state bodies were broken. The AAPA also changed its name to the American Institute of Accountants (AIA), becoming known generally, as the Institute. The new requirements further stalled the growth in membership while dissatisfaction increased over the AIA's unwillingness to have state branches. The controversy crystalized in 1921 over an anglophilic proposal within the Institute to apply for a federal charter incorporating an "institute of American Chartered Accountants." This plan precipitated the formation of yet another accountant's society by dissident members—the ASCPA. (Carey, 1969: 314–330).

THE AMERICAN SOCIETY OF CERTIFIED PUBLIC ACCOUNTANTS— 1921–1936

The American Society of CPAs (ASCPA, also referred to as the Society) was formally organized in December, 1921, and it operated continuously until the end of 1936. The ASCPA was a CPA association actively seeking government support. It wanted to raise standards and promote relations with the state societies. The ASCPA had only one membership class and it enforced discipline through its state societies, not the national organization. The Society supported reserving the practice of accounting to CPAs, published a monthly journal called the *Certified Public Accountant,* and in 1932 limited its membership to CPAs who were also members of state societies. Headquartered in Washington, the ASCPA "worked hard on federal

legislation and government agency matters affecting the profession"
(Carey, 1969: 330–331).

Competition from the ASCPA forced the AIA to modify its elit-
ism, and in 1922 the AIA opened its membership to CPAs passing
state non-AIA examinations. New AIA chapters were authorized, and
by 1924 Montgomery was even willing to sacrifice "the highest possible standards" for achievement of a national CPA society. Discussions
were also held with the ASCPA about possible cooperation on mutual
problems. In 1925 AIA membership requirements were eased for
foreign accountants, and throughout the thirties efforts continued to
liberalize the Institute and unite it with the Society. By the mid-
thirties both organizations were substantially national CPA organizations. The ASCPA served state societies better, promoted regulatory
legislation, and maintained relations with the federal government.
The AIA continued to concentrate on technical and ethical standards, published uniform CPA examinations, and worked with bankers and the New York Stock Exchange (Carey, 1969: 334–354).

ACADEME: THE AMERICAN ASSOCIATION OF ACCOUNTANTS—
1916 TO THE PRESENT

Accounting developed late as a professional subject taught by
full-time faculties, which explains the low status of the academic
within the profession, at least in the first decades of the century. Before 1900, only three commerce or business schools existed. Thirty-
seven were opened, however, between 1900 and 1915. New York
University gave the first professorships in accounting in 1900, and
in 1904 Henry Rand Hatfield became the first full-time accounting
professor at the University of Chicago. Adequate textbooks, course
coordination among universities, and the availability of competent instructors were poor until the 1920s. And, alas, the prestige of an accounting professor among university colleagues was low (Zeff, 1966:
5).

The academic accountants' association sprang from a meeting in
1915 of the Economic Association. The American Association of University Instructors in Accounting (AAUIA) also known as the Association, was incorporated December, 1916, and active members were
limited to those teaching accounting in college-rank institutions; associate nonvoting memberships were also offered. The restrictions on
membership prevented participation in the AAUIA by practitioners
and lower-level school instructors. The Association's initial concerns

were with standardizing and correlating university course work. Formal acknowledgment of its existence came from the AIA in 1918 when AAUIA members were permitted to use the AIA library.

Membership and attendance at annual meetings were low at first. Efforts to establish working relations or association with the practicing accountants' groups met little enthusiasm. When the AAUIA requested admission of accounting instructors to AIA membership, committee and general membership reacted favorably, but the leadership felt differently; "an unexplained delay ensued and the Association continued to encounter obstacles in dealing with the Institute's education committee" (Zeff, 1966: 13). The AAUIA had better luck with the ASCPA, which at inception admitted qualified instructors who were CPAs. In 1924 the AIA made a "major" concession: accounting instructors, if they were CPAs who had been teaching accounting for at least five years prior to their application, could join (Zeff, 1966: 11–14).

In 1926, after extended discussion, the AAUIA decided to publish a journal, the *Accounting Review,* which first appeared in March, 1926. Membership in the organization was then near 600 (Zeff, 1966: 14–29). In 1935, the AAUIA changed its name to the American Accounting Association (AAA), amid some practitioner opposition (see Chapter 9).

At the time of the crash and, later, the passage of the securities acts, the academic accountants were not a powerful body. Hostility from the AIA was a factor in its national status—and would continue to be (see Chapter 16); the prestige of accounting as a theoretical discipline was low, and the involvement of campus accountants with government was infrequent. Because relations with the AIA were tenuous, the academic's influence with the practitioners was minimal. All three factors help explain why academic accountants as a professional group had very little influence on the securities acts and the subsequent fight over whether the government or the practitioners should have authority for developing generally accepted accounting principles. The academics in the thirties were in a subsidiary position, one from which they never managed to extricate themselves.

Accountant-Government Interaction Prior to the Securities Acts

In 1906 President Theodore Roosevelt appointed the Keep Commission to examine U. S. government business and accounting methods. The AAPA was invited to cooperate and responded by forming a committee consisting of Henry A. Niles, Loomis, Dickinson, Sells, and Teele. Their meeting with the commission in May, 1906, was reported with satisfaction in the *Journal of Accountancy,* which later declared that "the best accounting talent in the country" was cooperating with the Keep Commission (Editorial, *JA,* February, 1907: 300–301). The AAPA Committee on Legislation was organized to examine federal legislation potentially important to accountants, including the newly passed (1906) Hepburn Act which required uniform accounting by the nation's railroads (*JA,* 1907: 72). Publicity of corporate accounts was supported by the AAPA, but apprehension was expressed about uniformity of accounting methods. It was hoped that "local peculiarities or . . . changing conditions" would be considered (Editorial, *JA,* November, 1907: 36).

Insurance company scandals in the first decade of the century created direct AAPA-state contacts regarding uniform accounting for insurance companies, which the accountants favored, in addition to mandatory audits. The accountants were not successful, though, in their efforts to achieve uniformity in the states.[2] Another AAPA committee, which pressed for employment of public accountants to prepare railroad statements under the Hepburn Act, was politely dismissed by the ICC chairman in 1906 (Carey, 1969: 58). After these rebuffs, however, accounting practitioner status turned up dramatically. New financial reporting requirements stemming from the 1909 and 1913 income tax laws, the 1913 Federal Reserve Act, and 1914 Federal Trade Commission Act brought accountants national attention. Indeed, the 1909 income tax precipitated a dispute between 12 accounting firms and Attorney General George W. Wickersham over proper income determination, a controversy finally settled by the Secretary of the Treasury. The law was "silly" and could not be enforced, commented Montgomery (Montgomery, 1939: 120), who testified before the House Ways and Means Committee in 1913 on behalf of fiscal-year reporting (Carey, 1969: 64–67). A 1915–1917 confrontation between the practitioners and the government over uniform systems of accounting revealed the limits of accountants' cooperation with the national government—and the line they would take later in their battle with the SEC. FTC Vice Chairman Edwin M. Hurley, in 1915, proposed establishing uniform accounting systems for the principal businesses in the United States. The plan allowed necessary variations, with the FTC acting as expert adviser. The Hurley proposal was obnoxious to the accountants.

Their position on the matter had been thrashed out in 1912 at the AAPA's annual meeting. Alexander Smith, a representative of a Chicago banking firm, argued that the investing public and bankers were as much the client of the accountant as business stockholders and owners; the AAPA, he said, should appoint a committee to study the possibility of adopting "exact and uniform principles of accounting." Dickinson contended that evils did exist, but that the solution was to provide better training and experience. There were no fixed rules for accountants, he maintained; each case had to be dealt with on its merits. Only broad principles could be stated, and conservatism and judgment were the keys (Carey, 1969: 63; 77–80).

Hurley also wanted a federal register of acceptable accountants whose audited statements would be taken by the FTC and the FRB. This was another threat to the accountants, because the accountants registered with the government would not be limited to AAPA members, which meant a crucial loss of control over the profession. Immediately after the AAPA's 1916 meeting, when they approved the new AIA organization, Hurley sent a letter to the new AIA formally making proposals in uniform accounting and for a federal accountant's register. The influential practitioner Sterrett suggested that the AAPA's Committee on Federal Legislation (Montgomery, May, and M. S. Chase) try to achieve an arrangement that would give the FTC proper accounting standards but allow the AAPA to retain professional control. Things then became very confused, and in the confusion, the accountants walked away winners.

The committee successfully persuaded the FTC and FRB that (1) AIA control over admission and ethics eliminated the need for a federal register of acceptable accountants, and (2) independent audit guidelines would meet any government requirements for a uniform accounting system. The government had wanted uniform industry accounting, which the accountants did not; what the accountants *did* want was to establish authoritative audit guidelines for financial statements. Probably capitalizing on Hurley's lack of knowledge about the distinction between uniform accounting and auditing, the accountants in 1917 simply developed and published a bulletin on auditing procedure called "Uniform Accounting" for the FRB. It was an hilarious—and bravura—performance. The preface referred to a tentative proposal for a uniform system of accounting, but the text dealt with audit procedures. Hurley resigned in 1917, and the same bulletin was reissued in 1918 by the FRB, the reference to uniform systems of accounting was omitted, and the name of the bulletin was changed to Approved Methods for the Preparation of Balance Sheet Statements. The bulletin had been used previously within Price Waterhouse (Carey, 1969: 129–135).

This revealing sleight of hand by the leaders of the accounting profession was a milestone. For the first time, the practicing accountants had an extended encounter with several government agencies over matters of vital interest to them and they won. The FRB may have gotten part of the auditing standards it wanted, but the FTC under Hurley did not. What the practicing accountants got was considerable: disciplinary control over their profession, rejection of a federal register of approved accountants, and rejection of a uniform system of accounting that would have reduced their control over accounting practices and thus reduced the value of their services. Accounting practitioners also gained the major voice in determining auditing standards. The victory of the accountants was particularly significant in view of the precedent set by the ICC which had been given the authority to determine uniform systems of accounts for railroads, and had exercised that authority. Finally, the accountants achieved working contacts with two important federal agencies.

It is noteworthy that in this 1915–1917 imbroglio, as with the SEC some twenty years later, the initial contact between a federal agency and the accountants took place when the agencies, the FTC and the FRB, were in their infancy. Fending off the FTC on the one hand and co-opting what could have been the exercise of a crucial function by the FRB on the other, the practicing accountants exercised remarkable finesse. They not only retained control over their profession, but left the encounter with more power than they had when they entered it.

The episode also illustrates how additional institutional structures, roles, and functions are developed and differentiated so that new tasks can be accomplished by a society that is daily growing more complicated. The new functions in this case were the need for better auditing reports and better standards for financial reporting. The question was whether an existing group (the accountants) or a newly created group (the FTC and the FRB) would perform them. The new operations, highly technical, were absorbed by the existing institution. The situation was to be repeated with variations, after the creation of the SEC. Interestingly enough, some of the players in 1934 were the same people who so effectively represented the interests of the practicing accountants in 1915–1917: among them, May and Montgomery.

Accountants were important to military and industrial mobilization in World War I. Afterward, the demand for accounting services grew in response to the corporate income tax, the new independent regulatory agencies, and the general demands of an elaborate industrial society (Rorem, 1928: 261–267). When the SEC was created in 1934, the practicing accountants had two stable, albeit competing, organizations, and a great deal of experience in dealing with political bodies and regulatory bureaucracies. By then the ASCPA, as well as the AIA, were better able to watch government activities affecting accountants' interests (Editorial, *CPA*, February, 1929: 69).

Accountants and the Financial System

Accountants were primarily involved with their clients, and among these the most important were the large corporations and banking institutions. As time passed, the practitioners became more integrated into the financial sector, were accepted as counselors by their clients, and developed a clear emotional identification as members of the private financial sector. Nevertheless, the accountants did not exert crucial influence in that sector prior to the 1930s. Not that available accounting techniques were not fully utilized by a rapacious financial community; they were. But the influence of the accounting profession upon the use of these techniques was limited. Part of the reason why the profession was unable to exert crucial influence was the absence of generally accepted standards for financial reporting, which gave clients the opportunity to pressure accountants to follow the client's wishes. The corollary of loose accounting standards was minimal control by the practitioner over the client.

Responsibility for industrial financial reporting, unlike that for transportation and utility industries already under federal regulation in the 1920s, could not be assumed, legally or practically, by any government or private institution. The AIA and the NYSE lacked either the mandate, prestige, or desire to assume this responsibility. Government institutions had no statutory authority to do so, and probably did not possess the required expertise even if they had the authority, though uniform systems of accounting were highly developed parts of the regulatory machinery of some independent agencies.

By the early 1930s the accountants were integrated into the private structure of the financial system, and the net result was their ability to resist federal efforts to assume responsibility for financial reporting principles, which in turn enhanced their influence within the financial system. The accountants owed a great deal to the stock market crash. Before 1929 their influence was small; after 1929, the upsurge in their prestige was dramatic—as their relations with the NYSE in the late 1920s illustrate.

Apparently severely wounded by the accusations of accounting and financial misdeeds made by Professor Ripley in his 1926 *Atlantic Monthly* articles, the AIA made its first overtures to the New York Stock Exchange in 1926. George O. May, then senior partner of Price Waterhouse & Co., suggested cooperative relations to encourage more comprehensive financial reports by listed companies.[3] The NYSE rejected formal relations with the AIA. Nevertheless, J. M. B. Hoxsey, executive assistant to the NYSE Committee on Stock List, which listed shares traded, asked May if Price Waterhouse would become consulting accountants to the exchange. May accepted in 1927, after the NYSE declined his countersuggestion that a committee of the AIA cooperate with the NYSE (Carey, 1969: 163–164). May's hiring as consultant was at the direction of Frank Altschul, chairman of the Committee on Stock List (Berle, 1938: 370).

After the crash, the attitude of the NYSE toward the AIA changed sharply. Hoxsey appeared at the Institute's annual meeting in September, 1930, to suggest that certain areas of financial reporting needed attention, and the NYSE would be happy to cooperate on this problem with a committee from the Institute (Taylor, 1941: 193). A committee headed by May was appointed, and immediately began to work with the exchange (Carey, 1969: 162–166). It was too late, of course, to accomplish anything that would redeem the stock market situation, but the establishment of relations between AIA and NYSE further integrated the practicing accountants into the financial system at a crucial time. Federal investigations were just beginning and New Deal legislation was close. When it arrived, the New York Stock Exchange and the practicing accountants provided each other with mutual support.

Over the years, as time increasingly separated the participants from the event, it became the fashion for practicing accountants to cite the AIA-NYSE-May interaction of 1926–1930 as evidence that "the profession" tried to drag a reluctant NYSE toward an improvement of corporate-financial statements. The claim is largely frivolous, as contemporary observations suggest, if one equates "the profession" with the AIA. An AIA study in the mid-twenties of the possibility of classifying auditing—with an eye toward developing a series of standard certificates—was not accepted by members of the Institute because it would have limited their cherished "judgment." Even if the NYSE had cooperated with the AIA in 1927, AIA members would "have been unwilling to accept any drastic departure from commonly accepted auditing procedures. It is doubtful whether any constructive suggestions would have been accepted by the Institute's members. . . ." (Taylor, 1941: 193). The NYSE had, of course, tightened their requirements for financial information both from members and from investment trusts (Stegman: 1929: 361; Auld, 1929: 363) under May's influence, but this was far from moving toward more uniform and revealing financial statements from corporations listed on the exchange.

THE EDGE OF POWER

And so by 1933 the accounting practitioners were integrated into the nation's financial system, a system that also had regular contacts with the federal government. Their close interaction with the New York Stock Exchange occurred when the crash forced the brokers to call for help. Thereafter, AIA sympathies and efforts were fully allied with the exchanges. The attitude of academic accountants was less doctrinaire, but because they possessed little power and were virtually ignored by the practitioners and the government, their somewhat more enlightened approach made no difference. AIA and ASCPA committees monitored all government operations that might affect accountants' interests; both helped develop regulations under the 1933 and 1934 securities acts. By the time the SEC went into operation in the fall of 1934, it was clear that attention would have to be paid to the practicing accountants.

BOOM AND BUST IN THE 1920s STOCK MARKET

The stock-market failure of the 1920s was due partly to the failure of accountants to provide a sorely needed moderating influence, though they were without real power to influence events at that time. Still, it is fair to ask whether they sounded any warnings or made efforts toward financial moderation. The answer is they did not. Criticism of corporate reporting during the boom emanated from outside the profession. The practitioners were solidly allied with their corporate clients, and offered little criticism of what was happening in the stock market. As it was, a great deal was happening that "practical" men could be concerned about. Viewed against their unconcern before 1930, their subsequent calls for slow and moderate change and their pleas for self-regulation were going to sound hollow to New Deal administrators like law professor James M. Landis, the second chairman of the SEC.

Notes

1.   Membership designations were changed to "member" and "associate." Fellows of the association, associates with more than five years of practice, and others entitled to take a qualifying examination could be members. Associates in the future would be those who were recommended for the designation after taking an examination. No one was to be admitted to the organization after October 31, 1916 without examination for either member or associate status. The new Institute had 1169 members, compared with 1238 in the former association (Carey, 1969: 123–127).

2.   Accountants conferred with the Insurance Commissioner of the State of New York in reference to the adoption of uniform accounting for insurance companies; the State of Massachusetts was reported considering the same approach (Editorial, JA, August, 1906: 290–293). Dickinson suggested that the reporting forms ought to be remodeled and that periodic audits should be conducted by public accountants (JA, August, 1906: 297). Efforts by the accountants along these lines were unsuccessful, however, and periodic audits were not made mandatory (Carey, 1969: 57).

3.   It seems clear that May's initial overture to the NYSE was precipitated by Ripley's articles, which prompted May to reply to them at the Institute's annual meeting in September, 1926. Taking issue with Ripley on many points, May did agree that the Institute should take the initiative in attempting to improve information available to shareholders. May's overture and subsequent connection with the exchange followed thereafter.

chapter

5

The road to battle

Summer, 1933

The AIA's *Journal of Accountancy* reacted favorably to the Securities Act of 1933 in its July, 1933, editorial. It would think differently in very short order, but for the moment, the AIA was pleased by the FTC's call to it for advice and assistance, which gave "indicacation of an earnest desire to make the new law not only protective but also workable." The invitation was laudable, Institute members indicated, and meant that the law would not be administered without the advice of those "most qualified to suggest practical methods"—namely, of course, themselves. An AIA committee would cooperate with the FTC to draft rules and regulations. "The law as it stands may be regarded as a singularly satisfactory piece of legislation," said the editorial, hardly suggesting the alarm that would be evident in a matter of months. There might be some areas where opinions could differ, it went on to say, but prior investigation of securities was needed to safeguard investors and raise standards of security flotation. The temporary euphoria of the AIA is a tribute to the eternal wisdom of encouraging participation in government activities by interested parties—providing, of course, they can be kept under control.

The invitation extended to the AIA also went to the ASCPA, and both sent top-ranking practitioners to participate.[1] Baldwin B. Bane, chief of the FTC Securities Division, and chairman of the FTC group working on the reporting forms, later cited the ASCPA for its help. Durand Springer, the ASCPA secretary, volunteered the efforts of five people to help the FTC in its work. Bane was appropriately grateful, and "very nearly fell on Mr. Springer's neck and wept in accepting the offer." The volunteers put in 15-hour days for about two weeks (Bane, 1933: 587).

The ASCPA had a reasonably enlightened attitude toward securities market reform and government regulation. Its brief of April 1, 1933, to the FTC argued against exemption of state political entities from federal securities regulation. Members supported an FTC right of inquiry covering the entire period in which a security was registered, and believed that revocation investigations required profit and loss information for more than just one year (Editorial, *CPA*, December, 1933: 323–326). *The Certified Public Accountant*, published by the ASCPA, even contained an article approving of the Securities Act of 1933. "Recent Federal legislation has taken cognizance of the accountant as a definite force in the economic life of our nation," applauded its author, who also thought the Securities Act a milestone toward accountant independence. Civil liability provisions were hard, but the accountant's obligation was to the public, he thought (Herwood, 1933: 746–748). The FTC *had*, in fact, kept accountants independent of the federal government by affirming state certification of accountants, thus eliminating fears of federal licensing.

Not all was serene, however, among the accountants themselves. With the crash and the legislation being proposed by the New Deal, a growing cleavage was taking place between the practicing and academic accountants. After 1932, in the euphemistic words of a man close to accounting practice during the thirties, "the academic people became a thorn in the side." The American Accounting Association took a grim view of recent business behavior.

"And now that the collapse has come, what has the public discovered was occurring behind the scenes?" asked the AAA's *Accounting Review*. The answer was numerous business malpractices, unscrupulous directors, managements violating their trust in the interest of "their own private, immediate gain," while ignoring investors and responsibilities to society. Clearly, the AAA felt it was time to get a few things said. The business community was roasted for its rapacity in the editorial, and the AAA editor, Professor Eric Kohler, placed the AIA next in line for the same treatment.

The AIA had just published a pamphlet called *Facts and Purposes*, which, the AAA observed, "seeks to place the management of the Institute among the immortals. Let the pamphlet speak for itself, as it does on every page. . . ." Selections from the AIA document were chosen with pitiless sarcasm. The AAA editorial on the AIA pamphlet dropped all pretense of brotherliness between practitioners and academics, claiming that the AIA's reports were snobbish, lacked good taste, and showed "real ignorance of the things at stake in the accounting profession." Recognizing the futility of hesitating once beyond the point of no return, Kohler continued his appraisal of the AIA:

> There is no indication of any understanding of the problems that lie ahead; . . . The Institute as pictured in *Facts and Purposes* is the survival of another generation—a static supremely self-satisfied organization unashamed to tell the world how good it is, and not afraid to stretch and overstress facts in order to prove a point (Editorial, *AR*, June, 1933: 163–164).

Commenting on the AIA's publication, *Corporate Accounts and Reports* by G. O. May, Kohler called it a refreshing turn from the *Facts and Purposes Pamphlet*. Each corporation should choose its own accounting method and stick to it, May had asserted. Five fundamental accounting principles should be applicable to all corporate reporting, but otherwise each corporation should be free to adopt such procedures as it pleased, given adequate disclosure. His five principles were summarized as follows:

1. Profit is realized only through sales.
2. Capital surplus should not absorb charges applicable to present or future income.
3. Earned surplus of a subsidiary company prior to consolidation does not constitute a part of consolidated earned surplus.
4. Dividends on treasury stock are not income.
5. Notes and accounts due from persons other than customers must be differentiated therefrom.

Deviations from standard practices should be made known to investors.

Commendable, but not entirely satisfactory, thought Kohler. Though May had not been creative, he had at least demonstrated the limitations of accounting and accountants. May had, in fact, well summarized the practitioner's credo, in effect: educate the public, make financial statements more informative and consistent, and do not let the government make the rules. Kohler thought it was time that the weaknesses of this theory and the foot dragging of practitioners were revealed; he also questioned whether disclosure without more standardization would protect the investor.

The AIA's judgment of the Securities Act changed drastically between July and October, 1933. The July editorial in the *Journal of Accounting*, noted earlier, showed some guarded pleasure with the act and its prospective administration, but an editorial in October displayed anxiety bordering on hysteria. Accountants, it was pointed out, worked under "a heavy cloud of uncertainty" because of "potential perils" in some of the act's provisions. It was the liability question that now was preeminent and the subject of many conferences.

What had happened was this: the accountants, as well as other members of the financial sector, had been looking closely at the liability provisions in Section 11 of the act, and they decided they did not at all like what they saw. Section 11 was going to be the battleground that tested the limits of how far the new administration could go in imposing new structural conditions on the financial sector. Those limits were nearer than many New Deal people thought.

The New Liability under Section 11

Section 11 was a major departure in American law. Prior to the Securities Act, recovery by a plaintiff of losses sustained in a financial transaction was based on violation of some duty by the defendant which caused the loss. All very reasonable assuming that it was not too costly to the defendant to bring suit, and to satisfy the requirements of proving that a duty was owed, violated, and loss related. Usually, however, plaintiffs *did* have a costly, difficult time establishing the required proof, which made potential defendants in the financial sector, including accountants, relatively safe from suit. Section 11 did some astonishing things to the traditional common law. To recover from the defendant, plaintiffs had only to prove that the defendants omitted or misrepresented a material fact. Plaintiffs need not have relied on the defendant's statement, nor was it required that the misrepresentation or omission caused the loss! Furthermore, the plaintiff no longer had to prove the guilt of the defendant, as traditionally required for civil liability in a negligence action. Under Section 11, the defendant had to prove his own innocence. In one act, Congress had eliminated the traditional legal requirements of reliance (on the defendant's action), causality (that the defendant's action caused the loss), and burden of proof falling on the plaintiff. In addition, the important "privity of contract" defense (see below) against suits by "third" parties was essentially eliminated.

The new law looked Draconian to those placed under its provisions. Probaby much of the lasting hatred of the financial and business sectors for Roosevelt and the New Deal stemmed from the original Section 11 of the 1933 Securities Act. The specifics of the incident largely have been forgotten by now, but the feelings persisted and set a hostile cast to business-government relationships in the 1930s and helped establish Roosevelt as an archenemy in American business folklore. For the accountants, Section 11 could not have come at a worse time, because they were still smarting from an adverse court decision. Only two years before, Benjamin Cardozo, at the time Chief Justice of the New York Court of Appeals, had imposed added liability on accountants in the landmark *Ultramares* case. And now the Securities Act was raising that liability beyond all bearable limits, or so it seemed to the practitioners.

Section 11 was a long journey away from the privity of contract protection accountants could look to before the *Ultramares* decision in 1931. It looked like a new legal world to the accountants, and their shock at facing it can be comprehended only in terms of how far removed Section 11 was from some common law concepts about contracts. The violent reaction of the financial sector to Section 11, then, is certainly understandable, also reasonable, and quite possibly legally sound, based on existing legal precedents. In any event, Section 11 in its 1933 form (see Appendix B) never reached the Supreme Court for testing. Here is the frame of reference against which Section 11 was being judged in 1933–34.

PRIVITY OF CONTRACT AND THIRD PARTY LIABILITY

Anglo-American contract law is based on the idea that persons wishing to bind themselves to legal obligations ought to have the right to do so. Contract law does not intend to obligate one to do more than one bargained for. The enforceability of an obligation almost always depends on the exchange of something of value, called consideration, between the parties. Central to contract theory is the general rule that enforceable obligations exist only among the persons who are parties to the contract. Why, the reasoning goes, should a third party, a stranger to the contract, have the right to sue either of the parties to a contract, unless the contract was made for the express benefit of the third party? The doctrine is known as *privity of contract,* and its argument appeared so eminently reasonable that there had been few departures from it, with exceptions usually based on noncontract theories, like deliberate fraud, or public policy.

The accountants believed themselves protected by the privity of contract doctrine. They argued that because their employment contract was with the client, only the client had a right to sue for losses sustained because of the accountant's inadequate performance. If the accountant failed to record important liabilities, or failed to verify alleged inventories, or miscounted accounts receivable, and his erroneous financial statement harmed the client, the client could sue. But if the client used the accountant's certified but erroneous financial statements to secure a loan from a third party, should that third party also have the right to sue the accountant on the ground of being misled? Did the third party have the right to rely on the accountant's statement, and did the accountant have a legal duty to the third party? Under a strict privity of contract interpretation, the third party has no such right because the accountant has no contractual duty to the third party. The accountant, therefore, would not be liable. Privity of contract, under that interpretation, is an effective legal defense. The accountants relied on that defense against third parties—and then came the *Ultramares* case to challenge it.

Ultramares, Negligence, and Fraud

In the *Ultramares* case, an accounting firm certified a balance sheet that had been deliberately falsified by its client corporation.[2] The balance sheet indicated the client's net worth to be in excess of $1 million, whereas insolvency was the true condition. Reasonable diligence by the accountants would have revealed the false entries. The defendant accountants anticipated the balance sheet would be the basis for financial dealings, but they had no notice that a particular plaintiff would rely upon it as the basis for extending a loan. The plaintiff, the Ultramares Corporation, loaned money to the client corporation on the strength of the accountant's certificate, sustained a loss, and brought suit against the accounting firm for damages, claiming negligence and fraud. Were the accountants liable to the third party plaintiff? At stake was what Chief Justice Cardozo, writing the unanimous opinion, called the "citadel of privity." If the liability for negligence existed, he wrote, slips, blunders, and failure to detect forgeries, deceptive entries, or thefts might place accountants under intolerable uncertainties for indeterminate amounts and time periods to indeterminate parties. A concept of duty that forced a business to operate under such hazardous conditions was questionable. Cardozo found the defendants did not owe such a duty to the plaintiffs, and therefore were not guilty of negligence toward the plaintiffs. The privity of contract defense remained intact.

Cardozo preserved the legal concept, but he did not like the result it gave. He proceeded, therefore, to expand the law to permit the plaintiff to recover. What Cardozo did was not unusual. Judges make law all the time. They have to, because legislatures do not always act, because "gaps" exist in the law, because legislation is often ambiguous and needs interpretation, and because cases must be decided. Cardozo was considered an unusually able judge; his decisions were accorded great attention, and usually applauded.

Cardozo found the defendant accountants guilty—not of negligence, but of fraud. Their audit was "so negligent as to justify a finding that they had had no genuine belief in its adequacy, for this again is fraud." Their audit was a reckless misstatement of fact or an insincere profession of an opinion, which went beyond honest blunder. Cardozo stated as a legal principle "that negligence or blindness, even when not equivalent to fraud, is nonetheless evidence to sustain an inference of fraud. At least this is so if the negligence is gross." The accountants certified as true something beyond their knowledge, and, therefore, they could be found not to have had a genuine belief that the certified balance sheet faithfully reflected the condition of the business.

The accountants were disturbed. The privity of contract principle may have been preserved, which was important to lawyers, but accountants were now liable to third parties on a new legal theory, albeit narrower than simple negligence. Either gross negligence as sufficient to sustain inference of fraud, or just good old, plain negligence, was just as sweet to a plaintiff if one or the other enabled him to collect money from a defendant—money, alas, that might increasingly come from the accounting practitioners' coffers.

Before *Ultramares* accountants boldly proclaimed their responsibility to the public, in the sure knowledge that they were not *legally* responsible. The *Ultramares* decision changed all of that. Even before the final decision, the accounting practitioners were warned that their vulnerability was increasing. Attorney Charles D. Hamel told the ASCPA members at their September, 1930, meeting that they were encountering a new liability because they influenced the life and actions of the community much more than other professionals. The liability of the accountant to the outside world was based on tort relationships, not contracts. There were two important questions involved in the issue of liability, said Hamel: negligence and reliance on the accountant's statement. He predicted accountants' responsibility for negligence to unknown third parties who rely on them would increase because business life was becoming more and more complex. Hamel disagreed with the accountants' contention that their "opinion" should have the same protection as a lawyer's. The lawyer's opinion applied known rules to facts; lawyers had considerable discretion and were paid for judgment and experience, not for legal knowledge or for sifting facts. Opinion in that sense was negligible for accountants; the nearest approach to their rendering an opinion would be fulfilling a request for a statement of value. Lawyers resembled that role in assembling data for title abstracts, and had greater liability in that area as a consequence. To argue that *Ultramares* would make accountants liable for errors of judgment was "too great a strain of reasoning" (Hamel, 1930: 338).

After *Ultramares* accountants reluctantly and unhappily became accustomed to increased liability and to approaching auditing with greater care. But to the extent possible, accountants would continue to try to limit their liability by changing the form of the auditor's statement and limiting its scope (Schlesinger, 1931: 73–75; Wildman, 1931: 3–4, 26–27; Editorial, *CPA,* April, 1931: 107–111; Editorial, *CPA,* June, 1931: 163; Editorial, *AR,* June, 1931: 143–146).

Fall, 1933

ALARM!

The October, 1933, *JA* editorial identified correctly the principal aspects of liability imposed under Section 11. Omissions or misrepresentations of material facts would make an accountant (or others) signing the registration statement liable to persons suffering a loss to the extent of the value at which the security was first offered for sale. The plaintiff did not have to show that he was misled by the error or omission. The plaintiffs needed only attribute to the accountant the untrue or omitted fact, prove the acquisition of the security, and that the accountant consented to the use of his name. This effectively shifted the burden of proof of innocence to the defendant. The accountant could be sued only on those items in a corporate financial statement prepared or certified by him. Where the accountant relied upon other expert individuals, he had only to have reasonable grounds for believing, and in fact did believe, that the statements made by others were true, and that they were fair representations of the experts.

The editorial commented that there was a school of thought, "commendable if not exactly practical," that an accountant should never hesitate to assume full financial and moral responsibility for every figure in financial statements bearing his certificate. However, another, more popular and representative professional opinion maintained that the new liability was "an overwhelming burden," that an accountant's certificate is at best merely an honest opinion, and that the accountant was not infallible. Although courts were unlikely to construe the act literally, it was nevertheless "a grave danger, and the jeopardy imposed was neither just nor fair. Minor errors might result in enormous losses against which the accountant could not insure himself (Editorial, *JA*, October, 1933: 244).[3]

Without question, the Securities Act faced the nation's financial sector with new demands and responsibilities, and investment bankers, financial writers, attorneys, and public accountants gave it their careful scrutiny. The possibility that the new act overstressed the audit as a means of investor protection was also a matter of particular concern to the accountants. Audits did not guarantee profits, and management, not accountants, controlled the business. Organized accountants would have to advise legislators on "the form in which compulsory demands should be prescribed" (Watson, 1933: 253; 260). Attorney Hamel added little comfort. "The motif of the Securities Act," he said, "is pitiless publicity." Disclosure should end flotation of worthless securities and needless industrial expansion (Hamel, 1933: 594). The accountant was in effect the prospective security owner's legal representative, with fiduciary liability (Ibid., p. 597). The accountants, by the way, had little sympathy for the bankers; the practice of combining investment and commercial banking received their criticism, as did having investment counseling departments within commercial and investment banks (Blass, 1933: 37–38).

J. M. Landis Tries to Calm the Accountants

October, 1933, was a crosscurrent of many events, all shaping the final outcome of the future Securities Exchange Act. In early October, 1933, Landis was appointed to the Federal Trade Commission along with George C. Mathews, accountant, long-time employee of Wisconsin utility commissions, and, since 1931, director of the securities division and Chief Examiner of the Wisconsin Public Service Commission. Both were to be transferred to the Securities Exchange Commission when it was formed. The New York CPAs noted the occasion by sending Landis congratulations: "Count on our cooperation," they cabled (N.Y. State Society of CPAs to Landis, 10/9/33: JMLPHULL). Benjamin V. Cohen, who had worked with Landis in drafting the Securities Act, also greeted the appointment with approval. Writing on October 9 to Felix Frankfurter who was in England for the year, Cohen expressed pleasure that the Securities Act had survived the efforts of the bankers to weaken it. Landis and Mathews would be strong bulwarks against the bankers, but the propaganda campaign that the act was interfering with recovery was a real danger.[4] Cohen was also concerned about an ineffectual committee appointed by Roosevelt to study the problem of regulating the stock exchange. It was a poor contrast to the appointment of Landis and Mathews, Cohen thought. Of the appointees, only Berle could be counted on to try for "the proper regulation."[5]

Landis wanted to alleviate the accountants' concern over the liability provisions of the act, and he accepted an invitation to speak to the New York CPAs on October 30, 1933. It was an important event, and Landis used it to make a policy statement that would clarify the act and to still the growing fury from the financial sector. He succeeded in the first objective. As for the second, he probably confirmed the misgivings of those most afraid of the act (Landis, 1933: 656–662).

Landis was well aware of the divisiveness created by the act, and he started his speech by stressing the need for calmness and recognition of the act's legitimacy. Misconceptions about it abounded, he said. Opponents and adherents were moving into separate camps; dispassionate consideration was largely lacking; intemperate attitudes were tragic. A public versus bankers confrontation was threatening, and not enough consideration was being given to the best interests of the public. The act was passed without emotionalism, Landis said; in five weeks of "unremitting labor" by a House subcommittee over the details of the legislation, there was hardly any major opposition. The vote in both the House and the Senate was unanimously in favor of the new law.

Section 11, which dealt with liability, got the greatest attention from Landis. It was "utterly erroneous" that all would be liable in the event that a misstatement was made. Every fact relevant to the value of the security need not be stated. Distinctions would be made among directors and underwriters regarding liability. "Section 11," he declared, "likens the standard of reasonableness to be applied to that which the law commonly requires of a person occupying a fiduciary relationship."

Landis then asked the question most important to his audience: if there was a misstatement or omission with reference to material fact, would a person be excused from liability if he had exercised reasonable care and had reason to believe that the statements were true? That, he said, depended upon the circumstances. Sometimes the standard would require personal knowledge of the facts assumed to be true. Delegation of duties to others was also possible. The director of a special committee, for example, could rely upon those things within the knowledge of that committee. Section 11 did not prevent reasonable delegation between underwriters and commission dealers, said Landis. These answers were of little comfort to the accountants, but his discussion of the damages issue confirmed their deepening anxieties.

Damages could never exceed the offering price of the securities, said Landis. This stipulation applied whether recision or damages were the method of recovery, he told the accountants, adding that "theoretically . . . each person . . . liable can be held to a liability equivalent to that of the total offering price of the issue. Practically, of course, no such large liability exists. Several factors will operate to keep the liability within much smaller bounds. . . ." For example, he explained, security values were unlikely to reach zero; all purchasers would not be likely to bring suits; liability was triable; and each defendant had the right of contribution against others also liable, unless fraud was involved. The penalties were not insignificant, but they should not frighten those seeking new financing through public issues. Landis criticized the legal profession as alarmists, commenting that its "opinions upon matters such as this are too often dictated by the interests of its clients," and "the opinion of the bar reflects too accurately the condition of the capital market."

The principle of legal liability under which an individual could return a chattel if it did not contain all of the qualities represented by the seller, even though the value of the chattel had fallen for reason other than the misrepresentation, was now being applied to securities, Landis patiently explained. Landis also claimed that a "second justification for the principle of noncompensatory damages in the Securities Act is their in terrorem quality" (his choice of the term "in terrorem" was to prove disastrous). Recent history indicated that common law liability or fear of criminal law prosecutions were insufficient to prevent some people from circulating erroneous information about stocks:

> . . . My good friends tell me of a reformed investment profession, that refuses to make secret profits or refuses to manipulate a market to unload its own securities under the excuse of maintaining the market during the period of secondary distribution, or refuses to engage in practices that were too current during the boom time of another era. I devoutly hope that this is true. But the evidence of even a sudden conversion is lacking, wholly irrespective of its permanency (Landis, 1933: 660).

Securities issues had been hurried to become effective prior to the act. The reluctance with which statements were amended to reveal "unpleasant information" involved the fly-by-night and "persons generally deemed by the Street to fall well within the bounds of respectability."

The FTC's regulatory powers were of great consequence, Landis argued. Practically all the accounting regulations were subject to the commission's jurisdiction. The commission could relax or strengthen registration statement requirements, and define trade terms. The commission had been "sparing" in using its powers thus far but with rapidly accumulating experience the time for "close fitting of general expressions of the Act to typical complex situations is about ripe." The regulations had the force of law and there was no "right to review general regulations of this character, except to determine whether they fall within the delegated powers of the commission" (Landis, 1933: 661). There were inherent flexibilities in the act that would permit the FTC to consider the needs of the financial sector.[6]

All in all, it was a straightforward presentation, but from the accountants' viewpoint, it was full of menace. They did not react well to it at the time,[7] and they later used it as a rally point. An evidence of the hardening attitude was NYCPA President Walter A. Staub's belated acknowledgment of Landis's October 30 speech.

Staub wrote to Landis on December 14, 1933, mentioning his "interesting contribution" (Staub to Landis, 12/14/33: JMLPHLL).

A. A. Berle, Jr., Makes Matters a Little Worse

While Landis was trying to defuse the situation, the comments of A. A. Berle, Jr., law professor and White House confidant, were guaranteed to make things worse. Berle wrote a paper for presentation to the AIA annual meeting in New Orleans in October, 1933. Because Berle could not make the meeting, the paper was read for him by Staub. The paper discussed development of consistent accounting principles that would not only aid investors and firms, but would achieve comparability among different firms in the same industry. The men to do this work were, Berle said, the "accountants themselves, acting through the medium of bodies such as the American Institute of Accountants." Yet it was questionable whether they could do the work alone:

> There is a strong body of sentiment slowly growing up to the effect that the experience of the Interstate Commerce Commission with the railroads ought to be more widely extended. So far as companies engaged in interstate commerce exceeding a minimum size are concerned, it has been argued that a bureau should be set up, presumably in the Department of Commerce, where accounts should be filed, and that this bureau should be asked to standardize accounting practices in various industries and firms.

Government control would probably be necessary to attain the result desired.

> Whatever may be said for individualism elsewhere, modern business is not individual. Upon it and the control of it and the appraisal of it and the result of its operations, there is now being erected a great structure. To my mind, that structure can only succeed as it is based on an accurate accounting system (Berle, 1933: 006–007).

It was essential that those developing the system have impartial minds. Unfortunately, impartiality was not possible for an accountant because "the job being done" by him "lies wholly in the control of his client," with the accountant "invariably" working under instructions. For the first time "in recorded history, the public is perfectly helpless in the hands of the accounting technician."

It was not easy to create a paper abrasive enough to be certain of offending just about everyone, but Berle, always the innocent progressive, managed to bring it off. Almost any one of the several allegations and suggestions made were sure to make wild men of the usually controlled, placid, practicing accountants: comparability of firm accounts within an industry! a government bureau to develop accounting systems! standardized accounting! no individualism in business! accountants wholly directed by their clients!

The sense of persecution evident in the statements of the AIA leaders at about this time must have been reinforced by Berle's comments. Berle was, after all, reputedly a White House adviser, and his remarks might well have been taken as an expression of the administration's intent. It was bad enough that the Berle paper helped commit the practicing accountants to a determined opposition to the Securities Act. In addition, it now appeared to the accountants that the new administration was truly an ideological, political, and economic enemy. Perhaps Berle was wise in staying away from the meeting and having Staub read the paper for him. The *Journal of Accountancy* never published it.[8] It must have been a marvelous evening.

Fall-Winter, 1933

THE OPPOSITION STIFFENS

Between October and December, 1933, the attitude of the practicing accountants hardened against the new Securities Act. The intense rhetoric of the December, 1933, *JA* editorial is noteworthy. It cited "widespread objection" to the "unwise policies" contained in many Securities Act provisions, and it claimed that the Act was drying up securities flotation because of "penalties which are staggering." There were some "altogether commendable" things about the Securities Act, but there was too much "impractical idealism."

The *JA* editorial stressed the key line of the Wall Street counterattack. The act, it was asserted, had brought to a standstill the financial operations prerequisite to the resumption of economic activity. People were made responsible for things entirely outside their control. There should be liability for wrongdoing, "but perils which attach to directors, bankers, lawyers, accountants and all others who have to do with the issuance of securities are absolutely prohibitive." No sane person would "assume the fantastic responsibilities" of the act; theoretical fancy had intruded "absurd and excessively extended liability." Washington was cognizant of the "destructiveness" of the Securities Act; reform might be expected at the next session of Congress, but practical men had to modify and "make practicable the ambitions of pious theory" (pp. 409–410). The more cautious and reasoned arguments in the July and even the October editorials, were now abandoned altogether. Emotionalism and fear had completely taken over.

The intensity of the practicing accountant's reaction to the apparent threat of Section 11 was based on an assumption that the liability provisions would be literally interpreted and enforced by the FTC. The accountants maintained that no audit *can* check every transaction, that their testing could miss something that might be seriously wrong. If they followed accepted methods, even after *Ultramares*, they would not be guilty of negligence if something were overlooked. But now, under Section 11, even that defense was unavailable. The accountants felt entirely vulnerable and afraid.[9]

The practicing accountants, it will be recalled, had little influence on the development of the 1933 Securities Act, which came "as something of a surprise to the profession." The AIA had no prepared strategy to deal with the legislation, or any constructive proposals for that matter, but they arranged with an influential Washington attorney, former Judge Harry Covington, to watch over the bill. Covington may have advised the AIA not to appear formally at the hearings, because "the profession's record in developing standards of financial reporting was not impressive" (Carey, 1969: 183). The AIA did make a suggestion to the congressional committee, however, which was subsequently adopted, that all registered financial statements be audited.[10]

Though the practitioners had little influence on the development of the Securities Act, once it had passed, the AIA had considerable interaction with the FTC, influencing regulations, the form of financial statements, accountant's certificates, and so forth. Nevertheless, the accountants remained unreconciled to the legislation. Although most contemporary writers on the subject believed that the Securities Act responded to public needs, they also knew that the act meant more work for the accountants. An impressive succession of articles appeared in which the liability provisions of the act were given the most attention. One commentator thought that if certain procedural auditing steps were followed, liability under Section 11 might be avoided (Hall, 1933: 452–461). Another wrote that the basis for liability was going to depend upon the determination of the reasonableness of the accountant's behavior and beliefs. It was clear that a key question was how literally the act was going to be interpreted (Gordon, 1933: 438–451).

Along with greater recognition of the accounting profession had come "truly appalling" responsibility. Some believed the Securities Act had "rather careless preparation," and they were among those pressing for repeal of the harshest provisions. Some accountants also realized that the new law was trying to broaden investor protection, but they were among those who felt the liability section was "oppressive" and out of proportion. Almost all were of the opinion that a drive was under way to create a new federal authority to govern security issues (Weidenhammer, 1933: 272–278). The accountants believed that though scrutinization of the financial system was inevitable in view of the recent debacle, they understood, and by and large faithfully discharged, their responsibility. They occasionally argued that auditors should be directly responsible to stockholders and not management. Their more frequent plea was that owners ought not to expect too much of the accountant, whose liabilities under the new act were disproportionate, because a CPA statement did not guarantee an enterprise's integrity. Accountants could only confirm the accuracy of the information given by management, but that did not mean that the public ought to be content with the situation (Andrews, 1934: 55–65).

As the year closed, it was evident that accountants, along with others in the financial sector, were recovering from their earlier paralysis. Something had gone wrong with the system, and they all knew it. One would have had to be completely out of touch with reality not to have recognized that. But while the words used by many accountants acknowledged partial responsibility, their *sense* of responsibility was certainly not widely or deeply felt. Guilt never is easy to bear, but actual punishment is usually worse, particularly when one does not really accept the guilt. As far as the accountants were concerned, they were being punished unjustly, and they intended to do something about it, if they could. They had a lot of company. Clearly, 1934 would witness a bitter fight between the administration and the financial sector.

Notes

1.   The AIA was represented at different times during the discussions by T. Edward Ross of Lybrand, Ross Bros. & Montgomery; by Joseph E. Sterrett, William B. Campbell, Percival F. Brundage, and Leland G. Sutherland of Price Waterhouse; by George P. Auld of Haskins & Sells; by Herbert M. Temple of Temple, Brissman and Co.; by John L. Carey, of the AIA; and by Harry Covington, attorney. Members of the ASCPA appointed to a special committee to meet with the FTC were Joseph J. Klein, of Klein, Hinds and Finke, New York; Frederick A. Tilton, ex-resident partner of Haskins & Sells in Detroit and recently third assistant postmaster general; Robert E. Payne, managing partner for the western division of Lawrence Scudder and Co.; Horace P. Griffith of Griffith and Co., Philadelphia; Carl Penner of Riley, Penner and Benton, Milwaukee; the secretary of the Society, Durand Springer; and Walter A. Staub, of Lybrand, Ross Bros. & Montgomery. All ASCPA representatives were present or past presidents of their state CPA societies (Cole, 1933: 386–388).

2.   *Ultramares Corporation* vs. *Touche, Niven & Co.* 225 N.Y. 170, 174, N.E. 441, (1931). Ultramares was one of those landmark decisions that represented a milestone in defining rights and liabilities of third parties. It is a curious decision, because it denied negligence as a right for recovery for third parties in a strict sense, yet in effect permitted the recovery on that ground if gross negligence was found. The plaintiff could recover, but it would have to fall under the "fraud" heading, which traditionally permitted third party recovery. The decision has come under attack recently, but is still influential as a leading case on the subject of professional liability to third parties. See Prosser on Torts, pp. 689; 716–724; "Public Accountants-Liability," in 46 ALR 3d, 980–1012; Dawson, Joseph P., "Auditors' Third Party Liability: An Ill-Considered Extension of the Law," *Washington Law Review* 46 (1971): 675–707.

3.   The editorial used the horrible example technique to "illustrate in a somewhat fantastic manner the dangers which some accountants think they have detected in the act." An investor whose $100,000 interest in stocks had declined to $10,000 could recover the difference from an accountant on the basis of a "minor error in the financial statement." This was "reductio ad absurdum," but portions of the act lent some possibility to the argument. The accountant's concern was not with negligence but with inadvertence. Accountancy was not an exact science, only the exercise of experience, knowledge, and integrity applied to facts and figures. And consequently certificates were honest expressions of carefully weighed opinion (p. 246).

4.   Cohen wrote that the "Securities Act seems to have emerged triumphant from what appeared to be a losing fight. Despite denials, I fear

that the bankers were making genuine inroads in certain official quarters. But the appointment of Jim and Mathews certainly form a bulwark that it will not be easy for the bankers to tear down. The fight, however, will be hard and one must not be over-confident because any propoganda to the effect that anything interferes with recovery is devastating in its effects. Few people are willing to pay any price for any real progress" (Cohen to Frankfurter, 10/9/33: FFPLC Box 115, Cohen folder).

5.   " 'The right hand knoweth not what the left hand doeth'. Simultaneously with the appointment of Jim and Mathews on the Trade Commission, the President apparently has constituted a committee, although official announcement remains to be made, to study the problem of regulating the Stock Exchanges. The members of this Committee consist of Berle, Dickinson, Arthur Dean, Achison, and Stanley of the Department of Justice. While I believe Berle will try to the best of his ability to fight for the proper regulation, I doubt whether he will succeed in getting anywhere with the committee appointed. My guess is that the real purpose of the Committee will be to delay rather than to encourage proper legislation. And Berle was pretty badly hoodwinked in the railroad bankruptcy legislation, as you know" (Cohen to Frankfurter, 10/9/33: FFPLC Box 115, Cohen folder).

6.   "Indeed," Landis said, "if half of the energy that has been expended in fulminating against the Act and propagandizing for amendments were enlisted in the effort to advise the commission in the wise exercise of its powers, the government and issuers, bankers, lawyers, and accountants would be far nearer to a solution of their problems" (Landis, 1933: 662).

7.   The comments following Landis's presentation emphasized that the apparently "unlimited" liability placed upon accountants was out of proportion to the possible damage. The need for certainty was a problem, too. Exception also seems to have been taken to Landis's remarks that indicated some accountants were not cooperating with the act and, in fact, were "fulminating" against it. The commentators reiterated a desire to cooperate, but under more certain circumstances (CPA, November, 1933: 662–66).

8.   The paper was called "Public Interest in Principles of Accounting." It was typeset by the Journal of Accountancy, and run off, but never published. The copy in their files is marked "Confidential," but there is no indication why the paper was so designated at the time.

9.   Some large accounting firms previously doing corporate reports that now had to be filed with the FTC abandoned that aspect of their business and devoted themselves only to auditing after the 1933 act (conversation with Carman Blough, 10/19/72).

10.   The senior partner of Haskins & Sells, Arthur H. Carter, decided to testify at hearings before the Senate Committee on Banking and Cur-

rency. Carter argued that accountants are capable only of giving their opinion; it would be hard to establish a standard of bookkeeping, but that one could rely upon principles of accounting. Each industry by itself could have a unique set of accounts. Audits by independent accountants were firmly endorsed (Carey, 1969: 193).

chapter

6

Wall Street goes on "strike"

George Oliver May Speaks to the Accountants

George Oliver May, senior partner of Price Waterhouse & Co., intellectual leader of the practicing accountants, was as influential as any practitioner in the country. Formidable, conservative, and resistant to the trends threatening his profession, his views carried immense weight and typified the attitude of the AIA toward accounting theory and technique, and toward the government. He never acknowledged publicly any responsibility on the part of the accounting profession for the speculative excesses of the 1920s. May's views seemed always to carry the "snobbish," self-satisfied AIA assurance that the AAA complained about. Most important, May's attitude set the tone for the practicing accountants' future interaction with the Securities and Exchange Commission.

May went right to the heart of the matter in a December, 1933, speech published the following month. The two crucial flaws in the new Securities Act, he said, were liability of accountants under Section 11 and the powers of the Federal Trade Commission to define accounting terms and make regulations under Section 19. The act might have been natural or inevitable, but its liability provisions were too drastic and "will place the distribution of securities in the worse possible hands" (May, 1934: 10). "There is reason to fear," May said pointedly, "that responsible people will refuse to accept the unfair liability imposed on them by Congress under this act, and will continue to refuse until juster provisions are enacted" (Ibid., p. 11).

To May, Section 11 was clearly punitive regarding the account- ant's limited services on new issues—which were, as he saw it, to express honest and informed judgments about the financial position and the operating results of the issuer "according to some acceptable standard of accounting conventions" (Ibid., p. 12). Reviewing Lan- dis's now familiar statement before the New York CPAs, May con- cluded no prudent businessman would assume such large liability. The fees received by accountants for new financing work were small, percentagewise; why jeopardize their entire earnings? The public interest would be better served by limiting the financial responsibility of accountants to errors of professional judgment. Ingenuously, May claimed there was "nothing in the history of accounting in recent years to warrant such an attitude towards the profession or that pro- vision which puts on the accountant the burden of proving his inno- cence" (Ibid., p. 15). Professional requirements were sufficient to enforce care and thoroughness; disproportionate personal liability would only discourage people from offering opinions.

Investors were really at fault, May argued. Accountants could have done more to discourage investors from taking accountants' opinions as facts, but their certificates had always said "in our opinion." Matters subject to accountants' opinions were the fairness of the balance sheet and its supporting accounting principles, how those principles were applied to the facts, and how the results were presented. Accountants, he threatened, would not fully accept ap- pointments unless Congress amended the Securities Act.[1] Definition of balance sheet and profit and loss statement should be done by the FTC, in addition to indicating acceptable accounting principles sanc- tioning "in many instances alternative methods . . . mutually con- sistent and . . . consistently applied" (May, 1934: 21). What May was saying was that it was all right for the FTC to set some minimal definitions and standards, but that the FTC ought not to do too much. Particularly, the FTC should not limit accountants' flexibility. The problem was also partially institutional, May seemed to think, be- cause commercial securities were hazardous and unsuitable for the small investor.[2]

THE WALL STREET "STRIKE"

The tone of May's speech was deceivingly mild. Behind it lay a campaign involving the major actors in the nation's financial sector to undermine the Securities Act. The commercial bankers, investment bankers, the New York Stock Exchange, the Wall Street law firms, and the accountants were all allied in a claim that the absence of capital investment resulted from the financial sector's deliberate refusal to participate in new capital flotations because of the liability provisions of the act. Amend the act and capital would flow into industry, they promised. Fail to amend it, and capital investors would continue to boycott new offerings. That too was a promise. But was the absence of new capital issues due to economic conditions or the recalcitrance of the financial sector? It was difficult to tell for certain, and for a nation economically prostrate, it was hard to resist the possibility that if the act were amended, things might improve. Those in the financial sector may have believed their own rhetoric, but many not in it noted that even securities exempt from FTC registration were not coming into the market, and that the Investment Bankers Association's "violent opposition" was partly for selfish reasons. Still, Commissioner James M. Landis's October 29, 1933, speech had merely confirmed the impression of most accountants that the liability section was "oppressive." The question was whether the New Deal administration would hold out against Wall Street's "strike," whether it would be worth the gamble to hold out. What it amounted to was this: the depression was real, but was the Wall Street "strike"?

J. M. LANDIS WRITES TO F. D. ROOSEVELT

The "best evidence," Landis wrote to Roosevelt on December 4, 1933, in an 11-page, carefully reasoned memorandum, lent practically no support to the assertion that the dearth of new capital issues was attributable to the Securities Act. Claims to that effect by bankers and their counsel were not genuine. There were so many reasons behind the drying up of new issues, that relating it causally to the act was impossible:

> One says that the directors refuse to assume the liabilities, though the bankers are willing to do so. Another reverses this unwillingness. The third ascribes it to a campaign of legal terrorizing brought about by the lawyers. Though the reasons given are diverse, all unite in saying that the fear of the liabilities under the Act is a fact that exists independent of its justification; but all admit that whether this fear will actually be a block to the capital market has met no real test and is not likely to do so under present conditions.

The failure of several issues to be floated in the market was more an indication of the inability of the bankers to handle it than of their lack of desire to do so because of the act, said Landis. Furthermore, refunding (of old issues) appeared to have been no major problem.

"Innumerable amendments" had been suggested to weaken the act. The amendment to limit the right of suit to those relying on untrue and misleading statements in the prospectus or registration statement appeared fair on its face, but it could also open an enormous loophole for evasion. Investor reliance on the registration statement, which need only be filed with the FTC, would hardly ever occur. Reliance on the prospectus could be minimized because the act did not compel delivery of a prospectus in an intrastate transaction. But buyer reliance on the registration statement and the prospectus, Landis argued, rested on those documents because they were the basic inducements for purchase.

A second proposed amendment designed to clarify omissions of material facts was based upon an initial misconstruction by the IBA, later expressly clarified in the act, that omissions of material facts were grounds for liability only when the material facts had been required by the registration statement or where the statements of facts were so partial as to be in substance untrue. A third proposed amendment was designed to eliminate the right to return the security and demand the purchase price and to limit the damages to those caused by the misleading or untrue statements. Landis opposed the suggestion, although he acknowledged some arguments in favor of it.[3] The practical difficulties, Landis indicated, in proving an amount of loss caused by misconduct of directors, underwriters, and accountants were so great as to make the liability theoretical rather than real. Civil damages "of a primitive character" were common in the law and were needed to assure compliance with the act. Amendments the FTC forced upon registrants were a tragic record of avoidance, and intentional concealment of facts from the public was obvious.

> Indeed, as compared with the disclosures now being made before the Senate Investigating Committee, these seem worse because they illustrate such a permeating disregard of what you happily designated as "the high standards of trusteeship."
>
> . . . Too many of the misleading circulars [about the act] . . . have been written by the very legal firms that in ordinary

times do the work for the reputedly respectable investment banking houses (Landis to Roosevelt, 12/4/33: JMLPLC, Box 94, FTC file).

These included an outstanding legal firm and "an accounting firm of wide reputation."[4]

Landis offered a series of amendments that might strengthen the act, though he advised the President that the act had not yet had the opportunity "to operate under conditions that permit its effects to be appreciated." Landis suggested requiring periodic certified financial reports from corporations whose securities were already in the hands of the public; eliminating exempted securities from the provisions of the act, licensing security dealers, extending registration and publicity requirements to proxy solicitation and to the exchange of securities, and creating certain minimum requirements with respect to the issuance of any securities. He also suggested the "creation of a Bureau of Financial Statistics whose functions would be both to make public unbiased general investment facts and also to develop adequate methods for comparable corporation accounting." This latter suggestion would have meant an enormous reduction of autonomy for accountants. It was never implemented.

Whether corporate management would default rather than work under the act was still merely speculative. "Threats, of course, are made but with the avowed purpose of thereby forcing emasculation of the Act," said Landis. He did not believe that experience had shown that modifications were advisable. "The hope that the Act will be shortly modified has been responsible for the organization of 'strike' activities against the Act. . . ." Landis's description of the campaign against the act was blunt.

> Ever since the passage of the Act, a campaign designed to undo its principles has been launched against it. . . . What financial criticism that existed in the beginning that was favorable to the Act has ceased.
>
> In Washington, the critics of the Act have been unusually active. A sabotage, based upon a misconstruction of the Act, seems to have been directed against a proposed government bond issue, only to evaporate after action by the Federal Trade Commission. Lawyers, who acted as counsel for the Investment Bankers Association during the passage of the Act and who destroyed themselves before a Congressional Committee by the patently crude jokers they sought to write into the draft bill have been constantly active. . . . That these men will continue to in-

sinuate themselves into government counsels is hardly to be doubted. The amendments that they have prepared and submitted for consideration are still not free from the vice of seeking to do much more than they pretend.

The Securities Act was one of the outstanding achievements of the New Deal; to go back upon its principles was unthinkable, Landis urged. "Changes seemingly innocuous may open wide opportunities for evasion, and the delegation of this task to those not wholeheartedly for the effectuation of the principles of the Act is an invitation to subversion of its major objectives," he said, echoing Cohen's reservations in an oblique reference to the committee Roosevelt appointed to look into the matter. The only safe course was to remain adamant. Revision would not bring forth capital investment, ground gained would be lost, "and the accumulation of experience, so badly needed must begin anew" (Landis to Roosevelt, 12/4/33: JMLPLC, Box 94, FTC file, 1933).

Winter-Spring, 1934

Was the "Strike" against Capital Investment Real?

The attack on the Securities Act was taking two lines, according to Bernard Flexner, a lawyer with a considerable amount of experience in Wall Street. The first was a general technical raking over of the act, with the attackers using "suppositious" cases to suggest that its provisions were uncertain or contained injustices. The second "really insidious" attack was in the guise of a "practical" argument. It's import was that whether or not the act was expedient on a long-term basis, it had to be abolished; otherwise, bankers and company directors would not cooperate with the President's recovery plans (Flexner, 1934: 232–250).

The similarity between the Landis letter to Roosevelt and an article by Flexner in the *Atlantic Monthly* indicates a possible collaboration between them.[5] Flexner agreed new securities were lacking, but it was because the brokers were unable, not unwilling, to handle them. The real issue was the attack upon the spirit of the act, upon its civil liability provisions; the act had been deliberately misinterpreted by those made liable. In a suit for damages "with the burden of proof on the investor, Wall Street lawyers would win every time," he wrote. If liability of a director to an investor was going to be effective, it had to be in the "nature of recision." The threat that no one will act as a director in view of the risks is nonsense, he argued. Directors operate as such because of prestige and information, not because of fees. Experts involved also ought to carry their share of liability. The argument of the "practical men" that disclosure would protect the investor was in fact not practical.

> Utopian theories of teaching the small investor overnight that he should not sink his money in securities until he has made the kind of investigation which he is not qualified to make—and which, in any event he lacks the power to make—are not a practical answer. It is a *condition* which confronts us—not a theory (Flexner, 1934: 246).

Other critics of Wall Street's stance argued it was unlikely the act stopped financing or refinancing. "Recently there seems to be a drive upon the part of certain interests to prove that because there are no new capital flotations or refunding of outstanding securities," wrote Deneen A. Watson, secretary of the National Association of Securities Commissioners, "that the same is caused by the enactment of the Federal Securities Act." But financing, he concluded, would have stopped on its own[6] (Watson, 1933: 603–604). Baldwin B. Bane also argued against the reality of the "strike." When 1929 arrived it was evident that it would be futile to expect reforms from the financial world, Bane told an ASCPA meeting in Milwaukee. Investors' rights and sponsors' liabilities were reasonable; the act was intrinsically fair. "One fails to understand the complaints, the legal manifestations of an insistence upon misinterpreting plain meanings, unless one realizes that the irresponsible and reckless selfishness that launched the host of unsound securities is not dead" (Bane, 1933: 590–591). Accountants' certifications of registration statements and prospectuses were on behalf of the issuer, but accountants also had an obligation to the investing public; otherwise there would be no need for the certification. The act required the accountant to be independent of the issuer, and therefore indemnification contracts on behalf of the accountant by the issuer were not desirable.[7]

Spring, 1934

"THE STOCK EXCHANGE BILL IS RECEIVING A TERRIFIC BATTERING"

Demands for stock-exchange regulation, even from many businessmen, intensified after the market broke again in late 1933. Short selling and bear pools had been present on Wall Street. The experience hardened Roosevelt's attitude toward the New York Stock Exchange. Stock exchange regulations had not been included in the 1933 Securities Act when their adoption would have involved less of a fight. Roosevelt's early 1933 decision to separate the regulation of securities into a Securities Act and the regulation of the stock exchange into a Securities Exchange Act probably made both measures weaker than if passed together. Sam Rayburn's domination of the House Interstate Commerce Committee peaked during consideration of the first act, but when the time came for securities exchange regulation, circumstances had changed. Felix Frankfurter, an important guide of the '33 act, was visiting England. Duncan Fletcher's Senate Banking and Currency Committee was eager to take a stronger role in the drafting of the new act.[8] Congress was reverting to its characteristic slowness when a crisis atmosphere wanes. Those representing the stock exchange were better prepared for the legislative challenge than the bankers had been on the securities bill. The desire to regulate stock margins meant that Congress had to consider the Federal Reserve System, which automatically involved the Federal Reserve Board and powerful Senator Carter Glass, who was much concerned about any proposals that would affect the Fed. And, finally, Roosevelt's committee of appointees, about which Cohen had expressed skepticism to evaluate the possibilities of the new security act had accomplished little.[9]

Landis had been working independently on a stock exchange bill within the FTC, but joined Cohen and Corcoran in discussions about the proposed legislation at the end of December. Federal Reserve Board power over margin requirements was acceptable to Landis, but not to Cohen and Corcoran. All three wanted the exchange's internal organization revised. Cohen was the principal draftsman of the bill with advice, criticism, and help of Landis, Corcoran, Flynn, and Winfield Riefler, a statistician with the Federal Reserve Board. Introduced February 10, 1934, in both the House and Senate, the securities-exchange measure known as the Rayburn-Fletcher Bill, limited both the credit for trading on the exchanges and the activities of the individual exchange members. Trading by directors, officers, and principal stockholders of listed corporations, and the financial affairs of listed corporations, would become public record under FTC control. The major innovation, Section 10, in effect limited exchange membership to commission brokers executing orders for the public; floor trading for their own account was abolished and transactions had to be effected on fixed price orders (Parrish, 1970: 109–118).

From the standpoint of greater economic stability and improved business morals, the first Rayburn-Fletcher Bill was, as Frankfurter observed, brilliantly conceived and expertly drawn. But from the standpoint of political possibilities in the fourth year of depression, it was doomed to revision. Seldom has one measure antagonized so many different constituencies (Parrish: 1970: 121).

Proud, influential, elitist Richard Whitney, president of the New York Stock Exchange, led the opposition. "For Whitney the notion of federal regulation of the Stock Exchange was practically lèse-majesté." His objections to the initial bill covered almost all of its aspects. If passed, the bill would give the FTC "absolute power to manage and to operate" the exchanges, Whitney claimed, and it was likely to freeze the liquid securities market just as the 1933 act had frozen the capital securities market. If that happened, a tremendous withdrawal of corporations from the exchanges would occur. Federal regulation was undesirable and the bill unconstitutional, he contended. Whitney did more than just talk against the bill; he became a very busy activist:

Four days after Roosevelt's (February 9) message Whitney called in representatives of the thirty principal wire houses to plan a campaign against the bill. In another two days he sent a letter to all members of the Exchange and the presidents of eighty large corporations. When debate began, he rented a house in Washington in order to direct the fight in person. Businessmen across the country rallied to his leadership (Schlesinger, 1958: 462–463).

"The New Deal," historian Arthur Schlesinger, Jr., has observed, "had not thus far confronted such an outburst of business indignation." Sam Rayburn called it "the most powerful lobby ever organized against any bill which ever came up in Congress." Opposition to the bill centered on the fixed margin requirements and *the provision for the FTC as the administering agency!* Whitney favored a seven man *special commission* with two members representing the stock exchanges and one from the Federal Reserve Banks, and in this idea he was helped by Senator Glass who led the fight for a separate commission" (Schlesinger, 1958: 464–465). The Federal Reserve also had its reservations about the bill, and even Wall Street moderates were not too happy about it. As Michael Parrish has pointed out, the "reform sentiment within the business and financial community, always a fleeting commodity, vanished suddenly" (Parrish, 1970: 122). For the first three weeks after the hearings began, investment banking and Exchange leaders appeared before the Rayburn and Fletcher committees. They condemned the proposed legislation as unnecessary, unworkable, and un-American. And under their barrage, "the original draftsmen, smothered by an avalanche of abuse, lacking positive support from any segment of business or finance, and criticized by cabinet members, retreated from the first Rayburn-Fletcher Bill" (Parrish, 1970: 124). Internal divisions among the protagonists had not helped either. Flynn and Cohen wanted explicit statutory prohibitions and requirements, and Landis favored more administration and less legislation. Obviously, concessions were going to have to be made to secure support for the bill.

"The Stock Exchange Bill is receiving a terrific battering," Landis wrote to Frankfurter on March 6, 1934. "All the corporate wealth of this country has gone into the attack and carried it all the way up to the White House. I think F.D.R. will stand very firm on its essentials, however." If Landis had little respect for the financiers and their legal counsel,[10] he had had a great deal for the President: "I am always delighted in F.D.'s sense of realities in this struggle. A man with less political sense would take as genuine much of the mouthings which are nothing but cleverly devised means of political maneuvering."

Nevertheless, Landis was pleased with the way the struggle over the amendment of Securities Act of 1933 was developing. It was going to be amended, but the persons really concerned with its objectives were the ones who were going to write the amendments. Causality would be amended and the underwriters' liability would be limited to participation.[11] He was more impressed than ever with Sam Rayburn, and the fact that the FTC was doing well and Congress was about to give another half million for administration of the act was also a source of gratification, although both he and Frankfurter shared a growing sense of impatience with the lack of support from sources they felt should be more sympathetic.[12]

Landis knew, however, how the accountants felt about the bill. They were concerned that a large federal agency would preempt CPA auditing standards, take over the role of determining who could do the certification, and prescribe accounting forms and methods. Communications had been exchanged between Landis and Walter A. Staub, then president of the New York CPAs, and Louis H. Renn,

Staub's executive assistant. Some of the anxieties of the CPAs had been revealed in an undated Renn memo to Landis appending two newspaper clippings from the March 23, 1934, *New York Journal of Commerce*. One article suggested the exchange bill might set up "a large bureaucracy to audit accounts of corporations and thereby threaten the work of fifty years or more in this country toward building up the standard of audits by independent certified public accountants." Was this a serious possibility, Renn asked? The article also suggested that the proposed law required certification of corporate financial reports by independent public accountants or as the commission may prescribe. The other clipping reported on the brief by J.M.B. Hoxsey presented to the House Committee on Interstate Commerce by Whitney. The article said:

> Section 12(b), covering the authority of the Commission to prescribe corporation accounting forms should be left out entirely, declared Mr. Hoxsey, commenting that such success cannot attend the legal prescribing of accounting methods. He asserted that such a section would "prevent all future progress in the accounting art." He asked for a new paragraph in Section 18 to require corporations to state the method of accounting used. He also took cognizance of a late stock exchange ruling requiring a statement annually that the accounting methods used are consistently applied, by suggesting such a paragraph in the law (Renn to Landis 3/3/34: JMLPHLL).

Landis' reply to Renn was prophetic. It was the first time he indicated that the federal agency in charge of setting corporate financial reporting standards would hesitate to use that authority. It was three months before the creation of the SEC. The fear of "that portion of the Stock Exchange Bill giving the Commission power to develop uniform systems of reporting and accounting" had no foundation in fact, Landis said.

> We ought eventually to move toward some uniformity in accounting, but it will be obviously a long time before that can be done. . . . That section of the bill as I see it in operation will mean that the Commission would work towards an end of that type, cooperating very fully with a particular interest involved. Surely that is sensible, and ought not to give rise to any fear (Landis to Renn, 3/26/34: JMLPHLL).

Landis knew the value of compromise. He also recognized the accountants' vital interest in corporate financial reporting authority. His attitude would typify SEC operations subsequently. The accountants did not realize it at the time, but they had little to fear.

The accountants had established a general "party line" by then. Staub, for example, gave the impression that he really thought investors were entitled to more information and that the pending legislation was warranted. But he also took the position that "progress is much more likely to come from unhampered development of the profession than by the prescription of stereotyped forms and methods which become more or less frozen if made the subject of legal restriction"[13]—a reference, superficially, to the accountants' preoccupation with the forms developed by the FTC. More significant was Staub's picturization of the government as a malevolent beast, thoughtlessly and rigidly creating accounting requirements that would inevitably stifle creative thought and individual initiative in corporate financial reporting technical development. It was a shameless strawman creation, but one that became a persistent part of the accountants' policy thereafter, as will be shown. Staub also was concerned with the public's "tendency" to treat certifications as fact rather than opinion, but even Landis knew better than to consider certifications as fact, he implied.[14] Staub also opposed the Security Exchange Act's liability provisions (Renn to Landis, 3/27/34: JMLPHLL).

The Last Phase of the Fight

In early March "Whitney's counter-offensive" was affecting even the administration, which became divided over the issue. New allies were needed by Landis, Cohen, and Corcoran, who approached the FRB, the Treasury, and the New York brokerage houses. A modified bill offered on March 19 gave the FRB margin requirement jurisdiction, although Cohen opposed the modifications, feeling that the Fed was too much under Wall Street influence. Provisions for segregation of exchange functions were weakened, but the sections on manipulative devices, corporate reports, listing requirements, proxies, and trading by directors underwent no substantial revision" (Parrish, 1970: 128).

The New York brokerage houses, through their representative Raoul Desverine, proposed that a Securities Exchange Commission be created. The proposal, however, was not adopted at this point because Roosevelt's basic idea was credit limitation to curb speculation. The rejection of Desverine's major suggestions, unfortunately, "left the Commission Houses more antagonistic than before." They, too, now regarded the bill as "punishment." Whitney did not even like this new proposal: he wanted the bill significantly weakened, and also urged creation of a special commission. Whitney's suggestions angered Rayburn, and Whitney "returned to New York where, in a desperate effort to unite his constituency, he began to circulate the idea that the legislation had been written 'by a bunch of Jews out to get (J.P.) Morgan" (Parrish, 1970: 129–130). With the regional exchanges, floor traders, and specialists continuing their opposition, the debates degenerated into low farce as the hearings considered allegations that the bill was Communist inspired—a red herring swimming slowly into April (Schlesinger, 1958: 457–459; Parrish, 1970: 131).

Significant changes were made to appease the vocal opposition, much of it in the Senate and House. Rayburn weakened the measure between March 24 and April 2 by reducing margin requirements and watering down further the separation of functions in the exchanges. On April 9 Fletcher's Senate committee adopted an amendment by Senator Glass abolishing jurisdiction over stock exchange regulation by both the Federal Reserve Board and the Federal Trade Commission and creating a three-man Securities and Exchange Commission to be appointed by the President. Proposed SEC authority over margin requirements created some alarm among the Federal Reserve Board, the New York Stock Exchange, and others, and on April 11 a compromise was adopted permitting the SEC to fix margin requirements for brokers to customers, and the Fed prescribing bank credit margins to brokers. Statutory margin guidelines were eliminated, technically isolating the Fed from the stock market. On April 17, Senator James Byrnes, reputedly a White House spokesman, proposed increasing the new commission's membership from three to five. The amendment passed, and the Senate bill then went to conference with the House bill. Prior to the acceptance of a new Securities and Exchange Commission on April 17, the FTC was instructed to prescribe the form of reports by corporations "in accordance with accepted principles of accounting," a provision eliminated in the final version of the act.

"Poor Tom Has Had to Bear Much More than His Fair Share of the Battle"

The fight affected the Cohen-Landis-Corcoran group physically and emotionally. "Poor Tom [Corcoran] has had to bear much more than his fair share of the battle," Cohen wrote to Frankfurter on May 11. "Because of his sheer ability as well as his brilliant fluency and superb advocacy, I have left him to bear the brunt of the attack. And because of his strength, he has been the more feared by far of the two of us."

> The result is that attempts are made to poison people's minds against him, the most hostile members of the house committee, for example, talk against him, pretend to dislike him in particular and at times even to express relative confidence in me—a doubtful compliment indeed. Of course Tom understands it all. But still he is a very tender and sensitive soul, much more so than his usual cheerful mien would lead one to believe. And he has been dreadfully alone in the battle. Because of his strength, few people realize that even he may be a bit disheartened and discouraged at times. And worst of all there are few about with mind and heart equal to his to give him a word of cheer. A god cannot be consoled by a fool.

"Ray Moley has been most helpful with the skipper," Cohen wrote, but even Moley seemed to have wavered in the fight. Should Frankfurter return?

> . . . there is no question of the need of real direction, real understanding, and some real personal force over here. The men attached to you are working hard, but their spirits are a little low and the consciousness of any coherent program is somewhat dulled (Cohen to Frankfurter, 5/11/34: FFPLC, Box 115).

By April's end, the pattern of regulation was settled. The government would be allowed to investigate, compel disclosure, control margins, and control exchange rules. Toward the end of May the House accepted a new commission and the Senate consented to nominal limitation of margins and permission of Federal Reserve Board intervention. In its final version, the Rayburn-Fletcher Bill "in effect confided to the discretion of the new Securities and Exchange

Commission much of the authority over the stock market which the earlier version had made mandatory in the statute" (Schlesinger, 1958: 466–467).

Amendments to the Securities Act of 1933

As the Rayburn-Fletcher Bill wound its way through Congress, the previously passed Securities Act also came in for further attack—and revision. Amendments to the 1933 act were attached as riders to the stock-exchange bill. The Roper committee recommended major changes in the 1933 act to the President, primarily because it assumed the liability provisions were interfering with the flow of capital on Wall Street. It proposed civil liability limitation to damages reasonably attributable to an untrue statement or the omission of facts where the purchaser relied on the registration statement; it also proposed that liability be apportioned among the underwriters based on their participation. The committee also recommended that a "reasonable" standard of care should be imposed on those liable for the registration statement. Similar amendments drafted by the American Bar Association, which would have made a shambles of many of the control provisions, were also coupled with major revisions in the schedule of information required for registration.[15]

The President, however, "kept a tight reign on the final amending process." He turned to a group including Landis, Cohen, and the Treasury's Oliphant to review the final amendments, and they salvaged as much as they could of the original bill. Concessions included a reduction on the time limit for civil suits. Causality was introduced as a defense by relating the decline in a security's value to the significance of the error or omission in the registration statement. Reasonable care was defined as that of a prudent man in the management of his own property. The original liability standard in the 1933 Act placed upon directors a positive requirement to satisfy that reasonable grounds existed to believe, and they did believe, that the statements were true. This liability was significantly eased through an amendment which now freed directors of responsibility for experts' reports in the absence of reasonable ground to believe they were untrue. Underwriters liability was limited to participation. Courts were instructed to assess full costs against parties presenting unmeritorious claims or defenses. However, no concession was made to the demand that purchasers rely upon the registration statement.

Most important from the point of view of regulatory control, no changes were made in the statutory requirements for financial data (Parrish, 1970: 195–196); the commission still had the right to prescribe accounting rules (Appendix B).

The business community's overwhelming opposition to the New Deal's legislation on securities reform and stock exchange regulation reflected its concern that vast power might be given to a commission if it had authority to control a corporation's books. From the point of view of the drafters of the securities acts, it was more critical to get the important powers into the commission than to have all the powers they would have liked to see assigned to the new regulatory group. The retreat from the Securities Act of 1933 was partially due to the impression created that the government was becoming a tyrant. Many amendments were designed to appease the financial community, but even so, little new private investment appeared. The claim that amendment of the liability provisions would unloose a torrent of new private investment was, after all, nonsense. The Wall Street "strike," in other words, was a myth.

Initially, the drafters of the Securities Exchange Act believed the powers would be retained in the FTC, but the "Wall Street people" wanted a separate, specialized commission under the assumption that they could control it better than one more general, like the FTC, and they got their wish. The financial sector was unsuccessful, however, in opposing the provisions for controlling corporate reporting, an opposition in which the accounting firms and the IBA played leading parts. The accountants had also cooperated with the lawyers in backing the opposition, which was led by the New York Stock Exchange, the Association of Stock Brokers, and the American Stock Exchange.

What did the writers of the Securities Acts intend about treatment of accounting principles and financial reporting rules? Did they intend to have the Securities and Exchange Commission prescribe detailed accounting techniques, or simply insure full or fair disclosure? Did they seriously consider directing the SEC to prescribe mandatory accounting principles? Benjamin Cohen recalled the ultimate idea was to obtain power for the commission so it could develop and make final decisions on "sound" accounting principles, with provision for some leeway. There would have been "quite a fight," if the SEC was going to dictate accounting procedures or develop a uniform system of accounting. Therefore, they avoided making the provisions mandatory. In addition, they had the feeling that it might also be too much of a straightjacket for the commission to have to follow (conversation with Benjamin V. Cohen, 10/18/72).

At the insistence of the Senate, no requirement was made in the 1934 act for the SEC to follow "accepted principles of accounting" (Parrish, 1970: 141–142). Instead, the final version of Section 13 covering reporting requirements authorized the SEC to prescribe the form of corporate registration statements. Congress gave the SEC extensive rule making authority; but specific requirements were not imposed, which was just as well because generally accepted principles of accounting were an illusion.

The financial sector, and in particular the practicing accountants, won a partial victory in staving off complete government regulation, and achieving reduction of liability to investors. The diminution of accountant autonomy, compared with the 1920s, was enormous, but things could have been worse, and they knew it.

> It is interesting to note that although accountants realized the inherent weakness in their techniques and the growing financial and economic complexities attendant with the concentration of capital in the corporate form of business enterprise, they were unwilling to accept self-imposed restrictions. Yet, in the thirties, they had to accept restrictions imposed by external groups (Taylor, 1941: 193).

Administrative discretion rather than mandates would thereafter determine the development and substance of corporate financial accounting rules under the two acts. How the American Institute of Accountants felt about this matter was clear. Their problem was to see to it that the Securities and Exchange Commission exerted as little of its statutory powers as possible.

Notes

1.   "Clearly," May said, "only action by congress can remove the fundamental and, as I feel, insuperable obstacles to the free acceptance of appointments under the act by accountants which have been created by the imposition of a liability bearing no relation either to the injury caused by the accountants or the compensation received by him. If, however, this major difficulty could be removed, the remaining problem could probably be solved by judicious use by the commission of the powers conferred on it under Section 19" (May, 1934: 21).

2. Realistically, three markets seemed needed, May wrote: (1) a govermentally fostered system for the safe investment of small savings, (2) a broad market subject to requirements for frank disclosure without undue drastic penalties for business investments, and (3) some medium entirely divorced from the idea of investment for the gratification of the "seemingly ineradicable instinct for gambling" (May, 1934: 22–23).

3. Landis acknowledged that theoretically eliminating recision was fair, that it would bring the Securities Act into "better alignment with the British Companies Act" although the latter was also a general incorporation statute providing many additional controls lacking in the Securities Act; it would solve the problem of successive purchasers' suits; and, finally, it would conceivably lead to a more liberal construction of what a material misstatement is. Courts might "so hesitate to impose the larger liabilities of the present Act that they will be led to construe the Act with unwarranted strictness against the investor—a tendency not unknown to the law."

Other proposed amendments dealt with elimination of Section 15, which made a person controlling another equally responsible person liable with him; the shortening of the period within which purchasers could sue; and, an amendment designed to limit litigation to the federal courts. Landis opposed all three.

4. A subsequent memorandum by Landis in response to an F.D.R. inquiry identified these as John Foster Dulles's firm in Wall Street, and Lybrand, Ross Bros. & Montgomery (JMLPLC, Box 94, FTC, file, 1933).

5. There appears to have been a close relationship between Flexner and Landis. Somewhat after these events, on September 27, 1935, Flexner wrote to Landis congratulating him on his thirty-sixth birthday and indicating reassurance in "this part of the business world" on his selection for the chairmanship of the SEC (Flexner to Landis, 9/27/35: JMLPLC, Folder A, Box 9). Landis replied to Flexner on October 8 and thanked him for his note, adding: "I hope very much that you will be here in Washington before long, because there are many problems upon which I would like to get your point of view and your sense of direction" (Landis to Flexner, 10/8/35: JMLPLC, Folder A, Box 9).

6. Funding and refunding had become successively less since 1929, Watson cited. For the eight months ending August 31, 1929, corporate, foreign government, agricultural, and municipal financing was $8.1 billion; for 1930, it was $6.1 billion; for 1931, $3.4 billion; for 1932, $1.2 billion; and for 1933, $.7 billion. Corporate issues, including new capital and refunding issues, in the United States for the eight months ending August 31, 1929, totaled $7.2 billion; for 1930, $4.6 billion; for 1931, $2.2 billion; for 1932, $.5 billion; for 1933, $.3 billion. "These figures clearly indicate to me that the new securities issues and refunding of outstanding issues have

dropped in large amounts each year since 1929. My conclusion, therefore, is that the Federal Securities Act of 1933 has not stopped such activities as I believe the situation would have prevailed anyway" (Watson, 1933: 604).

7.   The risk could probably be distributed by insurance arrangements throughout the profession or through that part of it that was involved in registration and prospectus examinations, Bane thought. "The risk is at most a moderate one to the accountant who upholds his professional standards, while at the same time the importance, dignity and value of his public services are conspiciously enhanced by the reliance which this new law places upon him" (Bane, 1933: 593).

8.   Max Lowenthal and John P. Flynn of Senator Fletcher's staff wanted to impress their ideas upon the new legislation. Flynn in particular had always been an arch-enemy of the Wall Street establishment.

9.   Included on the committee were Secretary of Commerce Daniel C. Roper and Assistant Secretary John Dickinson, Landis, Berle, and Arthur Dean of the Wall Street law firm of Sullivan & Cromwell.

10.   "The job that has been done in the Senate for the past two years has taught the general run of human beings a very deep lesson. Blandishment such as that of witness Eustace Seligman and my friends of the Street, is one of their chief weapons. It is an insidious thing, because no one always wants to appear as an unreasonable, unthinking and malicious devil.

"My office for the last three weeks has been a general reception room for brokers, bankers and the like who come in and tell me their troubles. I listen honestly and conscientiously, and always reaffirm my confidence that both Congress and the President will see to it that a good and fair Stock Exchange Bill will eventually be written. It is easy, though, to lose one's perspective in this whole turmoil, either to be too easy or too hard. When I think of what you did to me by making me, over night, an authority on finance, I am not sure whether you acted wisely or not. But one thing I am fairly certain, and that is that we have plenty of authorities on security distribution who are not worth the name" (Landis to Frankfurter, 3/6/34: FFPLC, Box 117).

11.   Landis wrote Frankfurter that "it looks as if we are going to introduce an element of causality into the damages that are recoverable"; underwriters' damages would be limited to the extent of their participation; judges could assess cost against both plaintiffs and defendants; Section 15 would be rewritten to do what it really is supposed to do, that is, to thrust liability back where it should be thrust back, and yet not to destroy the concept of limited liability where that device is used appropriately to serve the functions for which it was created. Section 15 I have always

thought was very badly done, but good enough considering the circumstances under which it was written" (Ibid.).

12.   "I rarely get home these days until midnight, and I find that that does not even enable me to keep up with the demands of the job." Speaking of the NRA and the difficulty of getting industry to work with government, Landis said that "to me it is somewhat amazing how our younger men are falling for this idea of partnership with industry without any recognition of the significance of keeping an independent judgment together with an independent leeway of action" (Landis to Frankfurter, 3/6/34: FFPLC, Box 117).

Frankfurter responded on March 17, 1934. Landis was driving himself too hard. Speaking of the legislation at hand, Frankfurter said:

> What you write about the Stock Exchange Bill and the Securities Act is full of the promise of good sense. Evidently the President knows his Street and isn't taken in by the large-sounding jargon and crocodile tears for the small investor of which we hear so much of these days.

He sympathized with Landis' comments about the Wall Street crowd: "Well, from the Eustace Seligmans [a lawyer with the New York firm of Sullivan & Cromwell] one expects their performance. Dyers are apt to be stained by the colors with which they work" (Frankfurter to Landis, 3/17/34: FFPLC, Box 117). And even the professors, like W.O. Douglas, who were writing on the subject were also perhaps impractical:

> . . . even Bill Douglas is trying to reflect too much the people in the big offices and the business schools, among whom he likes to appear as a sound and knowing fellow. I wrote him a letter the other day, in a half-saucy, half-severe strain, apropos of his private letters to Max and me respectively, telling how much he is for us and for what we want, and intimating that his public articles against our measures are a form of high strategy. Well, it's too high for my eyes to scale (Frankfurter to Landis, 3/17/34, FFPLC, Box 117).

The Amendments sounded like "sense," said Frankfurter; he agreed with Landis' appraisal of Rayburn:

> . . . and especially do I agree with what you say about the romantic simplicity of some of our friends, particularly among the younger lawyers, in their view of a "partnership with industry." And they are all so bitten with a touching confidence in regulation, and with a strange inability to understand the difficulty of regulating powerful forces (Frankfurter to Landis, 3/17/34: FFPLC, Box 117).

13.   Renn forwarded to Landis a copy of Staub's statement, which had been published in large part on March 27, 1934, in the *New York World Telegram* (Renn to Landis, 3/27/34: JMLPHLL).

14.   Staub said, "Dr. Landis' emphasis on the accounting certificate being, primarily, an expression of opinion merely recognized what those in the business and financial world already knew, but which perhaps needed to be stressed for the information of the many lesser informed investors." What was crucial was "the way of determining that the statements had been based upon sound accounting principles" with respect to certification by independent public accountants (Renn to Landis, 3/27/34: JMLPHLL).

15.   "The Bar Association said the schedule could be simplified by eliminating: the names of the underwriters; the names of persons holding ten percent of the capital stock; the amount of securities held by officers and directors; the proceeds from previous issues; payments to promoters; and material contracts not made in the ordinary course of business" (Parrish, 1970: 194).

chapter

7

To regulate or abdicate?

The SEC under the Securities Acts

The Securities and Exchange Commission, despite the weakening of the Securities Exchange Act of 1934 and the amendments to the Securities Act of 1933, still had specific administrative powers with enormous financial and economic potential for its regulatees and the nation at large. Most important were its authorities to determine the standards for corporate financial reporting. The authority to regulate the stock exchanges was comparatively unimportant. Its registration and corporate reporting controls, however, could influence or determine reported corporate earnings, profitability, and hence share prices, which in turn affect wealth and economic power, and, as a result, political and social power. On paper, at least, the SEC had the authority to determine accounting rules, establish uniform accounting systems, and force comparability of accounting between firms and industries. That was how far the SEC could go. But how far would it go? That distance would depend mostly on two things: how the commissioners and other key SEC people interpreted their mandate, and how effectively the accountants could contain SEC initiative.

Sweeping financial reporting authorities were written into the securities acts, but the commissioners disagreed among themselves about their mandate to press them. The initial commissioners had three paths they could follow: they could try to establish comprehensive accounting codes and drag (or try to drag) a reluctant financial sector behind them; they could defer to the financial sector entirely and let it set the financial conventions, as it had always done in the past; or, as a middle course, they could try to set some fundamental rules and still permit the financial sector autonomy within an acceptable range—a "push" rather than a "drag" approach. The SEC chose to follow the mid-course, and in so doing rapidly fell into a trap—partly planned by the accountants, partly acquiesced to by the SEC—in which they were to defer almost entirely to the accountants. Within three years after the SEC began functioning, the full initiative for developing rules of financial reporting had been passed to an eager accounting profession. It was an astonishing performance by both the SEC and the accounting practitioners, and it was one that challenges many of the conventional notions about what the operations of independent regulatory agencies (IRAs) are supposed to be like in their formative years.

Independent Regulatory Agencies

Much material has been written on such independent regulatory agencies as the SEC, the Interstate Commerce Commission (ICC), the Federal Trade Commission (FTC), and the Federal Communications Commission (FCC). Most of it concludes that these agencies operate in the interest of the regulated group, that if they maximize somebody's definition of the "public interest" they do so by accident. A variety of explanations have been advanced to acount for this perverse phenomenon in which the operations of IRAs have been precisely the opposite of those expected by some of their creators—namely, to regulate a given private-interest group so that it would be unable to victimize the public autonomously. After all, it was the economic depredations of the early railroads that had brought about the creation of the first of the IRAs, the Interstate Commerce Commission, in 1887.

Most explanations of a regulatory agency's behavior usually begin by assuming that the agency is co-opted by the regulatee, and that the process of co-optation is in some way a function of power positions. The co-optation assumption, however, begs the consistency of other assumptions—for example, the assumption that to become co-opted, one must initially be free. Along with this assumption, it is fashionable to make the simplistic one that at the outset IRA commissioners are aggressive and seek to establish themselves in an energetic manner in order to control the recalcitrant regulatee. Another hypothesis assumes that a regulatory agency is created to control an antisocial regulatee; that assumption may be accurate for the ICC, but it certainly does not fit the circumstances behind the creation of other IRAs like the Civil Aeronautics Board (CAB) or the Federal Radio Commission (FRC, later the FCC). In the case of the CAB and FRC, both were established by the regulated industries to operate a cartel in their behalf, and both have behaved according to the expectations of their creators, restricting entry and maintaining prices and industry profits. Under such circumstances, only the innocent would expect vigorous attempts by commissioners to control the regulatees. The more likely mode of operation, and the one most evident, is that the commissioners would look to the regulatees for their cues.

Thus there are two models to consider when evaluating the genesis of any independent regulatory agency: the agency created through public uproar and designed to control an anti-social group versus the agency created by some interest group to provide political protection for its monopolistic activities. Which of these two models best describes the SEC? Elements of both models—the ICC versus the FRC—can be seen. The public uproar over the stock market collapse did support creation of the FTC's new regulatory authorities, on the one hand. But on the other, the private sector's battle to have that authority relocated in a new agency—the SEC—where it could be controlled more easily, was successful. And of the SEC's early behavior, was there anything that suggested an aggressive, crusading enterprise willing to fight to control the financial-corporate sector? Close inspection of its formative years reveals little evidence of any such willingness, of any real conflict between the agency and the interest group. On the contrary, what is revealed is the unexpectedly quick erosion of the entire purpose behind creating the SEC, one that proceeded so naturally it was hardly noted as such at the time. The sequence of that breakdown makes a fascinating study of the difficulties of regulating powerful constituencies.

Immediate Pressures on the SEC

To its first commissioners, the mandate of the SEC was not clear, even though it had been invested with comprehensive financial reporting authorities. The disagreement between Cohen and Landis about regulation versus administration carried over into the SEC itself. It became clear rather early that the majority of the SEC commissioners did not intend to do much more than press for "adequate" disclosure of corporate financial data. This intention seems consistent with what Frankfurter also had in mind. "The greatest speculative carnival in the world's history" had brought on securities regulation, he said. Initially, adequate disclosure would be tried; more drastic remedies, like federal incorporation or direct control over investments, could be used if the act failed. Frankfurter thought the "evolution of model financial accounting methods" could have "far reaching beneficial effects on American corporate practices" (Frankfurter, 1934: 54–55; 108).[1] But the SEC's concept of "adequate disclosure" was unknown at first—and therefore cause for anxiety in the financial sector. Unfortunately for the SEC, its first commissioners had a great deal of work to do and almost no time to think about how they were going to do it.

During the last hectic months of thrashing out the Securities Exchange Act, no thought was given to the administrative structure of the new agency. As a result, its organization was evolving when crucial decisions had to be made about accounting forms and procedures for corporate compliance with the 1934 act (Cohen conversation, 10/18/72). Landis, who had been transferred from the FTC to the SEC, did take along with him the work he had been doing at the FTC pursuant to the 1933 act. Still, the first SEC commissioners— Chairman Joseph P. Kennedy, Landis, Mathews (also transferred from the FTC), Robert E. Healy, and Pecora—had to set up the administrative machinery almost completely and without much to guide them. Their first job was to develop forms for use by corporate registrants. The SEC tried to devise them as promptly as possible—a priority that was superficially commendable but ultimately unfortunate. For in trying to develop the forms quickly, the SEC members not only set a permanent short-term, operating mode for the agency, but placed themselves in the position of having to rely excessively upon outside assistance.

THE STRUGGLE FOR EFFECTIVE ORGANIZATION

The organization of the SEC had to proceed rapidly because the new forms were to be used soon. Its operations began on October 1, 1934. By December, 1934, the commission had developed a temporary means for registering securities until permanent registration forms, "which will portray with a minimum of burden and a maximum of clarity the status of a corporation's affairs to present and prospective investors," could be prepared. Studies of the national exchanges and special stock trading practices were also undertaken (Landis, 1934a; 41–42).

When Carman G. Blough (later the SEC's first chief accountant) joined the SEC as a financial analyst on December 1, 1934, work was still taking place in the commission's Forms and Registration Division on the forms required under the acts. Three specialists had already been brought in for temporary duty, though they remained well into 1935: Thomas H. Sanders, a professor of accounting at the Harvard Graduate School of Business; Donald McCruden, a financial analyst from New York, later to become head of Moody's; and Jerry Dunn, a Chicago investment banker (Blough conversation, 10/19/72).[2]

THE REGISTRATION DIVISION

The SEC's registration division was the key operation. In view of how quickly it had to be operational, the division was remarkably well organized and economically staffed. It was headed by a director with four assistant directors who reported to him. One assistant director did special work under the exchange act for permanent registrations; another was a legal adviser. The other two were in charge of six examining groups that reported directly to them; these groups reviewed data going to and from registrants. Each group was headed by a security analyst who was assisted by an accountant, an attorney, and three to five examiners. One group examined only public utility filings; the others reviewed all registrations in the order in which they were filed. A separate engineering staff analyzed property evaluation data. By law, the SEC had only twenty days to issue stop orders on deficient corporate registrations. Within five of those days, deficiency reports were to be prepared and given to the reviewing analyst. An assistant director then reviewed deficiency letters to registrants before they were sent out under the director's signature. The commissioners served as referees, settling serious differences between the director and his four assistants. The greatest amount of argument and debate within the registration division occurred over corporate accounting practices and financial statements (Smith, C.A., 1935: 325–327).

Developing the Reporting Forms

Form A–1, designed for corporations reporting new issues under the '33 act, was widely opposed in the business community because of its extensive requirements. Chairman Kennedy acknowledged this flaw, and promised "other and briefer forms . . . more suitable to special classes of business" (Kennedy, 1934b: 726). Form 10 for listed securities, authorized by the 1934 act, was issued on December 21, 1934; on January 12, 1935, virtually the same requirements were embodied in Form A–2 (which replaced A–1). Fundamental to Form 10 was full disclosure of financial facts and accounting practices from the registrant, although the form did not prescribe accounting methods, or even reporting methods, in detail. Form 10 was considered a minimum requirement, and consistent with what was then generally regarded as good acounting practice. Current financial changes were emphasized. Forms 10 and A–2 seem to have been well received by the practitioners (Sanders, 1935b: 11–15; Smith, C. A., 1935: 328). In both, the SEC had followed and improved upon the reporting lines adopted by the major securities exchanges. Eventually, however, it became apparent that progress in improving the quality of disclosed corporate financial data was more rapid under the SEC than "through the actions of individual exchanges" (Smith, F. P., 1937: 153).

Those in the SEC who were drawing up its new rules and forms, let it be emphasized, did not work in isolation. They received a good deal of help from the accounting practitioners of the AIA and the ASCPA and some corporate controllers and experts from the financial reporting organizations (Smith, C. A., 1935: 328; Sanders, 1935b: 15). Understandably, there were many observers satisfied with the results. Professor Kohler wrote: The SEC "in one month . . . set effective reasonable standards—necessarily incomplete, of course—for the profession, which years of futile committee work within the professional societies have not been able to produce or even begin to produce" (editorial, AR, March, 1935: 102). The group from the AIA had been invited by the SEC to take part in the creation of the rules and regulations soon after the SEC was set up. The AIA representatives met with the SEC in the first weeks of October, 1934, and were delighted with the cooperative attitude of the SEC (Starkey, 1934: 444). These early ties between the practitioners and the SEC helped allay fears fostered within the accounting profession by the FTC's Form A–1. Moreover, the cooperation of prominent accountants sought by the SEC helped obtain endorsement of Forms 10 and A–2 from the AIA and the New York State Society of Certified Public Accountants. Harmony, it was asserted at the time, existed between the profession and the SEC, and harmony was essential. Indeed, the contacts made between them during formulation of the SEC forms continued and helped Landis work with the financial sector.

In a speech to the New York CPAs in January, 1935, Landis tried to reconcile the New York financial community to the new securities acts. He stressed the cooperation achieved in developing registration forms as evidence of the community of interest between the SEC and the accounting practitioners. The SEC's administration would be flexible and beneficial to the accountants, Landis cajoled; the association of the SEC, AIA, ASCPA, and NYCPA in composing the registration forms was a mutual learning experience:

> . . . the story is one of long days, and long nights of work. On our side your reports and your memoranda were considered carefully; on your side our series of tentative drafts were subject to severe and weighty criticism. In many matters we were convinced by your arguments and in some matters we convinced you. It was an experience which, I know, we enjoyed, but more from which we learned to know and respect each other. I cannot pass this by without publicly expressing thanks for your generous effort and your wise contributions (Landis, 1935a: 18).

Landis explained the rationale behind the forms in some detail. The objective was to give the investing public adequate information, he said, but the SEC intended to be flexible regarding financial reporting methods. An accountant's certificate was required to indicate the audit's scope and the accounting principles employed, but its form was not prescribed. Landis cited some specific offensive accounting practices, such as writing off debt discount and expense against arbitrary credits, and he defended the reporting requirement for gross sales and costs of goods sold (Ibid., 22–23). He ended the speech with a call for mutual cooperation based on mutual need, and a hint that the SEC was needed by accountants to strengthen them in dealing with their corporate clients.

By the end of 1935, Landis was confident about the effectiveness of the registration program. Great refunding in 1935 had taken place under the new form A–2, accounting costs had declined, and business now accepted the theory of the independent government audit.

Information never before seen on American corporations was now available. These factors were all to the credit of the SEC. Yet in most instances the new information available on a corporation's financial status could only be evaluated by experts. It was still beyond the reach of the average investor (Landis, 1935b: 3–4). That the average investor could not benefit from the information became characteristic of SEC policy: investors were not going to have available to them, as a matter of course, the information submitted to the commission.

Not all private sector people applauded the SEC's forms, of course, and complaints of complex SEC accounting requirements persisted throughout the thirties. Hoxsey, in 1939, was still convinced of the correctness of his 1934–35 view that the forms had excessive detail, and he wrote about it to McCruden, the New York analyst who had worked on the development of the forms.[3] McCruden sent the letter to Landis, by then Harvard Law School dean. Landis was unimpressed with Hoxsey's argument, but he *was* concerned that the accountants were responsible for developing voluminous footnotes which they were appending to the forms. (Landis to McCruden, 3/9/39: JMLPLC, Box 25, McCruden file). The following year Landis again confirmed to McCruden his satisfaction with Form 10.[4]

In 1938 Healy, still an SEC commissioner, looked back on the work that had gone into the preparation of the early forms and lauded those from the private sector who had made important contributions, including Hoxsey, Dunn, McCruden, and Sanders (Healy, 1938: 1–2). The forms had been effective, Healy contended, but they could be and would be improved. Form A–2 would probably be changed and somewhat simplified, and the established-company prospectus would be shortened (Healy, 1938: 8). The emphasis at the SEC was still clearly on data submitted to the commission rather than to the investor—a curious circumstance inasmuch as the primary purpose of the acts was to supply *investors* with meaningful information. As time passed, that objective was less and less in evidence.

THE CHIEF ACCOUNTANT

An Office of the Chief Accountant was not included in the SEC's initial organization. One year after he joined the SEC in December, 1934, however, Blough became the first SEC chief accountant. His appointment to this position is extremely important because he opposed the view of the minority commissioners that the SEC should actively develop accounting principles and aim for a uniform system of accounting for registrant corporations.

Blough was not part of the eastern accounting establishment and thus it cannot be claimed that "Wall Street" had placed in a crucial position someone known to be sympathetic to their views[5] He went into the SEC as head of filings, an important post created under the 1933 act in which only commissioners could override his decisions. In 1935 it became obvious that the internal conflicts and differing criteria among the SEC staff and the commissioners necessitated the establishment of an Office of the Chief Accountant.

Two incidents seem to have triggered the inception of the office. Charles Sprague, responsible for SEC administration under the Public Utility Act of 1935, ordered a company to change its accounting report to meet his particular standards. The company later registered with the SEC using Sprague's instructions and methods. An assistant of Blough's, however, did not approve of the company's accounting methods, and he was upheld by Blough who said that Sprague was wrong. The company complained to the commission, and Sprague and Blough were called to account before the entire commission in November, 1935, thus emphasizing the need for a chief accountant. In an earlier incident, Blough had been overruled by Chairman Landis when Blough wanted a stop order issued on a particular finance company. Several months later, toward the end of 1935, the company defaulted to the extent of about a half million dollars. The incident apparently strengthened Blough in his insistence that one accountant ought to have policy-recommendation authority over all SEC accountants (conversation with Blough, 10/19/72). Blough filled the post of chief accountant until May, 1938, when he took a position with Arthur Andersen & Co. in Chicago, remaining there until he went to the War Production Board in the fall of 1942. In 1944 Blough joined the American Institute of Accountants as its first full-time director of research.[6]

The Establishment of SEC Policy

EARLY OBJECTIVES

The first SEC commissioners went out of their way to explain the objectives of the acts and to assure accountants and the rest of the financial community that they had nothing to fear and everything to gain from the SEC. The spearhead of this public relations campaign was Landis.

In December, 1934, Landis specified three main objectives of the acts (Landis, 1934a). The first was to control the speculative use of credit for exchange operations, an authority that was vested in the Federal Reserve Board. The second was to insure that the exchanges would not contribute unduly to excessive speculation, which required that offensive speculation practices be outlawed. Landis cited the third objective as the most significant—that all securities traded upon the exchanges be registered and that the SEC be furnished with certain information before trading could be permitted. The stock exchanges had a similar requirement, he said, but a public body administering requirements had greater impact. The exchanges obtained only incomplete information, said Landis; their power frequently was noncoercive, and the information they provided the stockholder was inadequate. Landis also noted that accounting practices were contributing to misleading asset and earnings reports.[7] Closely allied to the registration objective were provisions permitting the commission to prescribe rules for proxy solicitation; for director, officer, and equity holdings; and for corporate recovery of profits made by the rapid turnover of securities. Landis also stressed SEC powers in the over-the-counter markets (Landis, 1934a: 42).

Some six months later, addressing the New York Stock Exchange Institute in June, 1935, Landis's view of the acts' objectives had changed somewhat, and one year of operation had made the SEC's aims clearer to both the commission members and the public, he indicated. The objectives now were regulating credit for speculative purposes, achieving fairer practices in security transactions, and giving investors better knowledge and information. Landis stressed self-regulation. The less governmental regulation the better "and the better the self-government, the less need for . . . [public] regulation." That premise was the basis on which the SEC was dealing with the exchanges, Landis said, and he maintained that "sound and effective methods of cooperation" were being built (Landis, 1935c: 3). Educate rather than regulate; bring out the facts significant to securities; these were the ideas behind the acts, according to Landis (Ibid., p. 5).

By October, 1935, Landis was assuming that one of the principal purposes of the securities acts was generally known—namely, "to secure for issues publicly offered, adequate publicity for those facts necessary for an intelligent judgment of their value." Landis was giving a status report to an overflow crowd attending an American

Management Association Financial Conference. The tone of his speech was conciliatory, as usual, and he did his best to convince those in the audience that the acts were *good* for them. The basic problem, Landis said, was to perfect administrative techniques to achieve the disclosure objectives without unnecessarily burdening registrants. The simplification of forms, and greater familiarity with them, had decreased registration expenses. The acts' requirements were achieving routine status, Landis contended, and they were not violent departures from regular operations.[8] Speculative promotion remained a problem, and the accounting profession needed to assume added tasks.

Landis continued to find it necessary to defend prospectus information requirements on the grounds of investor protection and the need for general data. Again he mentioned that a briefer prospectus for average investors might be advantageous. Persons following SEC instructions would be protected from liability, he said, but the careful preparation of reports should not result in any delay under the twenty day filing period rule (Ibid., pp. 5–8).

Landis carried the brunt of the SEC public relations campaign, though Kennedy also helped. Their approaches were compatible. Kennedy's address to the National Press Club on July 25, 1934, tried to assure the financial community that it would not be persecuted in the process of protecting the investor. The antispeculative purposes of the act were not discussed. The SEC would accent publicity, disclosure, and information, said Kennedy, not close surveillance and regulation of the financial community. Wherever possible, flexibility would be given to those preparing the financial statements. The SEC would be businesslike and not indulge in political publicity of any sort; its task, he added, was "one of the most delicate . . . ever given a Governmental Agency." Businessmen were not "viewed with suspicion"; on the contrary, "we regard ourselves, as the President has said, as partners in a cooperative enterprise." The SEC was not a prosecutor; business had been seriously wounded in the Great Depression and had to be nursed back to health. Interpretations of the acts would not be vindictive; "only those who see things crookedly will find them harsh." "The greater the publicity [of corporate accounts]," Kennedy declared, "the more protected the public will be, and the more correct is the influence upon the financiers" (Kennedy, 1934a: 454–456).

Kennedy was still on the defensive in December of 1934. There was no left or right in the processes of the Securities and Exchange Commission, he indicated; all commission members were trying to do was to go forward (Kennedy, 1934b: 723). The new law would protect investors against the abuses of high-pressure salesmanship. The government was not judging business values, nor was it giving advice on or approving certain business values. The acts merely made deception more difficult—and conviction certain. Business cooperation was earnestly requested; government supervision would not destroy honest enterprise; there was nothing to fear. "This commission will destroy nothing in our business life that is worth preserving." The liability provisions were not burdensome and had not halted investment, Kennedy said. Advancement and protection of decent business, and the restoration of confidence, were the SEC's goals (Ibid., p. 728).

The 3–2 Split

Landis and Kennedy's conciliatory attitude toward the financial community was endorsed by Mathews and represented the majority view on the SEC. The other commissioners, however, had more militant perspectives; rather than cooperation and persuasion, they favored coercion where necessary. Mathews, among the other three original commissioners, was a former head of the Wisconsin Public Utility Commission, a public accountant, and, as noted earlier, a member of the FTC when appointed to the SEC. Healy, a lawyer, was chief counsel of the FTC at the time of his SEC appointment. Pecora, Senator Fletcher's former chief counsel, remained on the commission less than a year; he was succeeded by James D. Ross, an electrical engineer from Washington State who had been involved with the Municipal Power System in Seattle. Ross remained on the SEC until 1937 when he became an administrator of the Bonneville Dam Project.

When Kennedy resigned in 1935, Landis became chairman and William O. Douglas was appointed to the commission, serving until 1939 when he was named to the U.S. Supreme Court. Landis resigned in 1937 to accept the deanship of the Harvard Law School and was replaced by Douglas as Chairman, and Jerome N. Frank, a lawyer working for the government at the time, was appointed to the commission. Frank became a law professor and a U.S. Court of Appeals judge, resigning from the SEC in 1941. Three other SEC commissioners were appointed during the thirties: John W. Hanes, a New York stock broker, who served in 1938; Edward C. Eicher, a lawyer and congressman, who served from 1938 to 1942; and Leon Henderson, an economist, who served from 1939 to 1941. In total, eleven persons were appointed to the SEC from its inception in mid-1934 to the end of the decade (see Appendix C).

Between 1934 and the end of 1937, the commissioners made the crucial decisions that transferred accounting control back to the private sector. Among the original members, Pecora and Healy did not go along with the policy of conciliating the practicing accountants and the financial sector. They were advocates of a more aggressive approach. Later, the split was between Landis, Mathews, and Ross on the one side, and Healy and Douglas on the other.

The Road to Impotence

ACCOUNTING FLEXIBILITY AND DISCLOSURE

When the original SEC commissioners agreed with the accounting practitioners in the fall of 1934 that flexibility in accounting treatment would be permitted corporations in filing their registration forms, the first giant step was taken toward the abdication of SEC authority over corporate financial reporting. The second, absolutely crucial stride along the path of relinquishing control occurred in early 1935. At issue was how much pressure the SEC should exert on accountants and their client corporations to disclose relevant financial data.

THE NORTHERN STATES POWER COMPANY CASE

Would corporations whose reporting was found deficient be required to revise their forms according to specified standards? Or would they be permitted to disclose in a footnote that they had used an alternate standard? The answer evoked a major conflict among the SEC commissioners. The "most furious differences of opinion that have ever occurred among the Commissioners centered about an accounting problem, and yet . . . there was no difference of opinion as to the accounting," Commissioner Healy wrote three years after the 1935 incident.

The case involved the Northern States Power Company and its practice of amortizing debt discount. Prior to registration, Northern had written up assets based on reproduction cost, crediting half the write up to the retirement reserve and half to a capital surplus account, against which the company subsequently wrote off substantially all of its unamortized debt discount. This offset relieved the income account of a sum amounting to about $5 million. Northern's accounting practice had been common during the twenties but was much less acceptable in 1935. The company's auditors neither approved nor disapproved of the questionable accounting procedure. All SEC commissioners did disapprove of the accounting procedure, however, but because there had been a complete disclosure the majority felt a stop order was inappropriate. They also believed that the accountants' certificate in effect indirectly condemned the accounting method. Healy and Pecora believed the accountants had not expressed an opinion even indirectly, and they thought the company's earnings record and earned surplus balance were untrue, amounting to misrepresentation and, therefore, statute violation (Healy, 1938: 2–3). As Healy recognized, the differences among the commissioners were about the law, not accounting (Ibid.,: 5). The distinction, though, was highly significant for it indicated the commission's legalistic approach toward the acts—that is, it indicated a concern with what the law demanded rather than with what was required for a fair statement of the facts. Kennedy, Landis, Healy, and Pecora, were all lawyers; only Mathews was an accountant, and Mathews voted with the majority.

Healy remained unreconciled to the SEC footnote-disclosure policy.

> I regret that an attempt was not made in these cases to establish the principle that if an earnings statement and a balance sheet reflect the results of improper accounting, they amount to misrepresentations or misleading statements in violation of the Securities Act. In the absence of a court decision I have no right to go further than to reiterate the regret that an effort to have the questions settled by a court decision was not made (Ibid.).

One of the reasons the SEC chose not to proceed more stringently against Northern, Healy said, was the majority's feeling that it would be unfair to do so because the SEC had not promulgated accounting rules. This reasoning had some justification, of course, but in this case the thought was a crutch that crippled the user. If one thinks about the SEC rationale for just a moment, the magnificence of its circularity becomes apparent. In effect the commission majority was saying that as it had done nothing it could do nothing, which is simply carrying the ex post facto approach too far. Thus the key to impotence was avoidance of definitive rules because in their absence precise requirements became impossible. The logic is inexorable, but it is not the logic of action, and the subsequent frustration of Healy and Douglas with the SEC majority becomes understandable in this context.

Still, Healy had hopes in 1938 that something really affirmative might yet be done by the SEC in setting accounting rules. In that year, he said, the SEC was trying to develop a procedure to "express a few standards as to principles which we believe are accepted by a majority of good accountants, especially of those who do not assume the role of special pleaders for their more lucrative clients." Inflexible rules could not then be made:

> But it cannot be that there are no real standards in accounting. It seems to me, that one great difficulty has been that there has been no body which had the authority to fix and maintain standards. I believe that such a body now exists in the Securities and Exchange Commission. Its success or failure will depend in large measure on how wisely it exercises this function (Ibid.).

Healy proved quite right. SEC failure to exercise accounting rule-making authority placed the agency in a permanently emasculated position. Healy had taken a hard line about the accounting practices of public utilities when he served on the FTC; he was consistent in this attitude while with the SEC. In the continuing debate over whether the SEC should establish accounting principles and a uniform system of accounts, Douglas and Healy were the minority. The question was finally settled late in 1938 when Accounting Series Release [Rule] No. 4 was issued by the SEC. ASR No. 4 was a compromise favoring the majority view. Disclosure was established as the prime requirement, but if the registrant could show that his accounting procedure had substantial precedent, it would be accepted by the SEC, providing the commission had not made a contrary rule. ASR No. 4 thus affirmed the Northern States Power Company case. The SEC ruling made little difference, however; by then the accounting rule makers were the accounting practitioners. Landis and Kennedy were no longer with the SEC. Mathews left the agency in 1940. In one of the great coincidences of regulatory history, he became the vice president and controller of the Northern States Power Company.

THE DISCLOSURE MENTALITY

The basis for "flexibility" and disclosure in corporate accounting, then, was made by early 1935 in the Northern States Power Company case, and it was carefully noted at the time (Smith, C. A., 1935: 330; Sanders, 1937: 204; Kaplan and Reaugh, 1939: 223; Healy, 1938: 3; Blough and Allen E. Throop conversations: 10/72). Two years later the SEC's reluctance to undertake development of generally accepted accounting principles, except as a last resort, was confirmed as policy (Blough, 1937b: 37). ASR No. 4 in 1938 made alternate accounting conventions official—and encouraged confusing footnotes. It was going to take more than just the average investor to decipher corporate reports. The SEC had seen to that.

That SEC rules permitted the registrant considerable leeway was generally recognized. Corporations did not, for example, have to follow commission standards in making out their stockholder reports (Kaplan and Reaugh, 1939: 204). The flexibility available to practicing accountants was underscored as fact and necessity by numerous writers, within both the SEC and the accounting profession (Landis, 1935a: 21; Sanders, 1935b: 18; Starkey, 1936: 31; Broad, 1935: 24; May, 1940: 82).

The legalistic approach of the SEC was a major factor behind the disclosure mentality, and even as early as 1935 it was evident to outsiders that the SEC was administering a disclosure rather than a regulatory statute. The commission, for example, worked on the theory that item 56 of Form A–1 did not require a complete consolidation of the financial facts regarding a corporation's subsidiaries, even though it was obvious that the effect of not consolidating financial information on subsidiaries resulted in a misleading financial picture; it was content with requiring footnotes to the financial statements setting forth an explanation of various contradictory financial facts. In short, the commission was willing to approve financial statements that were deficient in setting forth accepted accounting practice provided the certifying accountant clearly pointed out the deficiency in footnotes and stated what the effect would be had a more acceptable practice been followed. Its reasoning for adopting this policy resulted from the fact that it was administering a disclosure rather than a regulatory act and that a statement from the corporate accountant concerning the accounting practice of the registrant gave a better picture of the managerial policy of his company than if the independent accountant were to revise the registrant's balance sheet and income statement to reflect more generally accepted principles and practices (Smith, C. A., 1935: 331). Whether the results of this policy were misleading accounting statements did not seem to matter. Footnote disclosure met the test of legality, which meant accountants would not change many questionable practices. Moreover the disclosure approach relieved the SEC and everyone else from the immediate pressure of undertaking the establishment of systematic accounting principles as uniform requirements.

The Early SEC: Accounting Principles and Accountants

SEC accounting requirements were specified in the securities acts of 1933 and 1934. They were also set forth in commission (1) rules and regulations, (2) instructions and forms, (3) published opinions and findings, and (4) opinions and rulings relating to unpublished financial statements. Section 19 of the 1933 act authorized the SEC to define accounting terms; prescribe forms for presenting financial information, including the details to be shown in income and balance sheets; and designate methods to be followed in preparing accounts and valuation techniques. The commission could require accepted accounting principles, formulate new principles to be used by the accounting profession in filing registration statements, or both. In 1935 the possibility still existed that the SEC would try to publish comprehensive accounting regulations, in spite of ominous signs indicating the contrary. At that stage only minimum rules were specified under the various forms, and the commission's inclination was to permit accountants to draw up "accepted accounting principles and practices."

The accountants watching and working with the SEC knew that if the SEC set financial accounting standards, those standards would become the nation's authoritative practice. That assumption was the basis of what became the standard "warning" to the practitioners, nowhere better stated than by Professor C. A. Smith in 1935:

> If the practitioners, after sufficient time has elapsed, have not come to some substantial agreement as to what are or should be considered accepted accounting principles and practices, we may well expect the Commission's staff accountants to prepare, and the Commission to publish what it shall demand in the way of such practices. . . . (Smith, C. A., 1935: 327).

The "warning" was repeated incessantly thereafter by acountants and government personnel alike, gaining a fundamental place in their dialogues. Many gave it superficial lip service, and the credulous accepted it as fact long after any likelihood of SEC intervention had passed.

Impediments to the creation of SEC accounting principles were formidable. One consisted of a large bloc of people who thought the SEC should defer to the accounting practitioners for accounting rules. It may not have seemed odd at the time, but important support for this tack came from the academic community. An outspoken academic advocate of practitioner leadership in accounting theory was Harvard Professor Sanders, who, as might be expected, was held in high regard by the practitioners. In early 1935 Sanders was working within the SEC to help devise their reporting forms and procedures.

Sanders summed up his attitude toward accounting practice and principles in September, 1934. Investment, he said, was critical to the economy, and investor protection could best be achieved if corporate financial reports were revealing and made up in accordance with "sound principles of accounting and classification." Differences in company practice and among professional accountants meant that choices among accounting alternatives were to be expected and that even principles could never substitute for judgment and experience. Many aspects of accounting theory had shaken down to substantially accepted practices, he believed, and these "generally accepted principles of accounting" included a number of permissible alternative practices. A "high degree of continuity" was desirable in the reports of different corporations, Sanders argued; moreover, complete uniformity in accounting practice was probably not attainable. Any attempt to achieve it would "inevitably result in a standard far below the accounting practices of leading business concerns at the present time." Conservatism—that is, understating rather than overstating corporate values and accounts—was the criterion (Sanders, 1934: 201–208).

Understandably, Sanders provided crucial support for the practitioners during the fight over the control of accounting principles. His views remained consistent. "The work of the Securities and Exchange Commission," he wrote a few months later, "is bound to have a vital influence in defining and giving effect to accounting principles." Flexibility in rules was critical, and it was important that the SEC not shackle business by creating meaningless requirements. Few rigid rules were to be found in the commission's regulations, he said, although full and complete disclosure of financial methods and company rules was required (Sanders, 1935a: 100–101).

The overriding question facing the SEC was whether certain tasks should be assigned to the corporate accountants or whether duties and rules should be imposed upon them. One purpose of the acts was interpreted to be that of educating rather than regulating, and in so doing to bring out the significant facts regarding securities (Landis, 1935c: 5). But how were the private accountants to fit into this scheme, especially when they were used as consultants to the SEC, especially when they were given free rein in completing the forms required by their clients for registration under the acts? The principle of disclosure contained in the acts was designed to give the investor the maximum amount of protection, according to Landis. This was to be accomplished through the use of SEC forms and by giving the support of the SEC "to the accountant who has a true sense of his responsibility to the investing public in whose behalf he is employed" (Landis speech to the Economic Club of Chicago, 4/29/36: JMLPHLL).

CRACKS IN THE COOPERATIVE WALL

By 1936, it was absolutely clear to Landis that the loyalty of the accountant was to his client, not to the investor, and Landis criticized that orientation in December of that year in an address to the Investment Bankers Association annual conference. It was the first time the constant battle and hostility between the SEC and the accountants got unmistakable attention from an SEC commissioner—and from no less a commission member than the chairman.

Landis had been doing his best to conciliate and cultivate members of the financial community, though he was by now well on his guard. In private he had strong resentments about some members of that community. He took exception to comments about the securities acts written to him by Eustace Seligman, an attorney with Sullivan & Cromwell, a Wall Street legal firm. On January 19, 1935, Landis had written to Frankfurter, who also had been corresponding with Seligman:

> With a typical genius of the New York Bar for devious misconstruction, he places upon us all the onus of the *in terrorem* quality of the legislation. As a lawyer he knew I was using that

term to describe to others that civil penalties, even if only com-
pensatory, possess an *in terrorem* quality. For him to pick up
a phrase like that and say it manifests a sadistic desire to punish
purely for punishment purposes, is typical of the verbal twist-
ing he and his ilk are always ready to indulge in . . . (Landis
to Frankfurter, 1/19/35: FFPLC, Box 74, Landis folder).

In his speech to the IBA, Landis asserted that those involved in
preparing corporate financial statements were in danger of having
their sense of responsibility dulled by the 1936 sellers' market.

Indeed one can draw a strange contrast before the almost tear-
ful protestations of originators and experts against the provisions
of the liability sections of the 1933 Act, even after its amendment, and the current tendency of these same individuals to
cut corners in the matter of forthright disclosure. *The impact
of almost daily tilts with accountants, some of them called
leaders in their profession often leaves little doubt that their
loyalties to management are stronger than their sense of responsibility to the investor* . . . [italics supplied] (Landis
speech to the IBA, 12/4/36: JMLPHLL).

The remark was to have far-reaching effects on SEC-accountant relations.

The private accountant's loyalty to clients rather than investors nettled other members of the SEC as well as it did Landis
(Mathews, 1938: 230; Blough, 1939: 163–164; Frank, 1939: 296;
Healy, 1938: 7). An interesting view of the accounting function was
made by Chairman Frank, in November, 1939, after he had replaced
Douglas. "I suspect that the accounting profession needs a Holmes;
that what he said of law is, in large measure, true of accounting; that
it needs to question its own first principles, . . ." (Frank, 1939: 295).
The idea of "soundness" was a fiction based on a guess, Frank argued.
It was an illusion to assume an investment was absolutely safe or
sound. "Accountants thus need to be both more modest—that is, to
indicate more adequately the restricted function of their work, and
at the same time to be more conscientious and exacting in the performance of their limited function" (Ibid.: 300–301). Those who are
engaged in accounting, Frank said, "sometimes forget to ask themselves just what is the social function of their work" (Ibid.: 296).

Frank's attitude toward accounting principles at the end of 1939
showed relatively little variation from those expressed by Landis

somewhat earlier in that year when he gave a series of lectures at the Harvard Law School on the Securities Exchange Act of 1934. In retrospect, Landis said, accounting opinions falling outside the range of reasonable differences were treated by the SEC as misstatements. The SEC differentiated between three types of accounting principles:

> . . . those that are recognized as being accepted by the best accounting authorities, those that are not recognized as acceptable and definitely beyond the pale, and then an intermediate ground where reasonable differences of opinion as to the correctness of a certain accounting principle can exist, and in that field all that is required is disclosure of the particular accounting principle that has been applied (Landis, 2/17/39: JMLPHLL, Misc. set, vol. 2, 1938–1939).

The statement recalls Landis's earlier views about disclosure, accountants' use of flexibility, alternate accounting principles, acceptability of submitting financial statements in various forms, and about not prescribing the form of the accountant's certificate (Landis, 1935a: 21).

The absence of generally accepted agreement among accountants about important accounting practices was also noted by Blough. The lack of agreement, he said, made it difficult for the SEC to take a position on many controversial issues—which forced compromises by the SEC. "Where highly thought of practitioners followed questionable procedures," Blough said, "sometimes the SEC hesitated to oppose them, and frequently disclosure was accepted where the matter was questionable, rather than 'insisting upon a revision of accounting statements'" (Blough: 1938, 110). Disclosure, therefore, became the standard technique of getting around the lack of accounting principles (Blough, 1939: 163). Although the SEC still asserted accounting should give the investor an opportunity to appraise the earning power of the corporation, firm rules were still avoided (Frank, 1939: 295–299; Healy, 1938: 227) .

PRIVATE OPINIONS

Landis had a public stance and a private stance on the subject of cooperation with the public accountants and their contributions. Shortly after the SEC was set up, Landis said in public that the commission was giving important support to the accountants and that the SEC in turn was getting important technical and moral support from them (Landis, 1935a: 18). But his January letter to Frankfurter manifested serious misgivings: "I wish I had seen you in New York the other night. I was up the night before and talked to some accountants—a strange class of people [who] I suppose by the very nature of their profession are without any humor" (Landis to Frankfurter, 1/19/35: FFPLC, Box 74, Landis folder). In mid-1936 Landis was anticipating an adverse reaction from Wall Street to a recent SEC report,[9] and it is evident that in general the Street had little of his respect. Landis again wrote to Frankfurter about his disappointment:

> It is interesting to see just how the propaganda machine works in this connection. Our friends, the Times, have clearly fallen for the so-called experience of the Street, and we have all too few friends on the other side who recognize that this experience is nothing more than wishful thinking (Landis to Frankfurter, 7/6/36: JMLPLC, Box 10, Frankfurter folder).

Three days earlier, Landis had written to Berle about the same report, and observed that objections "naturally arise when anybody suggests that there should be some change in the ordinary tenure of our institutional life," an attitude which had been most evident in 1934. (Landis to Berle, 7/3/36: JMLPLC, Box 9, "B" folder). A sense of overwork, weariness, and depression comes through in Landis's private writings in 1936—a condition that probably affected his decision that year to let the AIA assume certain authority over accounting determinations and ethics violations. Criticism from the liberal press did not help Landis's frame of mind either. He wrote to Frankfurter about a critical article in the *New Republic* that accused the SEC of not using all its powers and acting as "almost the champion of unlisted markets." Landis expressed his dismay with the article in a paragraph that, curiously, he later crossed out, though he sent the letter to Frankfurter anyway:

> . . . I am impressed by the tragedy of affairs. I sit here every day, taking it on the chin, psychologically speaking, from this group that hate every effort for general reform in the field of finance, and to find those who may really be more liberal, more radical—and perhaps be right in being so—weakening the strength that needs not only to be conserved, but needs to be built up, is an extraordinary bit of irony. If there is anything that you can do to give a little bit of education to these fellows,

to make them appreciate the things that are significant, and discard those that have no fundamental merit, since nobody can have a batting average of 100 per cent, it might be of some help (Landis to Frankfurter, 6/6/36: JMLPLC, Box 10, Frankfurter folder).

In March, 1939, Landis, safely back in Cambridge as dean of the Harvard Law School, still had some fond memories of the accountants, and in particular, of George O. May. "What is really needed is a good spanking for the accountants as a whole rather than refinement of the accounting form. They just won't take the responsibility of eliminating voluminous footnotes, which they could easily eliminate if they really insisted upon doing a thorough accounting job for their clients. . . . As long as you have the May leadership in the accounting situation, I have very little hope of seeing them accomplish much" (Landis to McCruden, 3/9/39: JMLPLC, Box 25, McCruden file). The accountants, in possession of the field by then, would not have been much concerned by the comment.

Notes

1.   Frankfurter's statement was a defense of the 1933 Securities Act. It appeared, belatedly, in a *Fortune* article in September, 1934—well after the ruckus on the Exchange Act was over.

2.   The three had apparently been invited by Kennedy. They began working on the rules and regulations in the fall of 1934 (conversation with Throop, 10/18/72).

3.   "As time went on and my actual experience with the reports increased, I became very strong in this view. . . . The mass of detail became so difficult . . . to understand . . . footnotes I found particularly objectionable. . . . The old-type annual report, where the auditors include merely such footnotes as are essential for clarity, is, I am sure, much better for the investor's own use (Hoxsey to McCruden, 2/14/39: JMLPLC, Box 25, McCruden file).

4.   "What a tremendous difference there is between the material that you have on companies who report to the SEC and companies who do not make such reports. Those that report to the SEC simply spoil you for the others and as you look over these reports you see an extraordinary difference before and after 1934. The old Form 10 certainly did the job" (J. M. Landis to D. McCruden, July 18, 1940: JMLPLC Box 25, Donald McCruden File).

5.   Blough was doing postgraduate work at Harvard in 1934, on leave from his position at Armour Institute, which, like many schools in the

1930s, was in financial trouble. While at Harvard, Blough was contacted by an ex-fellow Ph.D. student at Wisconsin, Don Montgomery, about an SEC appointment. Mathews had also known Blough in Wisconsin when Mathews was reviewing security filings in Wisconsin. Blough thinks Mathews was behind his appointment (conversation with Blough, 11/19/72).

6.   Blough worked at the AIA part time until the WPB went out of existence in December, 1945 (conversation with Blough, 10/19/72).

7.   "Furthermore, accounting practices, aided by lax state corporation laws, have too frequently permitted corporations to render reports misleading both as to assets and earnings. The importance of adequate and effective administration of . . . the Securities Exchange Act cannot be over-estimated" (Landis, 1934a: 41).

8.   Increased audit costs were not too severe, Landis argued, because the various schedules and supporting data were always needed and now had only to be prepared for the SEC in final form. Time required in conferences with SEC officers pursuant to registrations would decrease as familiarity increased (Landis, 1935b: 4–5).

9.   "The recent report that we got out on the segregation of broker and dealer functions came something of a bombshell to the Street. I am afraid that they will not accept it and its conclusions with any degree of alacrity. After making these recommendations, I thought it would be best to allow the report to be digested and to think for awhile and after a month or so to then take up the definite problem of bringing this recommendation into effect" (Landis to Frankfurter, 7/6/36: JMLPLC, Box 10, Frankfurter folder).

"We have survived the SEC, which has done a good job"

The Regulated Respond

The reaction of the nation's financial sector to the advent of the Securities and Exchange Commission and the security laws reflected the turmoil and conflict of the months before June, 1934. The accountants in particular were uncertain about the future behavior of the commission. The liability provisions of the 1933 act had been attenuated, but how would the SEC administer its responsibility for controlling corporate financial reporting? Would the commission prescribe rigid rules and regulations? Exasperation with the length of the prospectus required under Form A–1 only accenuated these anxieties, and some critics of the amended '33 act still objected that the theory of recision remained available to plaintiffs (Starkey, 1934: 433).

Antigovernment, anti-SEC, and antiregulation sentiment was much in evidence. Indeed, a significant number of accountants lamented the very existence of the SEC. Fearing rigid regulation and inflexible rules, few would acknowledge or refer to the financial abuses of the preceding years. Even when the collapse was mentioned, and the inevitability of some regulation recognized, regret about the SEC still manifested itself, which is probably understandable. There is an enormous difference between no regulation and some regulation, compared with some regulation and more regulation. In addition, antigovernment feeling was an inherent part of the business ideology of the time, and a constant propaganda barrage was directed against government regulation in general.

Toward the close of 1937, however, after the SEC had become "safe," the attitude of the financial community toward the SEC changed from anxious to condescending. After 1937 the practicing accountants found it increasingly easy to praise the commission. What made the SEC "safe" in 1937 was its decision to pass to the practicing accountants the responsibility for developing generally accepted accounting principles. It was the most important abdication of authority the SEC would ever make, and it set the pattern for SEC impotence thereafter.

Initial Reactions

Following the start of SEC operations in October, 1934, articles appearing in the accounting journals generally followed three lines in evaluating the SEC and the theory behind it. The first was adamant opposition to government regulation on any account and this approach persisted throughout the rest of the thirties. A second theme was what the SEC *might* do, rather than what it was doing. The third theme expressed the very specific set of notions held by accountants on what the SEC should *not* do.

Healy's hint that the SEC might license accountants to practice before it seemed to crystallize some of the fears of the accounting practitioners. These fears about possible SEC actions sparked demands among the practicing accountants for solidarity and the establishment of a single national standard for admission to practice. Control of the profession was lacking, they thought; moreover, the public interest was conflicting with the duties of the accountant to keep his confidential relations with the client. Both factors represented a dilemma, and evoked references to the accountants' "social responsibility" (Ellis, 1934a: 451–453). And now and then a prominent accountant would become carried away with the theme and rashly assert that the privity of contract defense had to be eliminated and that the ultimate client was the investor (Starkey, 1934: 438).

The threat of government licensing dramatized the existence of two accounting practitioners' organizations, the AIA and the ASCPA.

Many practicing accountants sensed their professional vulnerability, and their anxiety focused on the fear of additional legislation and SEC administrative action. Along with the securities acts "a new and very real danger appeared, the threat of bureaucratic control," wrote Rodney F. Starkey, partner in Price Waterhouse, and an intimate in AIA ruling circles, a man with a deft hand for the rhetoric and cliché to fit any occasion. He was also a relentless and effective opponent of the SEC. Unreconciled to regulation, his paean to self-regulation is a near-classic.

> A voluntary movement can always attain higher standards because of its flexibility. Regulation . . . no matter how intelligently and sympathetically administered, of necessity has a rigidity which must prove irksome, and, because of such rigidity, the standards set never can reach as high a plane of perfection as can the more flexible standards adopted and followed voluntarily without regulation. The first method is undoubtedly the more progressive and more satisfactory method. Self-government with a minimum of regulation will always be the ideal of an intelligent people (Ibid., pp. 434–435).

However, the AIA was willing to cooperate, Starkey stressed, and he cited recommendations submitted to the SEC by an AIA committee, one of which offered a lovely sleight of hand: "Uniformity of major accounting principles in a particular industry is desirable as an ultimate objective, though uniformity in their application may be undesirable." Other recommendations, though, did not offer much hope for the voluntary changes Starkey was touting:

> For the present, corporations should be required merely to indicate the principles which are followed.
> No standardized forms of financial statements should be prescribed. Statements in the form and detail best adapted to the particular conditions should be accepted.
> The commission should endeavor to advise investors as to limitations of financial statements as guides to the value of investments.

Still, one ought not to be uncharitable—everyone has a right to protect what they have. And fair warning is fair warning. Starkey did, after all, indicate his belief that the most important recommendation was the last (Starkey, 1934: 455).

A SOFTENING OF ACCOUNTANT'S ATTITUDES

Attitudes accountants expressed toward the SEC gradually softened as it became apparent that the influence of the SEC was not to be seriously disruptive. By 1937 the outright hostility of 1934 had been transformed into frank expressions of faint praise.

The conciliatory message Landis and Kennedy had broadcast during 1935 started getting through. The SEC's slow and evolutionary approach began to be noted, as had the idea that the SEC seemed to have a beneficial effect on accounting principles and procedures. Practitioners were relieved by the fact that SEC practices were accenting disclosure and were not forcing revisions in the registration statement. Professor Smith observed that if a government agency was to conduct a study of accounting principles, the SEC was as impartial as any to do it (C. A. Smith, 1935: 332). A *Journal of Accountancy* editorial in March, 1935, acknowledged the importance of the present epoch in the history of accountancy and predicted that a new form of accountancy would emerge. Amid praise for the SEC, the *JA* nonetheless had reservations about disclosure requirements for gross sales, costs, and profits and about maintaining trade secrets. In July, 1935, after the Supreme Court declared the NRA unconstitutional, the *JA*'s editorial reflected relief and vindication. The "sudden subversion" of existing society with "grotesque," "precarious" structures showed real progress possible only by slow evolution. "Members of Congress," it asserted, "were given warning that no longer could they play fast and loose with the government of the country."

Without question, the Supreme Court's NRA decision began to make the accountants, along with others in the financial community, more sure of themselves. The Court's ruling, coupled with the relief practitioners and their supporters felt when the SEC failed to impose rigid rules and regulations, resulted in a relaxation of suspicion toward the SEC and the two securities acts. Harvard Professor Sanders, who had been called in to work for the commission when it was first formed, was favorably impressed with SEC operations and the commissioners. Securities legislation was going to be permanent, Sanders knew. That made it essential for the SEC to "maintain the judicial attitude" that it had "already assumed," an attitude of sympathy toward both business and the investor, who needed protecting (Sanders, 1935b: 11). Sanders' approval of SEC performance is noteworthy because his professional orientation and political alignment was the same as George O. May's when it came to who should establish accounting principles. Sanders was much opposed to rigid accounting rules, and had been quick to point out that the SEC had not adopted that tack (Sanders, 1935a: 101).

Some reservations were voiced that the acts might require further amendment, and the SEC's emphasis on detail was criticized. But the SEC's sincerity in administering the acts was early associated with the idea that it was going out of its way to avoid making rigid rules. This stance pleased the practicing accountants and others, and resulted in favorable statements about the commission's broad-mindedness, its trustworthiness, and its "judicial attitude." (Henderson, 1934: 458; Haskell, 1936: 274; Smith, C. A., 1935: 332; Crane, 1935: 374). Some accountants also understood that the SEC had helped allay the financial community's fears, and believed it helped overcome the restriction of investment (Crane, 1935: 372). Praise for SEC operations in 1935 showed up in the *Journal of Accountancy's* editorials, and Professor Kohler, editor of the *Accounting Review*, joined in. In the one month since Form 10 had been issued he wrote, the SEC had "set effective and . . . reasonable standards—necessarily incomplete, of course—for the profession, which years of futile committee work within the professional societies have not been able to produce or even begin to produce" (Editorial *AR*, March, 1935: 102).

The SEC was even a less controversial part of the accounting scene in 1936. Comments about SEC administration continued generally favorable. Sanders, writing in early 1936, discussed SEC influence on accounting principles, reiterating his beliefs that flexibility was required and uniform accounting was undesirable. Flexibility, liberal spirit, and adherence to broad principles of accounting, had made the SEC's regulations mostly acceptable (Sanders, 1936a: 70). May, too, noted that SEC policy permitted registrants to follow their own accounting methods providing they were "not obviously unacceptable and were clearly disclosed" (May, 1936a: 12); furthermore, he thought added information required by the commission was reasonable.[1]

Practitioner Strategy against the SEC

May relentlessly continued his attack on regulatory legislation, if not on the SEC. He claimed that "even the members of the Securities Commision seemed to have developed doubts on the question whether the acts were really necessary or will prove beneficial in relation to issues of securities by seasoned corporations" (May, 1936b: 101). The acts created expectations they could not satisfy, he said, and would be more useful, more remedial and practical, if they were less theoretical and punitive: "Indeed, one of the dangers of the admitted excellence of administration by the Securities Commission up to the present time is that it may tend to blind us to the inherent defects of the law" (Ibid., p. 102). May's remarks illustrate a kind of ideological paralysis. His commitment against government regulation was so deep that it produced the conclusion that even if the law was working, it could not be because the law was good but because the commissioners administering it happened to be excellent. May's attitude was unwavering, and added to the frustration and anger disclosed privately by Landis.

The antigovernment attitude may have been ideological, but it was also self-serving. As such, it was a part of the practitioner's deliberate strategy to keep the SEC on the defensive. The practitioners, in effect, developed a dual approach in which they were consistent. On the one hand, praise the "flexibility" of the SEC, which permitted maximum accountant autonomy; on the other, continuously raise the spectral straw man of rigid, straight-jacketing regulation, and maintain the generic, ideological attacks on regulation as regulation. It was a game played best by Starkey and May, the latter by far the more powerful of the two.

The revision of audit procedures by the American Institute of Accountants in January, 1936, was prompted by the danger that the government might act in that field. "No profession such as accountancy in which individual integrity and business judgment are of the highest importance," said Starkey, "can stand being enveloped in a straight-jacket of rigid rules and regulations, which is the real hazard of the assumption of authority by a Federal commission" (Starkey, 1936: 27). Starkey invoked the horrors of the ICC's accounting requirements, in which the dangers "of regimentation, of uniformity, and of rigidity in accounting and auditing" were present. The profession, he added, was in a "precarious position" because of the threat of "excessive regulation" (Ibid., p. 30).

Following the same theme in an article purposefully entitled "Eating Peas with Your knife," May made a novel argument that excessive amounts of data required by the SEC in financial statements "destroys the implications which could fairly be drawn if [the information] were made voluntarily" (May, 1937c: 17). Statements required of an accountant did not carry the same implications as if made voluntarily, he believed. May also shed some tears for the fate that had befallen the profession: "You may feel, as I confess I do, a certain regret that the accounts to which you and we put our names that appear in prospectuses today are not as illuminating as those which we used to put out in the old days" (Ibid., p. 19). Yet that might not be bad, he continued, if the legislation, which he saw in the nature of a leveling process, resulted in a greater leveling up of the standard of the less satisfactory prospectuses that used to be issued (Ibid., pp. 19–22).

Merger of the ASCPA into the AIA: 1936

An important secondary effect of the securities acts was that they precipitated a major organizational unification of the accounting practitioners. The possibility of an ASCPA-AIA merger had received favorable comment within the AIA council in the early 1930s; the securities acts made the pressure to merge acute. In 1933 Walter A. Staub, president of the NYCPA and partner of R. H. Montgomery in the Lybrand, Ross Brothers & Montgomery accounting firm, initiated the talks that finally led to the merger in 1936 (Edwards, 1960: 180; Carey, 1969: 354). Montgomery's interest in a merger was well known (Carey, 1969: 358; Montgomery, 1939, 307–308; 334–335) and his membership in the ASCPA was primarily a move to try to bring it back into the AIA. He was not unusual in this respect (Edwards, 1960: 129–130).

Would the merger have occurred without the securities acts and the SEC? Probably, but not until later. Interest in a merger existed almost since the split in 1921, but only two years elapsed between the formation of the SEC and the consummation of the merger. Voluminous references in the accounting literature of 1933–1936 to the necessity for "solidarity" and "one organization" support the conclusion that the securities acts triggered the merger. Action to smooth the way toward merger of the two groups was taken by a joint committee in 1934 and 1935, and in 1936 a merger plan was submitted to and approved by the membership of each. The result was a re-united national organization of practicing accountants (Edwards, 1960: 179–181; Carey, 1969: 354–360). All ASCPA members in good standing were transferred to the AIA. A proposal to insert the words "Certified Public" in the name of the organization was defeated by membership vote. New applicants were required to hold CPA certificates. The organization was controlled by a council of 35, 7 of whom were to be elected each year. No more than 6 council members could come from the same state, and by custom, no more than 2 from the same firm (Edwards, 1960: 180–185).

The test of strength between the merger and antimerger factions crystallized in the presidential battle between Montgomery, representing the merger forces, and Will A. Clader, representing those in opposition. The Peat, Marwick, Mitchell company of New York was the only major accounting firm backing Clader; Haskins & Sells backed Montgomery. Price Waterhouse & Co. may have given merger tacit support, but in any event they stayed out of the controversy and did not oppose it. Montgomery won the election, 1210 to 438. After the merger total membership was 4105, compared with 2135 ASCPA and 2239 AIA members beforehand. In the year following the merger, membership approached 5000.

Even with the merger of the AIA and the ASCPA, competing CPA organizations made it impossible for practitioners to speak with one voice. Nonetheless, the leaders of all groups realized that professional control depended on unity, that federal licensing or regulation was always a danger. To achieve effective control, Montgomery thought, accountants needed only one organization per geographical district—and all should keep their eye on what Washington was doing: "Legislation affecting the profession should be watched and fostered or opposed by societies of accountants acting privately and accountable only to the members of the profession" (Montgomery, 1939: 274). The securities acts made Montgomery's wish for a national organization of CPAs possible. The practitioners were more indebted to the government, particularly to the securities acts, than they were willing to admit.

The AIA Is Given Charge

By mid-1937, even antiregulation practitioners like Starkey had become convinced of the essentially benign character of SEC operations—and with good reason. The AIA Special Committee on Cooperation with the SEC, which Starkey chaired, had responded to the commission's request for opinions on several accounting problems. More importantly, Starkey, in his concern about Landis's critical remarks about accountants in December, 1936, had contacted the commissioner. In addressing an annual conference of the Investment

Bankers Association of America, Landis had referred to "almost daily tilts with accountants" and to "loyalties to management . . . stronger than . . . responsibility to the investor." Landis had gone on to say:

> Such an experience does not lead readily to acquiescence in the plea recently made by one of the leaders of the accounting profession that the form of statement can be less rigidly controlled and left more largely to professional responsibility alone. Simplicity and more adequate presentation is of course an end much to be desired, but a simplicity that misleads is not to be tolerated. The choice here of more or less regulation is an open one for the profession. It is a "Hobson's choice" for Government (Landis, speech to 25th annual conference of the IBA, December 4, 1936: JMLPHLL).

If you are correct, Starkey told Landis, the AIA's Committee on Cooperation with the SEC still had a lot of work to do, and would want to do, to avoid future criticism. Landis was willing to cooperate, and suggested that Starkey contact Blough, the commission's chief accountant. Starkey did so. Blough, with Chairman Landis's approval, agreed that the Securities and Exchange Commission would refer to the AIA Committee on Cooperation with the SEC all accounting questions coming before the SEC with which the commission took issue with the accountants who had signed the statements. Details of different cases involving stop orders would also be sent to the committee. Furthermore, violation cases would be turned over to the AIA Ethics Committee for action. Shortly thereafter, in January, 1937, Blough sent Starkey the first set of accounting questions from the SEC.

The SEC's agreement to turn over to the AIA certain questions of accounting practice, as well as disciplinary matters, was the critical turning point that led to institutionalizing the responsibility for accounting principles in the hands of the private sector. The agreement was the second major event defining the SEC's permanent relationship with the practicing accountants. The SEC had already adopted the practice of permitting corporations wide latitude in the manner in which they disclosed financial information, consistently applied, in preference to imposing mandatory reporting methods. Both events implied the abandonment of any possible development of uniform systems of accounting by the SEC, and of course, by the practitioners. Both events, representing an abdication of public authority to the private sector, took the SEC far down the path to impotence.

Starkey's April 12, 1937, report indicated satisfaction with these arrangements (Starkey, 1937: 434–443). There was a significant absence of the anxieties he had expressed less than three years earlier over whether the SEC was going to exercise control over accounting functions.

Starkey's impression of the position the SEC was taking on accounting principles, uniform accounting, and the role of practicing accountants was solidly based. In a speech in October, 1936, Blough had defined the relationship of the SEC to the accountant and noted mutual SEC-practitioner assistance. The commission, Blough had said, had sought and received cooperation in developing efficient accounting practices and statements, remarks (published in January, 1937) that confirmed that the Kennedy-Landis position in 1935 had been institutionalized by fall, 1936.

> The commission has depended a great deal upon the ability of the independent public accountants, and has not attempted to lay down hard and fast rules regarding the type of audit or the specified form of the financial statements required. Certain minimum requirements are specified in each form, but much is left to the judgment of the accountant (Blough, 1937a: 25).

The registration forms were for so widely diversified a group it was impossible to incorporate a fixed procedure in the preparation of each statement; the accountant, consequently, had "enough leeway to express adequately the information for varying types of businesses" (Ibid., p. 26). The accountant was only required to specify the principles and procedures followed, and whether he had a major difference of opinion with his client. "There is, of course," Blough had said, "a dividing line between acceptable and unacceptable accounting practices; that line is a hair line, the location of which is a matter for the individual judgment of the accountant" (Ibid., p. 29). The hair line was to become one of the broadest ever recorded.

As SEC policies became clearly compatible with the interests of the practicing accountants, the latter's comments about SEC operation and administration became consistently favorable, although the acts themselves and government regulation in general remained fair game. In any enterprise, an accountant's value vanished under government ownership or operating control, Warren W. Nissley, partner in the "big eight" firm of Arthur Young & Co., wrote in early 1937. He assumed auditing work would not be transferred to the government, in spite of Landis's exasperation over "almost daily tilts" with the accounting profession. Nissley chose to rationalize away the Landis statement. First of all, management decided on the auditor's appointment, which put the public accountant in a difficult situation. Secondly, Landis could only be referring to a few isolated cases. Accounting was an art, not an exact science. For example, differences of opinion were bound to exist between accountant and management regarding the forms of financial statements; accountants faced with such a disagreement could either withdraw or attempt to reconcile the two views, though the latter course was better. Disagreements had tended to decrease since 1934 "because management is now much more aware of its responsibilities." The SEC could now assist the accountants by requiring that each listed company have its public auditor elected by stockholders (Nissley, 1937: 100–102).

EDUCATE THE INVESTOR!

To prevent financial speculations, the practitioners, who regarded themselves as practical men, consistently reiterated the impractical solution that the SEC "educate" the investor about the limitations of financial statements (Starkey, 1934; 438; Nissley, 1937: 103–104). The suggestion, if it was not frivolous, can be understood as a psychological attempt to avoid responsibility for promoting confusing or outright misleading financial statements. The ignorant citizen-gambler, the little man of little means, uneducated, unable to appraise financial reports and therefore inappropriately in the market, was a convenient scapegoat.[2] It was also argued, by George O. May, that SEC preoccupation with investors not being misled "obscured the desirability of enlightening them" (May, 1938: 359).

May's campaign of backhanded praise for the SEC continued in 1937 via an address at the Harvard Graduate School of Business Administration, invitation courtesy of Professor Sanders. A "major accomplishment" of the SEC, said May, has been the creation of a clearer understanding than ever before within the private sector of the practicable and the impossible ways in which investors can be informed. The commission also deserved congratulations for insisting that changes in reserves now required explanation. Still, the SEC should seek "improvement in financial accounts through sympathetic and patient encouragement of progress . . . and . . . not attempt . . . rigid rules of accounting as . . . some times . . . suggested . . ." (May, 1938: 366).

"We Have Survived the Securities and Exchange Commission, Which Has Done a Good Job"

By early 1937, the SEC had decisively relinquished its most important regulatory authorities over corporate financial reporting requirements. The commission had encouraged variations in methods of treating and reporting corporate financial accounts, promoted a "footnote disclosure" policy, and permitted public accountants to police their own ethics violations. All that remained to complete the capitulation was to announce as official policy that the SEC would avoid creating comprehensive accounting standards, in favor of the accounting practitioners. As described by Carman Blough, that decision was made by the commission in 1937 and communicated to the AIA, by Blough, at the Institute's annual fall meeting. The message was that the decision had been made to let the AIA make the accounting rules, though the message was accompanied by the threat that if the AIA did not do it, the SEC would. Early the next year, the AIA Committee on Accounting Procedure was reconstituted to undertake the task (conversation with Blough, 10/19/72).

Blough's official announcement was climactic. It provided the resolution of the conflict begun in 1933. It was an apt confirmation of the capitulation of the government agency, that the message had been delivered by the chief accountant.

Following the relinquishment by the SEC of responsibility for developing generally accepted accounting principles, some salient comments were made by R. H. Montgomery, then president of the AIA, at its fiftieth anniversary. Satisfied with the advance of the profession, Montgomery entitled his address "What Have We Done, and How? Relations with government and business would not remain static; a consolidation of accountants' strength was needed. "If anyone outside the profession—governmental or private, client or friend—is stronger than we are and is able to tell us what to do, is able to influence a statement or a report against our best judgment, from that moment the profession will deteriorate. It is not so today" (Montgomery, 1937: 337). The more government became involved in business and finance, the less there would be for the professional accountant to do. Montgomery's speech almost caricatured the values of the conservative practitioner. It was antigovernment, anti-union, anticontrol, anti-anything adversely affecting practitioner interests. Montgomery sounded the cry for accountants to fight any threats to CPA independence "by rules or regulations or business pressure."

In a bravura ending, he called upon the accounting profession to "fight bunk whenever and wherever it appears." His real message, however, was delivered in an earlier sentence with two beautifully antithetical observations: "We have survived the Securities and Exchange Commission, which has done a good job" (Montgomery, 1937: 348, 346).

AFTERMATH

When the practicing accountants fully realized that the Securities and Exchange Commission had relinquished its authority to establish rules for financial reporting, their attitudes toward the SEC became much more benign. Reminders to the SEC not to overstep its bounds were couched in terms of compatible AIA-commission aims. Even history was reinterpreted. Since the beginning, claimed the editor of the *Journal of Accountancy*, accountants fortunately had excellent relations with the SEC, in spite of the fact that on occasion there had been criticism. The commission was now seen as helpful to the accountants in their practice, who, backed by the authority of the SEC, had registered substantial improvements. Approval was also bestowed on the commission because the very few requirements it had adopted on specific accounting practices were those already receiving general acceptance. The editorial noted that inflexibility was still a danger, however, and that accounting problems ought to be treated as they come up, rather than in any systematic form (Editorial, *JA*, February, 1938: 91–92; July, 1938; 2–3; see also Broad, 1938: 78–79; 88–89; Fiske, 1938: 310). Cautious praise continued, even from May: the SEC was now "the most important single influence in the country in the determination of the course of accounting development." But, he added, it was the AIA committees "cooperating with the Securities and Exchange Commission, other regulatory commissions, stock exchanges, and others, [which] have unobtrusively accomplished substantial results." Confirming the events of the past four years, May announced that the dangers of laying down fixed rules had been recognized by accountants and SEC alike (May, 1938: 3; 7–8). Other practitioners kept hammering away at the theme that the accounting profession should always have the responsibility for developing accounting principles (Stempf, 1938: 12–16; Haskell, 1938: 293–294). As a corollary, and following May's lead, they characterized SEC achievements as supplementary to or merely consolidations of those of the practitioners (Stempf, 1939: 23–24; Stewart, 1941: 464).

By 1941, when Andrew Stewart, a partner in the "big eight" firm of Haskins & Sells, looked at the arena, the game was over. Relations between SEC and the accountants had already settled into a cozy pattern. Primary initiative for developing accounting rules had passed to the practicing accountants and investigation into accounting problems would be conducted by them on an ad hoc basis. Attempts to develop accounting knowledge in a systematic way were to be avoided for the next 20 years within the AIA by a large committee, almost all of whom were practitioners and none of whom could bind their accounting firms to the committee's decisions. The practicing accountants had won the power struggle. Their behavior in the ensuing years was to depend on several preconceived notions held by their leadership and shared, apparently, by the main body of practitioners. Practitioners of the AIA for the next three decades would dominate attitudes toward the function of accounting, uniform accounting systems, and the development of accounting principles, all to the substantial exclusion of the SEC and other accounting bodies.

Notes

1. It was "not surprising," May said, that the SEC had called for statements beyond the balance sheet and the income and surplus accounts in connection with the growing requirements of financial reporting (May, 1936a: 22).

2. "Much is heard about the gamblers in Wall Street. There are gamblers in that locality, of course. But there are millions of gamblers scattered throughout the cities, villages and hamlets of the United States who have a very large aggregate purchasing power and who are willing, and eager, to buy securities regardless of any consideration other than a belief that they can sell them for more. I do not believe there is the slightest hope of changing their gambling spirit by any method, but the extent of their gambling might be reduced by education so that they would be able to understand the odds better. Lacking such an understanding, security prices are affected unduly by mob psychology since the transactions of the uninitiated cloud the effect of the transactions of the experts" (Nissley, 1937: 103–104).

chapter

9

Was the organization of the Committee on Accounting Procedure an accident?

The CAP: 1938–1959

"It had to be an accident because no one would ever design it that way," a wit once quipped, on observing a monstrously impossible travesty of a presumably functional design. He could have made a similar observation about the structure and operation of the American Institute of Accountants' Committee on Accounting Procedure (CAP). The committee was re-organized in 1938 to conduct research that would lead to a body of generally accepted accounting principles. As organized, it was impossible for the CAP to accomplish that objective. Those who believe in accidents could also believe that the practitioners gave their best, and failed. Determinists, those who believe that all acts have purpose, consciously or unconsciously, are deliberately motivated, and therefore are no accidents, would conclude, however, that the AIA wanted the CAP to fail in its ostensible mission. I tend toward the latter view, hence the skepticism apparent throughout this chapter.

Late in 1938 the AIA reconstituted its Committee on Accounting Procedure to implement the decision of the Securities and Exchange Commission to encourage the accounting practitioners to develop "generally accepted accounting principles" (GAAPs). With George O. May at its head and Professor T. H. Sanders its director of accounting research, the CAP became a committee in its own right. No longer would it be composed of chairmen of other committees. Now it would have 22 members with the president of the AIA as chairman. Members were intended to come from many geographic locations, different size firms, and the teaching profession. A permanent research "staff" was organized consisting of two members: the director and one full-time research assistant. Expenses were covered by special membership contributions pending AIA budgeting. Committee decisions would not require the approval of the AIA's executive committee for publication, because some executive committee or council members would always be on the CAP (Bailey, 1940: 52).

The committee's pronouncements "could have no authority beyond that of the standing and integrity of the participants in the decision and the reasoning behind it," explained Bailey. In other words, AIA members did not necessarily have to abide by the committee's decisions. Opinions required at least two-thirds approval for release, and deadlocked issues were to be presented to the profession for discussion and crystallization (Ibid., p. 53).

PUTTING OUT BRUSH FIRES

About 30 years after the inaugural meeting of the CAP, Carman Blough described what happened. The main concern of those at the meeting was how to proceed. At first a comprehensive statement of accounting principles was considered to guide daily practice, but committee members realized such a document would have to be extensive to be useful. "After extended discussion," they agreed a statement of principles would take "as long as five years" to complete. Fear of SEC action if steps were not immediately taken to "reduce areas of differences in accounting procedures" led the committee to decide it could not wait that long.

> Instead it concluded that it should set to work as quickly as possible to resolve some of the more pressing controversial matters that were responsible for the criticisms leveled at financial reporting and for the concern of the SEC. This decision was described by members of the Committee as 'a decision to put out the brush fires before they created a conflagration' (Blough, 1967: 7-8).

In July, 1940, George D. Bailey, partner in the "big eight" firm of Ernst & Ernst and a member of the AIA Committee on Accounting Procedure, drew a distinction between what Professor William A. Paton of the University of Michigan called true research and research into areas where controversy was "localized." Accounting, Bailey indicated, was a practical tool and its research should be primarily along practical lines. The CAP thought the first phase of its research was like that undertaken by the American Law Institute— it was the sort of thing that should have been carried on in the universities but not exclusively by them. The shift in accounting emphasis from the balance sheet to the income statement and growing demand for more uniformity in accounting were cited by Bailey, who commented that "experienced accountants abhorred uniformity as such" but they thought it "possible for two different accountants working with the same set of facts to arrive at the same determination of the proper principle." In any case, the committee's initial work was a long, drawn-out procedure. As Bailey saw it, it was an "admittedly slow process of wide discussions and free interchange of ideas during the formative stages of the study of any particular project as well as in the early stages of the relevant releases" (Bailey, 1940: 52). The result was more likely to be sound, and of educational value to the Committee members and the profession, but even so, the committee did "explore some additional methods by which it may speed up its work without losing any of the benefits of the slow democratic process" (Ibid., p. 53). When Sanders asked if CAP research subjects would cover large or small questions, he was told that "the ideal answer obviously lies in the judicious combination of the two." "Practical" research would be followed as opposed to the theoretical, recognizing the demand to "clear up" differences of accounting practice and to "speed up" general acceptance of recognized principles (Ibid., p. 54). The CAP would begin with carefully selected individual problems that would point toward future broader studies and "what may be called pure research activities."

Bailey then inadvertently demonstrated some farcical aspects of the CAP process and the results of its dedication to "flexibility" in his description of the first problem discussed by the CAP: how to treat unamortized discount and redemption premium on refunded bonds. First the committee discussed the problem, then turned it over to the research staff (Sanders and his assistant) for study and analysis. The staff memorandum was sent to each committee member for comment. The replies were then sent to all committee members to permit consideration of all points of view. Another draft of the preliminary release was then presented to the committee at another

meeting. What was the result? "In the end," said Bailey, "the committee felt that the immediate charge-off theory and the future
charge-off theory each had sufficient theoretical and practical merit
to make it impossible to agree upon either theory to the complete
exclusion of the other, but it did express a preference" (Ibid., p. 55).
Understandably, the committee had been accused of "compromising
and temporizing" in the release, he admitted. But the absence of
"authoritative definition" of many accounting terms had been a
handicap. Therefore another committee was needed. Accordingly,
a Committee on Terminology, with three members of the CAP, was
appointed to help solve that problem.

The organization and operation of the AIA Committee on Accounting Procedure thus promised to be a pathetic attempt in democratic research on the lowest intellectual level. Is it unfair to be so
critical? The AIA prided itself as an agglomeration of practical men,
and its members must have realized that no substantive results could
come from a committee hampered by the procedural and objectives
limitations they had imposed. Several organizational mistakes are
quite obvious. A geographically distributed committee of 22 was too
unwieldy to permit effective discussion or rapid decisions. Membership criteria for the CAP was vague, and probably depended more
on accounting-firm affiliation than on scholarly pretentions. The committee had 15 full-time practitioners listed in the 1938 Yearbook, of
whom six represented five of the "big eight" firms: May and Starkey
(Price Waterhouse); Samuel J. Broad (Peat, Marwick, Mitchell);
Arthur H. Carter (Haskins & Sells); Bailey (Ernst & Ernst); and
Victor H. Stempf (Touche, Niven). All six opposed government
regulation, uniformity, SEC control of accounting principles, and
were dedicated to "flexibility."

Moreover, a part-time director and one full-time research assistant clearly could produce little research. The selection of Sanders as
research director guaranteed an approach to the issues faced by the
accounting profession that was compatable with the views of the
most conservative practitioners. At best, the work of the research
"staff" could have only an ad hoc quality, thereby thwarting the
achievement of any results.

Devotion to the "slow democratic process," and the two-third
vote requirement before an opinion could be released reduced
chances of producing timely research beyond a low consensus level.
The unwillingness of the AIA to make decisions binding on its mem-

bership threatened to compromise the committee's decisions, and unmasked the lack of control the AIA had over its members, particularly over the prestigious accounting firms, in spite of illusions some CAP members had about their own personal leadership. The committee no doubt wanted to avoid the promulgation of required accounting rules. They were all "flexibility" advocates. Finally, the hope that selection of individual problems would lead the way to future, broader studies is difficult to take seriously because of (1) the logical shortcomings of the notion, which should have been obvious to the committee itself; and (2) the practitioners' generally anti-intellectual orientation.

As "practical" men, the members of the Committee on Accounting Procedure probably realized that they were part of an organization that was quite certain to accomplish almost nothing. Was the committee structure deliberately designed for that purpose? To repeat, if one believes that few, if any, things are accidental, and that a series of deliberate choices can be construed in relation to their likely consequences, it is fair to conclude that the AIA only intended to maintain the status quo, retaining the power it had already obtained from the SEC. Was the choice conscious, or unconscious? In all probability, both. A conscious desire can be seen not to proceed too fast, to retain flexibility, and to keep the control over accounting principles in the hands of the practicing accountants. Unconscious elements, however, are also apparent in the rationalized superstructure of ideological commitments common to the practitioners of the time. The construction of the committee was so deftly designed to accomplish the minimal development of a comprehensive body of accounting knowledge that the cleverness of its formation may not have been consciously recognized by the AIA leaders. The only reasonable conclusion possible is that the practitioners never meant for the committee to achieve any effective results, otherwise it would have been designed differently. The ideological perspective of the CAP members was limited, but their intelligence was not. The cumbersomeness of the organization was deliberate, and it put significant limits on what the CAP could do. But had the CAP been the best of organizations, it is still questionable how much it could have accomplished. Three other entrenched, debilitating factors worked against the practitioners and the CAP: their limited ideological perspectives toward government and business, their anti-intellectualism, and their ad hoc approach toward accounting as a body of knowledge.

Ideologies

The resistance of the practicing accountants to the increased liabilities of the 1933 and 1934 acts was based on a limited conception of the client-accountant relationship. The increase in responsibility specified in the securities act was frequently regarded as "radical." The burden of proof placed on accountants signing a registration statement under the Securities Act of 1933 was feared to be impossible to sustain (Starkey, 1934: 438–439). Lawyer A. I. Henderson, discussing accountants' liability under the acts in 1934 on the platform with Starkey at the 1934 AIA annual meeting, recognized that the greatest importance of the acts would be on general accounting principles, methods of accounting, and financial statements. In other words, the acts would force significant changes in accounting practices and methods, particularly as the Securities Exchange Act of 1934 covered every listed corporation.

The securities acts altered the accountant's previous impression he was legally responsible to his client as a practical matter, and not to the public, although the *Ultramares* case had somewhat qualified that perspective. The test, Henderson believed—some forty years ahead of his time—would be what the corporation's financial statements conveyed to a person not familiar with accounting practices and conventions. Accountants would therefore be well advised, he thought, to place themselves in the position of the layman (Henderson, 1934: 448–449). In Henderson's view, the accountants had an indefensible belief that they merely certified the clients' corporate statements, and that therefore they were not responsible or liable for them. Nor would it be possible, he felt, to avoid liability for balance sheet defects through the device of an accountant's certificate that stated that a certain account had not been checked. Henderson's comments anticipated the 1939 McKesson-Robbins case: "I think it is doubtful if a statement that the accountant did not check the accounts receivable will relieve him of liability, in the absence of valid reasons for not making such a check" (Ibid., p. 456).

The securities acts substantially changed the accountant's liability to the investor, but the practitioners found it difficult to adjust to the new situation. They quite naturally preferred the previous strict interpretation of liability based on a privity of contract relationship with the client whereby no legal duty was owed the investor, under ordinary circumstances. But if the practitioners believed they should not be liable to investors, what did they perceive about their relation to clients? Because many thought they did not have to guarantee the accounts they audited, it followed that they considered it proper that there be limits on how far they should be required to check those accounts. Leading accountants felt they ought not to be responsible for the verification of inventories, for example, and that the real responsibility for this particular operation lay with the corporate executive. The layman had to learn that the accountant was not an appraiser, and that the determination of corporate asset values was the board of directors' responsibility. The function of the accountant was only to describe the basis of stating such values (Andersen, 1935: 333–334). Accountants, then, were recorders of facts. This attitude was reflected by some academic accountants as well (Sanders, 1936a: 71–72). In this sense, accountants were also seen as advisers to business (Andersen, 1935: 331), and as such they envisioned themselves as part of the business community. Even so, they preferred not to consider themselves as employees of business. Accordingly, some writers would refer to the necessity for "cooperation" between the profession and business (Stempf, 1939: 27).

Accountants also asserted that clients had to be resisted when their demands conflicted with the accountants' concept of good accounting. It was a theme they constantly reiterated. Consequently, the SEC's concern that too many accountants were susceptible to undue client pressure became a sore point, though this type of pressure was apparently frequent (Smith, C. A., 1935: 332). Because the accountant-client relation was a tight contractual arrangement, it followed that if the investor was to be educated for his own protection, it ought to be up to the Securities and Exchange Commission to undertake the job (May, 1937a: 343; Stewart, 1938: 40). While some writers might acknowledge that the investor was the ultimate client, they obviously did not like the idea (Starkey, 1934: 438)

The accountants' perception of the information investors needed was expanding, but it was also becoming less realistic. May, for example, thought investors ought to appreciate depreciation effects on income (May, 1937a: 344; 365). Nevertheless, the practicing accountants portrayed the average investor as not being astute, usually unwise, and basically interested in and very susceptible to speculative promises (Montgomery, 1937: 338–339). The fear that investors would misunderstand the nature of the SEC and would

assume that it accredited securities was also occasionally mentioned
(Starkey, 1934: 437).

One of the persistent rationales that permitted accountants to
adhere to the idea that investors should not be allowed to rely on
their certificates was that accounting was, after all, merely a matter
of opinion (May, 1937a: 345; Haskell, 1936: 276; Stempf, 1940: 523),
which, of course, contradicts the view of themselves as merely "re-
corder of facts." The corollary to the rationale that accounting was
only an opinion was that uniformity was neither possible nor desirable, a hypothesis that worked to the disadvantage of the accounting profession (Greer, 1938: 215). The stress upon nonuniformity was
generally concomitant with the belief in accounting "flexibility."

Practitioner's attitudes were essentially defensive. *Ultramares*
and the securities acts destroyed the public relations pose that the
accountant was responsible to investors. The Cardozo decision and
the two New Deal laws forced reliance on an alternative posture,
namely, that the accountant was the agent of the client and had no
authority to dictate rules or presentation styles to the client, which
would imply liability for the advice given; his sole function was to
follow the client's wishes and present properly the information supplied by the client. Verification of this data should be limited only to
what the client submitted. It was a peculiarly narrow, self-serving
view. It was also peculiarly unrealistic, seen against the background
of the two securities acts and the new emphasis for better investor
information on the one hand, and the practitioners' insistence on the
other that the SEC stay out of the business of specifying accounting
rules. If the client was the ultimate judge of what information would
be presented, and how it was to be shown, as many of the practitioners insisted should be the case, then clearly all the accountants
were superflous. That was not the case, of course, and so the argument was ultimately untenable. Nevertheless, the practitioners and
their supporters maintained that position as long as they could, which
was a long time indeed, and they bolstered it with a very large dose
of antigovernment ideology.

ATTITUDES TOWARD GOVERNMENT

The practitioners' attitude toward government was predictable,
based as it was on their fundamental opposition to the securities acts.
Reconciled, finally, to the SEC as a permanent addition to the institutional scene, many practicing accountants still disliked the idea

of government regulation, although they frequently accorded grudging respect to the commission as an administrative group. Nevertheless, some accountants chose to emphasize the 1932–1933 cooperation of the New York Stock Exchange and the AIA as evidence of real improvements in corporate financial reporting (Haskell, 1938: 294; Sanders, 1937: 192). The SEC was seen as permanent, and partially benign with respect to its influence on the accounting function and the relationship of accountants to their clients (Sanders, 1935b: 10; May, 1937a: 333; Watson, A. J., 1935: 445; Sanders, 1937: 196; May, 1938: 3) and as mentioned before, the constant barrage of anti-government invective continued even after the SEC became "safe." Even so, the overall attitude of the practicing accountants toward the government was not quite so simple.

THE RELATION TO SOCIETY AT LARGE

Though saccharine references to the purity of accountancy in the past can be found, the period of the late thirties saw a growing awareness on the part of the profession that it was becoming increasingly subject to public scrutiny because of the influence of accounting techniques upon society at large. R. H. Montgomery, looking back on the AIA's 50 years, felt himself satisfied with what the accountants had done. Most accountants were only partly trained, he conceded; still, the public accountant was nonetheless a vital factor in business, financial, and social affairs, and could not be disregarded. Accountants were charged with public as well as private duties, and he saw no reason to "apologize for the importance of educating the business public to pay big enough fees to professional accountants to enable us to remain as independent as we are today" (Montgomery, 1937: 334). But in the new scheme of things, he added, accountants had to cooperate with government in order to avoid more regulation. Other accountants accented minimizing friction with lawyers, thus developing a better cooperative attitude with the legal profession (Byerly, 1938: 154–160); it was a perspective that could also be interpreted as an attempt by accountants to get lawyers to agree on keeping monopoly boundary lines clear. And some did seek cooperation with the SEC in the interest of the investor and tried to convince clients to disclose more meaningful information (Watson, A. J., 1935: 445).

With rare exceptions, however, practitioners of the late thirties either never really understood or refused to admit the influence of accounting technique upon the national economy. Most references to the issue were limited to the effect of accounting technique on corporate balance sheets and income statements. G. O. May, for example, treated the effects of the changing emphasis in corporate accounting in a series of lectures and articles in the late 1930s and early 1940s, citing the changing emphasis from capital valuation to income. Capital gains laws, he recognized, were "obviously, if unconsciously, framed in the interest of the short-time speculator for the rise rather than of the long-time investor for the yield" (May, 1936b: 101). May traced the developing stress on the income account from an earlier period when the preparation of accounts was dominated by their use for credit purposes. With the increasing distribution of stock ownership and the separation of ownership from management, a new demand for accounting services occurred as people became concerned with a greater dividend-paying capacity than with corporate liquidated value. Increasing stock volume in the twenties brought about greater interest on the New York Stock Exchange in the form and content of corporate reports. "The shift of emphasis from the balance sheet to the income account was a natural incident . . ." (May, 1940: 73–74).

A series of securities scandals in the late thirties—the Trans America, Associated Gas and Electric, and Missouri Pacific Railroad delisting proceedings and the McKesson-Robbins auditing investigation—made it clear that "to a considerable extent, the fight for protection of the interests of investors and public regulation of corporate enterprise . . . shifted to the accounting front" (Kaplan and Reaugh, 1939: 203). Accountants and investment analysts agreed that the income statement was much more important to the investor than the balance sheet. The value of a business depended on earning capacity, not historical cost (Ibid., p. 206).

The importance of earnings became institutionalized. In the future, varying accounting devices would be invented or adapted to inflate or to give an appearance of greater corporate earnings. During the conglomerate merger movement, this widespread practice was to focus attention once again on the accounting scene.

Pragmatism and Anti-intellectualism

In the 1930s, the accounting practitioners and their supporters revealed themselves as ultimate pragmatists. There are some unfortunate limitations to pure pragmatism. Pragmatism breeds anti-intellectualism because it ignores intellectualism. Avoiding the broader context of the use of the intellect produces a potentially destructive ad hocism that justifies decisions for expediency's sake and promotes successive rationalizations without reference to ultimate objectives. Those who choose to follow the path of the purely pragmatic are likely eventually to fail to be taken seriously. And their efforts are likely to be discarded as their pragmatism fails, or is replaced by a more powerful pragmatism or by the pragmatism of the more powerful. The latter happened to the accounting practitioners on two separate, dramatic occasions; they were victimized by their own pragmatism, anti-intellectualism, and resultant ad hocism, all of which were evident in the latter half of the 1930s.

This is not to imply that the practitioners of the time were immoral, malevolent, more unreasonable than their business contemporaries, or more interested in protecting themselves than any of their contemporaries engaged with the government. Their behavior was what one would expect of people trying to protect what they have, no more and no less. If they were little concerned with the broader implications of what they were doing, or if their values differed from some of those of today, that was to be expected also.

The overall concern here is *why* certain specific events took place. First, why the SEC relinquished its most important authorities to the private sector. Second, why that part of the private sector, the accounting practitioners, that took over the relinquished authority failed to accomplish meaningful results with it. And third, why the practitioners in turn were forced to surrender a large share of that authority. My contention is that the seeds of the practitioners' failure were in certain attitudes that made their failure inevitable. Their debilitating ideological limitations were considered previously; their anti-intellectualism and its effects will now be examined.

PRACTITIONER HOSTILITY TOWARD THE ACADEMIC BRANCH

The accounting profession has had more than its share of intramural conflict. As an existential matter, this conflict reflects the newness of accounting as a profession. The squabbling that took place was over which group of accountants ought to be responsible for theoretical developments, and it took place because of the hostility of the practitioners toward the academics and the low opinion the practitioners had of intellectual activity.

Pulitzer prize-winning historian Richard Hofstadter pointed out that in a popular sense, intelligence is always esteemed, and never used as a kind of epithet. Intellect, on the other hand, is often looked on with suspicion, and not always associated with intelligence.

> . . . intelligence is an excellence of mind that is employed within a fairly narrow, immediate, and predictable range; it is a manipulative, adjustive, unfailingly practical quality—one of the most eminent and endearing of the animal virtues. Intelligence works within the framework of limited but clearly stated goals, and may be quick to shear away questions of thought that do not seem to help in reaching them. Finally, it is of such universal use that it can daily be seen at work and admired alike by simple or complex minds.
>
> Intellect, on the other hand, is the critical, creative, and contemplative side of mind. Whereas intelligence seeks to grasp, manipulate, re-order, adjust, intellect examines, ponders, wonders, theorizes, criticizes, imagines. Intelligence will seize the immediate meaning in a situation and evaluate it. Intellect evaluates evaluations, and looks for the meanings of situations as a whole. Intelligence can be praised as a quality in animals; intellect, being a unique manifestation of human dignity, is both praised and assailed as a quality in men. When the difference is so defined, it becomes easier to understand why we sometimes say that a mind of admittedly penetrating intelligence is relatively unintellectual; and why, by the same token, we see among minds that are unmistakably intellectual a considerable range of intelligence (Hofstadter, 1962: 25).

Anti-intellectualism has always been an important part of American business ideology; the businessman has always been characterized as the enemy of intellect (Ibid., pp. 233–252). Within the business community, to be accused of being "intellectual" is to be accused of being "impractical" or of being too "theoretical." The hostility between the accountant practitioner and the academic can very frequently be placed within this context. It was an opposition that on occasion burst open for all to see. More often, it vibrated below the vocal-written level, though it was apparent enough to any careful between-the-lines reader.

An episode that reveals this hostility centered around the effort of the practitioners to keep the academics out of research. Oddly, the affair was an outgrowth of a seemingly trivial notion—the desire of the American Association of University Instructors in Accounting to change its name. The proposed new name was the American Accounting Association, the idea of Professor Paton. The proposal was introduced and defeated in 1924 and again in 1931, and the academics continued to be burdened with the ungainly appelation. Besides opposition within the AAUIA to the name change, some practitioners were also against the proposed name because it might suggest equality with the AIA. The ubiquitous R. H. Montgomery was so vigorously opposed to Paton's proposal in 1931 that he incorporated the name "American Accounting Association" in several states to forestall the action (Zeff, 1966: 36). But Montgomery's gambit was unavailing. Some important AAUIA members went ahead and incorporated themselves under "American Accounting Association" in Illinois, where Montgomery had not preempted them. The AAUIA membership at its 1935 annual meeting, was then convinced to "join" the "new" group. Important backing was given by Carman Blough, then the first chief accountant of the new SEC. And so it was done: the AAUIA became the AAA—the American Accounting Association.

The AIA, then contending with the Securities and Exchange Commission over control of financial reporting rules, objected to a competing group in the research field. The academics also wanted to keep the government away from setting financial rules, and though they had not developed any meaningful research operations within their organization, they felt the time had come, as their official journal put it, to end the research "drift" of the profession in order to avoid SEC intervention (Editorial, *AR*, December, 1934: 334).

The systematic development of a consistent and useful body of knowledge is an important indicator of an advanced profession. The contributors of such knowledge usually enjoy high prestige and are well integrated into the professional hierarchy. Law and medicine are such professions, where pro-academic and pro-intellectual attitudes are characteristic. The accounting practitioners aspired to the professional status of law and medicine. It is an anomaly, therefore, that a strong and continual current of antiacademic, anti-intellectual tradition runs through the professional practitioners. It is doubly curious because the practicing accountants so self-consciously courted and asserted professional status in the eyes of the larger society. Anti-intellectual bias is observable among the practicing accountants in several ways. For instance, admission standards for the national accounting organizations have in the past specified nearly prohibitive practice requirements for academics. Leading directorship posts in the national accounting practitioners' associations have seldom, if ever, been filled by academics. Academic accountants had only a limited influence within the AICPA committees developing accounting principles, from the original Committee on Accounting Procedure through the Accounting Principles Board to the Financial Accounting Standards Board.

Even today the academic accountants are poorly integrated into the accounting profession. Efforts by the practitioners to achieve a "truly national organization" originally did not include them, and their addition afterward followed considerable dispute. Furthermore, they are still effectively excluded from meaningful participation in the affairs of the AICPA. It is striking that unlike the older professional groups the accountants have developed a noticeably segregated profession, though the underlying reasons for this circumstance are understandable. For one thing, the practicing accountants have always been involved in situations where power and financial gain were very much at stake for them and other members of the financial system. From that point of view, the presence of academic accountants in their midst could only be regarded as a disruptive influence relative to maintaining control over professional practices and standards. In a relatively arbitrary arena where conventional skills exist on an unsystematic, ad hoc level, compared with medicine or engineering, the contributions and prestige of the academic component could be considered as superfluous.

Exclusion of academics from real participation in the affairs of the AIA was a conscious effort. More than likely, it had its unconscious components also, reflecting the anti-intellectual tradition of both American business and British accounting. The exclusion served the practicing accountants well. The academics have had little demonstrable influence over them, and less over the government, leaving the practitioners to have things pretty much their own way. Organization of the academic accountants occurred well after that of the practitioners, and the academics never made much effort to work with government. Developing some strength and status only in the mid-thirties, it was too late for them to share with the practitioners the authority wrested from the SEC. Thereafter, the power balance between practitioner and academic remained relatively constant. The AIA regarded the academic accountants as poor relations, and it was duly resented. Both groups were, of course, accountants, and as such believed that the development of financial principles by the SEC would have been a diminution of power for the profession. Although neither AAUIA nor the AIA had warned against the financial and accounting excesses nurturing the 1920s boom, past performance was forgotten, all in the accounting profession sought to protect their most important, albeit dormant, role: autonomy to develop and administer the rules for corporate financial accounting. The newly dubbed AAA was ready to assist in the process, but vainly waited for the chance. The AIA was already there, and after getting control of the financial reporting principles from the SEC, retained it. The AIA was, after all, by far the most worldly of the two groups, and already an integral part of the financial system. It had a considerable financial stake in seeing to it that the never-exercised but much-talked-about function of developing accounting principles did not remain in the hands of the SEC—or slip into those of the academics.

The Freezing Out of Academe

The academic accountants irritated the AIA members with their efforts to become somehow involved in the development of financial accounting standards. The practitioner dwelt on the theme of the "impractical, theoretical" academic. Discussing the AAA's Tentative Statement on Accounting Principles, F. P. Byerly, a practicing accountant, said with an unctuous air that it "revealed the idealistic aspirations characteristic of the academic mind" (Byerly, 1937: 94). Defending the practitioner's reliance on precedent and authority rather than on scientific methods, it was observed rather snidely that it was "perhaps not unnatural that the authors of the [Tentative Statement] are men of academic or regulatory body training" (Byrne, 1937: 365). Professor Sanders also shared in the anti-academic feeling. He believed the accounting profession, which he equated with the practicing accountants, would accept the cooperation of teachers of accounting "provided," he said haughtily, "the latter are willing to go to the trouble of acquainting themselves thoroughly with the problems in hand" (Sanders, 1935a: 101). Rigid rules or attempts to establish them would unfortunately place practitioners and teachers in opposite camps, he claimed. Categorical requirements were impossible because of variations in business conditions, management, and changes in economic and political movements; only "practical wisdom" would consider those variables (Ibid.). Along this line Stempf, a fairly prestigious practitioner, objected that "the argument that a rule of practice can't be right if it doesn't have a foundation in sound theory provokes the unsound assumption that what *is* good in theory *must* be good in practice" (Stempf, 1940: 525). Something might appear excellent from the standpoint of theory, Charles Couchman added in 1934, but may prove to be unsatisfactory when faced with the limitations of practical application (Couchman, 1934: 348). Practitioner Couchman summed up the point with some succinct ideological nonsense: "Theory is principle; practice is experience. Theory thinks; practice acts. Theory says: practice does. Theory idealizes; practice penalizes. Theory plans; practice proves" (Ibid., pp. 351–352). The antipathy of the practicing accountants to their academic counterparts also appeared when the AIA merged with the ASCPA. No consideration was given to incorporating the AAA into the new organization.

In 1935, a proposal was made by Professor A. C. Littleton of the University of Illinois for an independent board of financial review for accounting matters, a "court" that would also license accountants to practice before it (Littleton, 1935a: 283–291). He argued the practicing accountant was very much subject to the client's whims. The new Securities and Exchange Commission and the promulgation of its rules, together with an Accounting Board of Review, would give accountants additional independence because they would be able to appeal to a significant authority.

An answer to this proposal appeared several months later. In the judgment of its author, who opposed the licensing idea, the adoption of Littleton's suggestions would "bind accountancy in the fetters of an inevitably mediocre bureaucracy" (Hunt, 1935: 453). Littleton took exception to this criticism. "License," he countered, was a "hobgoblin" of a word and need not be feared, and the proposal would not result in regimentation. Furthermore, there was no need to tie the proposed Accountancy Board to the SEC. Littleton was willing to make modifications on the proposal, though he denied that it would inevitably result in a "mediocre bureaucracy." Littleton was really thinking in terms of professional rulings set by the accountants' peers:

> Such a court would be better prepared to comprehend the issues than one in which the personnel was untrained in accounting. And it would probably be easier to find accountants also educated in law (for nomination to the court) than it is to find attorneys also educated in accounting for places as judges in the regular law courts (Littleton, 1935b: 269).

Little further comment on the proposal was to be found in the *Journal of Accountancy*. From the practitioners' view, it was clear that the proposal would have reduced their autonomy. Independence of the profession as a whole might increase, but the loss of flexibility would be disastrous. It was better to ignore the proposal.

The idea of a new institution to deal with accounting matters surfaced again some three years later. A. A. Berle, Jr. argued that a more systematic method of evolving standard, evolutionary rules of accounting was necessary because rules of accounting had in large measure become rules of law and those rules were not wholly satisfactory (Berle, 1938: 368). Accounting was a part of the business scene, and the accountant had become inextricably related to the mechanism of government control. Perhaps accountants had been too preoccupied with taxation problems to have devoted themselves to the more general development of the profession, he said. The accountants assisting in drawing forms and regulations in 1933 "really found themselves faced with the job of codifying, unofficially, a huge field of accounting in a few weeks—and that in a profession which had only begun to agree on terminology" (Ibid., p. 370). Accountancy had been driven from the private into the legislative arena within a very few years, Berle noted, and the SEC had probably been the most effective force in thrusting accounting rules into the legal structure even though there were dangers in administrative rulings (Berle, 1938: 371–372).[1]

Berle pointed out that if a deficiency letter was issued by the commission and challenged an accounting point, the corporate applicant submitting the information could argue the matter before the commission. If the SEC still disagreed, the applicant could either comply, withdraw the registration, or appear at a commission hearing on whether a stop order should be issued. Berle argued that the last alternative would be taken only if the SEC felt the registrant might be an "irresponsible swindler" and wanted to find out if he were committing a fraud. Nonetheless, said Berle, such stop order hearings mean that most questions of accounting are settled by the star-chamber process, and chiefly by subexaminers" (Ibid., p. 372). No sane man would follow the course of appealing to the commission, Berle argued, which was an unsatisfactory state of affairs. In arguing for the new institution, Berle pointed out that SEC decisions were not recorded or available to others, not necessarily uniform, reasoned, or systematic decisions, and not reviewed by any competent authority. Whether such decisions were based on valid precedent or whether they were purely arbitrary determinations depended on the capability and integrity of the commission's staff at any given moment. This unsatisfactory mechanism meant that administrative law was writing accounting rules into living law without self-criticism, the bulwark of the common law.

> The plain fact remains that effective accounting rules are made in camera, without system, without effective submission to criticism, with little guaranty against arbitrary determination, and without the continuous and open self-examination which must go into rulings which attain to the sanction and dignity of law (Ibid., p. 374).

Berle proposed three ways in which rules made by government bodies could be challenged. Provide (1) the opportunity for full argument on both sides before a decision is reached, (2) require publicly announced, reasoned decisions, and (3) permit review of decisions upon appeal to a higher tribunal. "It should be within the realm of possibility to create a board of accounting appeals to which accounting questions could be referred, and which, by training, personnel, and equipment would be capable of rendering swift decision on such problems" (Ibid., p. 372). The board could be formal or informal but would have to be authoritative; it would provide not so much a judicial proceeding as a forum for the airing of the best prevailing thought on accounting issues. The board could decide either a specific problem or issue an advisory opinion in advance of a controversy or for general application. The doctrine of stare decisis ought not to be followed—that is, precedent should not be binding, said Berle. "Rather, we ought to borrow from the experience of our European friends who practice the Roman law, and follow the system by which the writers, the scholars, the commentators are as persuasive authority as are the decisions of the group itself" (Ibid., p. 375).

If the suggestion of a review board was too innovative, a less ambitious expedient might be employed, Berle said. A special division of the SEC could rule on problems of accounting and issue published opinions after hearing arguments. It could be assigned the task of ruling on such matters as the accounting provisions of new regulations, the requirements of new forms, and the need to change old forms. "Then, and not until then, will we begin to have something more satisfactory in the way of effective accounting opinion" (Ibid., p. 376).

Berle's paper was presented before the AAA in December of 1937, and appeared in its *Accounting Review* in March, 1938. It was reprinted in May, 1938, in the *Journal of Accountancy,* and was therefore readily available for accountants' comment. Like Littleton's suggestion before it, however, it received relatively little. An Accounting Board of Review apparently represented too much of a threat to the autonomy and independence of both the academic and the practitioner.

Meanwhile, the squabbling between them continued, as Professor Paton's negative reaction to the AIA Statement of Accounting Principles evidenced (Paton, 1938: 196–207). Professor DR Scott of the University of Missouri argued that the development of accounting principles was unsatisfactory, that accounting should be based on social theory rather than on practice, and that leadership was required of more parties than of just practitioners (Scott, 1939a: 70–76). Professor Kohler's editorial in the *Accounting Review* of March, 1935, had claimed that one month of the SEC had done more for accounting than years of futile AIA committee work; his comments on the first three bulletins issued by the AIA Committee on Accounting Procedure continued to be savage. The bulletins unfortunately did not show the promise held out for them by the CAP. To Kohler, they "succeeded in being little more than attempts to explain and justify practices existing among professional accountants" (Editorial, *AR,* December, 1939: 453), adding that it was unlikely the CAP would make any serious theoretical contribution.[2]

In the same issue of the *Accounting Review,* Professor Scott argued that it was no longer open to question that accounts would constitute a central feature of the system of economic control in the future. "The danger is . . . doctrinaire or half-baked formulations of principles . . . frozen into the rigid requirements of law. And the surest way to bring about the adoption of such half-baked principles is for leadership in the accounting profession to take the position that public accounting practice cannot be subordinated to a system of accounting principles or theory" (Scott, 1939b: 401). The latest hard feelings between the two groups had been prompted by the appearance of the AAA's Tentative Statement of Accounting Principles and the subsequent appearance of the AIA's "Statement." Members of the AAA believed the AIA precipitated publication of its statement to compete with the AAA. As later described by Professor Hiram T. Scovill of the University of Illinois:

> Some very harsh words were used in describing the attitude of
> the Council of the Institute as one of jealousy. On the other

hand, it is likely that some practitioners in the Institute referred
to the Tentative Statement of Accounting Principles as the attempt of some pedagogues to tell the profession what it ought
to do (Scovill, 1941: 173).

Efforts were made to reconcile the two groups, and by 1939 Professor Scovill believed that some significant steps had been taken
toward that end (Ibid.) Professor Scovill was wrong on that point.
There was a community of interest between the practitioners and the
academics over the rules for financial standards, and both were opposed to government intervention. But the division of authority between them was too lopsided for reconciliation. Furthermore, the
cleavage on theoretical grounds was increasing rapidly. The ad hoc
approach of the practitioners would become less and less acceptable
to the academics as time passed. Nowhere was this gathering disagreement more evident than in the attitude of the two groups toward
the development of accounting principles, which was, after all, what
the entire affair was all about.

Notes

1.   "There is always danger, where accounting rules are made by specialized administrative tribunals, that the resulting body of doctrine may
be lop-sided, if not positively dangerous, however conscientiously the rulings have been made from the point of view of the administrators making
them" (Berle, 1938: 372).

2.   "But the Committee, exemplifying the arbitrary and unreasoning
approach of a boastfully practical man, did not 'deem it opportune to discuss the theoretical soundness and practicability of adopting an alternative treatment of bonds which would recognize in some respect the nominal
character of the terms "principle" and "interest" '. . . . The early adoption
of a 'rule' without giving it extended consideration is likely to impede if
not make impossible any serious contribution by the Committee to accounting theory" (Editorial, AR, December, 1939: 455–456).

The practice versus theory controversy

Practitioners and Principles

No single accounting topic received more attention during the late 1930s than the question of generally accepted accounting principles. Its consideration encompassed uniform accounting and the entire system of control by the Securities and Exchange Commission over financial reporting practices. It provided much of the focus for the power struggle between the SEC and the accountants.

Most of the practitioners' discussions of generally accepted accounting principles was vapid, and the alleged "principles" they advocated were the precedent-established practices of the larger firms. No serious attempt was made to develop a codification of accounting principles in the thirties. There was, toward the end of the decade, a growing literature among the academic accountants that began to suggest that some systematic development of general accounting principles should be possible and could be undertaken, but by then the authority to develop them had passed from the SEC to the academics' practicing counterparts, and the commission had become committed to an ad hoc approach toward accounting rules. It was an approach that became a permanent operating mode.

"GOOD ACCOUNTING PRACTICE IS MERELY THE PRACTICE OF GOOD ACCOUNTANTS"

"Good accounting practice is merely the practice of good accountants" R. H. Montgomery had written in 1921 (Montgomery, 1939: 471).[1] The remark emphasizes the practitioner's reliance on precedent and individual judgment. Montgomery's attitude typified that held by most accountants in the years following World War I and the coming of the New Deal. It was no wonder, then, that there had grown up a large variety of inconsistent accounting conventions. The consensus among practicing accountants at about the time the SEC was created was that generally accepted accounting principles did exist, and, moreover, supported a wide variety of accounting practices.

Toward the end of the thirties, however, a marked shift in opinion took place. Accountants no longer asserted that a definite body of generally accepted accounting principles existed. Instead, they wrote that few definite accounting principles could be identified, and considerable controversy occurred over the rationality or effectiveness of even those. If generally accepted accounting principles did exist, they were so broad as to support a broad range of financial treatments. In any case, the practitioners drew the conclusion that "flexibility" was essential. Alternately, when practitioners asserted that GAAPs did not exist, their conclusion was interpreted to mean that judgment, therefore, *had* to be relied upon.

The practicing accountants claimed, of course, that they, and only they, were in the best position to determine which practices would be most reasonable. As a result, practicing accountants dwelt continually on the idea of "flexibility" and opposed the establishment of rigid accounting rules and procedures—which they successfully resisted. The outcome of the controversy was the direct and conscious transfer from the SEC to the accounting practitioners of the responsibility for the development of accounting principles. Once transferred, the responsibility became part of the institutionalized activities of the practicing accountants.

THE EARLY PERSPECTIVE

The AIA appointed a Special Committee on Development of Accounting Principles in 1933. Its objectives were to survey and analyze the underlying principles "which should govern the practice of accountancy." The appointment of the committee "was merely putting in a more concrete form" the purpose of the Institute's organization. The subject was important. The committee consisted of the chairmen of several other of the Institute's committees and thus was "representative of a large group of competent accountants" (Editorial, *JA*, December, 1934: 407).

Many phases of accounting theory and practice in the early thirties were "still in the controversial stage," according to Harvard's Professor Sanders. Summing up the perspective taken by the practitioners and their supporters at that time, Sanders said that for accounts to be reliable they should be "set up in accord with sound principles of accounting and classification." He implied, however, that even if "sound" principles of accounting and classification were followed, corporate financial reports could not be sufficiently uniform to provide comparisons. Operating variations among companies and differences of opinion among accountants prevented comparability. These difficulties forced reliance on accountants of

> experience, disinterestedness, and sound judgment to . . . make the best choices among alternatives. As experience accumulates, however, it becomes possible to embody it in general principles. . . . not that these . . . can ever . . . substitute for judgment and experience, but they may . . . supplement these . . . and . . . reduce the area . . . of . . . judgment. . . ." (Sanders, 1934: 202).

One of Sanders' "practical" recommendations was that investors should be educated about "the character of balance sheets and income statements, and especially of their unavoidable limitations (Sanders, 1934: 203). Financial reports were not predictions, he said, but only limited indicators of corporate value. Sanders held that many aspects of accounting theory were accepted practice, and that generally accepted principles of accounting included permissible alternatives. What was essential was year-to-year continuity, because complete uniformity in accounting practices for business would not be ideal, even if attainable. To Sanders, any attempt to standardize accounting procedures for all business would "inevitably" result in lowering standards far below the accounting practices of leading business; evolutionary accounting progress would be stifled. Except for well-known basic principles, effective accounting systems for a particular company needed to be specifically designed for its peculiar requirements (Sanders, 1934: 205). The latter point was one Sanders continually emphasized throughout the 1930s; it was also one that was continually echoed by numerous others. Practitioner Starkey, for example, shared Sanders' view favoring accountant flexibility, declaring that "corporations should be required merely to indicate the principles which are followed" (Starkey, 1934: 445).

The import of the Sanders-Starkey position was clear: practitioners did not want to be tied to required reporting procedures. The AIA committee chaired by Samuel J. Broad, revising the 1929 auditing pamphlet, *Verification of Financial Statements,* published its bulletin in late 1935. It, too, stressed the importance of flexibility and slow evolution, allegedly needed in any program of audit procedures. The new auditing bulletin was abreast, but not ahead, of the prevailing opinion within the profession (Broad, 1935: 23–26).

The practitioner's commitment to recording rather than leading business practices unfortunately guaranteed that uniform accounting principles would not be developed. Arthur Andersen, founder of the firm carrying his name, however, seemed unaware of the relationship. In 1935 he wrote that one of the problems inherent in the preparation and interpretation of financial statements lay in the lack of precise and uniform principles within the profession. "Accountancy," said Andersen, "has thus far accumulated little technique, for it is still in the process of steady development of fundamental principles . . . developed as a composite of the best and most enlightened business experience" (Andersen, 1935: 332). He saw accounting policies as a management province, but noted that the comprehension of financial statements depended on accompanying statements of the principles used. Andersen's was a typical "business precedent" orientation that assured a constant flux in accounting practice, because accounting practices would change according to corporate interests. By that standard, accounting "principles" were potentially infinite.

Not everyone, of course, upheld the practitioners' view. From academe came the opinion of Professor Smith in late 1935 that there was a "growing awareness . . . that 'in accordance with the accepted accounting principles' is a most indefinite characterization of what should be a fairly definite concept." Too often, he declared, "accepted accounting principles" were simply what each practitioner considered acceptable. A critical disinterested study was needed "so that . . . practitioner and teacher alike may know what is or is not really acceptable by a majority of the better accountants" (Smith, 1935: 332).

But Sanders continued to assert that a viable set of accounting principles did exist, stressing, at same time, the importance of judgment in accounting and noting, with relief, that the SEC permitted optimal accounting practices. The SEC mode of operation was firm by 1937, institutionalizing the Northern States Power case, and Sanders stated what had become the government's policy: that "the commission has in its accounting regulations not sought to prescribe accounting methods, but has prescribed full disclosure of whatever accounting methods the company had chosen to adopt" (Sanders, 1937: 204).

The AIA's official approach toward accounting principles also appeared in 1937 in a report of the AIA Special Committee on Cooperation with the SEC. The report was in response to several inquiries on the appropriate treatment of certain accounting problems submitted to the AIA by Carman Blough, and it described different ways in which an accounting problem could be treated:

> The broad question which you [Blough] have raised, . . . is open to so many reasonable differences of opinion that the committee feels that full disclosure of the particular method used, the justification for its use, and consistency in its application are primarily the important features.

Still,

> . . . cases have arisen in which it has been considered proper to depart from the strict interpretation of this rule.

On the other hand:

> It is not intended to convey the impression that these two examples constitute the only exceptions to the general rule (Starkey, 1937: 438–442).

Several months previously Starkey had answered criticism of the new AIA bulletin on auditing procedures. There were complaints, he said, that rules of practice and procedure were insufficient to furnish the average practitioners with a satisfactory guide. "In my opinion," Starkey had written, "the very fact that such criticism could be leveled at this booklet is indicative of its real value" (Starkey, 1936: 28).

THE LATER VIEW

George O. May's attitude toward flexibility remained fairly consistent throughout the 1930s, but by 1940 his belief in the existence of generally accepted accounting principles had pretty well dissolved. "Accounting is a tool of business," he wrote in 1936, "and . . . like the development of business law, has been determined by the practices of the business man" (May, 1936a: 11). Accounting in principle and authority involved recognition of custom, convention, and judgment, not the application of rigid and unvarying rules. The "clamor for an unattainable combination of completeness, precision and simplicity and for a uniformity [was] superficial and illusory" (Ibid., p. 22).

No higher principles existed than those of general economic advantage and justice by which accounting practices should be governed and judged, May indicated.[2] Conventions based partly on theory and partly on practical considerations formed the determination of income and the preparation of balance sheets. Improving accounting conventions and increasing the uniformity ought not to be based on "purely metaphysical concepts," but through "careful consideration of what is fair and in the best interest of those having a legitimate interest in accounts. . . . No rule . . . contrary to the interests of all of the parties should be established on the sole ground that it conforms to some abstract notion of what is sound accounting" (May, 1936c: 183–184).

A year later May's ideas about the identifiability of accounting principles showed some signs of modification. "When you hear a reference made to an accounting 'principle,'" he told an audience at the Harvard Business School in 1937, "you may find that in reality it is nothing more exalted than a convention or a rule of convenience." The AIA tried establishing some basic principles of modern accounting, he said, but it was unable to suggest more than half a dozen as generally acceptable—and these were rules rather than principles, and, as such, were subject to exception (May, 1937a: 334–335). Accounts might therefore properly differ according to the purposes for which they were prepared (May, 1937a: 336). If there were generally accepted accounting principles, therefore, they "must be few in number and extremely general in character" (May, 1937b: 424).

Accounting conventions sought to be determined by the results they produce, he said in 1938. The so-called principles of accounting were not fixed laws of the natural world. They were principles in the sense of "rules adopted or professed as a guide to action"; hence, they were neither inevitable nor immutable. They depended upon the usefulness for which they were employed for their continued recognition (May, 1938: 8).

By 1940, May had about given up the quest for accounting principles, asserting that "consistency" and "conservatism" were the two principles where most agreement among accountants was to be found. There was no unanimity regarding questions of capital and income (May, 1940: 75–76). May's 1940 attempt to conclude on accounting principles smacks of desperation.

> . . . I am disposed to follow the example of James Bryce in his *Modern Democracy*. You may recall that his chapter discussing definitions of democracy reaches the conclusion that no satisfactory definition can be evolved, but that it is not really necessary to evolve one because everyone knows broadly what democracy means. There are no precise criteria by which the existence of democracy in a state may be determined, and there are none by which the appropriate accounting treatment of a transaction may surely be judged. In both instances a decision must be reached upon the basis of some rather broad concepts and an appraisal of the essential facts in relation to the objectives sought to be attained (May, 1940: 78).

May's opinions about general accounting principles were highly significant. He was widely considered the intellectual leader of the practitioners, a reputation he guarded jealously, and, although not very well known throughout the profession, he wielded great influence on Wall Street and within the AIA.

When May's book, *Twenty Five Years of Accounting Responsibility*, was published in 1936, Professor Sanders gave the book almost obsequious praise. He hailed the book's appearance an "outstanding event" that would "add to the stature of the accounting profession." "The breadth of spirit with which [accounting] was treated would command respect." "The author's broad grasp, penetrating insights, lucid, cogent style, serenity of spirit" clearly conveyed the respect Sanders accorded May (Sanders, 1936b: 390–392). The intellectual compatibility between Sanders and May was later confirmed when Sanders was named the part-time research director for the AIA's Committee on Accounting Procedure.

May had the endorsement of others besides Sanders in the form of numerous imitators who followed his line that generally accepted accounting principles were scarce, that few could be developed, and that therefore no one "best way" could be applied. It was a tenet that led them to conclude that "sound" judgment in choice of accounts and techniques had to be left to the practitioners (Byerly, 1937: 94–95; Stewart, 1938: 36; Starkey, 1937: 439; Byrne, 1937: 367–370; Broad, 1938: 78–79; Haskell, 1938: 300; Stewart, 1941: 464–466).

But if generally accepted accounting principles were hard to find, and when found incapable of broad application and treatment, how could the practicing accountants assert that it was imperative to follow some accounting procedures? They answered with the idea that certain accounting principles were verities, but that subrules permitted various treatments under each accounting principle. The prize essay for the AIA's fiftieth anniversary was Gilbert R. Byrne's "To What Extent Can the Practice of Accounting be Reduced to Rules and Standards?" said Byrne:

> As to the fundamental principles of accounting, there can be no more question of their "general acceptance" than of the moral rightness of the ethical principle that it is wrong to kill. But there are legal rules derived from the moral command, "Thou shalt not kill," which have differed at times and in different countries.
>
> The principles of accounting remain the same, and about them there should be no substantial disagreement; as to the body of accounting rules, practices and conventions derived from those principles, there may well be differences of opinion as to their validity in a particular case (Byrne, 1937: 369–370).

The fundamental principles were, therefore, presumed known and used by accountants examining financial statements (Ibid., p. 372). Thus, Byrne developed the general argument that parent principles could be distinguished from the rules derived from them.

Practitioner Broad followed a similar approach in claiming that accountants' opinions distinguished between an accounting principle and its application, "and the distinction between an accounting principle and an accounting rule" (Broad, 1938: 87). Inflexible rules were neither expedient nor supportable, he argued. The dangers of inflexibility were extremely obvious when one considered the different methods of valuing inventories and appraising fixed balance sheet assets.

The Statements of Accounting Principles

Although the practicing accountants were satisfied with a distinction between accounting principles and the rules derived from them, their academic counterparts, with the exception of Sanders and a few others, were less convinced. The difference of opinion between practitioners and academics created considerable friction, and helped exclude academicians from the AIA and its development of accounting principles.

Part of the animosity between the AAA and the AIA stemmed from their direct confrontation over generally accepted accounting principles. Some of the best contemporary accounting writers took issue with the practitioners on the state of the art of accounting and its reliance on ad hoc analyses. The AAA issued a document called "A Tentative Statement of Accounting Principles" in June, 1936, that was the first major attempt by either academics or practitioners to develop a formal set of accounting principles. Its authors were Professors Paton, Littleton, Kohler, and Howard C. Greer, who wrote the paper in four months.

The "Tentative Statement" advanced three propositions: (1) corporate transactions should be recorded at cost rather than value, (2) the all-inclusive concept of the income statement should be used, and (3) a clear distinction should exist between paid in capital and accumulated earnings. Neither of the last two propositions was generally accepted in 1936. The "Tentative Statement" was initially ignored by the *Journal of Accountancy*. In 1938 the AIA published "A Statement of Accounting Principles," authored by Professors Sanders and Henry Rand Hatfield, and lawyer Underhill Moore.[3]

The Academics Attack the AIA's "Statement"

The AAA's "Tentative Statement" used an approach quite different from the AIA's later "Statement on Accounting Principles." The academics' "Tentative Statement" tended to follow a deductive approach, whereas the "Statement" was based exclusively on accepted practice. The difference became magnified over the years. Academic accountants increasingly tried to develop accounting rules within systems; practitioners continued to approach accounting problems individually. And because development of rules for financial reporting was officially in the hands of the AIA, the practitioners could ignore the academics' opinions.

When the Institute's "Statement" was published, some of the reviews by academics were biting. Professor Paton expressed "keen disappointment," considering the "distinguished authorship." He had anticipated an outstanding scholarly approach. He found few substantive recommendations, and he perceived the "Statement's" irritatingly constant use of expressions such as "sound business management" as "abnegation" and "subservience" to business (Paton, 1938: 196–197). Other reviewers were less blunt but equally condemning. The authors of the "Statement" had interpreted it as their job to report on the weight of opinion and authority on principles for preparing financial statements, wrote Prof. Wyman P. Fiske of the Massachusetts Institute of Technology. The report represented current practice, and as an authoritative code it was a real contribution. But in spite of its strengths, the report was nevertheless disappointing to those concerned with broader professional progress. There was an unfortunate absence of aggressive leadership and too much attention to rules instead of truths (Fiske, 1938: 308–316).

Andrew Barr, then making a transition from teaching accounting at Yale University to a staff accountant's position with the SEC, becoming chief accountant of the SEC in 1956, agreed that Paton was correct in being disappointed. A better title for the "Statement," Barr suggested, would have been "A Statement of Accounting Practices." "Principles should grow out of a sound economic analysis, rather than a codification of current conventions or practices (Barr, 1938: 318–319). Barr also took the opportunity, however, to look askance at some of the campus accountants. Too many teachers of accounting, he indicated, assumed with practitioners that business management methods must be right.

"Fundamental truths in accounting," Professor Littleton observed, "may . . . be generalized out of practical experience or deducted from stated premises . . . accepted as true in themselves, or prove to be true by argument. . . . When both methods yield similar results we . . . have obtained . . . fundamental truth" (Littleton, 1938: 17). The differences between these two processes were not always kept in mind, however. Littleton wanted a method of arranging propositions in order to examine their logical interdependence. He argued that good practices and sound principles were supplementary rather than contradictory, but "accounting literature has yet to present . . . the means . . . of what is sound, consistent, logical doctrine . . . ; most of the literature . . . offers only what . . . authors conceive to be accepted accounting practices, although many titles use the word "principles" (Ibid., pp 23–24)

Professor Scott pointed to the connection between accounts and accounting and economic control. Accounting, he said, was being brought into the modern law as a method of adjusting economic interests, similar to the way in which Elizabethan jurists took over the Law Merchant and incorporated it into the common law. Development of a comprehensive set of principles, necessary to guide and support the accounting profession, should not, therefore, be feared. "It is only a means to an end. The important consideration is the result of such practice in terms of a more effective social control over economic processes" (Scott, 1939b: 400). To Scott, accounting was a system transcending the authority of business management, and the public accountant occupied a position of public trust.

Earlier in the year Scott, in commenting on the AIA's "Statement of Accounting Principles" had said that it was reasonable and sure to win practitioner support, but he disagreed with "the tenacity with which the accounting profession clings to the dogma of conservatism" (Scott, 1939a: 74). The "Statement's" purposes were to coordinate, standardize, and correct developed rules and to improve the social orientation of accountancy within society; even so, principles ought not be subordinated to applications, and theory ought to dominate all professions, including accounting.[4] The formulations of subsequent accounting principles should discuss the relation between accounting theory and practice (Ibid., pp. 75–76).

Obviously, the AAA and AIA were split on the practice versus theory issue. No wonder, then, that the AIA ignored and eliminated the AAA organization from participation in the genesis of accounting principles. The academicians were damned as impractical and idle theorists incapable of contributing to business needs.

The SEC Looks at Accounting Principles

The Securities and Exchange Commission never tried to establish rigid financial reporting rules or a uniform system of accounts for industrial corporations. According to its chief accountant, Carman Blough, commission concerns about accounting practice fell into two major areas: whether disclosure was sufficient to make acceptable otherwise questionable accounting procedures, and whether the commission itself should undertake the development of accounting principles. As to the second concern, the commission decided against such an undertaking and, instead, sought "material assistance in solving controversial questions" from the profession. Hard rules were not established by the SEC for audits or financial reports; much was left to the individual accountant's judgment (Blough, 1937a: 23–25). The accountant's opinion on the accounting principles and procedures had to be stated under the SEC certification requirements, and the accountant was obliged to indicate where his client's accounting practice violated accepted practices.

Blough's comments on the AAA's "Tentative Statement of Accounting Principles" therefore, came as no surprise. His mistrust of the academic wing was apparent. The "Tentative Statement" was a real contribution, he said, and in general he agreed with it. But practicing accountants would accuse the college professors of being too theoretical, he thought. "Because of this, it is important that the Association judiciously consider its pronouncements and consult widely with practical accountants before recommending principles for adoption by the profession" (Blough, 1937b: 30). Blough said though the SEC felt a great need for a more generally recognized body of accounting principles, it was almost impossible to find uniform opinion among all accountants on many questions. With little time for extensive research or consultation with leaders in the field, the SEC hesitated to take positive stands when highly thought of practitioners followed contrary procedures. In urging the academics to get together with the practitioners on establishing accounting principles, he sweetened the suggestion by saying that the AAA was looked to for leadership in expressing "sound" principles.

Somewhat in dismay, Blough said he had found no satisfactory definition of generally accepted accounting principles, although the term was widely used.[5]

> Almost daily, principles that for years I had thought were definitely accepted among the members of the profession are violated in a registration statement prepared by some accountant in whom I have high confidence. Indeed, an examination of hundreds of statements filed with our Commission almost leads one to the conclusion that aside from the simple rules of double entry bookkeeping, there are very few principles of accounting upon which the accountants of this country are in agreement (Ibid., p. 31).

Those depending upon precedent usually were content to find a number of cases sufficient to support their position, without any substantial effort on their part to examine the extent to which other practices were followed. The SEC, nevertheless, would undertake the prescription of principles only as a last resort (Ibid., p. 37).

The following year, Blough reported that the SEC was still unsatisfied with the progress being made toward creating acceptable accounting principles. Accountants and registrants argued before the SEC that if statements were drawn in accordance with accounting principles peculiar to a given industry, they should be accepted. "Our attitude, on the contrary," said Blough, "is that accounting principles followed in a particular industry need explaining if they differ from principles generally accepted throughout business as a whole" (Blough, 1938: 110). Disclosure in lieu of revised accounting statements frequently resulted in voluminous footnotes, he said, noting that a better method had to be developed.

SEC Commissioner George C. Mathews expressed ideas compatible with Blough's. The commission, Mathews indicated, is quite responsive to the accountant's desire not to be given too rigid a standard to follow, considering that he has the first-hand experience with actual materials and business problems. The SEC "dared not stifle" the accountant. It had, therefore, established general rules setting forth requirements, but the specific form to be used had been left to the certifying accountant (Mathews, 1938: 227–228).

Accounting has multiple functions, asserted Commissioner Jerome N. Frank in late 1939, following the by then well established SEC position. In accounting as in law, many rules and principles were not certain. The facts were also "often matters about which reasonable men can differ" (Frank, 1939: 296). Frank did concede that there was no good argument for deceiving the investor about the inherent uncertainties behind the facade of the accountant's report, which had so many conditions it was imperfect. The ultimate objective was to disclose the prospective net earning power, and financial statements for investors ought to be designed toward that view (Ibid., pp. 297, 301).

By 1940 the SEC had formalized its position for maximum communality with the practitioners, who had finally concluded that if any "generally accepted accounting principles" did exist, they were extremely hard to find and even more difficult to agree upon. Obligingly sympathetic toward the practitioners' plight, the SEC had failed to establish any absolute requirements for corporate registrations other than for disclosure of significant financial data. Quoting Mathews' January, 1937, address, the SEC's Barr affirmed that accounting professionals should be encouraged to take responsibility for setting up

GAAPs. Where they failed the public duty to recognize and apply adequate standards, the responsible agency must eventually move in, Barr threatened. He quoted Accounting Series Release No. 4 as a fundamental authority document.[6] SEC accounting research was based on supplying the investor with consistent and accurate information, he added, and to the extent that optional accounting treatment of business transactions met that objective, it would be accepted (Barr, 1940: 91–94).

These comments by Blough, Mathews, and Barr, coupled with those of Landis and Kennedy, indicate that by 1940 the Securities and Exchange Commission had completely abandoned any attempt on its own part to undertake comprehensive research. This also meant that uniform accounting systems were by then a dead issue.

UNIFORM ACCOUNTING AS AN ISSUE AND OBJECTIVE

Whether a uniform accounting system should be developed was debated vigorously in the years immediately after the creation of the SEC. As has been noted, the practicing accountants were very much against any such attempt. In that attitude they were seconded by the academic accountants. Not even the SEC expressed much interest in uniform accounting, although on two separate occasions the commission did advocate the development of comprehensive, recognized, accounting principles. Ultimately, uniformity in treating some specific situations did take place on a minor scale. Individual accounting problems were discussed and settled, either through bulletins released by the AIA (later the AICPA) or by the SEC. Nevertheless, at no time was there any sustained effort to develop a body of uniform accounting rules and regulations.

Practitioners viewed uniform accounting with even greater fear than they did the development of accounting principles by the SEC. After all, uniform accounting would be a second step after GAAPs were formulated. One could have a large body of GAAPs without uniform accounting, but uniform accounting required a *comprehensive* set of GAAPs. This explains the revulsion felt by practitioners for the idea of uniform accounting. Practitioner Couchman argued that uniform financial statements presupposed uniform accounting, which assumed developing an enormous number of accounts; to create a set of uniform accounts so perfect that they would not be misleading was impossible. The task would be immense (Couchman,

1934: 340) and the loss of discretion would be enormous.[7] The AIA urged the SEC not to standardize financial statements (Starkey, 1934: 445). To practitioner Mongtomery,

> . . . standardization of accounting practice or procedure . . . would mean the substitution of fixed rules for opinion and discretion. In fifty years we have learned much. If we had been standardized or unionized at any time during those fifty years, I am sure we would have lost one of our choicest possessions—independence to express our convictions in each particular case submitted to us, and most cases differ from every other case (Montgomery, 1937: 345).

The consensus of practitioner opposition to uniform accounting was in earnest. Some regulatory commissions, such as the ICC, had developed uniform systems of accounts, and many accountants thought these systems straitjacketed accountants and corporations alike. Once posited, such systems, the practitioners felt, were almost impossible to change. What would happen they asked, if a uniform system of accounts were to be developed for a group of unrelated industries? Not only would the development of a sufficient variety of accounts to take into consideration all requirements be unlikely, but the problems of consolidating these accounts to get meaningful statistics would be insurmountable. As practitioner May put it, extraordinary transactions often required exceptional treatment. "Uniformity" becomes illusory if each corporation determines when to depart from ordinary practice, which "implies a demand for an external authority" to determine permissible variations (May, 1937a: 356). That was a *real* problem as May saw it, because a scheme of regulation was offensive to him. Control by government authority of a uniform accounting system would result only in adherence to minimum standards, and would necessarily involve a retreat from conservative accounting practices. Regulating bodies, academics and practicing accountants wanted alternative modes of treatment and flexibility in the application of uniform principles, May believed. Raising the inevitable straw man again, May asked the rhetorical question whether accounting should be based on inexorable principles resting on purely scientific grounds or should it be determined by the usefulness of its results? His predictable answer was that accounting ought to "be largely conventional, . . . each convention must be decided by the practical results . . . it produces" (May, 1938: 1).[8]

Uniformity was often discussed relative to specialized areas where it was used, like by the Interstate Commerce Commission, the Federal Power Commission, and the SEC under the Public Utility Holding Co. Act of 1935. But little hope was ever given for the development of uniform systems of accounts for industrial corporations under SEC jurisdiction. In almost all cases, the practitioners' plea was for continued cooperation between themselves and the SEC (Stewart, 1938: 33–60). Academic accountants frequently took the same anti-uniformity approach as their practitioner counterparts. The large number of industries involved was often cited as an impediment to the development of effective uniform accounting practices (Sanders, 1936a: 67). Other writers took a lofty antigovernment approach, asserting that codification "enthrones authority, rather than reason and judgment" (Fiske, 1938: 313). By 1940 SEC ad hoc decisions were producing some minimal uniformity, but the commission never tried to establish fixed rules for reporting (Barr, 1940: 89–92; Healy, 1938: 1–9).

Notes

1.   I am indebted to Professor James S. Schindler for bringing this quotation to my attention.

2.   "Some accountants believe that there are such principles, and it has been suggested that the American Institute of Accountants, or some other body, should undertake to lay them down. It is difficult, however, to see why this should be true of accounting, when it is obviously not true in respect of law or of economics" (May, 1936c: 183).

3.   The study had been commissioned in early 1935 by the Haskins & Sells Foundation (Zeff, 1966: 43–49).

4.   "Some hold that practice of the profession cannot be controlled by any formulation or general acceptance of principles. Others hold that accounting practice may be standardized and controlled by generalized rules based upon such practice. The first view in effect denies the existence of accounting theory, leaving only practical rules of thumb and personal judgment to guide the practicing accountant. The second view looks upon accounting theory as a body of rules or generalizations which summarizes the experience of the profession. It tends to subordinate theory to the practice from which it is assumed to be drawn. . . .

"Neither of the foregoing views is the one adopted in this discussion. Principles cannot be subordinated to their application" (Scott, 1939a: 75). The appeal lies to still more general principles which underlie broader aspects of social organization, Scott claimed: "Thus accounting theory must tie in with more general principles of social theory. It is theory, in this broad sense which should dominate and control the practice of all professions" (Ibid., p. 76).

5.   ". . . It would seem that the proper interpretation to give to the term "generally accepted principle" in the field of accounting is that it is a procedure for handling the recording and interpretation of a particular type of business transaction so extensively followed that it may be considered to be generally accepted. If this is a proper interpretation of the term, I am very much afraid that it is difficult to name very many principles that are generally accepted" (Blough, 1937b: 31).

6.   Barr reaffirmed the understanding pursuant to ASR No. 4, which indicated that accounting principles followed by practitioners in submitting financial statements had to have authoritative support, but where there was a difference of opinion between the commission and the registrant, then, despite the precedent that the registrant might offer, a previously published rule, regulation, or other official releases of the commission, including the opinions of a chief accountant, would be controlling (Barr, 1940: 91).

7.   "A uniform balance-sheet designed for all industry, or even a uniform balance-sheet designed for a specific industry, could scarcely be made sufficiently flexible to permit a proper display of current assets and current liabilities in every organization which would be compelled to use the form. Discretion and judgment are necessary in each case, but results depending upon specific judgment and discretion are not compatible with the term 'uniform.' In other words, a uniform accounting system, if I understand the term correctly, involves a predetermination of the method of treatment of each item involved so that there will be no necessity and, unfortunately, no opportunity for the exercise of discretion" (Couchman, 1934: 341).

8.   Neither the "Tentative Statement of Accounting Principles" put out by the AAA, or the "Statement of Accounting Principles" issued by the AIA recommend the establishment of uniformity in accounting, although the academics' "Tentative Statement" seemed to imply that more rather than less uniformity be established, May argued. Uniformity was not a goal in itself, but only a possible aid in making accounts more valuable (May, 1938: 6–8).

chapter

11

The difficulties of regulating powerful constituencies

The SEC Just before World War II

Some conclusions can be drawn about the history of the SEC and the accounting profession prior to the outbreak of World War II. We have seen how—in only a few short years following the worst stock market crash in the history of Western Capitalism—the resurgent power of America's financial-industrial sector in the early months of the New Deal forced the transfer of financial control over corporations from the Féderal Trade Commission to a new independent regulatory agency, the Securities and Exchange Commission. We have also seen how, after 1934, the continuing harassment of the SEC by the accountants and others in the financial-industrial sector finally resulted in the commission's agreement in 1936–1937 to relinquish its statutory authority to develop rules for financial accounting and transfer it informally to the American Institute of Accountants, the foremost national organization of practicing accountants. That transfer was completed in 1938 when the AIA reconstituted its Committee on Accounting Procedure to develop accounting principles. Events surrounding the nondevelopment of comprehensive, effective accounting principles and the collapse of the CAP and the Accounting Principles Board following World War II were logical outgrowths of the early struggle between the financial sector and the government. Though the accountants failed to devise a set of uniform principles, the SEC never seriously attempted to regain the power it had relinquished to the practitioners. As time passed, the pattern established in the thirties between those in the private sector and the SEC commissioners became firmly planted in the minds of both.

The authority for development of rules for financial reporting became increasingly institutionalized in the private sector. When the successive accounting principles research organizations developed by the accounting practitioners collapsed because they failed to carry through their mandate to establish principles, the authority to formulate the standards never reverted to the SEC. By 1972–1973 it was lodged in a composite financial group consisting of organizations from the financial and industrial sectors, plus the traditional, token inclusion of the academic accountants. The accession to power of the Financial Executives Institute and, to a lesser extent, the Financial Analysts Federation, demonstrates the critical institutional change that shifted the authority for developing financial standards away from the accounting practitioners. The failure of the academic accountants to make successful, or at least serious, efforts to absorb some of that authority on their own is almost as striking as the SEC's abandonment of its power to do so to the financial-industrial sector.

The Struggle to Control Standards of Financial Reporting

The failure of the Securities and Exchange Commission to assert and maintain its authority to prescribe standards of financial reporting at the earliest opportunity was fatal. The commission was never again able to assert that power. The lesson suggested by the experience of the SEC is that an independent regulatory agency should utilize the full range of its power at the outset of its existence, or forego the opportunity subsequently to use them as effective instruments of public policy.

The transfer of power from the SEC to the accounting practitioners between 1936 and 1938 was the result of a set of complex circumstances. Continuing pressure from the financial sector gradually broke down whatever will there was on the part of the early SEC commissioners to retain control of accounting principles. The effectiveness of this pressure was enhanced by the fact that a majority of the commissioners believed the private sector should have maximum opportunity to determine their own operating rules. The urgings of the financial sector combined with the orientation of the

SEC toward self regulation wherever feasible provided a perfect setting for the transfer of the authority for developing accounting principles to the American Institute of Accountants. This shift in power was abetted by the political maturity of the accounting profession in the 1930s. Prior to World War I and continuing through the depression period, the accounting profession had numerous contacts with the government. Although the accounting practitioners were divided into two main national groups, the real power in the practitioner ranks lay within the AIA, and to some extent with the New York Society of Certified Public Accountants. The American Society of Certified Public Accountants, the other national organization, was more favorably disposed toward the SEC and toward government regulation, but even it resented the idea of extensive SEC control. The advent of the Securities and Exchange Commission provided the motive for the merger of the AIA and the Society in 1936–1937. The history of the thirties, as witnessed particularly by the accounting and financial literature, plus the private letters of SEC Commissioner James M. Landis and Harvard law professor Felix Frankfurter, indicate that the financial community, and the accountants in particular, were never reconciled to government regulation by the Roosevelt administration—and that the SEC was much aware of that attitude. By the end of 1933, the business community, which had so recently been at its lowest prestige point since the turn of the century, had regained some of its strength and was able to mount an effective attack against the Securities Act of 1933.

A great deal was at stake for the financial community in the provisions of the new regulatory law. The right to determine the composition and treatment of financial reports was also, within limits, the right to control reported earnings, which was and still is critical to the valuation of corporate entities. The right to control corporate financial reporting standards by which corporate profits were represented to the public, was of absolute importance. Earnings reports were also critical to corporate financial relations with Wall Street and banking institutions. The abuses of financial statements in the late 1920s, notwithstanding, corporations insisted on maintaining maximum flexibility in presenting their accounts, and the spokesmen for the corporations in this matter were the accounting practitioners. Accountant and corporate perspectives on the issue of SEC regulation were indistinguishable. The need for accounting flexibility, so frequently asserted by the accounting practitioners, appeared in the guise of a need for accountants to be able to exercise their own personal judgment. Otherwise, it was argued, accountants would be robots. In fact, of course, one of the fundamental reasons for advocating flexibility was to facilitate catering by the accountants to client needs. The rationale of the accountants was highly compatible with the interests of their clients—and, therefore, to their own interests as well. It is a rationale that explains much of the tenacity with which the accounting profession traditionally fights any challenge to the notion of flexibility in the application of accounting principles.

The practitioners of the AIA well understood the significance of the authority given them by the Securities and Exchange Commission. A codified set of accounting rules would certainly reduce their opportunity to apply alternative financial-reporting methods, which, in turn, would curtail practitioner discretion, importance, and, hence, earning power. Furthermore, an aggressive SEC could easily force consideration of certain accounting problems that the financial community preferred to avoid. The practitioners, therefore, were adamantly opposed to both the establishment of comprehensive accounting rules and any concerted SEC activity toward that end. The assumption by the AIA of responsibility for developing accounting "principles" thus relieved both anxieties, and the elimination of these twin threats thereafter permitted the practitioners to look upon the commission with a degree of fondness.

By August, 1938, Samuel J. Broad, senior partner of Peat, Marwick, Mitchell & Co., one of the "big eight" accounting firms, and a member of two important AIA committees—the Committee on Cooperation with the Securities and Exchange Commission and the Committee on Accounting Procedure—was able to write of the "helpfulness" of the SEC to the practicing accountants and of the cooperative activities between the two groups.

> . . . the Commission has made very few requirements as to the adoption of specific accounting practices and those were only such as had already received general acceptance; . . . The Commission has expressed reluctance to undertake the prescription of principles to be followed, but as time passed, has increasingly urged accountants, both those in practice and those engaged in educational activity, to undertake accounting research looking to the development of a greater degree of uniformity (Broad, 1938: 78).

Before the end of the year, the AIA reconstituted its Committee on Accounting Procedure to undertake the development of accounting principles for the entire profession, for the SEC, and, *for the nation.* Predictably, the accounting practitioners failed badly in their task of developing the rules for financial reporting, as we shall see. Their failure was almost entirely deliberate, and largely conscious, and the reasons for their failure are observable in the accounting ethic of the 1930s.

Practitioners of the thirties self-servingly equated comprehensive rules of financial reporting with rigid, foolish and arbitrary directives enforced by hostile and incompetent bureaucrats. This ideological commitment became ritualized in the fight over the control of accounting principles, and persisted thereafter. The practitioners argued that maximum flexibility in applying accounting conventions was necessary because financial situations, companies, and industries differed and, consequently, merited different accounting treatment. This perspective, incidentally, was also of great benefit to corporate clients who frequently could count on accountant "flexibility" to improve otherwise unimpressive financial statements. It was, therefore, an impossibility for a set of comprehensive (as opposed to ad hoc) accounting principles to emanate from the accounting practitioners. Furthermore, their negative attitude toward a comprehensive code of accounting rules became a ritualized belief.

The failure to develop accounting principles along systematic lines also stemmed from the practitioners' narrow view of the function of accounting, which they saw primarily as a device utilized for the benefit of individual concerns rather than as a means of social control or as a technique for measuring and comparing the financial status of corporations. The effects of the these practitioner beliefs and narrow perspectives became highly important in later years. The conglomerate merger movement of the 1960s, for example, had much of its basis in the early interaction between the SEC and the accounting profession. Individuals associated with both groups played controlling roles. The institutionalization of an ad hoc, precedent-oriented concept of financial reporting, and the deliberate rejection of systematic accounting schemes took place within the first three years of the SEC's formation and set the subsequent pattern of interaction between the SEC and the accounting profession. Virtual exclusion of the academic accountants' organization from the formulation of accounting principles had its sanctioned start in the 1930s also. It too persists to the present.

How Much of Its Accounting Powers Did the SEC Use?

By 1941 the SEC's relations with the AIA were fixed. They were clearly expressed by CPA Andrew Stewart. "I am gratified to state that it has been and it still is the practice of the Commission to obtain the advice of the accounting profession," he wrote that year, "and to allow ample time for comments and suggestions before any new form of regulation or any amendment thereto is adopted." AIA committees were constantly in touch with the commission, and "the result of this procedure has been that no important instruction or regulation relating to accounting has been issued by the Commission which has not had fairly general approval by members of our profession" (Stewart, 1941: 459). The SEC commissioners had neither attempted to prescribe the form or content of annual stockholder reports nor tried to establish criteria for accountants to satisfy themselves that financial statements filed with the commission fairly represented the financial conditions and operating results of registrant corporations. Where new forms or regulations were proposed, Stewart explained,

> . . . the Chief Accountant of the Commission has invariably consulted our profession through the appropriate committee and in perhaps most cases modifications have been made of the original draft to meet the view of our profession. As a result accounting principles enunciated in these opinions are recognized by the profession generally (Ibid., p. 462).

The more important improvements in professional standards had emanated from the profession, that is, the practicing accountants, rather than from the Securities and Exchange Commission, Stewart pointed out. The CAP was working continually "in the preparation and promulgation of accounting research bulletins," and the SEC was not promulgating extensive rules and regulations to govern auditing. Stewart's attitude showed the practitioner was triumphant, and detractors were to be disregarded. "Critics of our profession," said Stewart, "who are principally teachers of accounting and lawyers, the latter usually fresh from law school, fail to understand this incontrovertible fact of the variety of business organizations, policies and transactions and the diverse views of individuals" (Ibid., p. 465). The SEC's perspective corresponded with Stewart's appraisal. The SEC was not publishing extensive rules; the main path of progress, such as it was, was going to be entrusted to the practicing accountants (Barr, 1940; Frank, 1939).

The theme of SEC cooperation with the accounting profession had been carried to its logical conclusion following Landis's 1935 efforts toward conciliation (Landis, 1935a). In assigning some of its powers to the AIA and in avoiding the use of others, the SEC helped the cause of peace with the financial community. The SEC, for example, had the power to prescribe information requirements for newly listed corporations and call for corporate quarterly reports, but it had avoided using its power to require that stockholder reports be filed with it, which would have made these reports subject to statutory liability under the Securities Act of 1933 and the Securities Exchange Act of 1934. The cooperation between the SEC and the practitioner had been effective in reducing conflict, but it had cost the SEC a tremendous amount of power.

Specifically what power had the SEC lost? The loss was in potential power rather than in a diminution of exercised authority. The SEC never exercised its power to prescribe comprehensive accounting principles, for instance. Several reasons explain SEC inaction. The general feeling within the SEC, according to its first chief accountant, Carman Blough, was that the commission was in no position to undertake the development of accounting principles. The SEC staff was too small and not adequately trained. Blough estimated, when he was with the SEC, that it would have taken several people at least five years to do the job. Afterwards, he decided that five years was an underestimate. Moreover, it was believed within the SEC that an effort on its part to develop generally accepted accounting principles would have encountered tremendous opposition from both the practicing accountants and Wall Street. Blough's impression about the stubborn resistance of the financial community is shared by Throop and Benjamin V. Cohen. In fact, Allan E. Throop, second chief counsel of the SEC, citing the adverse decision of the U.S. Supreme Court on the constitutionality of the NRA, believes that if the SEC had tried to impose comprehensive accounting principles, it would have been challenged legally and probably would have lost. An equally important, but more subtle, reason for SEC nonfeasance was its legalistic orientation.

The SEC's Legalistic Approach

Viewed in retrospect, the early SEC commissioners were political moderates. Most important, their legal training caused them to approach the securities acts as essentially disclosure statutes. Although more extensive regulations would have been desirable—and some SEC commissioners acknowledged as much from time to time—their conviction that disclosure was the overriding objective prevented them from pursuing or advocating more stringent control over the nation's financial-industrial sector. Even on the matter of disclosure the SEC could, of course, have required more specific financial information. Greater financial detail could have been called for in the SEC's registration forms, and uniformity of accounting treatment could have been required.

The assumption that disclosure, even in the form of footnotes, was sufficient for investor use is indicative of the legalistic approach taken by the commissioners. Disclosure of material information automatically meant that investors were warned. Having been warned, investors were on their own in trying to understand the reported information, which often required great expertise to comprehend. With even sophisticated investors sometimes finding it impossible to interpret the revealed financial information, average investors were usually faced with a hopeless task.

It must be recognized that the commissioners believed they were administering a disclosure statute rather than a primarily regulatory, or punitive, measure. The distinction is fundamental. Convinced that disclosure was the prime rationale behind the securities acts, and that that disclosure would best serve the investor, the SEC commissioners oriented their approach toward forcing corporations to reveal crucial details about their financial operations. If the individual investor was interested in a particular corporation, the SEC reasoned, the revelation of all pertinent data would be sufficient for his or her purposes. The disclosure policy carried with it several unfortunate limitations. It permitted the absurdity of voluminous footnotes, which, although they presumably revealed the necessary information, allowed accountants to include provisos indicating they had little faith in the information itself or in the style of its presentation. The emphasis on disclosure policy, followed from the outset by the SEC, also resulted in noncomparable financial data from industry to industry, and from corporation to corporation within each industry. Noncomparability made it extremely difficult for investors to evaluate one corporation against another, assuming to begin with that they had sufficient sophistication to read the financial statements.

From one public policy viewpoint the results were a disaster. Noncomparability significantly hampered the use of the highly individualized corporate statistics for broader purposes than just investor information. Economists, government personnel, and public institutions, among others, were thus forced to use a mass of noncomparable corporate data for analytical purposes, much of which when aggregated was likely to be meaningless because of the variety of accounting techniques and presentations used. In narrowly interpreting its mandate and authority under the two securities laws, the SEC oriented itself toward investors, not toward the univeral use of corporate statistics and the control of corporate financial reporting in the public's interest—toward the small technical problems of financial accounting rather than toward the broader implications of the problem itself. Nowhere was this restricted preoccupation to be better illustrated than by SEC inaction during the conglomerate merger movement.

The dominance of lawyers on the early SEC also supported the disclosure mentality and insured reliance upon precedent. The trend was to continue. Only a few SEC commissioners have been accountants—the most notable being Commissioner Mathews and, more recently, James J. Needham, who became head of the New York Stock Exchange after a relatively short tenure on the SEC. For the most part, SEC commissioners have been lawyers or politicians or both. Representation from other fields has been relatively small; Leon Henderson, for example, was the only economist ever appointed an SEC commissioner. The predominance of lawyers on the commission affords added understanding of why it permitted the financial-industrial sector to administer the rules for financial reporting. The lack of training and knowledge in accounting on the part of SEC commissioners, plus their ingrained reliance as lawyers on precedent, has always provided the basis for their supporting the ad hoc development of accounting principles by a private group (see Frank, 1939: 296).

Reliance on precedent instead of upon systematic codes is a part of the America's Anglo-Saxon legal inheritance: precedent is the foundation of common law. Systematic legal codification is the method of the civil code nations, but not that of Britain and the United States. Almost all references to the law by accountants and commissioners drew comparisons with common law procedures. Except for a few writers like Berle and Paton, the idea of codification was hardly discussed, although information was available to the profession and the commissioners that codification of accounting rules was operative in several countries, including Germany (Krollmuller, 1934a; 1934b; 1934c). The development of comprehensive codes has played little part in American law. Thus it was logical that the legally trained SEC commissioners did not seek to institute a comprehensive code of accounting procedures for the corporations under their jurisdiction. In the first place, they did not know how to develop a code in an unfamiliar professional area. And secondly, the idea was not compatible with their own training and philosophical views.

GOVERNMENT REGULATION VERSUS SELF-REGULATION

We have seen how various representatives of the Securities and Exchange Commission endeavored to achieve a cooperative relationship with the accounting profession. The accountants had been assiduously courted to secure their support and cooperation (Landis, 1933; 1934a; 1935a, b, c; Blough, 1937a, b; Frank, 1939; Lane, 1938; Kennedy, 1934a, b). The accounting profession, or at least the practicing accountants, was unimpressed with the proffered hand, at least until mid-1937 when the commission largely relinquished its power to develop required principles of accounting. Practitioner reaction was partly a function of general antiregulation attitude, and partly due to their anxious appreciation of the potential and real encroachment of the SEC. Some of the objections of the practicing accountants to government regulation approached a caricature of the ultraconservative mind. Montgomery's statement in December of 1937 rings with antigovernment regulation statements, distrust of government bureaucrats, and anti-union feeling, not to mention the miserly plea for a way in which to reduce the salaries of junior accountants (Montgomery, 1937).[1] Other leading accountants also followed the same antigovernment regulation tack with monotonous platitudes.[2] Voluntary regulation generally was believed to be the route toward obtaining higher standards (Starkey, 1934: 434–435; May, 1937a, c). Reservations about whether real progress could come from government regulation was a frequent theme of the heads of the "big eight," like Andersen, Broad, Montgomery, and May.

Though social problems were causing increasing control over accountancy, noted Andersen, improvements in accounting practices and corporate reporting could never result from legislation or government regulation. "The regulations laid down by a governmental bureau serve a good purpose but can never successfully take the place of individual initiative, intelligence and courage" (Andersen, 1935: 343). May, as was noted previously, thought the government should simply hand over its powers to develop accounting principles to the accounting profession (May, 1940: 82). Whenever possible SEC action could conceivably threaten the profession, a *Journal of Accountancy* editorial was quick to point out the danger. The *JA's* attitude toward a federal bill licensing accountants, for example, was totally negative, (editorial, *JA*, 1938a: 92–94), as it was when the SEC reserved the right to review the credentials of persons appearing before it (editorial, *JA*, 1938b; 137–138). The idea that the federal government might license corporations was equally abhorrent to the AIA's *Journal of Accountancy*, though the proposal never got very far (Payne, 1935: 84). Antiregulation opinion continued to emanate from the practicing accountants throughout the last half of the 1930s, much of it aimed by the accountants at the SEC.[3]

SELF-REGULATION AND MINIMUM REGULATION

Self-regulation has always been part of the American political and business ethic, and deviations from that standard have usually been attempted only after major abuses occur in a private sector. When a group has exceeded its legitimate behavior, regulation has sometimes been imposed. But even after the crash of 1929, and the revelation of financial malpractices had precipitated the securities acts, business self-regulation still remained a desirable objective for a substantial number of Americans. The majority of the early SEC commissioners, for example, especially Landis, still had a strong preference for self-regulation by the private sector. Financial community pressures for permission to regulate itself, therefore, received a sympathetic audience.

The development of corporate reporting forms by the early SEC was nonetheless a considerable accomplishment. This accomplishment was particularly notable because little corporate financial information was required prior to the enactment of the two securities acts. The SEC commissioners did require, then, minimum standards of disclosure compatible with available accounting techniques.

Even so, the state of the accounting art in the thirties, although advanced from the turn of the century, could not have provided the basis for a comprehensive set of accounting rules by the commission, even had it been desired. The SEC accounting staff was relatively small and completely engaged in the day-to-day surveillance of corporate statements and the resolution of immediate problems. There was neither time, personnel, nor funds to engage in a serious study of accounting principles and comprehensive accounting systems. This fact, combined with a belief in the ethic of self-regulation by Landis and by such a key staff member as Blough, insured that the SEC was going to take a nonbelligerent stance over both a required accounting format and a definition of and adherence to accounting principles. The moderate approach of Chairmen Kennedy and Landis, compared with what might have happened if a more militant chief commissioner had been appointed—Pecora, for example—meant that careful but minimal disclosure would be sufficient to satisfy the reporting requirements under the statutes.

Could the SEC Have Been More Aggressive about Accounting Principles?

The Securities and Exchange Commission did not want to develop a comprehensive set of generally accepted accounting principles, the practicing accountants had no intention of doing so, and the academic accountants were not asked to. If any of the three groups *had* wanted to develop accounting principles in the 1930s, would it have been possible to do so from a technical and methodological point of view? Probably not. Accounting at the time lacked the technical basis for establishing a comprehensive, compelling set of accounting principles. Given the state of the art as revealed in the controversies in the accounting literature of the period, both the necessary points of agreement on accounting technique and the willingness to have an official accounting code were lacking.

Development of a comprehensive set of noncontradictory accounting principles requires either an approach to accounting similar to that toward legal codification in civil law countries or an approach to accounting as an integrated system. Any ad hoc treatment of individual problems leads inevitably, as a matter of logic, to internal contradictions. Codification is a lengthy, scholarly undertaking. The only genuine legal attempt at codification in the United States took place during the nineteenth century, but it failed. Some states like California have codes, but they are not relied on as the almost-exclusive authority, as in civil law countries; instead, case precedents, judicial comments, articles, and so forth are used to augment the code. American law is based on precedent, and the accounting practitioners looked to the legal model. Almost all comparisons between accounting and legal development by accountants in the 1930s were based on the assumption of common law-like progress for accounting. The absence of a "sytems" orientation, which is more a product of the post-World War II period, also prevented development of comprehensive accounting principles in the late 1930s.

Nevertheless, the SEC could still have attempted to improve far more significantly the state of accounting by scholarly work within the SEC, or it could have underwritten such an assignment within the academic community. Obviously, both alternatives would have been opposed by the practitioners, and the SEC lacked the interest and the will to see the task undertaken. The path of least resistance was followed; it assigned the duty to the AIA, which doomed any possibility of developing systematic accounting principles. Both May and Sanders, important figures on the AIA Committee for Accounting Procedure, were stated adversaries of a comprehensive set of principles. Besides, the AIA had carefully designed the CAP to guarantee that it would accomplish very little. A few CAP seats were assigned to the academics, but the AAA was never encouraged by the AIA to embark upon the job of developing accounting principles. Indeed, the presence of AAA people on the AIA committee may have helped preempt the AAA from the task. Besides, a lack of funds precluded the AAA from doing the job without support. The AAA probably had the requisite talent, but the AIA had the money and the mandate.

Landis, an astute negotiator and brilliant legal analyst, was well aware of the limitations on the power of the new SEC. The battle that had taken place after the passage of the 1933 act clearly left its mark on the protagonists. The financial community and the accountants had won a qualified victory, while the New Deal had avoided a major defeat. The people involved with the SEC in the early days anticipated a stiff, if not a losing, fight if they tried to push the question of uniform accounting or general accounting principles too far. The entire process illustrates the limited power of an independent regulatory agency in the face of massive resistance from its regulated constituency. Landis, the best man in the entire event, seems finally to have been worn down by both the opposition and the rigors of the job.

Of the original commissioners, Landis, Kennedy, and Mathews were moderate liberals. Pecora, who stayed only a short time, and Healy, were more militant, but hardly radicals. Thus, the personalities of the first commissioners were not conducive to an aggressive take-over of accounting and financial reporting conventions. A persistent tendency to appoint lawyers to the SEC also defeated subsequent chances of the SEC's assuming a vigorous stance on accounting principles and procedures. In addition to receiving professional training emphasizing precedent, most U.S. lawyers are innocent of detailed accounting practices and theory. Because it is difficult for a nonexpert to supervise studies requiring specialized knowledge, it is somewhat understandable that the SEC commissioners avoided entering the area of accounting theory.

Since the transfer of accounting principle development to the practicing accountants took place early in the SEC's history and was rapidly institutionalized, subsequent attempts to regain that authority would have been resisted with determination. No such attempts were made, however, and control over accounting principles passed through the hands of several ill-fated AIA committees in the following years —with extremely serious consequences for the national economy.

Notes

1.   Compensation of top practitioners during the thirties was handsome. Conversation with persons active in the accounting world of the 1930s revealed their belief that heads of some of the "big eight" accounting firms, like May of Price Waterhouse, Mongtomery of Lybrand, Ross Bros. & Montgomery, and Andersen of Arthur Andersen & Co., were earning about half a million dollars a year, a considerable amount in those depression days. I must add that I have not taken any steps to confirm these estimates.

2.   Charles B. Couchman, for example, a partner in Barrow, Wade & Guthrie, an active participant in the inner councils of the AIA, and a deft hand with platitudes, offered the following broadside, among others, against uniform accounting for industry:

> It is doubtful if the various attempts to prescribe uniform accounting or uniform financial statements, made not only in the United States but also in other countries, have resulted in more accurate and more useful statements than had been obtained where uniform accounting restrictions do not control. There is a strong opinion, expressed by many who had given intelligent thought to the subject, that the greatest progress in the improvement of accounting methods and state-

ments has been accomplished where no such restriction prevailed. It must not be overlooked that minimum requirements almost always become maximum accomplishments (Couchman, 1934: 347).

3.   Rodney F. Starkey's comment was as typical as any: "No profession such as accountancy in which individual integrity and business judgment are of the highest importance can stand being enveloped in a straight-jacket of rigid rules and regulations, which is the real hazard of the assumption of authority by a federal commission" (Starkey, 1936: 27).

chapter

12

The art of maintaining the status quo

The Committee on Accounting Procedure: 1938–1959

The American Institute of Accountants' enlarged Committee on Accounting Procedure ostensibly assumed the responsibility of bringing some order to accounting principles, but it worked under severe handicaps. The support of the Securities and Exchange Commission was uncertain, and there was some continuing anxiety, however unrealistic, that the SEC would eventually step in. Backing within the profession was tenuous. CAP opinions were not binding upon the profession. The Committee members were committed to an ad hoc approach, which meant that clear direction for consistent research would be absent.

Ideologically, the main problem was that the practitioner CAP members did not *want* to be limited by comprehensive accounting principles. The leaders were men devoted to the concept that only "principles" offering "flexibility" were desirable—not rules that prescribed accounting treatment without possible variation. Then, too, the academic accountants on the CAP had no real influence. Their token membership on the committee helped to forestall effective pressure from the American Association of Accountants to undertake an intensive and continuing program of developing principles on its own. The anti-intellectualism of the practitioners was not to be offset by a rival group of academic accountants.

Opposition to government regulation had resulted in a transfer of authority for accounting principles to the practitioners, and an attitude which had given such salutary results was not to be abandoned. Antipathy toward the national government firmed the practitioners' alliance with their corporate clients; thus independence of their clients became virtually impossible. The committee's subsequent experience with the release of its Accounting Research Bulletins (ARBs) featured some dramatic examples of CAP/AIA retreat in the face of determined client opposition.

The consequence was that comprehensive, generally accepted accounting principles were not developed during the 20-odd years of the existence of the Committee on Accounting Procedure. The committee's organization made it impossible to achieve quick or controversial results beyond a threshold agreement level. If the internal organization of the CAP did not guarantee its near paralysis in developing accounting principles, the external pressures of its clients and the Wall Street institutions, plus SEC apathy, made its immobility certain. Nevertheless, the practitioners managed to maintain, by and large, the control over accounting they had achieved. Their lack of significant activity during the history of the CAP resulted in its collapse and abandonment in 1959 in favor of a new organization called the Accounting Principles Board—again under their auspices.

The Committee on Accounting Procedure began to issue Accounting Research Bulletins in 1939. By the time the United States was involved in World War II, 12 ARB's had been published (Carey, 1970: 14–15). Wartime conditions caused some significant changes in CAP operations. Sanders relinquished his research directorship to Professor James L. Dohr of Columbia, who stayed a short time before he, too, departed for war duty. The urgencies of war diverted attention from the question of accounting principles as accountants became involved in the control and costing of military goods. The question remained, but in the early forties there was a temporary quietus in the controversies over accounting principles. The silencing of argument appeared to one writer to be a "minor bright spot in the whole tragedy of global war" (Gilman, 1944: 109).

THE MCKESSON & ROBBINS CASE

The most traumatic event for the accountants between 1939 and the entrance of the United States in the war was the McKesson & Robbins case. In that case Price Waterhouse & Co.—one of the "big eight"—was found negligent in its auditing responsibilities. McKesson & Robbins' fraudulent inventories and accounts receivable had not been discovered by the auditors. The controversy centered on the relationship between auditors and client. The critical allegation was that auditors were too much influenced by their employers. Ordinary auditing practices were inadequate to deal with cases of deliberate fraud. In the SEC investigation, Price Waterhouse was found guilty of not having been sufficiently vigilant, though the SEC softened its censure by saying that the practicing accountants in general had made significant improvements in auditing techniques. It was a dramatic example of the regulatory agency engaging in client advocacy. Furthermore, the SEC affirmed its stance about not interfering with AIA self-regulation; until experience indicated that the SEC should prescribe the scope and procedures of accounting, it would leave it to the practitioners to improve matters. "The profession had," as John L. Carey put it, "survived another crisis" (Carey, 1970: 37). The McKesson & Robbins case illustrated the established commitment of the Securities and Exchange Commission to noninterference with the practitioners, if at all possible.

Changes took place during the 1940s not only within the CAP but within the AIA leadership. None of them, however, indicated the likelihood of a change in attitude toward accounting principles. May relinquished his direction of the CAP in 1941 and was replaced by Staub, a practitioner as much opposed to uniform accounting and compulsory accounting principles and procedures as May. Many of the presidents of the Institute in the forties were men who held opinions compatible with May and Staub's, including C. Oliver Wellington (1940–1941), Norman L. McLaren (1941–1942), Victor H. Stempf (1943–1944), Samuel J. Broad (1944–1945), and George D. Bailey (1947–1948). In 1944, Carman Blough, former first chief accountant of the SEC, was appointed the first full-time director of accounting research within the CAP; Blough retained that position throughout the life of the CAP.

The CAP's Accounting Research Bulletins and ARB No. 48

The history of the CAP was marked by some accomplishments, most significant, the issuance of ARBs that brought standardization of accounting practices to certain areas of accounting. The bulletins became particularly important after the SEC announced it would not accept financial statements filed with it that did not follow the ARB recommendations. More characteristic of the bulletins was either their avoidance of controversial issues or recommendation of alternate accounting treatment when controversial questions could not be evaded. They were also a vehicle for backtracking. For example, a CAP attempt to develop a set of accounting principles was begun in 1949, but the "efforts were highly unsatisfactory to everyone concerned and the work was ultimately abandoned in favor of a revision and restatement of the bulletins that had previously been issued" (Blough, 1967: 11). The revision and restatement were published in 1953 as ARB No. 43. Several incidents in which the CAP did take a firm position in the bulletins resulted in so much opposition, either from the financial community, accounting practitioners, or the SEC, that the positions had to be abandoned. Dissatisfaction with CAP operations during the mid-fifties prompted formation of an investigating group that recommended its dissolution in favor of a more powerful and larger research effort.

A total of 51 ARBs were issued by the CAP between 1938 and 1959. One of them, ARB No. 48, dealing with business combinations, was to have important long-run effects in the conglomerate merger movement of the 1960s. ARB No. 48 specified that pooling of interest accounting for business combinations was an acceptable alternative to purchase accounting, provided that certain criteria were met. A gradual erosion of the criteria was permitted by the SEC, and pooling of interest provided the basis for most of the financial reporting slight of hand that typified the wilder aspects of the conglomerate merger movement.

Purchase accounting presumably had a built-in limitation upon an acquiring firm, preventing it from not paying too much for the acquisition because the excess of price paid over the market value would have to be charged against goodwill—provided, of course, that reduction of goodwill would be charged against future earnings, which was not always the case. Pooling criteria initially required several important conditions: (1) continuity of all the constituents of the business enterprise; (2) continuity of management; and (3) similarity in the size of the businesses—that is, that one corporation would not be substantially larger than the other. Under these circumstances, it appeared reasonable to justify simply adding together all the accounts of the two firms. There was no charge against goodwill, so if too much was paid for the acquired firm, there was no record of it in that account. If the capital stock account was reduced as a result of the pooling, earnings per share would increase because the combined earnings of the pooled companies would remain the same, which was the really important advantage to companies on the merger trail. The result was "instantaneous gains in earnings per share," known alternately, by critics, as "dirty pooling."

The difficulty with ARB No. 48 was a deficiency peculiar to many of the research bulletins; the wording was so ambiguous it could be interpreted to mean a wide variety of things, as indicated in the following excerpts [italics supplied]:

> 4. . . . After a pooling of interest, the net assets of all of the constituent corporations *will in a large number of cases* be held by a single corporation. . . .

> 5. . . . where a constituent corporation has had two or more classes of stock outstanding prior to the origin of the plan of combination, the redemption, retirement, or conversion of a class or classes of stock having senior or preferential rights as to assets and dividends *need not prevent the combination from being considered a pooling of interests.*

> 6. . . . Relative size of the constituents *may not necessarily be determinative,* especially where the smaller corporation con- tributes desired management personnel; however, where one of the constituent corporations is clearly dominant (for example, where the stockholders of one of the constituent corporations obtain 90% to 95% or more of the voting interest in the combined enterprise), *there is a presumption* that the transaction is a pur- chase rather than a pooling of interests.

Any accountant of average intelligence ought to have understood from all the qualifiers above that there was a great deal of leeway in deciding whether pooling of interests could qualify as business com- bination accounting, and that the "criteria" need not be taken too seriously. However, just in case there were some practitioners around who were a little dull, the following barn-door loophole was pro- vided:

> 7. *Not one of the factors discussed in paragraphs 5 and 6 would necessarily be determinative and one factor might have varying degrees of significance in different cases.* However, *their pres- ence or absence would be cumulative in effect. Since the*

conclusions to be drawn from consideration of these different relevant circumstances may be in conflict or partially so, determination as to whether a particular combination is a purchase or a pooling in interests should be made in the light of all such attendant circumstances (ARB No. 48, AICPA, 1971: 6081–6082).

That, should have done it. If an accountant was not bright enough to understand Section 7 as an open invitation to try to qualify almost any business combination as a pooling of interests, he was not bright enough to be an accountant.

Terminology similar to that used in the above excerpts was consistent with the Institute's desire to avoid making its ARB's mandatory upon the profession. After the SEC began to back the ARBs as "substantial authoritative support" for filings under the acts, however, accountants were bound to the ARBs irrespective of the wishes of the AIA. But establishing alternate methods of accounting would retain for accountants the opportunity to use different accounting treatments, according to the circumstances. The use of ambiguous wording was subsequently one of the major issues that brought the operations of the CAP to a close in the late fifties. Ambiguous wording and permissive alternatives were also symptomatic of the CAP's objective of retaining control over accounting principles, and to develop accounting rules favoring clients. The CAP approach appears to have been behind several differences of opinion that took place between them and the SEC.

THE SEC AND THE CAP BREAK SOME SMALL ANTLERS

The Securities and Exchange Commission in 1940 discontinued registration Forms A–2 and 10 in favor of a single financial-disclosure document, Regulation S-X. SEC accounting rules had not been codified, of course. The SEC's stance on accounting matters was dispersed, and for the registrant to discover. There were the SEC Accounting Series Releases, SEC reports to Congress, SEC formal decisions, SEC chief accountant conferences with corporations whose practices were being questioned, and informal SEC contacts with individuals and organizations. In addition, the results of discussions between the commission and registrants coming from deficiency proceedings were not disclosed (Zeff, 1971: 151–152). It was specifically this type of general obscurity in accounting standards to which Berle had objected in 1938 (Berle, 1938: 373–374).

It was logical that the commission, in the absence of its own set of accounting rules, would look to the CAP. The number of disagreements between them were few, but some were bitter. The encounters were over a variety of issues. Sometimes the SEC discouraged the CAP from issuing an ARB; sometimes the SEC failed to accept ARBs already issued.[1] As for the committee, actions taken by the SEC without prior consultation with the CAP were resented. For example, CAP inaction on the matter of preferred stock charges to capital surplus prompted the SEC to issue ASR No. 45 in 1943, which irritated the CAP enough to consider issuing a contrary ARB, which they did not do. A controversy over allocation of income taxes in 1944–1945 saw the SEC issue ASR No. 53, partly contradicting the CAP's prior ARB No. 23. (The CAP accordingly adjusted its position.) In 1945 SEC ASR No. 50 prohibited the write-off of intangibles against capital surplus, a practice merely discouraged by the CAP's ARB No: 24 issued a month earlier; the CAP had been on notice of the SEC's views for three years, but had chosen to disregard them. The committee did not adopt the SEC position until ARB No. 43 was isssued in 1953 (Zeff, 1971: 152–155).

Inflationary pressures after World War II prompted some corporations to revalue assets on a basis of replacement cost. The CAP gave the practice tenuous support in 1945, later withdrawing it due to SEC opposition. In 1950–1951, the question came up again, and again the CAP avoided publishing an ARB because of the SEC's position.

Two disputes between the Institute and the Securities and Exchange Commission were the subject of compromise. The first dealt with the treatment of extraordinary charges and credits, that the CAP wanted to charge or credit to earned surplus, which meant they would not affect the income account. The SEC, however, felt only dividends and capital adjustments should be reflected in surplus, that all items affecting income should be shown in the income account. The AIA-CAP view distinguished between ordinary earnings and extraordinary profits, which should have made corporate income statements more comparable. Bailey, then head of the CAP, urged this approach against strong internal AIA opposition. ARBs No. 32 (1947) and No. 35 (1948) followed Bailey's view. The SEC disagreed. A compromise was reached in 1949–1950. The S-X regulation would allow net income or loss to be shown before special items were included. The final figure was termed "Net income or loss and special items" (Carey, 1970: 165–167; Zeff, 1971: 157–158).

The second compromise involved the SEC's intention to include the contents of several ASRs, plus other principles not shown in them, in a revision of Regulation S-X. Both the AIA *and* the AAA objected. Chief Accountant Earle C. King agreed not to take action if the CAP "would, among other things, codify its series of Bulletins." "These two compromises by the Commission were regarded as positive achievements by the profession toward retaining a large measure of self determination of accounting principles" (Zeff, 1971: 159). King was chief accountant for the SEC from 1946 to 1957, and, according to some observers, was the most hostile of all SEC chief accountants toward the AIA. SEC activism at the time was at least partly attributed to King's personality. Other chief accountants, Blough (1935–1938), William W. Werntz (1938–1946), and Barr (1957–1972), were considered "friendly" to the AIA.

In any event, the compromises meant that the SEC had been forestalled once again. The CAP began to work on a codification, but abandoned the effort in 1953 in favor of a revision and restatement of the first 42 ARBs.

The CAP under Attack

These disagreements illustrate some SEC dissatisfaction with the AIA's performance in the area of accounting principles determination, but the more important point is that the profession once again vigorously and successfully defended its "right" to continue control over accounting principles. At no time was there a serious, sustained, and successful effort on the part of the CAP to develop a comprehensive, compulsory set of accounting principles. But then, the SEC itself and the academics hardly did any better, although several isolated attempts were made.

The SEC commissioners, according to King, "instructed the Chief Accountant to prepare a series of statements of accounting principles by industries." The order was apparently given in 1937 or 1938, but was never carried out or rescinded. The "enormity" of the task and lack of staff prevented its accomplishment (Zeff, 1971: 133). As for the academics, Professors Paton and Littleton, sponsored by the AAA, published in 1940 an expansion of the 1936 "Tentative Statement." It was named "An Introduction to Corporate Accounting Standards," and advanced the argument that income measurement should be based on matching costs and revenues, instead of asset and liability valuation (Carey, 1970: 16). In the following year the American Association of Accountants published another position on accounting principles, called "Accounting Principles Underlying Corporate Financial Statements"—no "Tentative" this time. But World War II and the apathy of the accounting practitioners assured that the AAA effort would have little effect.

The sum of AIA, AAA, and SEC activity was a continuation through the mid-fifties of the status quo: an ad hocism based on solving accounting problems as they arose, minimum disruption to practitioner "flexibility" and perpetuation of AIA prime responsibility for accounting principles. But if the Institute successfully defended itself against criticism from the SEC, it was less effective in fending off attacks on the CAP arising within the financial community. The most important assaults came from the Controllers Institute, and from specific charges against the committee by Leonard Spacek, managing partner of Arthur Andersen & Co.

The practitioners had continually castigated the academic accountants for their alleged impracticality. Members of the Institute, therefore, were greatly chagrined to have the same accusation leveled at them by men apparently more practical than themselves—the leaders of the Controllers Institute. The controllers' pique stemmed from their belief that they had not been adequately consulted by the AIA before ARBs were issued. Because the Controllers Institute (later renamed the Financial Executives Institute) represented the top financial people in the nation's corporations, they were very much concerned with what the AIA put into the research bulletins. Their disgruntlement came to a head with the issuance of three 1947 ARBs. The chairman of the Controllers Institute's Committee on Consideration of Mutual Problems with the American Institute of Accountants, observed rather snidely:

> Many of the bulletins of the American Institute of Accountants do not consider the practical business aspects of accounting problems. They reflect a lack of experience of independent public accountants in dealing with these problems. This is no criticism of our American Institute friends, for as consultants they are not expected to know the business details of these problems (Zeff, 1971: 145–146).

Strong stuff indeed. The criticism was part of a pattern of pressure on the AIA that increased in the mid-fifties to have proposed ARBs circulated among interested and affected parties before issue. By

1958 some 1400 copies of AIA exposure drafts were mailed out regularly.[2]

The hostile encounters in the 1940s and 1950s between the AIA and the Controllers Institute demonstrated the strains and tensions between them that have since broken into the open on several occasions. Opposition from the financial executives helped sink the CAP and its successor organization. The same antagonism was evident during 1972 in the fight over the composition of the Financial Accounting Standards Board.

Spacek began a series of speeches in 1956 that criticized the accounting profession for not establishing the foundation for accounting principles, not establishing the principles themselves, and for not using a public forum for their determination (Spacek, 1969: 1–143). Spacek's 1956–1957 speeches attacking the method of determining accounting principles, plus his allegation that the CAP had yielded to outside pressure, aroused widespread indignation among accounting practitioners and a good deal of interest from outsiders (Carey, 1970: 76–77; Zeff, 1971: 169–170). In August, 1957, Spacek proposed an Accounting Court to hear appeals from the CAP decisions (Spacek, 1969b: 27), and four months later the Institute appointed a 10-man special committee to look into Spacek's charges. The special committee had a diverse membership, including four of the "big eight" accounting firms, one medium size CPA firm, plus Barr, the SEC's chief accountant; Professor R. K. Mautz of the University of Illinois; Spacek; and industry and insurance company representatives (Zeff, 1971: 170).

Notes

1.   "In a historic confrontation, the SEC sought to incorporate several of its Accounting Series Releases dealing with accounting principles as well as a few accounting principles not contained in prior Releases, into its rulebook on financial disclosures, Regulation S-X. As part of this action, the SEC also proposed to issue a rule asserting its preferred solution to a controversy on which the SEC and the Committee on Accounting Procedure had been unable to reconcile their divergent views for many years" (Zeff, 1971: 152–153).

2.   The advance copies went to state societies of CPAs, groups and individuals within the Institute, and to 12 cooperating groups, including the AAA, the Controllers Institute, the National Association of (Cost) Accountants, the National Association of Financial Analysts Societies, Robert Morris Associates, the SEC, the New York Stock Exchange, and the American Petroleum Institute (Zeff, 1971: 147).

chapter

13

The life and hard times of the Accounting Principles Board

Today, CPAs alone are pretty much the high priests of accounting principles. In twenty years, will the users of accounting also be part of the hierarchy? (J. S. Seidman, 1959: 30)

"The High Priests of Accounting Principles" Create the Accounting Principles Board

Alvin R. Jennings, president of the American Institute of Certified Public Accountants—the new name adopted in 1957 for the old American Institute of Accountants—proposed in December, 1957, that an Accounting Research Foundation be organized. It was a radical suggestion. It provided that any foundation report approved by two-thirds of the Institute's council would be binding on the membership of the AICPA. The proposal also removed the responsibility for developing accounting principles from the direct control of the AICPA to the foundation, and for the first time *required* the adherence of AICPA members to approved accounting principles—a stipulation that threatened accountants' "flexibility." Not surprisingly, Jennings' recommendations were declined. The Special Committee appointed to check into the criticism leveled at accountants by the Controllers Institute proposed instead a much more conservative route. The AICPA would retain control over the development of principles. The Committees on Accounting Procedure and Terminology would be abandoned, and a larger research group would be organized and placed under the jurisdiction of a new Accounting Principles Board (APB). The research staff would have a director and up to eight analysts. Recommendations of the APB would *not* be binding on Institute membership; the APB's purpose was to advance generally accepted accounting principles for the "guidance" of the members, but reliance was to "be placed on persuasion rather than compulsion" (Report of the Special Committee on Research Program, 1958: 62–63).

According to the special committee, attention was required at four levels: postulates, principles, rules guiding specific application of principles, and research. Apparently the first three did not qualify as research, if the Special Committee is to be taken literally. The new, "streamlined" APB was to be composed of 18 members, rather than the cumbersome 22-member CAP it was replacing. All APB members had to be AICPA members, *but for the first time, members employed in industry (financial executives) could sit on the board.* Another innovation was designed to commit the big accounting firms to APB decisions; it required them to be represented by their managing partners. The 18-person roster of the new APB was to be as follows:

12 practicing public accountants, including partners from six of the "big eight" accounting firms.
3 university accounting professors.
2 financial executives.
1 director of research.

WEAKNESSES AND PORTENTS

A critical examination of the proposed board shows that it would hardly be better organized to develop generally accepted accounting principles than the prior CAP. Again, membership size was too large to permit efficient discussion. Again, APB decisions would not be binding on Institute members. Again, the research staff, though enlarged, would still be too small to conduct comprehensive research. The really significant change incorporated in the committee's recommendations, seen in retrospect, was the inclusion of financial executives on the APB. The addition of industry representatives was an official acknowledgment of the importance and influence of the corporate sector, which presumably had been excluded from any control over the determination of accounting principles—legally since the creation of the SEC, and administratively during the tenure of the CAP. The controversy precipitating formation of the APB partly was sparked by accusations of accountant subservience to clients' wishes; the de jure inclusion of corporate representatives on the APB was, therefore, ironic, at the least.

Operations of the APB

The APB functioned, more or less, for thirteen years—between 1959 and 1972—when it was discarded for substantially the same reasons as those for which the CAP was scrapped. The history of the APB illustrates the continuing quandary of a private, self-regulating professional group trying to develop governing principles and experiencing helplessness when confronted with controversial problems. The most dramatic incident in the entire history of the Accounting Principles Board was the controversy, or rather the avoidance of action, over how to deal with accounting for business combinations in the 1960s. An earlier imbroglio over accounting principles and postulates foretold the later incident.

Professor Maurice Moonitz of the University of California at Berkeley became the first permanent research director of the APB on July 1, 1960, and the APB's first research study, *The Basic Postulates of Accounting*, was written by him and published the following year (Moonitz, 1961: 1–57). Professor Stephen A. Zeff, an accountant and respected historian of accounting, has described the reaction to the booklet:

> In 55 pages of broad-ranging discussion, the author developed a framework of three tiers of postulates, comprehending the environment, the field of accounting itself, and imperatives. Since a study of this sort had few precedents in the accounting literature, it is probably fair to say that many readers, not to exclude the Board, did not know quite what to make of it. Seldom had accountants formalized this conceptual schemata in terms of postulates, whether or not rigorously derived (Zeff, 1971: 174–175).

In 1962 the third APB research study was co-authored by Moonitz and Robert T. Sprouse, who at that time was also an accounting professor at Berkeley. Some members of the profession had hoped that this study, *A Tentative Set of Broad Accounting Principles for Busi-*

ness Enterprises (Moonitz and Sprouse, 1962: 1–83) would make concrete the "abstractions and generalizations" of the first research study. In this hope, they were disappointed. The authors intended to formulate principles compatible with Research Study No. 1's postulates. Some of their recommended principles—for example, reflecting merchandise and plant at current values and showing cash settlement receivables and payables at present (discounted) values—were different from accepted practice—and "provided considerable controversy." Eight of the nine comments filed on the study by members of the AICPA's 12-man Project Advisory Committee for the principles study were, to say the least, unsympathetic. Indeed, controversy developed over whether the study should be published at all. The study was finally issued under Moonitz's authority as research director, but to avoid giving any impression that it had the "substantial authoritative support" of the AICPA, the Institute initiated what was in effect a disclaimer policy, that the research studies were not official AICPA policy. The warning was blatantly placed on the front cover and copyright page (Zeff, 1971: 175–176).

The AICPA clearly was not going to tolerate theoretically based research studies undermining or requiring major reforms of accepted practice. The hassle over Research Study No. 3 highlighted the issue, and pointed up the dilemma that would always arise when board members and researchers disagreed. When it came to advocating major changes in existing practice, the managers of the "big eight" firms could be surprisingly intractable. The APB majority expressed "deep dissatisfaction" with the study. It had not been tested with practical implementation, they believed, and it was unacceptable "as a foundation for future opinions."[1] Research Studies Nos. 1 and 3 were discarded, and the practitioners saw to it that there were to be no sequels. So much for theory; it was time to get back to the comforting codifications of existing practice.

The opening APB studies have been described by Professor Abraham Briloff of CUNY as "the most ambitious single venture in accounting research," one . . . "launched with much fanfare and high hopes" (Briloff, 1972: 327). Powell, the first chairman of the APB, forecasted that new approaches to theory would be considered, and even George O. May had written to say that the time had come for viewing the system as a whole, that mere patching up wouldn't do. But Studies Nos. 1 and 3 were too radical for implementation, and three years after his appointment Moonitz was replaced by Paul Grady, retired Price Waterhouse partner. His research Study No. 7 came out under the title *Inventory of Generally Accepted Accounting Principles for Business Enterprises;* it was merely a consolidation of practice in the best tradition of the AICPA. Even under Grady's successor, Reed Storey, research studies continued to deal with specific topics rather than broad concepts.

Some critics have been bitterly accusatory of the APB's research policy. Briloff, for example, said the APB "[went] its own way—issuing Opinions generally without prior formal research, at the least without any published studies" (Briloff, 1972: 328–329). His judgment is probably too harsh. The APB research staff worked hard enough, but it was hampered by an ingrained ad hoc, precedent oriented approach that probably set defined, implicit limits on what would be acceptable. If theoretical research was to be done, the events surrounding publication of Research Studies Nos. 1 and 3 conclusively proved that the AICPA was not the place to do it.

It was not entirely correct to say that the APB had gone "its own way," either. Actually, the APB *went* the way of the CAP before it, and was scrapped in favor of yet another attempt by the private financial sector to prescribe accounting principles. In 1972–1973 the Financial Accounting Standards Board—"principles" were apparently no longer in vogue—replaced the APB after the conglomerate merger movement revealed the inherent inability of the accounting profession-SEC arrangement to take positive action to put a halt to the accounting abuses underlying the merger mania of the 1960s. It was unfortunate, but it took a major economic and financial speculative event, with vast implications for the industrial power structure of the nation, to expose the continuing inadequacy of the standards for corporate financial reporting in the United States.

The Conglomerate Merger Movement

MERGER WAVES AND INDUSTRIAL CONCENTRATION

The United States has sustained three major industrial merger movements: 1895–1903, 1919–1930, and 1948–1969.[2] Almost all comment upon these merger waves discuss them as separate incidents, which is an unfortunately narrow perspective. Examination of these movements against the larger panorama of economic, social, and political history reveals that American industry has gone through a *continuous* concentration since the 1880s, interrupted only by wars and depressions, which, alas, have been all too frequent. Industrial concentration in the United States has been coincident with prosperity, prosperity has bred optimism, and optimism has spawned speculation. Speculation requires certain devices through which the gambling instinct can be satisfied, and the financial sector has never failed to supply them. Each merger wave has had its unique characteristics, but a necessary (not sufficient) condition of each has been the availability of financial conventions that enticed investors into participating in the movements by promising them the possibility of large capital gains. In the first movement, overcapitalization was characteristic (Nelson, 1959: 105). In the second merger wave, holding company and investment trust devices were fully utilized (see Chapter 2). In the conglomerate phase of the third movement (circa 1960–1969) the pooling of interest method of accounting for business combinations was the key device employed (FTC, 1969: 122).

Speculation, avarice, and the full participation of the financial community were crucial factors in all three waves. Each merger movement left behind it the increased concentration of American industry. The conglomerate merger movement brought the process of *asset* concentration to its most extreme level (FTC, 1969: 3). What was very different about the last merger wave compared with the first two was its new institutional setting. The Securities and Exchange Commission had been created to exercise control over financial reporting, and it was hoped, over precisely the kind of speculative activity capable of affecting the nation's economy adversely, that characterized the conglomerate mania. But the warm working relationship between the accounting profession and the SEC precluded the invoking of any means to cope with the abuses of the pooling of interest technique. The secondary effect of this organizational and administrative failure was not only further industrial concentration but the speculative activity that helped precipitate the recession between late 1969 and mid 1970.

Failure to control the use of pooling of interest accounting for financial combinations brought down the APB. More important, it permitted the most incredible stock market speculation seen in the United States since 1928–1929.

THE THIRD MERGER WAVE

The fight over business combinations accounting must be interpreted in the environment of the conglomerate merger movement. Unfortunately, there are no statistics that authoritatively define the progress of the conglomerate merger movement in its entirety; the evidence has to be pieced together. Nevertheless, there are several points that can be made about the "third" merger wave. First, the conglomerate merger movement was most likely the severest episode of concentration of business activity in the history of the United States.[3] Second, the most intense part of the concentration episode occurred between 1965 and 1969. Third, as the concentration movement progressed, large firms increasingly became active as acquirers of other business, definitely making the conglomerate merger movement a "big business" event.

Taking the big mergers first, columns 1 and 2 of Table 1 show the growth in importance of acquisitions of "large" mining and manufacturing firms having more than ten million dollars in asset value. There was an initial peak in the acquisition of these firms in 1955 when 67 firms with a combined asset value of over $2.1 billion were absorbed by other businesses. By 1961, merger activity again exceeded the $2.0 billion level, creeping to more than $3 billion in 1965 and 1966, exploding to $8.2 billion in 1967, peaking to $12.5 billion in 1968, and dropping to $10.9 billion in 1969. By 1971, the conglomerate phase of the merger movement was over, with the total value of acquisitions of large firms approximating 1963 activity. Roughly comparable figures from the FTC on the merger of all firms are available only from 1961 to 1971 (column 3). The FTC series on completed mergers of all firms between 1961 and 1971 shows acquisitions in the thousands, with the peak occurring in 1969. Since the W.T. Grimm & Co. data for 1968–1974 (column 4) include both announced and pending mergers, they are larger than and not necessarily consistent with the FTC data. Nevertheless, viewed as a whole, the merger panorama of the 1960s is one of a continuing build-up of activity during the decade, coming to a climax at the end of the period, and falling off rapidly thereafter. Throughout this period, the SEC remained apathetic, and the AICPA's APB continued to be ineffectual. In addition, the FTC and the Justice Department did nothing about the merger movement until it was over, which begs investigation because both had jurisdiction under the antitrust laws, and both knew that mergers had reached unprecedented levels. Why did not the FTC and the Justice Department act? The answer lies in some of the subtleties of antitrust law, and in some opaque aspects of politics.

Table 1

Acquisition Activity in the United States, 1948–1974

Date	Acquisition of Mining and Manufacturing Firms with Assets of More than $10 million[a]		Total Firms Acquired[b]	Total Acquisitions Completed or Pending as of Announcement[c]
	Number	Assets ($ mill.)		
1948	4	63.2		
1949	6	89.0		
1950	5	186.3		
1951	9	201.5		
1952	16	373.8		
1953	23	779.1		
1954	37	1444.5		
1955	67	2168.9		
1956	53	1882.0		
1957	47	1202.3		
1958	42	1070.6		
1959	49	1432.0		
1960	51	1535.1		
1961	46	2003.0	1724	
1962	65	2241.9	1667	
1963	54	2535.8	1479	
1964	73	2302.9	1797	
1965	62	3232.2	1893	
1966	75	3310.7	1476	
1967	138	8285.5	2384	
1968	173	12554.2	3932	4462
1969	136	10966.2	4542	6107
1970	90	5876.0	3089r	5152
1971	58	2443.4	2633p	4608
1972	58	1860.3		4801
1973	55p	2896.4p		4040
1974 (6 mo.)				1669p

a Source: Bureau of Economics, Federal Trade Commission.

b Source: Table 1, Statistical Report No. 10, Current Trends in Merger Activity, 1971," Bureau of Economics, Federal Trade Commission, Publication No. R6–15–14.

c Source: W. T. Grimm & Co.

p = preliminary.

r = revised.

The Failure of Antitrust Administration

Loopholes in Section 7 of the Clayton Act prior to 1950, permitted by a conservative Supreme Court in the 1920s and early 1930s, promoted increased industrial concentration during the 1919–1930 merger movement.[4] In 1950, the Celler-Kefauver amendment to Section 7 closed out vertical and horizontal mergers as serious possibilities for would-be acquirers, as a series of cases before the Supreme Court showed in the late 1950s and early 1960s. Conglomerate acquisitions then became the objectives of growth-thru-merger oriented firms. The Federal Trade Commission estimated that approximately 77% of all large firm mergers were of the conglomerate type between 1961 and 1970 (Table 2).

It was commonly held in the late 1950s that Section 7 of Clayton Antitrust Act could not touch conglomerate mergers. For the section to be operative, it was necessary to prove that the merger had caused a substantial lessening of competition along relevant market lines. But if the firms involved in a merger were not in compatible lines of commerce, a substantial lessening of competition was not likely.

Table 2

Acquisitions of Manufacturing and Mining Firms with Assets of $10 Million or More, by Type of Acquisition, 1961–1970

Type of Acquisition	1961–1970		1961–1970	
	No.[a]	Assets (million)	Percent	
			No.[a]	Assets
Horizontal	125	$6,902.9	11.0	11.7
Vertical	131	5,761.7	11.6	9.8
Conglomerate:	877	46,118.9	77.4	78.5
Product extension	567	23,252.6	50.0	39.6
Market extension	40	4,970.9	3.5	8.5
Other	270	17,895.4	23.8	30.4
Total	1,133	58,783.5	100.0	100.0

Source: Statistical Report No. 10, "Current Trends in Merger Activity, 1971," Bureau of Economics, Federal Trade Commission, May, 1972 Publication No. R6–15–14.

   [a] Total acquisitions shown in Table 2 are greater than those subsequently reported by the FTC, shown in Table 1, due to the inclusion of "private" acquisitions. Percentages do not add to 100.0 due to rounding.

Consequently, it was doubted that few, if any, true conglomerate merger suits would be brought because the standards of illegality seemed "wholly elusive," and it was unlikely that these cases would be entirely devoid of vertical and horizontal aspects, which, in themselves, would be sufficient to permit the application of existing laws (Kaysen and Turner, 1959: 131). Carl Kaysen, a noted economist at Harvard and later at the Massachusetts Institute of Technology, and Donald F. Turner, a Harvard law professor, later to become head of the Justice Department Antitrust Division under President Lyndon Johnson, accepted conglomerate mergers on the grounds that the "comparatively stringent ban on vertical or horizontal acquisition by firms with market power" made conglomerate acquisitions reasonable means to enter new markets, "perhaps barring some extreme cases where adverse effects are obvious or the concentration of wealth is huge, e.g., AT&T and U. S. Steel" (Ibid., pp. 134–135).

Turner's conviction that conglomerate mergers could not be attacked by Clayton Section 7 proved crucial in the development of the conglomerate merger movement. It accounted for his inaction as chief of the antitrust division in the face of increasing speculation and industrial concentration. Not until 1967 did Turner reverse his stand that conglomerate mergers were benign; some action was necessary, he conceded, though it would have to emanate from new legislation. (Statement before the Senate Small Business Committee hearings, April 6, 1967, quoted in ATRR No. 397, 2–18–69.)

The official position of the Justice Department on conglomerate mergers became more forceful when Richard W. McLaren was chosen by President Richard Nixon to head the Antitrust Division. McLaren asserted that Section 7 *did* cover conglomerate mergers. He thereupon instituted action against several large conglomerates intent on acquiring additional firms, including Ling Temco Vought for its take over of the Jones & Laughlin Steel Corp. and the International Telephone and Telegraph Corp. for its acquisition of the Hartford Fire and Life Insurance Co. Both cases, unhappily, were settled by consent decrees,[5] the latter subsequently coming under the cloud of scandal associated with the 1972 Republican presidential campaign. Nevertheless, the antitrust actions taken by McLaren seemed to dampen the conglomerate merger movement. The real dampener, however, was the weakening business conditions of late 1969 and the recession that developed in 1970. McLaren's view that Section 7 extends to conglomerate mergers was never tested in the Supreme Court.

While the conglomerate merger movement was in full swing, the consolidation of manufacturing and mining increased steadily, becoming a source of alarm in quarters fearing the unrestrained concentration of corporate power.

> In unprecedented fashion the current merger movement is centralizing and consolidating corporate control and decision making among a relatively few vast companies. By the end of 1968, the 200 largest industrial corporations controlled over 60 percent of the total assets held by all manufacturing corporations. This concentration of economic resources represents a substantial increase over previous levels that have earlier prompted major concern on the part of the United States Congress. Specifically, the share of manufacturing assets held by the 100 largest corporations in 1968 was greater than the share of manufacturing assets held by the 200 largest corporations in 1950. . . . The 200 largest manufacturing corporations in 1968 controlled a share of assets equal to that held by the 1,000 largest in 1941 (FTC, 1969: 3).

As conglomeration continued, it involved the acquisition of more and more large corporations. Between 1948 and 1968, it was estimated that companies with assets totaling $250 million or more absorbed 37 percent of all acquired companies, and 56 percent of the acquired assets (Ibid., p. 51). Furthermore, the companies taken over were frequently among the nation's leading firms. Of the 1000 largest firms in 1950, 327 had been swallowed up by 1968, many of them in highly concentrated industries (Ibid., p. 54).

The Movement's Economic Effects

The pure asset concentration impact of the conglomerate merger movement is undebatable, and stamps the merger wave as undesirable politically because it further concentrated private power within the United States. This evaluation assumes, of course, that one favors widely distributed power as a condition for the maintenance of effective democracy. A value judgment, of course.

Were there any identifiable economic effects of the merger wave in terms of greater market concentration or greater profits? The evidence is not conclusive. There would be a *presumption* of no added market concentration because of the operation of the antitrust laws. Added profitability because of the synergism effect had been claimed by conglomerators and their admirers. Have investigations so far borne out these presumptions?

With respect to the operations of conglomerates, some have concluded that decision making centers on financial impacts, not marketing, questions. Others have found that pricing and advertising decisions are left to operating and division heads, and therefore conjecture that reciprocity (favorable dealing among related firms to the disadvantage or exclusion of other firms outside the corporate umbrella) is less likely in conglomerates than in other firms (Markham, 1973: 90–91). Increase in the concentration of value added in manufacturing was evident for the largest 200 corporations, taking place between 1958 and 1970. In 1958 the largest 200 accounted for 38 percent of value added; in 1963, it had risen to 41 percent, and by 1970 it reached 43 percent (Ibid., pp. 116–117). A large portion of company diversification can unquestionably be attributed to acquisitions in the 1960s. Yet there was also an inverse relation between 1961–1970 acquisition activity and 1970 profitability; in other words, the most merger-active companies had the poorer earnings records (Ibid., pp. 159–162). But how should this be interpreted? Does it mean growth-oriented companies sacrificed earnings for growth? Does it mean poorer earning firms sought acquisitions to improve earnings? Does it mean earnings through acquisition are not effective? Or does it mean that by 1970 the overleveraged (too great a reliance on borrowed funds as opposed to ownership-equity-capital) conglomerates were in great trouble? There are no totally reliable answers to these questions at the moment, though the last two explanations seem to be the most valid.

Claims of superior conglomerate profit performance have relied on a comparison that removes the effect of leverage (Weston and Mansinghka, 1971: 933–934). But because the conglomerate merger movement was based to a large extent on the use of debt, it seems unreasonable to use a leverage adjustment. In any event, the profit performance of major conglomerates was very poor in 1970. To one observer the earnings performance of the conglomerates, when it did exist, was serendipitous (Reid, 1971: 945). Other analysts found "remarkably little hard evidence" that conglomerates did much harm —or good—and they felt that what evidence there was did not support the conclusion that government intervention was justified (Lorie and Halpern, 1970: 165). Still others saw signs of concentration of assets mainly in the top 51 to 150 firms, with acquisitions most heavily concentrated in the newer industries (Gort and Hogarty, 1970:

182–184). "The hypothesis that merger occurs to increase earning per share and common stock value via a favorable price-earnings ratio" was verified by another investigator (Conn, 1973: 757).

But the increase in the concentration of assets may also have increased the concentration of industry within market groups, particularly where the acquiring firms were giants in their industry. As one writer on corporate mergers put it, "the conclusion that large mergers contributed significantly to industry-group concentration appears inescapable" (Preston, 1973: 43–44).

The information and opinion now available on the conglomerate mergers indicates that there is at present no consensus by economists, on their effect. A reasonable generalization is that the conglomerate merger movement certainly increased the concentration of *assets*, that it probably increased *market* concentration somewhat, that it featured poor earnings performances for the most merger-active firms, and that it most certainly *failed* to deliver on the promises of outstanding growth through synergism, expert management, and so forth. The last claim was, after all, without substance.[6] The weight of available evidence suggests that conglomerates induce less, rather than more, economic efficiency.

Accounting Abuses and the Conglomerate Merger Movement

The pooling of interest method of accounting for business combinations was the principal instrument used for combining corporations during the conglomerate merger movement. The pooling method could be abused by manipulating the accounting to create "instantaneous gains in per share earnings" for the acquiring corporation. Assets obtained from the acquired company might have been seriously undervalued on its books, and the acquiring firm could record the undervalued assets at the acquired company's valuation, at the time of merger. Subsequently, if the assets were sold at a higher price than the recorded value, the difference would be registered as a profit. The profits were illusory, of course, because the acquiring company had paid for those assets, perhaps even at above market value, by purchasing the enterprise.

A second method of abuse in the pooling of interests was to add the earnings of both corporations while reducing the outstanding shares below original levels, which arithmetically increased the per share earnings for the merged firms. An eager stock market placed a premium on corporations showing consistent earnings "growth." The hope for capital appreciation of "growth stocks" created high price-earnings ratios for "glamour" issues, prompting many corporations to follow the merger trail with gluttonous monotony. Given a stock market evaluation based on a multiple of 20 to 30 times earnings—sometimes higher—smaller firms were provided with the economic basis for acquiring larger firms through exchanges of stock or debt securities. The *acquirer* benefited by obtaining a larger earnings base upon which the multiple would then generate even higher total valuations, thus supporting further acquisitions. The *acquired* benefited through receipt of a higher-than-market valuation for the relinquished shares. Continued growth in earnings that stemmed from successive mergers —for example, Gulf & Western made 26 acquisitions in 1967–1968— provided a speculative basis that was completely divorced from product or market realities. Once committed to the merger route, a corporation was dependent upon a continued high price-earnings market valuation to support further mergers. A firm with declining stock value was in no position to offer advantageous trading arrangements to a company that was a prospective acquisition. The stock market break in 1969–1970 was therefore instrumental in cooling off the merger-through-pooling boom.

A wide variety of accounting devices were also used during the conglomerate merger wave to create earnings growth, unrelated to corporate market or product activities. The enormous accounting flexibility available to conglomerators and corporate enterprises was sufficient to create illusory earnings in a great many cases. In addition to the use of pooling accounting, other accounting devices were used—defensible in and of themselves—to reflect situations that actually did not exist. For example, Gulf & Western, cited by the FTC as a particular offender, used accounting devices to increase earnings by switching the treatment of research and development accounts; failing to distinguish between extraordinary and normal operating earnings; recording long term rental contracts as income upon execution; and, through the use of pooling, reporting minimal related depreciation and amortization costs. Where preferred stock or debentures were used as the acquiring devices, earnings per share (related to common stock) would rise as long as the net addition to income was greater than the cost of preferred dividends or interest payments, thus offsetting substantial sums paid for an acquisition. Ling Temco Vought purchased all of Wilson & Co. (meatpackers) stock for cumulative preferred stock and cash, the latter financed by debt instruments. Wilson's earnings thus had maximum impact on LTV's earnings (FTC, 1969: 127–136).

Tax Structure Inducements

A further inducement to conglomerators was the highly favorable federal tax structure. The structure created a significant institutional bias in favor of using the pooling of interests technique over an outright purchase for cash or any other method of acquisition. During the height of the conglomerate merger movement, the pooling of interest mergers were tax free. A tax exemption was extended to the sale of a business where stock was exchanged for stock; this exemption permitted accumulated holdings to be sold without paying a capital gains tax. Of the 18 largest acquisitions in 1967–1968, with combined assets of nearly $7.6 billion, 14 were tax free. Tax free treatment appears to have been applicable in 85 percent of the mergers. The exemption had been instituted in 1921 as a temporary measure, but was never changed. In the 1960s conglomerators grasped the opportunities for manipulating tax free mergers that provided special incentives for investors.

The exchange of convertible debentures for stock, based on enabling provisions of the tax code, also became a speculative-acquisition device. Capital gains for the seller exchanging stock for debentures could be deferred for many years simply because no immediate profit was involved in the transaction. For the stock-acquiring company, the interest payments on the debentures could be deducted from income as an expense, thereby reducing its earnings and taxes. A stock for a cash transaction, of course, would have made the profit in the exchanged stock taxable to the seller. It has been estimated that tax-free, debt-equity switching transactions accounted for at least 20 percent of the large acquisitions consummated during 1968. Tax free exchanges coupled with deferral of the payment of capital gains as well as debt-equity switching were both eliminated in the 1969 revision of the tax code. The use of tax loss carryovers and ABC transactions[7]—available as tax avoidance techniques to corporations in the extractive industries—were also employed to facilitate mergers for the purpose of avoiding taxes (FTC, 1969: 143–159).

Clearly, some aspects of the federal tax structure actively fueled the conglomerate merger movement. The failure to revise the tax structure so that it would not induce mergers was an institutional public-policy omission in the same sense that the Justice Department and the Federal Trade Commission failed to take prompt legal action to halt the speculative activity that was causing industrial concentration. The availability of the pooling of interest accounting technique was, therefore, not solely responsible for the conglomerate merger movement. Nevertheless, it is doubtful that the merger movement could have assumed such incredible proportions without the pooling-purchase alternative. Accounting techniques, in their free-wheeling "flexibility," remained the prime factor in the conglomerate merger movement, although they were significantly abetted by a conducive tax structure and a flaccid antitrust policy. It was the pooling-purchase controversy that finally revealed the weakness of the APB and directly caused its abandonment.

Notes

1.   Stephen Zeff's book *Forging Accounting Principles in Five Countries* provides an outline of the events surounding the first research studies. I have used his description as the basis of my summary, which I supplemented with an examination of the documents and articles available dealing with the event, as well as with personal interviews with accountants active in the AICPA and APB at the time. More detail may be found on pages 167–186 in Zeff's book.

2.   See, for example, Nelson, 1959: 6–13; Eis, 1969: 267–296; and the Federal Trade Commission's *Economic Report on Corporate Mergers*, 1969.

3.   It is difficult to compare the three merger movements because of the differences in the way statistics describing each have been compiled. The first movement was measured in terms of numbers of firms involved and their capitalization. The second movement was described on the basis of the number of firms acquired and their asset valuations, as was the third movement, but differences in the value of the dollar and the growth of business firms in total obscure the comparison. The first and second movements added to horizontal and vertical concentration, while the third certainly produced greater asset concentration, and probably added to horizontal and vertical concentration as well. The Federal Trade Commission Staff Report was convinced that the conglomerate merger phase had exceeded both of the prior movements in importance, measured in terms of numbers of firms involved and the percent of total corporate manufacturing firm assets that were acquired (FTC, 1969: 37). The point is debatable, however; not all economists agree that the conglomerate merger wave was as important an industrial concentration phenomenon as the first merger phase.

4.   "Practically no legal constraints operated on mergers during the latter years of . . . [the 1919–1930] movement. Although the FTC issued 37 merger complaints between 1914 and 1926, the Supreme Court, in a series of decisions between 1926 and 1934, rendered Section 7 of the Clayton Act almost totally ineffective. Clearly, Section 7 had little impact on the rate or character of merger activity in the late 1920s" (FTC, 1969: 37).

5.   A consent decree is designed to save the expense of long trials and to permit speedy remedial action through agreement between the government and the offending corporation. A respondent company agreeing to a consent decree does not, however, admit its guilt. Consequently, the consent decree cannot be used against it in a civil trial. The decree, therefore, is attractive to the respondent, who in effect is saying, "I'm not guilty, but I won't do it again." The Justice Department is not required to reveal its reasons for accepting a consent decree, which unfortunately sets the stage for further abuses of the process, as alleged in the ITT case.

6.   There is a large and growing literature on the subject of the effects of the conglomerate merger movement. See, for example, *Studies of Industrial Concentration by the Conference Board, 1948–1972* (New York: Conference Board, 1973); Harry H. Lynch, *Financial Performance of Conglomerates* Graduate School of Business Administration, Harvard University, Boston, 1971; "Conglomerate Mergers and Acquisition: Opinions and Analysis," *St. John's Law Review* 44 (Spring, 1970), special edition. The bibliography of the referenced articles in the text also provides extensive source references.

7.   ABC transactions were tax avoidance devices available to corporations in the extractive industries. The technique involved a production payment carved out of the property and sold to a bank or lending institution, with the residual interest sold to another operating company. Extra depletion allowances result as long as the production payment was large compared to the residual working interest. "To realize a tax saving benefit, this transaction requires the sale of the original operating interest to another enterprise, which may encourage a merger" (FTC, 1969: 157).

chapter

14

Exit the Accounting Principles Board

The Pooling versus Purchase Controversy

There does not seem to be universal agreement among accountants on any one best way to account for a combining of businesses. Furthermore, there does not seem to be any way of designing a system of accounting for business combinations that cannot be abused one way or another in order to show something that does not exist, like huge assets, for example, or sizable earnings per share. Such deceptions were at the root of the controversy over pooling accounting versus purchase accounting, a controversy that grew out of the pooling abuses associated with the conglomerate merger movement. The pooling of interest technique was not designed by a group of malevolent accountants to further the rapacious aims of unscrupulous clients, although some people stung in the wild stock market of the 1960s may have thought so. The maddening thing about the pooling of interests method is that it was designed to correct purchase method abuses, by providing another alternative of accounting for business combinations.

The basic idea behind the purchase method is very simple. The acquirer buys, with cash or stock, the assets or stock of another company. One asset is traded for another if the purchase is made for cash, as the cash is traded for some other assets—say, plant and equipment. Because the assets of the acquired company are almost always recorded at historical cost, their fair market value is likely to be greater than shown on the books of the acquired company. This difference means that the amount paid is likely to be greater than the book value. The usual accounting technique would be to write up the value of some of the assets where justified, but where there was still some difference between the amount paid and the revalued assets, the difference would be recorded as an intangible asset value, called goodwill. Thus, if the amount paid was *very* much greater than the book value, it was probable that the amount of goodwill shown would be *very* large. A large goodwill account would only be a problem if the firm decided to reduce that amount, which could be done in several ways. A charge against reduction of retained earnings matching the reduction in goodwill might be made, for example. This charge reduced the asset value of the company, and was therefore seen as a reduction in the stockholder's equity. Or alternately, the firm might make a direct charge from the income account at year's end and reduce the goodwill by the same amount. This method would also reduce the stockholder's equity in the sense that less income would be shown, hence less earnings would be available for dividends, and a smaller earnings per share record for the year would be registered. For a stock market that made corporations thrive with consistently growing per share earnings year after year, this accounting device would be deadly. It was a method to be avoided if at all possible. A method of business combination accounting that would avoid that problem, therefore, would be very attractive. But because goodwill did not have to be retired in the 1960s, a large goodwill account might be an embarrassment, but not a threat.

The purchase method also presented another problem from the point of view of the investor and the Securities and Exchange Commission. A cash-for-assets transaction affected only the asset side of the books. But say the acquiring company did not buy the acquired company for cash, but gave stock for the assets instead, which was the more typical way of making the purchase. In a stock-for-assets transaction, there was less to restrain the acquiring company from putting *too high* a value on the assets of the acquired company. The acquirer could issue the desired amount of stock, and record the assets purchased at an amount equal to the market value of the exchanged stock, which could easily be well over the book value or the fair market value (or both) of the assets. This accounting device gave an illusory picture of the assets of the combined company, which could be important in securing loans, attracting investors, or raising the value of its stock in an atmosphere where one emphasized the balance sheet rather than the income statement. Obviously, the SEC was not going to care for this kind of arithmetic. The commissioners, in other words, were wary of the purchase method because of its potential for abuse via the revalued asset trick.

Revaluing assets could, then, always be a problem for the SEC, but one that was particularly acute in periods of inflation when defenders of the purchase method could argue convincingly that even though the business combination had been consummated through an exchange of stock, an exchange transaction had taken place. Therefore, their rationale was, the combined assets acquired a new accounting entity and should reflect the consideration given of their fair market value.[1] Nevertheless, the SEC had a continuing antipathy to asset revaluation, which frequently accompanied the use of the purchase method of accounting for busines combinations (conversation with Blough, 10/18/72; see also, Wyatt, 1963: 71–80).

POOLING BECOMES A WAY OF LIFE

The previous chapter discussed some of the objections that the Federal Trade Commission raised to pooling of interest abuses during the conglomerate merger movement. It also provided an idea of the way in which the pooling technique worked to produce gains in earnings per share just by virtue of arithmetic—namely, by keeping income constant while decreasing the number of shares (comparing the two companies before merger to the surviving combined firm). Some additional information on the manipulations under pooling of interest accounting must be mentioned. Furthermore, the technique raises some questions that must be asked and answered. For example, when did pooling become popular? Did the accounting community realize the pooling device was being abused? When did the SEC acknowledge the situation? What kind of criticism, if any, did pooling receive, and did the AICPA, through the Accounting Principles Board, ever consider the problem?

Criticism of Pooling Accounting before the Late 1960s

The term "pooling of interest" became popular during the 1940s.[2] No guidelines were established for qualifying combining businesses prior to 1950, but a 1945 case suggested that the relative size of the combining firms was not going to be considered as important as other criteria. Four tests for qualifying a business combination for the pooling of interest treatment were specified in Accounting Research Bulletin No. 40 of September, 1950: "Continuity of substantially the same proportionate equity interests, relative size, continuity of management, and similar or complimentary activities." The last yardstick was dropped and did not appear in ARB No. 48, published in January, 1957. Size and minority interests were questioned first. Where other tests were met, there was no objection to pooling when the smaller company accounted for 5 percent to 10 percent of the combined equity. Retention of top management personnel was taken as an indication of good faith that the plan for combining two businesses was a pooling and not a purchase.

The criteria noted in ARB No. 48 were stringent, but they were permitted to erode by the SEC (Harman, 1968: 83 ;Barr, 1969a: 4–5; 1969b: 10; Briloff, 1972: 63–65). The entire speculative frenzy of the conglomerate merger movement was characterized throughout by APB vacillation and SEC inaction. Pooling of interest remained the most common method of accounting for business combinations during the conglomerate craze, which lasted almost through 1969. Merger-active companies like Gulf & Western, LTV, Boise Cascade, ITT, Litton Industries, reported substantial increases in earnings per share on the basis of the arithmetic of pooling. "Aggressive" or "creative" accounting became the catchwords of Wall Street.

The speculative potential of the pooling method initially made little impression on the government or on academic accountants. As late as 1959 Andrew Barr, the SEC's chief accountant, was not alarmed about the use of pooling (Barr, 1959: 175–181) and between 1958 and 1961 the pages of the *Accounting Review* were almost entirely devoid of articles specifically evaluating accounting for business combinations.

By 1961 the ability of the pooling method to increase per share earnings immediately was being recognized publicly, though it was obvious that pooling had been widely used before then. Samuel R. Sapienza, an accounting professor, commented in 1961 that "there is little doubt that Bulletin No. 48 is being given a liberal interpretation. . . ." He also indicated that the pooling standards had been eroding since 1957 and needed clarification (Sapienza, 1961: 40). The press too had noted the effects of pooling on earnings (*New York Times*, "Mergers Create Financial Magic," April 30, 1961). Even to the legal profession the problem of accounting for business combinations was apparent (Kripke, 1961: 1028).

Pooling was becoming a management option, and the standards of ARB No. 48 did not seem to be interfering, commented Prof. Henry R. Jaenicke in late 1962. "When management wants to pool," the accountant could justify the pooling of interests treatment even if substantial changes in ownership had recurred; the critical point was that not one of the criteria suggested in Bulletin No. 48 was determinative (Jaenicke, 1962b: 63). Jaenicke also commented that the use of cash was becoming prevalent in pooling cases. Earlier in the year, Jaenicke observed that selection of the accounting method to be followed for business combinations depended upon the desired financial results, and thus the accounting treatment had become an "independent variable."[3] Jaenicke supported Sapienza's position, and offered specific examples of business combinations in which "there is every indication that accounting theory has been unjustifiably flouted in this area [of pooling]." Analyzing the St. Regis Paper Co. mergers, he stated, "At the very least, the study of St. Regis indicates the extent to which the pooling treatment leads to favorable operating results as compared with the purchase treatment" (Jaenicke, 1962a: 765). He confirmed that statements on business combination accounting recognized the advantage in pooling technique of avoiding large amortizable excesses of cost over book inherent in purchase accounting. Again in 1962, Sapienza cited pooling as a "vital force in the 'urge to merge,'" adding that "from a slow beginning, the tempo of poolings [has] accelerated appreciably." Sapienza based his 1962 article on data gathered from "hundreds of listings on the stock exchanges." To Sapienza, the serious detrioration in pooling guidelines was continuing, and he called 1950–1960 the period in which the doctrine of pooling was formulated (Sapienza, 1962: 278).

Relaxation of the pooling criteria was not accidental. Many practitioners regarded ARB No. 48 as too restrictive on the use of pooling (Arthur Andersen & Co., 1962: 73–74). Major accounting firms led in exploiting the advantages of pooling, although some thought differently about it later, when the fashion changed. Briloff, for example, mentions a firm that shed copious crocodile tears afterward at alleged SEC nonfeasance that permitted abuses of the pooling technique (Briloff, 1972: 105–107).

Important criticism of the pooling of interest method finally did come from within the AICPA in 1963. The AICPA's Accounting Research Study No. 5, made by Arthur R. Wyatt, a professor at the

University of Illinois, and entitled "A Critical Study of Accounting for Business Combinations," recommended complete elimination of pooling. He suggested that accounting for acquired assets be made at fair value (based on consideration given or assets received) and that the excess of fair value over book value be attributed to appropriate tangibles, with the balance to goodwill (Wyatt, 1963: 103–108). Wyatt later became a partner at Arthur Andersen & Co. His major recommendations received comment within the profession, but they were not adopted in subsequent APB Opinions.

An examination of the Flintkote Co.'s merger sequence showed how, according to Sapienza, "appreciably different results obtain if alternate accounting methods are used. Important financial differences of interest to stockholders arise from a consistent application of the pooling method as contrasted with a purchasing technique." Pooling—where outlay exceeded book value—resulted in the significant undervaluation of assets at the time of exchange, in earnings ratios overstating operational efficiency of management and in the worsening of debt to equity ratios when pooling techniques were consistently used. The acceptance of historical cost figures for acquired assets was also distorting many financial relationships (Sapienza, 1963: 101). Other writers acknowledged that the merger boom was "based mainly on the economic facts of life," and that tax considerations were important factors to buyer and seller (Berman and Cooper, 1963: 61).

By 1964 acquisition ⌐ ⌐ mergers were "an every day occurrence" —"all part of the effort of American business," said Leonard Spacek, "to serve the public and investors better." But accounting practices recording the business combinations transactions were diverse and totally inadequate, often distorting the results, he asserted. Pooling was an attempt "to achieve a proper accounting for the goodwill portion of the purchase price of a going concern," but pooling compounded the problem, said Spacek; it was a fiction, but a convenient makeshift, and the result was "accounting chaos" (Spacek, 1964b: 38). Others defended the pooling technique itself while finding fault with the way in which pooling was used when other accounting methods would do as well. It was clear that pooling would maximize the market value of the stockholder's investment, assuming "the stock market does not adjust for such reported earnings" (Phillips, 1965: 381). Other defenders of the pooling technique saw it as rational and useful where exchange of shares was the basis for the combination; in such cases the businesses were not affected subsantively. "On the strength of its acceptance during the past one and a half decades, it seems safe to say that pooling has come of age," commented R. C. Lauver, a partner in Price Waterhouse & Co. (Lauver, 1966: 74).

Others found it difficult to agree with some of the leading accounting practitioners that pooling was a valid accounting technique. Wyatt, for example, was concerned about APB inaction on the problem of business combinations. He feared further delays by the board, and complained that the criteria specified in ARB No. 48 were not being followed (Wyatt, 1965: 527–529). Another critic backed up Wyatt's 1963 conclusions. Martin M. Eigen concluded that all business combinations ought to be recorded as purchase transactions and that the use of pooling was a reaction against goodwill. Existing guidelines to deal with pooling were insufficient, said Eigen, and the criteria were not only inadequate but were being ignored. He recommended treating all combinations as purchases, and writing off goodwill immediately against retained earnings (Eigen, 1965: 536–540).

Criticism of Pooling Accounting in the Late 1960s

In the latter half of the 1960s the controversy over accounting for business combinations reached its climax. The SEC maintained a hands-off policy in spite of growing demands for action from some parts of the financial community and the Congress. Statements by SEC commissioners on problems relating to the interaction between the SEC and the accounting profession continued to concentrate on disclosure requirements for conglomerate corporations rather than on the pooling-purchase issue (Cohen, M. F., 1966a: 60–61). When the pooling problem *was* mentioned, it was with the hope that the AICPA would provide the necessary guidelines. Said the SEC's Barr: "It is evident that more definitive criteria are needed for the application of this [pooling] concept of business combinations. As noted previously, the Institute has sponsored a further study on goodwill and business combinations in an effort to resolve the problem" (Barr, 1967b: 14). The SEC hierarchy began in 1968 to take official notice that conglomerate companies were catering to investor pressures to increase earnings per share. Barr observed that a "recent decrease in the earnings return of a pioneer conglomerate has evoked comments in the financial press to the effect that the conglomerate's claims of a contingent increase through synergism and super-management may not be warranted after all" (Barr, 1968: 11). A year later he was showing some irritation with the AICPA for not having acted. The accounting problems created by corporation acquisition maneuvers were serious, he said; the merits of pooling versus purchase methods of accounting had been debated for the last twenty years, and the significant erosion of standards for pooling and purchase techniques required a thoughtful reexamination of the problem (Barr, 1969a: 4–5). All of which makes one wonder why the debate that had taken place since Wyatt's 1963 study did not qualify as thoughtful reexamination. What Barr's comments meant was that the SEC had become very much aware of the pooling-purchase problem but had deliberately remained apart from participation in its analysis and direct resolution.

Compared with earlier statements on pooling, comment in the late sixties became much more specific about accounting abuses and the SEC's involvement in them. In 1967 Prof. Abraham Briloff was publishing his direct assaults on the abuses of the pooling technique. His criticism of accounting distortions was straightforward. He was particularly critical that the adoption by the AICPA of APB Opinions 9 and 10 meant that pooling of interest accounting would be continued as an alternative to the purchase method until the entire subject of accounting for business combinations was considered. There was no question that pooling "lends itself to distortions," said Briloff, and that abuses were continuing with the full knowledge of the institutions concerned:

> . . . shareholder delusion through share dilution continues unabated. It can . . . be fairly inferred . . . this process goes on with the specific approval, and probably . . . guidance, of the independent auditors for the acquiring entity, and with the direct knowledge and consent of the Securities and Exchange Commission, as well as the committees on stock listing for the several exchanges, . . . (Briloff, 1967: 489).

The debate over pooling had reached its last, and most bitter, stage. With the AICPA committed (through delay) to supporting the use of pooling, and the SEC equally committed (through inaction) to supporting pooling, the debate began to spill over into other professions and the financial press. New York University law professor Homer Kripke, a member of the AICPA's Advisory Committee for APB Research Studies, regretted that the Institute had ignored the "wealth of legal talent" available to help analyze the purchase versus pooling topic. Abuses had been perpetrated by pooling, Kripke acknowledged, but under certain controlled circumstances pooling was useful and ought to be retained. He cited the disadvantages of reducing income under the purchase method to eliminate goodwill as a basis for preferring pooling. But to outlaw pooling "could have staggering effects in slowing down the current trend for acquisitions, particularly among conglomerate companies, and lawyers should be alert to the possibility." A company was purchased on the basis of its earnings, not its assets. Kripke thought, therefore, that the Accounting Principles Board would not adopt the recommendations of Accounting Research Studies 5 and 10 (Kripke, 1968: 91–95). He was quite correct.

The subject of accounting for goodwill was eventually treated in the AICPA Accounting Research Study No. 10, published in 1968; it came to the same conclusion as Study No. 5, that most business combinations were purchase transactions and should be accounted for in the same manner as other purchases. The recommendation of ARS No. 10 was that the total value paid for the transaction should be accounted for; the difference between the value of the consideration given and the fair value of the net separable resources and property rights acquired should be assigned to goodwill—that is, a reduction of stockholders equity. The study concluded that pooling of interest was an invalid concept, in particular, the practice of carrying forward the absorbed company's retained earnings (Catlett and Olsen, 1968: 105–106). Study No. 10 shared the same fate as Study No. 5, with which it agreed. Both received attention, but not enactment.

The criteria for pooling were sufficiently eroded and in doubt by 1968, and calls kept being made for new definitions and new guidelines (Fisch and Mellman, 1968: 48). The concern of the financial press by 1969 was illustrated by a *Fortune* article that characterized the conglomerate tide as "swollen into a colossal flood of mergers and take-overs . . . that seems virtually unstoppable" (Burck, 1969: 79). Describing "Mergers by Numbers," and "The Chain Letter Effect" the author spun out the conglomerate's reliance on external acquisition for earnings growth rather than on internal operations. It was predicted that when acquisitions ceased, per share earnings would fall and the "stockholders who are in at the end are left holding the bag" (Ibid., p. 81). No obstacles seemed to confront the conglomerate movement. Although some conglomerate stocks had faltered, the number of acquisitions had continued "and nothing in the way of immediate government intervention is likely to stop it" (Ibid., p. 161). Burck's predictions were probably the most brilliantly accurate and succinct of the entire event.

The Senate hearings in 1969 before the Subcommittee on Antitrust and Monopoly focused additional attention on the conglomerate merger problem. The FTC had been requested in 1968 to investigate the issue and undertook an analysis in July of that year, transmitting its report to the subcommittee in August, 1969. The report reviewed the conglomerate merger movement, identified the accounting abuses and tax merger incentives, recommended that pooling be eliminated (FTC, 1969: 1–753).

Between 1968 and 1970 the APB slowly considered the business combinations accounting problem. Under increasing pressure from the Securities and Exchange Commission and other groups inside the financial community, the APB invited other professional groups in 1969 to meet on "pre-exposure" drafts of proposed accounting rules.[4] In February, 1970, the APB finally circulated an exposure draft on business combinations that proposed a 3-to-1 size test for an acquisition to qualify under the pooling technique. The proposed criteria immediately came under attack. A vigorous write-in campaign was organized, apparently by the Financial Executives Institute, and the APB was flooded with letters opposing the proposed rule (Zeff, 1971: 214–215). In June, the test was modified to 9 to 1. On a 3-to-1 basis, many companies would have had to report a merger as a purchase rather than as a pooling. Corporation pressure against even the 9-to-1 ratio continued and was a critical factor in finally forcing elimination of *any* size criteria at all. To get APB Opinions 16 and 17 passed (Opinion 16 finally received a 12-to-6 vote and Opinion 17 a 13-to-5 vote), the size test was dropped entirely (Ibid., p. 216).

In June, 1970, the APB agreed that both pooling and purchase methods were to continue, but not as alternatives. Part-purchase and part-pooling were eliminated. George C. Watt, partner in Price Waterhouse & Co., and member of the APB, exulted that the problem had finally been solved and pooling had been retained, that the size requirement had been abandoned, and that the opportunity for abuses "cured" (Watt, 1970: 216–217; JA, August, 1970: 9).

The Opinions were issued in August, 1970. Opinion No. 16 dealt with "Business Combinations"; Opinion No. 17 with "Intangible Assets." ARB No. 48 pertaining to the bases of accounting for business combinations, which had remained on the books though steadily losing its effectiveness, was superseded. Opinions No. 16 and 17 established new criteria that still allowed enough leeway to permit pooling of interest accounting to continue; both testified to the fact that so far as the practitioner was concerned pooling of interest ac-

counting had significant financial advantages over purchase accounting (Briloff, 1972: 99–107). Publication of these two opinions culminated some ten years of active debate about both questions. They
exposed the weakness of both the SEC and the AICPA, emphasized
the shift in the power structure that had taken place within the financial system, and helped speed the demise of the Accounting Principles Board.

Why Did the APB Fail?

Throughout its history, the APB was subjected to mounting
criticism. At the beginning of its tenure this criticism involved outright demands that the board establish better methods for developing accounting principles and resolving accounting problems coupled
with skepticism that it could do so. Criticism at the outset came
mainly from within the accounting profession. Later on, the financial
community at large and the government added their voices. Finally,
in late 1971 a group was commissioned within the AICPA to examine
the operations of the board, its status, and the validity of the criticism
it had engendered. The upshot was a recommendation in 1972 that a
new research group, the Financial Accounting Standards Board, succeed the APB.

The APB suffered many of the deficiencies hampering the Committee on Accounting Procedure that it had replaced: (1) no sincere
effort or even intent to develop comprehensive accounting principles;
(2) too much part-time effort; (3) an ad hoc approach to accounting
problems; (4) lack of help from an SEC ever more eager to avoid
controversy and thus willing and happy to let the board carry the
brunt of the research effort; and (5) domination by accounting practitioners whose limited perspectives guaranteed limited results. And
in addition the APB also was handicapped by attacks from the corporate sector, operating mainly through the Financial Executives Institute. The corporations were anxious to play a larger role in the
development of the accounting and financial reporting conventions
that affected their earnings reports, and they were also determined
to protect the options of merging or divesting under circumstances
most favorable for earnings performance.

Thus from the outset, the APB was bound to fail. The brightest
hope would have been to develop a novel approach to the accounting principles problem, but the APB was merely an "improved" ver-

sion of the CAP. Leonard Spacek understood that, but even his influence was insufficient to sway the AICPA to adopt a significantly different approach. Spacek, whose criticism was instrumental in bringing about the dissolution of the CAP, believed the AICPA could successfully handle the problem of accounting principles through an accounting court. Fourteen years earlier Spacek had said that "if AICPA assumed the task, it could readily accomplish the objectives of a court of accounting principles." Even at that time Spacek had found the AICPA to be "seriously deficient" in exercising leadership of the practicing accountants although as an organization it was ideal for that purpose. Spacek did not want his proposed accounting court to operate within the government, nor did he advocate exclusive AICPA representation on the court (Spacek, 1958: 378–379).[5] Nevertheless, when the APB was formed in preference to an accounting court, Spacek became a member of the board.

Initial Confusions

Confusion about accounting principles was a principal point of concern in the accounting profession when the APB began operations in 1959. In the following year, George Catlett, partner in Arthur Andersen & Co., member of the APB from 1965–1971, and to co-author Accounting Research Study No. 10 on "Goodwill and Intangible Assets," wrote that accepted principles are not always sound and do not always result in the fair presentation of a corporation's financial status. The test of general acceptance had hindered accounting as much as it had helped, he thought, and alternative practices had flourished. The new APB had an outstanding opportunity to exercise leadership in developing financial standards (Catlett, 1960: 38). But there was still no clear-cut statement on generally accepted accounting principles, and at least Spacek and Prof. Charles J. Gaa of Michigan State University thought that this was a serious deficiency in the accounting profession (Peloubet, 1961: 35–41; Spacek, 1961: 41–46; Gaa, 1961: 47–51; Blough, 1961: 51–53).

Who would develop accounting principles, asked Professor Robert Anthony of the Harvard Business School? It was still too early (1963) to tell whether the APB would succeed, he thought, but if it failed the SEC would most likely have to act—and that would be unfortunate. Anthony, too, feared the straw man. Accounting principles formulated by the Securities and Exchange Commission would go beyond principles; the SEC would undoubtedly prescribe rules that would be frozen and stultify progress. Next, the auditing function would be taken from the accounting profession (Anthony, 1963: 105). The professor knew the SEC did not want the job, but it was "not inconceivable" that it would do it if necessary (Ibid., p. 102). The issue was urgent; it was an "eleventh hour," said Anthony, but he could not suggest how a feeling of urgency might be instilled within the profession.

Briloff endorsed Anthony's conclusion that the SEC would act if the profession did not, though it was his feeling that the AICPA was likely to fail (Briloff, 1964: 12–15). Accepting Berle's flimsy conclusion in *The American Economic Republic* that responsibility was now demanded of management because of the shift in corporate control from owners to managers,[6] Briloff noted an important dichotomy of interests. Citing several dilemmas, he wondered whether accountants could really achieve independence from clients. The theoretical structure of accounting in placing alternatives at the client's disposal offered the opportunity to select those "capable of seriously and vitally affecting reported earnings," such as depreciation, deferred research and development costs, compensation of executives and others, inventory valuation, cost attribution, and gains or losses on the disposition of fixed assets and inventories.

Universal accounting principles were far from attainment, Briloff thought, and an agonizing reappraisal of accounting problems was needed within the profession as well as a new approach to theoretical research. Practitioners allied with management could not do forthright research without irritating the client, and even if they could the public would be doubtful of the objectivity of the reports. Universities ought to do theoretical research under government or foundation grants, and the APB should broaden its membership base to include other areas of society (Ibid.).

Leonard Spacek was disillusioned with APB operations by 1964. In spite of all that had occurred since his speech six years earlier urging the establishment of an "Accounting Court," the basic problems with accounting principles were still unsolved and objectives still undefined. He described as naïve the belief in the profession's dedication to the fundamental objectives of accounting permitting fair and dispassionate self-examination. Pointing out deficiencies to a profession more concerned with concealing them did not lead to instant improvement. The profession continued to demand unanimity of opinion before acting—an impossible objective used as an excuse for inaction. To Spacek, the profession knew that it was not living up to the public's expectations. "Bear in mind that gross negligence can be construed as fraud," he cautioned. "I ask you, has not the profession been guilty of such negligence in not straightening up its house?" Professional inaction, moreover, was forcing the regulatory commissions to make accounting decisions for which they were unqualified.

Spacek pointed an accusing finger not only at the accounting profession but at the Securities and Exchange Commission as well. The SEC, he said, had misled Congress into believing investors were furnished financial information based on uniform reporting patterns and generally accepted accounting principles. How could the profession permit these misrepresentations to be submitted to Congress when the profession itself knew how far that was from actual practice? "We all know that the SEC accounting staff is aware of these defects; but does this relieve us of the responsibility to disclose the state of affairs to the Commission, or to Congress itself?" he asked (Spacek, 1964a: 282). Conclusions on accounting principles had to be reached soon; the APB could do it by exercising its available ability. Lack of initiative created the profession's dilemma, said Spacek, but heeding its conscience would lead to its assuming proper responsibility (Ibid., pp. 282–283).

Defensive reactions to the criticism directed at the APB came from some of its personnel. Reed K. Storey, director of research, tried to reconcile the need for research with the need for handling special problems: the director urged the profession to combine concept and practice if it was not to stand still or retrogress (Storey, 1964: 55). Weldon Powell, member of the APB, made a plea for continued research—and for patience. Both theoretical and empirical research were needed, he said, but the APB had to have a consensus before it could "crack down" (Powell, 1964: 40). Powell acknowledged that the attack on the APB from security analysts had some basis because comparable financial statements were being used (Ibid., pp. 40–41).

Wyatt complained about APB inaction in the two years since publication in 1963 of his study on business combinations accounting. He pointed out that the AICPA intended to wait until the board's "Study on Goodwill and Intangible Assets" was produced before doing anything further about issuing an Opinion on accounting for business combinations. But, Wyatt asked rhetorically, was it advisable to wait that long? The problem had been critical since 1960; to wait for the second study would mean that the APB could not act until 1966 or 1967 (Wyatt, 1965: 527–528). (Wyatt was optimistic. The APB did not act until 1970.) Wyatt considered several methods for reporting business combinations, and suggested some admittedly arbitrary working guides for the alternative selection of pooling and purchase (Ibid., pp. 530–535).

But the APB did not accelerate its consideration of the pooling-purchase problem. In 1967 Briloff, in an article entitled "Dirty Pooling," once again hoped the APB "would come around to discrediting and disowning the pooling device in the interest of fair and relevant reporting of corporate economic data" (Briloff, 1967: 496). By 1968 dissatisfaction with the APB reached critical proportions. Noted Zeff: "The four years between January, 1968 and December, 1971 brimmed with controversy over Board Opinions and with criticism of the Board as a viable institution for promoting improvement in accounting practice" (Zeff, 1971: 205).

But were not these assessments of the APB and accountancy in general a matter of perspective, after all? In spite of the repeated criticisms, Executive Vice President Leonard Savoie of the AICPA, a former partner of Price Waterhouse & Co., insisted that the accounting profession and the board were receiving more favorable comment (Savoie, 1968: 38).

Criticism of the APB Reaches Its Apex

Savoie notwithstanding, the controversy over the APB forced the Institute to agree to a conference with allied, albeit critical, professional groups within the financial community: the Financial Executives Institute (FEI), the Financial Analysts Federation (TFAF), and Robert Morris Associates (RMA). This conference late in 1968 became known as the Seaview Symposium, notable in formally drawing together some of the main groups involved in forming the Financial Accounting Standards Board four years later. The conference considered accounting comparability and flexibility, among other topics, and discussed the APB and accounting research. Not surprisingly, the APB was still considered to be the appropriate group to work on accounting principles—in spite of the criticism leveled against it. The consensus of those at the Symposium was that non-CPAs were not required on the APB, although additional staff and more full-time people would be helpful. A topic-by-topic approach to research received a vague endorsement, and it was suggested that the APB issue a statement of accounting objectives (Burton, 1969: 4–8). The participants apparently thought their efforts worthwhile, and left the Symposium with what one of them described as "a feeling of warmth and accomplishment" (Ibid., p. 3), a feeling, however, that was not shared by members of the FEI who were at that moment protesting against their small role in the development of accounting Opinions (Zeff, 1971: 206).

The following year the AICPA obligingly invited pre-exposure comments on Opinion drafts, Congressional hearings on the conglomerate merger movement took place, and the FTC issued its "Report on Economic Concentration." Testimony by SEC Chairman Hamer H. Budge in 1969 contained a reluctant admission that the commission might be forced to step in (Zeff, 1971: 213), and revelations of the tenuous character of corporate earnings continued to be discussed in the financial press (*Wall Street Journal*, March 4 and July 24, 1969). It all added up to increasing pressure on the accounting profession.

In his end-of-the-decade article prognosticating likely accounting developments for the seventies, Chicago Business School Dean Sidney Davidson was not too optimistic either. The APB "despite many protests about its procrastination and indecisiveness, will probably continue to operate along traditional lines." Said Davidson: "We will probably progress at the rate of two steps forward and one step back throughout most of the 1970s, constantly wishing that some more effective agency would be developed but recognizing that self-government carries the cost of relatively slow action" (Davidson, 1969: 32). (Self-government would also produce some increases in market concentration, further increases in asset concentration, and rampant stock market speculation as additional prices paid for "relatively slow action.") Other writers viewed the past ten years of the APB as ones of substantial progress and predicted the future held even more promises of success (Hicks, 1969: 60).

As the seventies began, however, criticism of the APB became almost a daily occurence. The board often felt like "a lone tree in the midst of 1,000 dogs," noted APB member Professor Charles Horngren (Horngren, 1971: 8). But what "Board critics condemn as inexcusable may well be the same sort of 'muddling through' characteristic of policy-making in many other contexts," defended Dale L. Gerboth, a manager in the AICPA accounting research division (Gerboth, 1972: 47). It was too late for defenses by 1970. Accountants were reported to be on "the firing line" in Washington, with nine Congressional hearings occurring during 1969–1970 on conglomerates (Bryan, 1970: 28).

Attacks from within the profession were also having their effect. Marshall S. Armstrong, president-nominee of the AICPA, expressed some dismay in the fall of 1970 about internal faultfinding coming from a "vocal minority of our own professional family—those who enjoy stirring the waters with criticism but who fail to make full disclosure of the real progress we are making in establishing accounting principles and financial reporting standards" (Armstrong, 1970: 67). Criticism of the APB was based on lack of understanding, Armstrong contended; "our profession has long been urged from all sides to improve financial reporting, but as we do so we often encounter sniper fire from those affected by the improvements" (Ibid., p. 68). The functions and purposes of the APB were clear-cut, and the APB was moving toward those goals—namely: "To *further clarify*, and disseminate understanding of generally accepted accounting principles. To *narrow* areas of difference and inconsistency. To *take the lead* in thinking out and resolving unsettled and controversial issues" (Ibid., p. 69).

To outside observers, the foot-dragging of the APB was the main issue. The delay between the emergence of a question and the APB's dealing with it was the real problem. While research was going on, a problem could become hopelessly "fouled up," said attorney A. A. Sommer, citing the delay between Wyatt's study on combinations in 1963 and the issuance in October, 1970, of the APB Opinions on combinations and goodwill. Said Sommer, who later became a SEC commissioner: "During that . . . period billions of dollars of economic activity was accounted for in a manner that almost literally everyone knew was an inadequate and sometimes downright misleading method of dealing with the transactions" (Sommer, 1970: 211). The conflict of interest faced by accountants—between managers of enterprises and reports of their efforts—could only be eliminated by restricting the alternative accounting practices available in a given situation and by disclosure, Sommer argued, though departures from prescribed principles could be made with adequate reason. Accountants were "victims of the modern mania that attaches near-beatitude on the 'earnings per share' concept." Comparability still was the "transcendent goal," and earnings per share ought to be arrived at in roughly the same mathematical way for each company (Ibid., pp. 212–214).

Academicians also criticized the APB. The board had two major problems, according to Professor Paton. The first was its tendency to "explore details and endeavor to take a positive position on all sorts of minor points." The second problem was the APB's "dictatorial" tendencies in setting down hard-and-fast rules and directives. The board had become virtually an arm of the government, he said (Paton, 1971: 42). It was also apparent, said Professors R. K. Mautz and Jack Gray, that part-time research was not much help in solving practical problems. Trial and error was the characteristic research approach of the APB, and it had not been successful. "The genuine danger is that researchers, finding their strenuous and costly efforts to be of little apparent significance to the APB, will turn their efforts in other directions," the authors hinted darkly (Mautz and Gray, 1970: 57–58). The professors felt that coperative research between the practitioner and the academic should be helpful, particularly because additional and improved research was essential.

Criticism of the APB was summed up by accounting Professor John C. Burton of Columbia, editor of the Seaview Symposium, and successor to Barr as chief accountant of the SEC in 1972. Noting that criticism of the accounting profession was appearing "more and more frequently in the business press," Burton declared:

> In abdicating its professional responsibility, the accounting profession has pointed the finger at generally accepted accounting principles and thereby at the Accounting Principles Board. In so doing it has urged the Board to define accounting principles more precisely, so that the number of loopholes which exist for misleading reporting will be reduced.
>
> The Board had responded with increasingly long, complex and legalistic Opinions which have closed a number of loopholes after they have been exploited (Burton, 1971: 50).

The hesitant performance of the APB over the pooling-purchase controversy had destroyed its credibility as an effective organization capable of resolving a truly controversial, crucial financial reporting question. Clearly, the APB, its prestige destroyed inside and outside the accounting profession, would have to be completely reorganized or entirely abandoned. The severe condemnations of the APB and the accounting profession made it obvious that the AICPA would have to take some positive action. But what action could be taken? No longer in a position to decide autonomously how accounting principles would be formulated, the practitioners of the Institute were faced with a considerable tactical problem. The FEI and other financial sector groups were pressing hard for a large share in developing future accounting standards that would affect corporate financial reports. The SEC, quiescent until now, might be forced finally to take a significant initiating role in the rule making process. Both threats were very real and, if actuated, would result in an important loss of power for the accounting practitioners. Conceding that the APB was finished, the AICPA would try to keep the SEC out of any new organization developed to formulate accounting rules, and they would try to contain the demands of the other financial sector groups for a greater voice. The AICPA would succeed in the first objective, but would be only partly successful in the second. The device they would use to try to achieve both objectives would be to rely on the process of self-selection. Fortunately for them, the SEC was agreeable to the use of the tactic.

Notes

1.   Asset revaluation in inflation is always a problem posing a dilemma for government and financial people alike. Some nations with chronic inflation problems have made legislative provision for consistent revaluation of assets on an annual basis. In the United States, the problem has thus far received much attention but no final resolution. Advocates of retaining the historical cost orientation are opposed by those believing that historical cost is a costly fiction to preserve because it understates replacement costs and overstates profits, contrasted with following a LIFO [last in first out] inventory policy. If U.S. inflation continues for long at a 12 percent annual rate or higher, some standard methods will likely be adopted for asset revaluation—without, it is hoped, an inordinate number of "reasonable" alternatives.

2.   Andrew Barr stated he first heard of the term in a 1945 CAP report (Barr, 1959: 175–181).

3.   It depends on how one looks at the dependent-independent relation. If accounting treatment is seen as a function of what management wanted to show, the accounting treatment would be the dependent variable.

4.   Six symposia on different subjects were held in 1969, but due to APB preoccupation with business combinations and goodwill, none were held in 1970 (Zeff, 1971: 207).

5.   I am obliged to Mr. Spacek who corrected my original impression that he had advocated exclusive jurisdiction within the accounting profession.

6.   The shift in control idea was a tiresome doctrine widely but erroneously perpetuated among the more optimistic or naïve, many from the academic area. The doctrine was first stated by Berle and Gardiner C. Means, an economist, in 1932 in their classic *The Modern Corporation and Private Property*. The shortcomings in their statistics and analysis were ignored by people who should have known better, probably because their conclusion supports the egalitarian ideal and makes it easier, philosophically, to advocate either public ownership or management operation of a firm in the public interest because its ownership is widely dispersed anyhow. The actual separation of ownership from control has a long way to go, but that also is another story. See Phillip H. Burch, Jr., *The Managerial Revolution Reassessed* (Lexington, Mass.: D.C. Heath & Co., 1972) for a credible and creditable analysis.

chapter

15

The process of self-selection:
the FASB and its prospects

The Financial Accounting Standards Board, 1972–?

In January, 1971, an AICPA conference recommended appointment of two study groups to examine the operations of the APB and the objectives of financial statements. The AICPA Board of Directors approved the conference's recommendations, but permitted the first study group, headed by Francis M. Wheat, a lawyer and former Securities and Exchange commissioner, to consider more than APB operations. The second group was headed by Robert M. Trueblood, chairman of Touche Ross & Co., and a severe critic of the Accounting Principles Board (Zeff, 1971: 224–230; AICPA, 1972: 1–4).

The Wheat Committee met for a total of fourteen days during which its members held two days of public hearings, met with different private-interest groups, and conferred twice with the SEC and its staff. Background papers were prepared and viewpoints received from other groups in connection with its hearings (AICPA, 1972: 4–5). Most witnesses at the hearings were of the opinion that responsibility for establishing accounting principles should be retained "by the organized profession of public accounting as represented by the AICPA," and most thought that a vastly greater research effort was needed (*Journal of Accounting*, December, 1971: 9–12). The activities of the Wheat Committee were closely followed by the press, which noted that substantial changes in auditing were being recommended, and that managers and analysts might be given roles in shaping accounting standards (*Wall Street Journal*, October 17, 1971: 36; November 4, 1971: 10).

THE WHEAT COMMITTEE REPORT

The Wheat Committee submitted its report to the Board of Directors of the AICPA on March 29, 1972. In May the AICPA Council adopted its recommendations which included the formation of a Financial Accounting Foundation (FAF) to be governed by nine trustees "who would have the duty of appointing members to a Financial Accounting Standards Board (FASB) and of raising funds for its support. The seven-member FASB would be full-time and fully remunerated. A Financial Accounting Standards Advisory Council (FASAC) of not less than twenty members was also to be formed.

The original proposal intended that public CPAs would have five of the nine foundation trusteeships, one of whom would be the president of the AICPA and the other four CPAs in public practice. Two trustees were to be financial executives, one a financial analyst, and one an accounting educator. SEC Chief Commissioner William J. Casey supported the Wheat Committee's proposal, and the commission itself suggested that the operational procedures of the three new groups be widely exposed for public comment before adoption. It was intended that the FASB would be established by January 1, 1973 (*JA*, June, 1972: 9–10).

The Structure of Financial Standards Control

The most important aspects of the Wheat Report, in relation to the purposes of this study, concern the organization and composition of the financial standards mechanism, the degree to which the opinions of the FASB would bind accountants, and the relation of the FASB to the SEC.

The proposed structure of the three new organizations was adopted, by and large, as recommended, although there were some important changes. The CPAs are a majority of the FAF Trustees, but the presence of three trustees from the corporate and financial sectors revealed a significant shift of power away from the accounting practitioners when compared with the all-CPA composition of the Committee on Accounting Procedure and the Accounting Principles Board. The accounting "educator" trustee was to be nominated by the AAA. The same shift of power evident on the Financial Accounting Foundation was also seen in the composition of the FASB, where four of the seven members were to be CPAs from public practice; it was agreed that the other three members need not be CPAs, providing they were "well versed in problems of financial reporting."

A twenty-seven member FASAC (the advisory group) was named on March 1, 1973. The composition of the FASAC also emphasized the growing, de jure influence of the corporate and financial sectors. Only six of the advisory council's original members appeared to be associated with public accounting firms, compared with five members who were either financial executives or from industrial concerns, and eight who represented the financial sector, including the New York Stock Exchange, and brokerage, banking, and investment banking firms. Three were academics, two from law firms, two from government, and one, Barr, an ex-chief accountant of the Securities and Exchange Commission (Appendix A). The FASAC is intended to consist of persons with skills and expertise valuable to the Financial Accounting Standards Board, and is to assist the FASB on agendas, priorities, information concerning required research, and on any other accounting matters where its advice would be helpful (FAF, 1972: 25–26; 1973: 18–19). The FASAC may not issue opinions on financial standards, however.

Statements of Accounting Standards issued by the FASB are not to be binding on the accounting profession. Such Statements are apparently to have the same status as Opinions issued by the APB: they will represent authoritative support, but may be deviated from providing such deviations are disclosed and defended with an "adequate" reason. The Wheat Committee, in commenting on the operations of the APB which it was studying, took care in its report to note that FASB opinions should not be officially adopted as rules of the SEC.

> On balance, therefore, the Study believes that it would be unwise, as it is unnecessary, to attempt to institute an arrangement by which opinions of the APB (or its successor) would be proposed for adoption as formal rules of the SEC. It should be borne in mind that the SEC presently has power to overrule the Board and to reverse or amend its opinions, as it did in the episode involving APB Opinion No. 2 (AICPA, 1972: 67).

The bylaws of the Financial Accounting Foundation carefully specify that FASB Statements on financial standards not be mandatory with the accounting profession or its clients. Even the weak "purpose" section covering FASB Statements in the 1972 exposure draft was watered down in the final bylaws. The wording of the draft was as follows:

> The FASB shall issue Statements of Accounting Standards which shall set forth and establish standards of financial accounting and presentation for the education and guidance of persons and organizations issuing or using financial statements and of practicing certified public accountants (FAF, 1972: 23).

In the bylaws as finally adopted, ". . . shall set forth and establish standards of financial accounting . . ." was changed to:

> The FASB's Statements of Financial Accounting Standards shall be designed to establish or improve standards of financial accounting and reporting for the guidance and education of the public, investors, creditors, preparers and suppliers of financial information, reporting entities and certified public accountants (FAF, 1973: 15).

As a practical matter, deviations from APB rules are uncommon. Given the traditional amount of "flexibility" available to accountants, there is little reason for them to deviate. FASB rules will no doubt be adhered to by practitioners as a matter of course. However, should mandatory rules be specified where no alternatives are possible, revolts can be expected to occur.

PERSONNEL, RESPONSIBILITY, AND FUNDING

None of the foundation's trustees were drawn from the SEC or any other government agency, but one of the members of the FASB, Arthur L. Litke, was chief accountant at the Federal Power Commission prior to his FASB appointment. Once appointed to the FASB, members are required to sever their previous professional contacts. There are no restrictions on employment after serving on the FASB.

The Wheat Report also dealt with the "threshold" question of whether the responsibility for developing financial standards should be carried out by a government agency—that is, by the SEC. Quite predictably, the answer was negative. The committee offered the usual panoply of reasons, including the "dangers" of rigid rules, the susceptibility of a regulatory agency to political pressure, the sapping of "the vitality of the accounting profession," and the narrowness of the SEC's domain (AICPA, 1972: 21–24). Despite this negative stance toward the SEC, the commission itself appeared well disposed toward the FASB and will apparently support its opinions on financial standards.

> Marshall S. Armstrong, Chairman of the Financial Standards Board, has reported that the Securities and Exchange Commission has pledged support of FASB pronouncements. Speaking at a meeting of CPAs and investment analysts in Chicago, Mr. Armstrong said that he agreed with a comment of SEC Chief Accountant John C. Burton to the effect that the relationship between the two bodies should be one of "mutual nonsurprise" (*JA*, June, 1973: 5).

Funding requirements of the FASB were estimated in the Wheat Report at between $2.5 million and $3 million annually (AICPA, 1972: 78). The Financial Executives Institute agreed to provide $1.5 million for each of the first two years of FASB operation (FEI Bulletin Nov., 1972: No. 226). Contributions from the FEI, an organization of top-level financial people, should not be regarded as charitable donations. Of the original FASB members, Robert E. Mays, former controller of the Exxon Corp., was nominated by the FEI. The FAF certificate of incorporation specifies that of the two foundation trustees with "extensive experience as financial executives," one is to be nominated by the FEI and the other by the National Association of Accountants, the old Cost Accountants Association.[1]

But the inclusion of FEI representatives on the FAF, FASB, and FASAC should not obscure the continuing hostility between the FEI and the AICPA. The AICPA apparently had a great deal of difficulty in persuading the FEI to participate in the new organizations under the existing membership composition.[2]

A hint of things to come appeared in an article called "A Management Reaction to the Wheat Report" (van Pelt, 1972: 819–822). Appraising the new financial standards mechanism as a device permitting the accountants to retain control of financial standards, van Pelt, a financial vice-president of an industrial concern, questioned whether there was a persuasive basis for AICPA dominance. The objective of the foundation and the FASB should be true independence, van Pelt asserted. To achieve that objective, the AICPA president should not be a trustee, and not more than three trustees should be accounting practitioners. Three should come from the FEI. "The remaining Trustees might be selected on a rotating basis by the Financial Analysts Federation, the American Accounting Association, and the National Association of Accountants" (Ibid., p. 821).

Van Pelt's position was consistent with that of the FEI's policy paper submitted to the Wheat Committee on the operations of the Accounting Principles Board and the establishment of future accounting principles. In its statement the Financial Executives Institute once again scored the APB for having unbalanced representation which mitigated against the understanding and the resolution of "practical operating problems confronting the financial community in their attempts to apply rigid 'rulings' in diverse business situations" (Andersen & Co., 1972: 449). Apparently even the loose AICPA accounting policies were too "rigid" for the FEI. The FEI wanted equal representation with the AICPA on the new financial standards group, and suggested that together they should constitute as much as 80 percent of the membership.[3]

The Shift of Power

The new accounting standards organizations underscored several fundamental institutional changes and relationships among those in the financial community and between the community and the Securities and Exchange Commission. First, the shift in power from the accounting practitioners to the corporate and financial sectors was formally stated and institutionalized. Second, the relegation of the SEC to permanent status of onlooker was now completely unmistakable. Third, the sequence of events covering the history of the CAP, the APB, and the formation of the FASB continued to prompt the question of whether accountant "independence" was at best ever anything but wishful thinking. In a broader sense, the process of determining accounting principles, beginning with the stock market crash and ending with the formation of the FASB, has illustrated some of the limitations on regulating a private sector when a public independent regulatory agency is faced with the determined opposition of powerful forces. All these events, of course, augment our understanding of the public policy process.

Institutionalization of Financial Reporting Standards Authority within the Private Sector

During the three decades since passage of the Securities Act, the SEC generally has not exercised the broad authority over accounting granted to it by the Congress. It has issued relatively few rules in matters involving accounting principles and practices (SEC Chairman William L. Cary, 1963).

It was not inevitable at the outset of the Securities and Exchange Commission's operations that the authority for determining standards of financial reporting would be transferred to and institutionalized within the private sector. But for the SEC to have retained that authority, newly taken from the private sector by the Securities Acts, would have required an unusual set of circumstances, including a clear Congressional mandate, a militant chief commissioner, and a long-range, scholarly approach aimed at codifying and making uniform industrial accounting. Selection of a militant chief commissioner was not politically feasible, as the selection of Joseph Kennedy and his successor J. M. Landis, rather than Ferdinand Pecora, testifies. The legalistic perspectives of the SEC and the regeneration of the power of the financial-industrial sector following the stock market crash combined to limit the regulatory approach of the commission. The opposition of the accounting practitioner was also a particularly important factor in the SEC's failure to assert its authority to the fullest.

The cumulative effect of these factors, plus the wearing down of Landis's resistance by 1936 to practitioner obstinacy and Chief Accountant Carman Blough's belief that the SEC could not develop a set of accounting principles, precipitated the transfer in authority over accounting principles. Two critical, affirmative steps were taken by the SEC to effect the *return* of that authority to the private sector: the agreement to let the profession handle violations of accounting ethics, and the more important decision to permit the Institute to determine accounting principles.

Landis probably had little confidence that the accounting practitioners were going to do very much about the development of accounting principles. Why did he agree to the transfer? The most likely answer is that Landis was exhausted by the struggle by late 1936, and that he was also convinced that it would not be possible to determine accounting principles within the SEC. Given Blough's opinion that the SEC *could* not develop accounting principles, together with the preference of two other SEC commissioners that the SEC *should* not do so, Landis agreed that the accounting practitioners should try.

Was there any intention of letting this authority remain permanently in the private sector? The answer to that question is, probably.

Landis was hardly so naïve as to believe that authority once surrendered could be easily regained. Nowhere is there any evidence that the SEC merely intended to permit the accounting practitioners a trial period in which to develop accounting principles. The threat of SEC intervention and its reabsorption of authority over the formulation of accounting principles always remained present, but it was quickly reduced to the level of a ritual that supported the interaction between the commission and the practicing accountants.

By 1940 the transfer of authority seems to have been thoroughly accepted by the SEC commissioners. When World War II broke out the attention of both the SEC and the accountants was drawn away from the question of accounting principles. With the resurgence of business prestige after World War II, chances of the SEC retrieving its authority for the development of accounting principles declined significantly.

Why the SEC Failure?

The SEC has never made a formal authorization for the development of financial reporting standards to a private rule making group. Formal institutionalization, in the sense that the National Association of Security Dealers has been chartered and given certain powers by the government, was never extended to the CAP, the APB, or to their successor, the FASB. Consideration of this alternative was made but discarded in the Wheat Report. It is quite clear that at its option the SEC could have at any time legally retaken the authority for developing financial accounting standards. Why, then, did the SEC choose never to do this?

There are many reasons for the failure of the SEC to regain its power to determine accounting principles, beyond those that led to the initial transfer of authority. The rapid formal adoption of a plan to develop financial standards by the practicing accountants through the Committee on Accounting Procedure facilitated its acceptance by the SEC commissioners as an operating device for handling the accounting problems and issues with which they were faced. Once an interactive operating method is developed, deviations are likely to disturb seriously the equilibrium established among participating institutions. The SEC was unable to resist pressure from the financial sector to relinquish significant authority in 1934–1938; in 1968, when the conglomerate merger movement was at its zenith, and in spite of all of the abuses taking place within the nation's financial sector, the SEC followed the pattern instituted after 1938 and refused to act.

The arrangement with the AICPA's accounting principles groups had many advantages for the SEC. The AICPA was there to blame when things went wrong, and the SEC avoided the inevitable strife that would have occurred had it chosen to take on the job of developing accounting principles. Professor Horngren, in commenting in 1972 on the operating relationship established between the SEC and the AICPA, claimed that there was a partnership between the private and public sectors, with the SEC acting the role of top management and calling the direction of APB activities. Exasperation was evident in Horngren's article, understandable inasmuch as he had been a member of the much abused APB. Horngren overstated his case in using the top management analogy, but his other point comes through very persuasively, that there was an established communications network between the SEC and the AICPA for many years (Horngren, 1972: 37–41).

With the AICPA ostensibly on the job, the Securities and Exchange Commission could claim that the development of accounting principles was proceeding on an evolutionary basis and that the pattern of self-regulation was being maintained. Therefore it could be argued that government regulation was being both effective and benign with respect to the financial community. Whenever problems became sticky and pressures tightened, the SEC could always then proceed to issue its characteristic "warnings" that the accountants had better "act" on a problem or otherwise the SEC would "step in." This finger-shaking provided the appearance of action and the illusion of control, but in fact the entire sequence was an elaborate charade in which the AICPA and the SEC willingly participated over a period of more than 35 years. If the arrangement served the purposes of the SEC, it also worked to the advantage of the AICPA and the financial-industrial sector.

History was another important factor. To retrieve the responsibility for devising accounting standards from the AICPA would have taken another shock on the order of the 1929–1933 depression. Even the conglomerate merger movement was insufficient to get the power back into the hands of the SEC, or to force the Congress to make mandatory upon the SEC the determination of accounting principles.

A series of incidents surrounding the investment tax credit issue illustrate the vulnerability of both the commission and the Institute to political pressure from both the White House and the Congress, pressure that betokens the effectiveness of corporate lobbying. With a strange obstinacy, the practitioners have three times recommended spreading the investment tax credit over the life of a company's assets, but corporations have favored reflecting the profit effect entirely in the initial year. The ostensible intent of the legislative and executive branches in endorsing the investment tax credits has been to increase national investment levels—a debatable policy device to achieve that purpose. The more evident objective of the investment tax credit, however, is to make corporate profit statements look better.[4] On two separate occasions the SEC, after having agreed to remain neutral and permit the AICPA to recommend the application of the tax credit over a period of years, has reneged and subsequently supported the flow-through method.[5] Accountants, failing to appreciate the practical exigencies of the situation, continued to brood about the behavior of the SEC in the investment tax credit controversy, and remained committed to the "principle" involved. The incident demonstrates the vulnerability of the SEC to Congressional pressure when applied by the corporate lobby. The investment credit controversies also illustrate why the SEC has not been particularly eager to accept the responsibility for developing accounting principles (Carey, 1970: 98–108; 133–134; Zeff, 1971: 178–180; 201–202; 219–221; Barr, 1963: 23).

The tenacity of the accountants and the remainder of the financial community to keep accounting principles from being exercised by the SEC is explainable partly by the enormous financial stakes involved for both in the content of corporate financial statements. It appeared to some participants in the events of the 1930s that had the SEC tried to apply and develop accounting principles, there would have been a fight to the bitter end; and it was not at all clear whether the SEC would have won, that is, whether it would have been upheld by the Supreme Court. Though support of the Supreme Court is perhaps less questionable today, the SEC still remains vulnerable to Congressional and White House pressure, both of which in turn are very vulnerable to corporate pressure. Corporate prestige and power have completely recovered from the crisis of 1929–1938, and in the absence of another major financial and economic crisis it is now clearly too late for the SEC to regain control of the financial standards it granted to the private sector. From 1938 through 1959 little external pressure was generated for a major change in the established ways of doing things.

Moreover, individuals selected as SEC commissioners and chief accountants have never been oriented toward the development of sophisticated, comprehensive accounting codes. Most commissioners have been innocent of accounting intricacies, and almost all chief accountants have been complacent about SEC inaction on accounting principles. Earle C. King was the most vigorous of the chief accountants in trying to force the adoption of specific financial accounting principles, but the others have been content to have the responsibility for accounting principles remain with practitioners. John C. Burton, who has been chief accountant since 1972, has stated clearly that the development of financial reporting standards belongs in the private sector, and that he could not conceive of an occasion in which a duly adopted principle established by either the APB or the FASB would be vetoed by the SEC. Thus the determination of accounting principles remains firmly in the private sector—a prerogative reinforced by the recent and dramatic shift in power from the AICPA to the corporate and financial community.

The role of the chief accountant of the SEC is particularly important, and therefore, the criteria for his selection have always been crucial. Throughout the history of the SEC, the professional identification of the individual chief accountants primarily as accountants may have interefered with their effectiveness as government employees, at least to the degree that their attitudes toward the accounting practitioners were uncritical, with the probable exception of King. Of the four retired chief accountants, Blough, Werntz, and King took positions with private accounting firms after resigning from the SEC. Blough subsequently was research director in the AICPA; Barr became a consultant to the AICPA after his resignation. Burton, a former Columbia professor, was a senior accountant at Arthur Young & Co., where his father had been a partner. There could, of course, be important benefits to accounting if the chief accountant kept an eye on and actively encouraged the formulation and use of accounting principles; the prime deficiency of most chief accountants, however, has been their failure to take an adversary position against the AICPA and the corporate sector. Unfortunately, the process of selecting a chief accountant does not appear to allow this option. Burton, for example, was recommended by Arthur Young & Co. (*Business Week*, April 8, 1972: 21). Not that such a sponsor compromises Burton, but it does indicate his acceptability to accounting practitioners, which seems to be a requisite for holding the chief accountant's position. The selection of someone willing to challenge aggressively the established financial organizations on the issue of standards is very, very slim. The complacent stance of most SEC chief accountants has been a substantial impediment to the development of both accounting principles and a comprehensive set of accounting rules. In fairness, though, it must be noted that the attitudes of the SEC commissioners have been compatible with those of their chief accountants.

The FASB and the Transfer of Power to the Corporate Sector

> The period from 1926 to 1936 was a period of trial for the profession. At its end the profession had successfully restored the position that had been threatened in the early days of the Roosevelt Administration (George O. May, 1961).

The FASB and its supporting task forces include a considerable number of financial executives. Their inclusion is yet another manifestation of corporate power in America, a phenomena receiving much recent comment. The nation's financial executives once again have an official and crucial role in shaping the accounting principles that determine the income and profit reports of the corporate sector. The accounting abuses of the 1920s and the reaction against the 1929 crash resulted in the passage of two securities acts, both of which were intended to bring some order and meaningful disclosure to financial statements. The passage of the Securities Act in 1933 and the Securities Exchange Act in 1934 represented a rejection of the control over financial reporting previously held by the financial and corporate sectors. Some 40 years after the passage of these acts, the power to determine the principles behind financial reports has been partially transferred back to these sectors, and the transfer has received de facto recognition from the SEC. George O. May was only partly correct when he said the position of accountants that had existed before the Roosevelt era had been successfully restored in 1936. It was really the advent of the FASB that restored the pre-SEC status quo, wherein the financial and corporate sectors had control over accounting principles. It was only in the interim that the accountants exercised most of this power, at least outwardly.

Is the Accountant Dependent on the Client?

Was the exercise of power by accountants over accounting principles ever anything more than just a semblance of independence while in actuality they themselves were subservient to their clients' wishes? Probably the more accurate assessment is that the accounting practitioners have been as much dominated by their clients' interests as by their clients. The matter of independence has always been a point of concern and contention among the accounting practitioners. The Wheat Committee Report defensively asserted that the independence of the FASB was unchallengeable (AICPA, 1972: 10; 70–73). The claim was supported by stipulating that members had to renounce other affiliations once they joined the FASB. The assertion is naïve and misleading because it assumes that individuals forget their past orientations and associations and take on new identities when given new responsibilities. It is far more realistic to believe that the perspectives of FASB members will remain consistent with those they developed in prior positions. For the younger members of the FASB, the question of future employment is also important.

The practicing accountants seem always to have misunderstood the route toward independence, or else they have been deliberately misleading in their writings about it. Their preoccupation with freedom from government "interference" in the development of accounting principles subsided, however, after it became obvious that the SEC was not going to make a bid for its relinquished authority. But their claim that they are "independent" of their clients has always been challenged, within and outside of the accounting profession. The association of interest between corporation and accountant, in spite of accountant protestations to the contrary, has never really surmounted the fact that the accountant is dependent on his client. Accountant advocacy of "flexible" accounting rules favored client interests by protecting the client's financial options. During the conglomerate merger movement the positions taken by the large accounting firms for the most part favored continuation of the pooling of interest and purchase alternatives. Had the "big eight" accounting firms[6] wanted to eliminate pooling of interests, it could easily have been accomplished after the publication of Wyatt's 1963 study. What actually happened, however, was that the possible elimination of the pooling of interest technique prompted near revolts against the APB by at least two major accounting firms.

Accountants prefer to ignore the fact that the only basis on which they are likely to resist client pressure successfully is to be able to indicate that government regulations—that is SEC regulations—forbid accession to client wishes. In the absence of an outside authority to which the practitioner accountant could refer and appeal if necessary, and thereby persuade clients to accept less than optimal accounting treatment from their point of view, the accountant has little chance of achieving independence.

AUTHORITY REFERENCES

The identification by accountants of authority references (sometimes referred to as authority figures) to support or defend their procedures and opinions represents another important consideration. Accountants have always accepted the corporate sector as their legitimate authority reference, rather than the government. In this, accountants have been consistent with, or perhaps caricatures of, the espousers of the classical business creed (Sutton et al., 1956: 33–52). Business sector attitudes toward authority recognition within the United States, on which I have commented elsewhere (Chatov, 1973: 67) generally supports the accountant selection of the business sector rather than government as the prime authority figure. The very strong undercurrent of antigovernment feeling of the accountants has been cited in this book. Added to the financial interests of the accountants, which make them vulnerable to clients, their ideological perspectives reinforce an attitude whereby independence from the client cannot be realized.

POSSIBLE CONFLICTS OF INTEREST

Finally, the entry of "big eight" accounting firms into businesses other than accounting completes the identification of the large accounting firm with the corporate sector. Their expansion into management services, consulting services, and executive recruiting is too dependent upon the corporate structure to permit the maintenance of independent action and perspectives by individual accounting firms. Many have in effect become diversified businesses themselves, and are no longer simply auditors, analysts, and record keepers. For a considerable number of years, accountants have carried on within their journals a tedious discussion on whether or not a conflict of interest exists when an accounting firm is both the auditor of a corporation's books *and* its business consultant. The large accounting firms involved in these businesses have, quite naturally, defended the practice of dual operations, claiming that it is possible to carry out both functions without conflict. From an outside point of view, the assertion is hardly credible, though it is completely understandable. The problem has been recognized by the SEC (Cohen, M. H., 1966b: 57), but no action to counter the trend has ever been taken.

FINANCIAL-CORPORATE SECTOR DOMINANCE OF THE FASB

The membership composition of the FAF, the FASB, and the FASAC are extremely suspect because of their organizational biases. The nine FAF trustees are to be nominated by the AICPA (five, including the president of the AICPA); the FEI (one); the National Association of (Cost) Accountants (one); the Financial Analysts Federation (one); and the AAA (one). FASB membership is not specified by organization, its members are appointed by the FAF trustees. However, the previous organizational affiliation of the original FASB members were the AICPA (four), the FEI (one), the AAA (one), and the Federal Government Accountants Association (one) (Appendix A).

Representation by the corporate and financial sectors on FASB task forces is also large. The first three Status Reports issued by the FASB in 1973 identified the membership of four task forces that had been organized. Personnel from the corporate and financial sectors represented a majority on both the Accounting for Future Losses and the Diversified Companies task forces, and they constituted about half the membership of the Accounting for Certain Costs task force. Only on the Accounting for Foreign Currency Translation task force were they outnumbered by public and academic accountants combined. Other interested and affected organizations from the private sector—for example, the American Bar Association and the American Economic Association—have been carefully excluded. Economists and attorneys easily merit representation. They have as great an interest in the preparation, and availability of corporate financial statements as the FAF, FASB, and FASAC incumbents—and a broader perspective. Other organizations could doubtless make equal claim for FASB membership. Obviously, no criteria other than power have been established for FASB membership.

The AICPA is less vulnerable to criticism now that other groups are joined with it on the FASB. The AAA member lends some academic repectability to the organization, but the overall orientation of the FASB quite clearly favors the corporate and financial sectors rather than the government, the investor, or the general public. The situation is somewhat akin to the justice of the peace system wherein the justice has a financial interest in the outcome of the hearing: the greater the fine, the greater the justice's compensation. To have the users of accounting principles determine those principles is a self-serving absurdity, with predictable results. Historically, and viewed from the perspectives of private power and the circumspection of a public regulatory agency, the present situation is explainable, albeit undesirable.

Specialization, Industrialization, and the Growth of Power

Structural differentiation partially explains the shift of power from the accountants to the corporate and financial sectors. Structural differentiation involves the process whereby specialization takes place as functions become more complex. Functions are separated, and in the field of accountancy, for instance, practitioners become distinguished from each other by the special areas in which they work. Structural differentiation has been taking place within the accounting profession and the financial community in general since 1900. The accounting profession is broken down into several fairly distinct groups: the practitioners, including the cost accountants; tax accountants; auditors and general financial accountants; government accountants; and academic accountants. Earlier, many of these groups were lumped together, but as the economy became more complex, specialized functional groups carried out these particular assignments.

The structure of the accounting profession followed the changes in industrial operation. At the time the American Institute of Accountants first received its mandate to build accounting principles, the distinction between research and practice was fairly vague. Research had not achieved very advanced levels, and many of the individuals dealing with accounting theory were in fact accounting practitioners like May and Montgomery. But as accounting theory and research became more sophisticated, the accounting practitioners remained more or less within their 1930s' structure, and the gap between research and practice widened. To the accounting practitioners, research and theory by academicians became more and more "impractical" and "unrealistic." The difficulty of reconciliation was a product of increased specialization; the advancing level of knowledge made the practitioners increasingly defensive about their inability to exercise a theoretical, contemporary approach toward accounting.

Academicians became more and more devoted to deductive methods, beginning with postulates and progressing logically through to their consequences, which, of course, were inevitably bound to conflict with existing practices, particularly because alternative practices were available in many areas. As a result, practitioners had to reject the deductively oriented research being conducted in the academic field. The most striking incident in this regard was violent opposition of the accounting practitioners to the AICPA's Accounting Research Studies No. 1 and No. 3 authored by Professors Moonitz and Sprouse in the early sixties. Since then, the AICPA has undertaken no other comparable studies, nor was theoretical accounting carried much further by the APB (Carey, 1970: 97). The prospects are that the FASB will not be any more eager or adept at undertaking and implementing theoretical accounting studies than the APB.

Newspaper reports indicate that the FASB will operate on "urgent" problems affecting the profession and the financial community. Reports have also indicated that the FASB has decided to sidestep several controversial financial accounting problems at the present time (*Wall Street Journal*, April 5, 1973: 7). This kind of inaction is reminiscent of the operations of the CAP and the APB. FASB Statements, as pointed out before, will not be binding upon the accounting profession; they will merely be expressions of guidance, which the profession may either follow or deviate from if persuasive reasons exist for doing so. And to do so, of course, means preserving a set of options for future contingencies.

Thus the prospective change in the determination of accounting principles is of form rather than substance, and it is unlikely that the FASB will be more effective in developing accounting principles than its predecessor organizations, particularly in controversial areas. Because the combination of practicing accountants, their corporate clients, and the financial institutions now dominate the FASB, the APB orientation toward profit-generating flexibility and alternative accounting treatments should be perpetuated in FASB operations.

Notes

1.   The National Association of Cost Accountants (NACA) was organized in 1919. The purpose was to advance cost accounting as a branch of accounting. Membership was 2,000 by 1920, 44,000 by 1959, and 67,000 by 1969. Technical publications were assumed in 1955 with "Accounting Practice Reports" issued to the members. In 1957 the word "Cost" was dropped from the Association's name, a sign of the group's expanding in-

terest in accounting in general, and in management accounting in particular. The NAA started publication of a *Bulletin* in 1925; in 1965 the *Bulletin* became *Management Accounting* (NAA, 1969). Prior to the inclusion of the NAA in the FASB, its position in the development of general accounting principles was minimal. Its accession to some influence attests to the growth of its membership and its status within the corporate sector as an association appealing to public accountants, corporate accountants, and finance people.

2.   My source of information for this statement is a series of conversations I have had with persons within the AICPA, the FEI, and the new Financial Standards organization.

3.   "The body should be organized within the private sector; it should have an equal number of members representing the public accounting profession and the business management community, plus a lesser number of members drawn from public interest groups, such as financial analysts, the academic community, government, etc. . . . both the accounting and business groups should each have as much as 40% of the total membership of the body. Membership in the AICPA should not be a prerequisite for representatives other than the public accountants, and the selection of those members not representing the AICPA must be made only after careful consideration of the recommendations of the appropriate associations or groups who are actively engaged in the area of financial reporting" (Andersen & Co., 1972: 449–450).

4.   This is an arguable conclusion, I acknowledge. Economic analysts of the stimulating effect of the investment tax credit disagree. What cannot be denied, however, is that the investment tax credit improves profits in whatever year applied.

5.   Hearsay has it that President Kennedy personally intervened with the SEC after having been put under considerable pressure by the corporate sector. There is no adequate proof of this allegation, but it has some elements of plausibility and ought not be dismissed quickly. Presidential intervention in antitrust matters pertaining to the SEC, the Justice Department, and the FTC is believed by many to be fairly common. The alleged Nixon Administration intervention in the ITT antitrust case is a case in point.

6.   One should not believe the "big eight" firms always act in concert, although at times they do. Nonetheless, the predominant power among the accounting practitioners is in the major firms, and their positions have always been crucial.

chapter

16

On the sociology of government regulation

"The Threat" Ritual

Several important aspects of the interaction between accountants and the Securities and Exchange Commission have to be considered in a broad context to be fully appreciated. These aspects are especially meaningful when viewed as sociological phenomena: creating rituals, turning history into myth, and the drive toward professionalism.

After 1938 there developed a ritual threat mechanism ("the threat") that operated between the SEC and the accounting practitioners of the AIA/AICPA. This ritual helped maintain the authority for developing accounting principles within the AICPA and at the same time permitted the SEC to disguise its eroding control. The threat mechanism was very clearly operative prior to World War II. It was less utilized during the fifties, but in the sixties and early seventies it was in great use, even though the inaction of the SEC had become so institutionalized that the ritual threat mechanism should have lost all credibility.

"The threat" went into effect whenever a persisting accounting controversy or practice the AICPA and SEC could not resolve drew too much attention. When pressure from others could be ignored no longer, the SEC, through one of its commissioners or staff, would issue "the threat": if the CAP or the APB did not take steps to settle the issue, the SEC would "reluctantly" be forced to "step in." On the surface, the entire scenario is reminiscent of low comedy enjoyed more by the participants than the spectators, as somber versions of "the threat" are ceremoniously grumbled back and forth. Some samples of "the threat" at work in the early years of the SEC are as follows:

FROM THE ACCOUNTANTS:

It seems to be assumed that either accountants must speedily write their own principles in pretty definite terms, or the Commission will write them for us (Sanders, 1935a: 100).

If the practitioners, after sufficient time has elapsed, have not come to some substantial agreement as to what are or should be considered accepted accounting principles and practices, we may well expect the Commission to publish what it shall demand in the way of such practices . . . (Smith, C. A., 1935: 327).

With the widespread recognition of the importance of accounting in solving present-day problems of government and industry, practitioners and teachers of accounting have an unparalleled opportunity to make a constructive contribution. If we do not, the lawyers of the Securities Exchange Commission and other Government agencies will do it for us (Barr, 1938: 323).

The profession was warned that unless it could create a degree of uniformity in the practice of its members and in the treatment of accounts of different institutions by its own efforts, it would inevitably find that such uniformity would be imposed on it by external authority (May, 1940: 74).

In a profession such as ours, where new problems continually arise, it is obvious that the profession must itself take the initiative in setting forth acceptable practices and procedures in relation to such problems. Our profession also recognizes that its failure to do so would undoubtedly result in the promulgation of additional rules by the Commission (Stewart, 1941: 464).

FROM THE SEC:

What the future policy of the Commission will have to be, I am not prepared to say but we are reluctant to undertake the prescription of principles to be followed except as a last resort. It is hoped the profession will itself develop greater consistency in the many places where uniformity appears essential to avoid confusion in the presentation of financial data (Blough, 1937b: 37).

> If the profession fails in its public duty to recognize and apply adequate standards, I believe the agency whose duty it is to administer laws such as the Securities Act must eventually move in (Mathews, January 8, 1937; quoted in Barr, 1940: 91).

> We may, as we have not yet done, seek to develop our rule making power under the Securities Act for the formulation of accounting rules designed to impose minimum standards of accounting theory and practice upon accountants whose work is to be submitted to our scrutiny. . . . We should deplore as much as you [accountants] the necessity of going further, and imposing drastic government restriction and supervision on the practices of accountants (Lane, 1938: 9).

Was the threat mechanism ever real, or was it always a farce? Certainly in the late thirties it was still uncertain whether the SEC would continue to "support" the AIA's "efforts" to develop generally accepted accounting principles. The practitioners' Committee on Accounting Procedure was in operation in 1938, and by 1940 SEC Chairman Frank was complimenting the AIA on its development of principles (Carey, 1970: 63–64). Practitioner anxiety, then, should have been relieved by 1940. The truth of the matter seems to lie in the difference of "the threat" before and after World War II. Prior to the war it involved possible SEC absorption of the *entire* responsibility for formulation and enforcement of accounting principles; after World War II "the threat" usually encompassed SEC intervention and action in *individual* instances. There are no clear-cut statements by SEC officials in the sixties that suggest the commission might take back the entire authority for developing GAAPs.

Despite the critical difference in the before-and-after threats, the significant point is that the SEC had accepted the AICPA "management" of accounting principles development as a permanent part of the institutional structure, and it was happy to continue working on that basis, even though to do so meant the gradual erosion of SEC vitality and power. CAP-AIA influence was persuasive enough in 1950 to force the SEC to compromise on its plan to make mandatory upon reporting companies the "all-inclusive" income concept, that is, all items of revenue and expense recognized or recorded in a given year be included in the calculation of net income, whether or not those revenues and expenses pertained to that year. The Institute's objection to SEC "rule making" on accounting principles at the time was blunt and vigorous as it fought to protect its position (Barr, 1963: 21). The transition from the CAP to the APB was forced intramurally, for the most part, although criticism from other private groups—the Controllers Institute (later the FEI) and the Financial Analysts Federation—were important in bringing it about. The SEC maintained largely its passive role throughout that event.

The corporations also took issue with the SEC on accounting matters. Corporate pressure against steps that would make earnings more comparable became increasingly effective in the fifties, and helped remove SEC backing from the AICPA on the issue. Corporations were also instrumental in forcing the SEC to withdraw support from the AICPA in the second installment of the investment credit controversy in the early 1960s. And as the SEC sank deeper into passivity in the mid-1960s, the practitioners wondered whether it had softened its position on speeding the elimination of diverse accounting practices. House hearings in 1963–1964, in which SEC Chief Commissioner William L. Cary was questioned regarding the diversity of accounting principles, were interpreted as "a warning both to the SEC and the Institute to get on with the job" (Carey, 1970: 80–110).

After the mid-sixties the threat mechanism could hardly have been taken seriously by either the accounting practitioners or the corporations, though for some reason its implementation appeared to loom as a possibility to the academics. The SEC had "stepped in" on a few occasions, but there was obviously no intention whatsoever on its part to regain its authority to develop accounting principles from the practitioners. The ritual had served its purpose in the early years of the SEC in determining the relationship of the parties to each other. Its real meaning was the reaffirmation of the relationships between the two groups, while providing outside observers—the Congress, the White House, and the public—with the illusion that the intentions of the securities laws with respect to the determination of accounting principles were being carried out effectively.

The SEC as Onlooker

By the mid-sixties the SEC had adopted the role of onlooker when it came to the *general* area of developing rules for financial reporting. On some specific issues, however, it was more aggressive. For example, it pushed for product line reporting by diversified companies (Barr, 1967c: 2; 1968: 8; 1969b: 3–5; Casey, 1972i: 11; *WSJ,*

July 18, 1969: 8; October 27, 1970: 22; April 15, 1971: 1), and it suggested inclusion of profit forecasts in annual reports (Cook, 1973d: 5–10; 1973b: 15–16; *WSJ*, June 9, 1972: 8; December 11, 1972: 8). Whether SEC efforts to force disclosure of product line profits were effective, at least some attempt was made toward obtaining this information.

On the really important questions of which institution would exercise control and initiative for the development of financial standards and of how the pooling-versus-purchase controversy should be resolved, the SEC took a near-neutral position, carrying to its logical conclusion the passive role adopted first by the 1936–1938 commission, some two years after the SEC was founded. SEC spokesmen either ignored or were ignorant of the battle that had taken place within the SEC between 1934 and 1936 over whether the government should establish accounting principles. The cozy relationship that existed between the Institute and the SEC in the 1960s was presumed to have existed from the outset, and was mythicized by SEC representatives into a kind of faith (Barr, 1970b: 9; Needham, 1971b: 1; Owens, 1971: 2). Speaking to the AAA convention in September, 1964, SEC Chairman Manuel F. Cohen took the typical position on the subject:

> No one can dispute the assertion that the Commission has the power to decree "acceptable" accounting principles and practices. I think it is common knowledge that we have, at various times, been urged to do just that. However, from its *inception,* the Commission has preferred co-operation with the profession to governmental action and has actively encouraged accountants to take the initiative in regulating their practices and in setting standards of conduct. In response, the profession, although not the recipient of delegated power . . . , has performed an important service as a self-regulatory institution [italics supplied] (Cohen, M. F., 1965: 5–6).

Cohen also indicated the SEC's reliance on current practice, and, by indirection, its lack of activity in the field of research:

> Our forms and rules have been kept current through the joint efforts of the profession and our chief accountants office. [T]he Commission's accounting rules . . . represent a codification of the best practices . . . by leading professional accountants over the past 30 years. This has been accomplished in a spirit of co-operation and voluntary action (Ibid., p. 5).

Cooperation efforts between the accounting profession and the SEC have always been a major theme for SEC spokesmen (Barr, 1963: 12; 1968: 3; 1970b: 10; 1970d: 3; Owens, 1971: 23). Referring again in 1966 to the mythical "beginning" of relations between accountants and SEC, Cohen stated:

> From the beginning, the Commission has, in the main however, held that authority in reserve, in the expectation that the independent accountants would actively exercise the initiative they had sought and secured. With some exceptions, our expectations have been realized. To the extent that the profession has been willing to move ahead, we have been content to remain logically in the background, filling a vacuum when necessary in stimulating study and development of accounting and auditing principles on a continuing basis (Cohen, M. F., 1966b: 56–57).

To exercise the function assigned the accountants by the SEC, their independence was critical, Cohen said. The application of alternative accounting principles was an impediment to financial statement comparability, although he recognized that registrants under the 1933 and 1934 acts were permitted considerable leeway in accounting, compared with the detailed, uniform systems of accounts required of public utility holding companies under the 1935 act. The SEC was "a strong influence in the development of accounting standards generally. . . . informal, day to day activity of accountants and the role of the Chief Accountant had been important," said Cohen. The flexibility-uniformity debate was an important issue; comparability was good, but it was uncertain if it could be developed; uniformity was good, but the accountants had not been able to achieve it in many significant areas. The SEC would operate in cases where there were reconcilable differences between it and the profession. But in any event, the SEC would continue its cooperative activities with financial institutions (Cohen, M. F., 1966b: 56–60).

The SEC position thus had become stereotyped by the mid-sixties. It was further confirmed by SEC Commissioner Needham: "As far as accounting principles are concerned, the Commission has always believed that the profession should set the standards and that all others should voluntarily comply with them," although that opinion "wasn't universal," he added (*JA*, August, 1970: 10). To all intents and purposes, then, the SEC operated as if the formulation of accounting principles was taking place in another world, and that its function was merely advisory.

The speeches and articles written by SEC commissioners and the Chief Accountant in the 1960s reveal recurrent themes. The Commission continued to support the development of accounting principles by the profession, and stressed their prior examination of ARBs before release; the daily review activity of the SEC was also considered important (Barr, 1963: 12–14). The SEC claimed it worked closely with the AICPA and gave it their support (Barr, 1970d: 3; 1970b: 10; Owens, 1971: 2–3). The Financial Analysts were considered important (Casey, 1972i: 11–12; Barr, 1965: 21) particularly in view of the continuing reaffirmation of the SEC's emphasis on disclosure (Casey, 1972c: 9; 1972h: 14; 1972i: 1–10; Cook, 1973b: 1, 11–14; 1973d: 1–4; 1973e: 21; Barr, 1968: 2, 14; Barr and Koch, 1959: 176).

Major SEC nonfeasance occurred when corporate pressures were greatest. Even though the dangers regarding too much emphasis on earnings per share were manifest in 1965, nothing was done to remove them because the SEC was too committed to alternate methods of implementing generally accepted accounting principles (Barr, 1965: 16; 25). It was also recognized that the problem of business combinations needed to be resolved (Barr, 1967b: 13), that there were significant earnings per share abuses and that claims about corporate synergism might not be justified (Barr, 1968: 11). But here, too, corporate pressure and SEC lethargy allowed the problems to continue. The SEC finally acknowledged, too late, that there had been an erosion of pooling standards (Barr, 1969b: 10; 1970a: 8) and the Congress finally questioned the use of convertible debentures. The SEC was also fully aware of what was going on in the conglomerate merger movement and the use of pooling (Barr, 1969b: 15).

The SEC was incapable of taking direct action. Instead, AICPA action on the pooling rules, when it came, was described as joint action between the SEC and the APB, with the commission supporting the February, 1970, APB exposure draft—to which the Financial Executives Institute was opposed (Barr, 1970a: 10; 1970d: 4). The FEI was deeply involved in the business-combination controversy (Barr, 1970d: 4–5) and the SEC finally made concessions to get accountants and businessmen to accept the business combinations rules recommended by the APB (Owens, 1971: 4). It was claimed afterward that the SEC took the lead in urging the AICPA to develop rules covering the reporting of business combinations (Owens, 1971: 3).

After the rulings on accounting for business combinations were adopted, and the conglomerate merger movement waned, the SEC became more concerned about what had happened. There had been a great deal of slowness all around, according to William J. Casey, SEC Chairman. The accountants had been slow in tightening their pooling rules; the SEC was slow in not requiring disclosures to correct misleading impressions, and the analysts were slow in not putting the available information in proper perspective (Casey, 1971b: 8). Corporate operations had been obscured by accounting, and what was needed was an "honest count." "I believe," said Casey, "the public has lost more money through the use of permissible variations in accounting to exaggerate earnings and growth and to obscure declining performance than through the whole catalogue of things which we have made impermissible" (Casey, 1973: 4). Casey's solution, of course, was to require disclosure of both accounting policies and the significance of accounting variations.

On one matter, the SEC was of good assistance to the accounting practitioners. Corporations had not been averse to shopping around among accounting firms to find one that would agree with the treatment their management wanted (Barr, 1968: 16). In fairness, it must be noted that the SEC considered management primarily responsible for the presentation of accounts. Corporations also made efforts to pit one accounting firm against others in an effort to secure the best possible presentation of their accounts (Needham, 1971a: 3). The SEC did place a ruling into effect that corporate changes of auditors had to be reported to the commission (Casey, 1972h: 13).

The SEC's inability to take action compatible with its legislative responsibilities was commented upon eloquently by Professor Anthony in 1963 when it seemed impossible to believe the SEC would permanently remain quiescent in the face of AICPA paralysis.[1]

> . . . the SEC is responsible for safeguarding the public interest. It cannot tolerate indefinitely a situation in which the accounting reports submitted to it have less meaning than they should have because they are not constructed on a solid foundation of generally accepted accounting principles. The SEC has looked to the AICPA to fill this need; but if it concludes that the AICPA is not going to do so, then it presumably must take action on its own. Under these circumstances, for the SEC to refuse to act would be to abrogate its statutory responsibility to the public (Anthony, 1963: 102).

But the SEC *could* tolerate the situation indefinitely, and the presumption that the SEC would take action on its own proved wrong, abrogation of statutory responsibility to the public or not. In 1970 Professor Kripke concluded that the SEC failed in its duty between 1945 and 1970 by being so forbearing toward accountants on the matter of improving accounting. The "end of the 1960s was the worse period of corporate abuse since the end of the 1920s, and many of the problems lay exactly in the difference between something that is fairly presented in accordance with generally accepted accounting principles, and something that is fairly presented." The SEC ought to act as an early-warning system, and not be "mesmerized" by the auditing statements of leading firms (Kripke, 1970a: 289).

A suggestion of future SEC action on accounting principles, now referred to as financial standards, was offered by another utilization of "the threat" which surfaced in 1970:

> Concern about the possibility of the SEC's exercising its statutory powers is well founded in my view. If the board were to fail in its efforts to improve financial reporting, the SEC probably would step in—it has said so many times. Most of us think the job can best be done by the private sector.
>
> In February, 1969, SEC Chairman Homer Budge, appearing before a Congressional Committee, warned that if the profession didn't solve the pooling or purchase accounting problems soon, the Commission itself might have to do so (Armstrong, 1970: 68–69).

Pooling-purchase rules were issued; the FASB replaced the APB. Both events passively witnessed by the SEC. The present composition of the FASB, which permits the primary users of accounting principles to formulate those principles, places the SEC in a weaker position than ever before. Because the SEC approved the changeover from the APB to the FASB, apparently equating reorganization with improvement—it can be argued that it is now obliged to "give it a chance to work." If it does not work, of course, "the threat" can once again be invoked. As Chief Accountant Burton put it as recently as 1973: "We will continue to refer problems to the FASB and if we do not get a response, we might have to take a position."

The Curious Cases of ASR No. 146, and Lease Disclosure

Sometimes new personalities can breathe life into a near moribund operation. Various independent regulatory agencies from time to time take on added vigor, and in the process cause their regulatees some concern. The Federal Trade Commission went through such a period in the early 1970s, and it was still showing some important activity in 1974. In 1973–1974, the Securities and Exchange Commission caused considerable anguish among FASB members and their supporters over two accounting rules.

It was an amazing show of aggressiveness on accounting matters for the SEC. Chief Accountant Burton appears to have been the catalyst. The first incident involved an interpretation of APB Opinion No. 16's criteria for pooling. At issue was whether a company could use stock reacquired on the open market as the exchange basis for a pooling if the stock was acquired during the two years prior to the merger. Opinion No. 16 concluded that if cash or other assets were used, or liabilities were incurred to accomplish the business combination, it should be accounted for as a purchase. The fear was that a firm purchasing its own shares on the open market and using those shares to acquire the assets or stock of a firm it wanted to acquire, would thereby be circumventing the purchase accounting requirement under APB Opinion No. 16—that is, the stock of the acquired firm obtained and used in that manner was merely a device to avoid the purchase interpretation, and ASR No. 146 so interpreted it.

Issuance of ASR No. 146 by the SEC caused near apoplexy and actual revolt in the financial community, particularly among the accountants, who had advised their clients that treasury stock repurchased on the open market would qualify under pooling, not purchase, criteria. The practitioners were both shocked and embarrassed. The ruling was issued on August 24, 1973, and the accountants were quick to respond. And what a response! It was the best SEC-accountant fight since the investment credit imbroglio; it "provoked the strongest barrage of protest in memory from the accounting profession" (*Wall Street Journal*, October 8, 1973: 2). Arthur Andersen & Co. entered a law suit twenty days after the ruling was issued, asking for an injunction against it as a violation of the Administrative Procedure Act, which requires federal agencies to give regulatees the opportunity for comment by first making proposed rules public before putting them into effect. The commission had not invited comments. In addition to the Arthur Andersen law suit, Price Waterhouse & Co. formally petitioned the SEC to reconsider, and Peat, Marwick, Mitchell & Co., the nation's largest firm, "submitted a stiff letter" charging the SEC with "effectively circumventing" the FASB (Ibid.).

The SEC beat a hasty, but as it turned out, partly temporary retreat. It suspended ASR 146 as a rule in October, reclassified it as a proposal, and invited comments—which it got. This compromise led to another. In early April, 1974, the SEC affirmed the ruling, but said it would not apply it retroactively. This stipulation meant that stock purchased in the past two years would be exempt, but in the future, the two-year rule would apply. Chief Accountant Burton was quoted as saying the decision against not making the interpretation retroactive was a "significant concession" (*Wall Street Journal,* April 12, 1974, 12).

The other incident occurred in the fall of 1973 when the SEC adopted a proposal forcing firms to disclose more information about lease arrangements. The proposal was "widely opposed by businessmen and accountants" (*Wall Street Journal,* October 8, 1973: 2). It preempted the FASB, which had not expected to get to the matter until 1975, from ruling on it. Burton thought two years too long to wait, particularly because the SEC had tried to get the APB to deal with the issue satisfactorily in June, 1972. "The comission's new lease-disclosure rules drew 134 letters of comment, all negative" (Ibid., 8). The provision requiring earnings impact to be shown if "financing leases" were capitalized or treated as debt was the least popular. The new ruling also required companies to reveal the present value of their minimum commitments to future lease arrangements. The SEC thought these rules necessary to enhance comparability with firms that were financed through borrowing rather than leasing. Capitalizing leases means treating them like debt, and showing a larger annual charge against earnings. Businessmen disliked the requirement and they objected to the idea of having to record the transaction on the balance sheet, rather than treating it as an expense on the income statement only. The *Wall Street Journal's* reporting of the event even went so far as to refer to the SEC's "activist accounting staff."

Did these two incidents suggest that the SEC was heading toward a confrontation with the FASB and the accountants? Probably not, inasmuch as the SEC agreed to the formation of the FASB and is obliged to see that it operates for several years, at least. But they did show a side of the SEC that had not been in evidence for a long time. An article appearing in the *Financial Executive,* the journal of the FEI, put the matter succinctly: "The Financial Accounting Standards Board was set up to keep the standards-setting function within the private sector. ASR No. 146 comes perilously close to standards-setting by the public sector. This is perhaps the most important issue of all" (Foster, 1974a: 52). The two incidents do not mean that concern over the traditionally quiescent SEC may now be discarded, that a "new" SEC is on hand. The private sector did, after all, force the commission to back down on the ASR 146 question. But what it does mean, is that Chief Accountant John C. Burton may well deserve the Sly Fox of the Year Award.

Mythicizing the SEC-Accountant Relationship

Transformation of the early accountant-SEC history into myth requires a brief comment. There is little or no recognition in present writings by either accounting practitioners or SEC spokesmen of the struggle over the formation of the commission and the desire of the financial community in the 1930s to install an independent regulatory agency more susceptible than the FTC to its influence. Instead, one finds constant mention that the SEC *never* exercised any authority over the determination of accounting principles, that the commission and the practitioners have always enjoyed friendly relations. The first assertion is incorrect: about two and a half years elapsed before the accountants were given authority to develop accounting principles, during which the SEC vigorously established reporting forms and rules and set the limits of its influence. As for the second assertion, some factual basis does exist for stating that amicable relations were established between the two institutions, but considerable acrimony also erupted at different times, particularly at the outset of SEC operations. There has been a continuing undercurrent of mistrust of the SEC by the accountants since the thirties; it waned during World War II, but it has been periodically apparent since the war. For example, the two institutions were at odds over the investment credit issue and during consideration of Opinions 16 and 17, when the SEC failed to back the stronger (than finally adopted) pooling requirements recommended in the APB's February, 1970, exposure draft. Some specific reference can be found in print to the widespread resentment generated by the latter incident. Members of the AICPA felt that once again the SEC had failed to back the Accounting Principles Board (Savoie, 1973: 11–12). Mythicizing both the assignment of authority and the amicable relations facilitates the maintenance of cooperative relations between the two groups, but it undermines any attempt to take the ritualized threat mechanism seriously. Had SEC spokesmen really wanted "the threat" to be menacing rather than ceremonial, would it not have been more effective to refer to the less passive pre-1937 SEC stance and to the fact that only by a 3-to-2 vote were the accounting practitioners given the opportunity to develop accounting principles? Public statements about the constantly friendly relations between SEC and accountants both supports and disguises the true nature of their interaction. And thus both groups are given the opportunity to solidify their relations with each other, in private.

THE REVERSAL OF ROLES BETWEEN THE SEC AND THE ACCOUNTING PROFESSION

Role reversal has been one of the striking interaction characteristics between the SEC and the accounting profession, and emphasizes an authority relationship whereby the SEC looks toward the accounting profession for direction, rather than the reverse. This transposition of authority relationships does much to explain the process of institutionalization between the accountants and the SEC. In this sense, it is typical of the general mode of identification developed by independent regulatory agencies with client groups, and explains why IRA commissioners became so comfortable about taking their cues from their regulatees. It is both a path of least resistance and a very distinct identification process. It helps to develop a better understanding of the SEC when the commission is seen as part of a larger constituency, the nation's financial sector. The accounting practitioners are a part of that sector, and, to the SEC, they are seen as authority figures. An illustration of this mentality can be seen in the following quotation by a member of the accounting firm of Arthur Young & Co.: "Thus far, the Commission has chosen—in my view, wisely so—to leave the establishment of accounting principles to the AICPA. The SEC has, however, acted usefully as an interested and informed contributor to the Institute's activities" (Hicks, 1969: 59).

Note the marvelous, almost unconscious, reversal of roles made by the author; the SEC was useful to the accounting profession, rather than the reverse. It is a typical accounting practitioner perspective, one widely prevalent in the financial sector. It is striking how little the relations between SEC and accountants have changed since they were formalized between 1936 and 1938. The perspective of the accounting practitioners toward "proper" functions of the SEC remains consistent with their main thinking in the 1930s.[2]

A persuasive case can be argued that the corporate sector has always been the dominant influence behind the liaison between the accountants and the SEC in their interaction over the determination of accounting principles. This influence is periodically acknowledged by both the accountants and the SEC, particularly in reference to the client's selection of accounting principles. "It is plain that management *is* becoming very interested in the work of the board" said Savoie, the executive vice president of the AICPA, at the time the conglomerate merger movement was in full swing (Savoie, 1968: 38). Savoie's comment became more bitter subsequently, when he described the combination of industrial and accounting firms that forced the abandonment of the APB (Savoie, 1974: 11–12). The fact that the FEI had been extremely aggressive in pushing its views on the SEC when the commission was considering more detailed conglomerate reporting was also noted by SEC Chairman Cohen (Cohen, M. F., 1966b: 59). Leonard Spacek, the outspoken member of Arthur Andersen, Inc., has been very clear in indicating the extent of client influence.

> But what does the public accountant do in passing on financial statements that use alternative principles of accounting? Does he justify the alternative procedure used by determining whether it produces the most accurate and reliable end result in terms of income? Indeed not. Where alternative accounting principles or conventions are available, it is the client that makes the choice. All the public accountant can do is try to influence the client by persuasion, assuming he has a conviction one way or the other (Spacek, 1958: 371).

After the Wheat Committee Report was approved on May 2, 1972 by the Council of the AICPA, SEC Chairman Casey said, "We believe . . . development of accounting standards should stay in the private sector and hope that the new structure will increase public confidence in accounting principles and in financial reporting generally" (Johns, 1972: 534). The innocuous position of the SEC was thereby reaffirmed once again.

But not all persons approved of the SEC-AICPA operations. Professor Kripke noted the role reversal (Kripke, 1972: 393),[3] and indicated that in the case of an APB hearing on the valuation of marketable securities by insurance companies, the SEC had submitted position papers to the APB! In a proper relationship, the APB and other accountants would submit their views to the SEC, which would then announce the governing rules, he said. While Kripke argued the SEC should exert its accounting powers more forcefully, he questioned whether, considering the SEC's attitudes, it would be wise to have it actually intervene more forcefully!

But in spite of criticism like Kripke's, the ritualization of the SEC-accountant interaction continues, as witness the following report of a "sharply worded statement" on accounting profession non-feasance by Chairman Casey in late 1972:

> In a strongly worded speech before the American Institute of Certified Public Accountants in Denver, SEC Chairman William J. Casey asserted that after "looking back at the record," he is "virtually forced" to the view the commission should be "more vigorous" in overseeing the accounting profession.
>
> Mr. Casey's sharply worded statement wasn't at all that surprising, as the SEC in the recent past has suggested that it would take some action if the accounting profession didn't act to overcome its shortcomings. And, the accountants generally responded favorably to the speech (*Wall Street Journal,* Oct. 3, 1972, p. 3).

The reversed situation continued after the FASB began operations. Practitioners still express fear over possible SEC activism (Foster, 1974b: 31–32), and the government is described as a "vitally interested spectator" of private sector deliberations on how financial standards are to be developed (van Pelt, 1972b: 16).

Accountant Professionalism

American accountants have striven noisily for professional status since the turn of the century. Has this long-sought goal been achieved?

Measured in a political dimension, the professional achievements of practitioner accountants have been considerable. The amount of pressure they exerted upon Congress at the time of the debates over the Securities Exchange Act, and later on the SEC over the authority for formulating accounting principles, was impressive. In their ability to exercise influence on the public sector, the accountants achieved an advanced professional level by the 1930s. From an organizational standpoint, they also achieved professional maturity in the thirties, at the very latest when the AIA was reunited with the ASCPA in 1936. From the time of 1930s, then, there has been a very powerful accounting association speaking for members of the profession and guarding their interests. The later growth of the National Association of Accountants (NAA)—formerly the National Association of Cost

Accountants—in the 1960s further strengthened the professional power of the accountants.

The technical accomplishments of the accounting profession are more difficult to assess. Individual problems have been handled with great skill, and many are debated and researched with diligence in the journals. There is a broad range of accounting literature, much of it becoming more mathematical, sophisticated, and systems oriented. Also, the body of accounting knowledge has expanded commendably, though much of it is abstract and has obscure, if any, immediate application. Yet this is the problem, or advantage, of "pure" research in any field; applications cannot always be determined before the research is undertaken. The more important criticism to which the profession is subject, and which reflects on accounting professionalism as a whole, is that the *practice* of accounting and the resolution of accounting questions continues to be handled on an ad hoc basis. The price of this take-them-as-they-come attitude is internal inconsistency and a permissiveness of techniques that makes the resulting data difficult to understand, and sometimes even dangerous for investors and government to use. This critique was the essence of the attacks on the APB during the 1960s.

Another dimension of professionalism can be identified as devotion to the larger constituency, the public interest. In what sense have accountants measured up to this criterion? The grandiose assertions of accountant responsibility to the public are difficult to reconcile with the behavior of the accounting practitioners, particularly in terms of their reluctance to curtail the ruinous speculation associated with the conglomerate merger movement by eliminating the abuses of the pooling-purchase alternatives. In continually attempting to limit their liability to third parties, the public accounting practitioners might also be found wanting when it comes to the public interest. But no one, of course, is obliged to seek or accept additional liability, and accountants should not be criticized on this basis alone.

Perhaps a better test is whether accountants acquitted themselves of their professional responsibility to the public less well than some other professions, for example, medicine and law. Here again, it is difficult to make any comparative judgment. Medicine and law have been socially deficient in many areas, and have been criticized accordingly. The American Bar Association and the American Medical Association have never been slow to protect the interest of their members. If lawyers and doctors have accomplished more professionally than accountants, both law and medicine are older professions, and are far more oriented toward people than things. But one criticism does appear justified, and that is that the practitioners never went beyond a level of reluctant cooperation with government. Their consistent ideological antigovernment attitude hampered their performance in the public's interest: the client's interest got first, foremost, and in many cases, exclusive consideration.

Preempted Academics?

Another serious gap in accountant professionalism is the failure of the academic accountants to gain sufficient operational influence within their field. For one thing, they have been too deferential. Members of the American Accounting Association considered undertaking a study on accounting principles about the same time the Wheat Committee began its operations. When requested by the AICPA to withhold their study until the Wheat Report was completed, the AAA obliged. This submissiveness by the AAA was consistent with its traditionally compliant attitude toward practicing accountants. Academic accountants have been employed by the APB and in the AICPA to conduct research, but they have not fared well, as witness the fate of Research Studies 1, 3, and 5. The effects of accounting research as published in the *Accounting Review* had little effect upon APB Opinions. Like the practitioners, the academics have failed to move with determination toward development of a comprehensive accounting code; they also tend to share the practitioner's anti-government bias.

The difference between the status of academic accountants and academic legal scholars helps explain the fact that the academic accountants have less influence. Legal scholars enjoy considerably more prestige within their profession than academic accountants do in theirs. Traditionally, legal scholars, in their writings, have contributed a great deal toward improving jurisprudence, law in general, and legal procedure, largely because they have a very important audience whom they address: the courts. The accounting scholar's higher authority exists mostly in the form of the administrative authority present in the SEC. But the commission lacks the independence of the courts because of its political vulnerability and the limitations inherent in combining the functions of accuser and judge. Under the circumstances academic accountants, who for the most part are outside of the practitioner-client-SEC system, must play a less significant role, unless specifically assigned one legislatively.

The academics, however, have more or less acquiesced in this lesser role. They have never seriously engaged in consistent lobbying activities with the Congress or with the SEC to try to improve accounting principles. They have permitted themselves to be used by the accounting practitioners and by the financial community by holding secondary or token positions on the APB and the FASB, knowing that the real decisions would be dictated by either the AICPA or the FEI. But does the academic internal reward structure, at least within the first rank universities, encourage participation in the problems of administration and use of accounting conventions? The question is arguable, but to the extent that promotions are contingent on publication of abstract, mathematically based papers, there will be less liklihood of academic participation in the public policy oriented issues concerned with the determination of corporate financial reporting regulations.

Should Academics Abandon the FASB?

Should the academic accountants divorce themselves from the Financial Accounting Standards Board? The move would have some disadvantages in the short run for the academics because they would lose whatever token functions they have in the development of day-to-day accounting rules. Some also argue that because FASB rules provide for dissenting opinions when the requisite five-member vote of approval is obtained, they would have the opportunity to register variant opinions, and that consequently AAA representation on the FASB need not imply AAA endorsement of FASB opinions. It is a persuasive argument, but not persuasive enough.

The AAA should withdraw from the FASB and its associated groups for two reasons. First, the legitimacy of the FASB is very tenuous. The Securities and Exchange Commission may not have been directed by Congress to assume the responsibility for the development of accounting principles, but it is questionable whether the commission could have carried through its mission without developing GAAPs, something the Congress in 1934 may not have understood. It is even more questionable whether the SEC has the legal right to delegate the admittedly optional authority provision to determine financial standards. It is a point requiring clarification.[4] If the SEC does not have that legal right to delegate its authority, then SEC approval of the FASB is not legitimately conferred, and the FASB has no legal authorization to do what it is doing. AAA presence on the FASB lends de facto legitimacy to that group. And because the FASB is a private group performing a public function with predictable results under questionable legal authority, the AAA ought not to lend it its support.

Secondly, AAA participation on the FASB siphons attention from academic consideration of financial standards in their broader application to the requirements of public policy. Furthermore, it prevents academic consideration of those standards as a comprehensive, internally consistent, and reliably interpretable body of rules. FASB operations, like those of the CAP and APB before it, will be hampered by political considerations and client concerns. It is not an atmosphere in which unbiased research can be undertaken and thrive. Also, the AAA may not assume an adversary position toward the FASB if it is represented on it, which it could do if it were independent. It should be added, of course, that whether AAA representation on the FASB gives the Association's official sanction to FASB Statements is still subject to debate.

FUTURE RESEARCH

Academic accountants differ about what kind of research is desirable and who ought to do it. They appear to be too sensitive to the views of the practitioners, their former students. Professor Mautz made a plea in 1965 for practitioners to understand that research may not be immediately applicable, but is valuable nevertheless, and that practitioners really do not understand what is meant by research (Mautz, 1965: 299–300). Anyone who can do research, should, he believed, and greater support for research ought to be available. Unlike the physical sciences where researchers had funds from government and the military and from private sources, he pointed out that nothing comparable was available for accounting researchers. But Mautz did not recommend that the AAA try to generate these funds and undertake the research as an organization.

Professor Briloff, who by 1967 had given up on the APB doing anything timely about pooling abuses, hoped that the event would draw academic scholarly attention. They ought to "ferret . . . out . . . the cases . . . where generally accepted accounting principles have produced . . . anachronisms, and . . . give them the widest circulation" (Briloff, 1967: 496).

For academicians distrusting increased government activity on accounting principles, slow or no progress in the improvement of accounting appeared an inevitable price. Dean Sidney Davidson of the Chicago Graduate School of Business and member of the APB, looked at it this way: "The SEC has enormous power to prescribe accounting procedures. Fortunately, the Commission has chosen to let that power lie dormant but the spectre of its exercise is a forceful reminder to the accounting profession that there can be no relaxing in its search for improvement" (Davidson, 1969: 31). Radical departures from existing ways of accounting development were not recommended: "For those of us who accept the evolutionary nature of accounting, the starting point for the next decade is the framework of accounting as we know it today" (Ibid., p. 30). "Unfortunately," he added, "efforts to develop a set of accounting postulates and principles reveal the ad hoc nature of many of our present rules," which appeared likely to continue as the future research orientation of the profession. Efforts like ARS Nos. 1 and 3 would "continue to produce comments" that the proposed changes are too radically different for adoption at this time. This will force problems to be dealt with on a "one-by-one" basis (Davidson, 1969: 32).

The Briloff and Davidson approaches are compatible. Both suggest improvement through gradual development and by examination of current practice, with Briloff advocating more of an "exposure" orientation than Davidson. But is the evolutionary approach sufficient? Has it any promise of offering the kind of firm financial standards on which investors and government can rely? These questions are rhetorical, of course. Meaningful research in accounting and financial standards demand something beyond both the "exposure" and "evolution" approaches in order to prevent repetitions of the accounting abuses of the past, and to give some hope of substantial improvements in the future.

Notes

1.   "So far the SEC has not had the will to act. The Commissioners have hoped all along that the accounting profession itself would take the necessary action. Indeed, the Commission has done everything it could to encourage the development of principles through the mechanisms created by the profession. Although the SEC has been forced to make a few pronouncements on principles so as to meet urgent problems on which the profession was unwilling to take any action whatsoever, it has done so reluctantly and only after giving the profession full opportunity to carry the ball. Andrew Barr himself has made it abundantly clear that he dis-

270 CORPORATE FINANCIAL REPORTING

likes the thought of having accounting principles prescribed by a government agency" (Anthony, 1963: 10).

2.   Contrast the following quotations, for example, with those made by accounting practitioners during the thirties as recorded earlier.

> And the SEC, which has jurisdiction over certain of the reports of the group of companies relatively small in number but great in importance, has wisely confined its requirements to full and fair disclosure with only a minimum of prescription of accounting standards to be uniform for all (Bevis, 1961: 12).

> Thus it is clear that neither comparability among financial statements nor any other interests of investors are better served per se by centrally promulgated uniform accounting rules. Any group involved in promulgating pronouncements, whether the SEC or the accounting principles board must keep that carefully in mind (Bevis, 1966: 37).

Herman W. Bevis was former senior partner in Price Waterhouse & Co., active in the AICPA, and a Board member of the CASB. See p. 298.

3.   "The spectacle of the SEC submitting position papers to the APB as to what accounting principles should be in order that the APB can make a determination which the SEC will then enforce (presumably whether or not the board has agreed with the SEC's submission) reverses the appropriate state of affairs" (Kripke, 1972: 393).

4.   It is a debatable and interesting legal point, which deserves more attention from legal scholars than it has gotten.

17

Public or private control?

Financial Reporting and Public Policy

ACCOUNTANT'S LIABILITY, SEC INACTION, AND THE COURTS

The securities acts of the early thirties sought to force disclosure of relevant financial information for investors. The Securities and Exchange Commission received the mandate from Congress to determine what information ought to be disclosed, and it was given the authority to set rules for required financial reporting. The two new acts placed responsibility upon accountants for auditing financial statements. The SEC certainly did not do all that it could toward promoting disclosure. It did not bring stockholder reports under the securities acts. It took belated, ineffective steps for product line reporting. It never provided for comparability between the financial reports of different corporations, even in the same industry.

The commision abrogated its responsibility for setting rules of financial reporting by turning over that responsibility to the accountants. This transfer of authority also helped limit accountant liability to the public, a serious omission that has begun to be corrected by the courts, without regard to whether generally accepted accounting principles are followed. The broader the range of acceptable accounting alternatives that might be characterized as "generally accepted," the more easily could accountants avoid liability to third parties, as long as the criterion of acceptability was whether the principle followed had general or "substantial" acceptance. By permitting alternative accounting treatments, the SEC became party to limiting accountant liability, thus helping circumvent one of the broad objectives of the securities acts.

Steps toward reaffirming and tightening accountants' liability to third parties were taken during the 1960s by the courts, not by the SEC. This study can only give cursory treatment to the changes that occurred in the legal liability of accountants. The doctrine of *Ultramares* (1931) later was expanded by some jurisdictions when accountants were found liable to third parties for simple negligence if they foresaw that such third parties would rely on their statement. A cause of action was also found present if auditors remained silent after having discovered in the course of special studies that they had certified incorrect statements. In 1970 the case of *United States* v. *Simon*,[1] initiated by the U.S. Attorney for the Southern District of New York, provided a legal basis for further weakening the protective limits previously available to accountants, even if generally accepted accounting principles were followed. A footnote contained in a corporation's financial statement was alleged to have been materially misleading because it understated the magnitude and significance of certain advances it made to an affiliated company. Eight nationally recognized accountants testified that the defendant conformed to generally accepted accounting principles. The defendant, nevertheless, was convicted at a second trial, and the conviction was affirmed by the Second Circuit Court of Appeals. Attorney A. A. Sommer, prior to his SEC appointment,[2] offered an evaluation of what had happened:

> More disturbing to the accounting profession than the conviction itself was the language in which Judge Henry J. Friendly, surely one of the most knowledgeable of federal judges in financial and accounting matters, wrapped the affirmance. He said in effect that the first law for accountants was not compliance with generally accepted accounting principles, but rather full and fair disclosure, fair presentation, and if the principles did not produce this brand of disclosure, accountants could not hide behind the principles but had to go beyond them and make whatever additional disclosures were necessary for full disclosure. In a word, "present fairly" was a concept separate from "generally accepted accounting principles," and the latter did not necessarily result in the former (Sommer, 1970: 209).

The *Simon* case suggests that in the future accountants will not be able to rely upon having followed "generally accepted accounting principles" as a defense, if following them does not result in a fair presentation of the relevant facts, and damage is sustained as a result. Furthermore, the *Ultramares* rule is likely to erode rapidly as more courts permit third party recovery on a basis of negligence, particularly where the accountants have knowledge that the reports they prepare will be used by a particular party or class of parties. Here, of course, the determination of the parties to be protected is crucial. If the courts expand the definition of those persons who "rely" upon the accountant's statement, the accountant will become correspondingly vulnerable, and it looks as if greater accountant liability *will* be the wave of the future.[3] As a case in point, accountants presently are being challenged in the courts on their failure to discover fraudulent client internal accounting controls. In a Federal appeals court opinion delivered by Chief Judge Luther Merritt Swygert, it was held that one of the big eight firms, Ernst and Ernst, could be considered an abettor to a fraud of which "it admittedly had no knowledge. The firm would become liable if its audit had missed something important because of lack of due care, . . ." (*Wall Street Journal*, 9/19/74: 4). The decision, which is controversial and bound to be argued on rehearing, departs from the present legal rule that, to be considered to have abetted in a fraud, both knowledge and wrongdoing are required. The decision is another step in the present trend for courts to demand higher standards of accountant performance toward third parties.

Accountants were thus being subjected to an "unprecedented number of lawsuits" beginning in the late sixties. Some observers saw it as a time of both prosperity and peril, noted that the older cases like *Ultramares* and *McKesson-Robbins* were based mainly on auditing deficiencies, and blamed the increasing lawsuits on the greater articulation of accounting principles, which were making accountants more vulnerable to plaintiffs in "heretofore untested situations" (Reiling and Taussig, 1970: 39–41; 47).

Accounting practitioners were also concerned about research that would restrict accounting principles and perhaps make them more vulnerable legally. The problem had always been recognized and was the foundation of their demand for flexibility. If accounting principles became final and limited, it would make accountants an easier legal target because they would then have a specific standard to meet. This dilemma was recognized clearly by Spacek, who nevertheless argued in 1958 for greater certainty in accounting principles:

> . . . we must not permit alternative principles or conventions of accounting to be accepted. . . . There are those who

> say this would freeze accounting and prevent progress. How-
> ever, the reverse is true. Alternative accounting principles do
> not encourage improvement in accepted principles—they merely
> provide the leverage to eliminate the preferable principles in
> favor of those that produce less desirable or inaccurate results.
> Under alternative principles of accounting, most of the pressure
> is to follow the less desirable, not the most forthright (Spacek,
> 1958: 372–373).

At the time, accountants could avoid responsibility for the client's
election of accounting principles as long as it could be shown that the
principles were "generally accepted." Spacek thought, however, that
accountants should be responsible for the selection of the correct
principle (Ibid., p. 374).

In summary, it is evident that important changes in accountants'
liability are taking place as a matter of the common law process, not
through internal decisions by the accountants nor action by the SEC.
The prime agents of change are aggressive plaintiffs, U.S. attorneys,
and sophisticated judges. This activity in the courtroom suggests
that responsibiilty may be imposed more successfully upon the financial-industrial sector through appropriate court action, than through
the ordinary avenues of administrative law.

The SEC-accountant world has not yet been invaded by public-
interest litigation groups, to whom other areas of the public sector
have so far appeared more crucial, more accessible. It is only a question of time, however, before they attack corporate financial reporting. The SEC or the FASB or both may soon find themselves
defendants in cases challenging the present system of developing
rules governing accounting and financial standards.

Why Did the Accountants Fail to Develop Effective GAAPs?

The major reasons why the acounting profession failed to develop effective generally accepted accounting principles are apparent
from the operations of the Committee on Accounting Procedure in
1938 through the demise of the Accounting Principles Board in 1972–
1973. The accountants were guaranteed to fail by a combination of
circumstances.

The accounting practitioners of the AICPA were severely limited
by their method of approaching accounting research and the development of accounting principles. Such research as was done, was ad

hoc; each problem was taken as it arose. Those that were too controversial were avoided. The AICPA thereby created a group of
opinions without any necessary logical interrelation. No overall development plan for an accounting system was ever adopted.

The practitioners' cumbersome research organization also made
any significant accomplishments impossible. Part-time initially, the
research unit was always understaffed. The CAP and APB themselves
were both too large for efficient discussion and consideration and
neither was sufficiently backed by the AICPA council and a large
enough number of the controlling "big eight" firms. CAP and APB
Opinions were never officially mandatory upon the AICPA membership, and the two-thirds vote for adoption of Opinions promoted approval at the lowest level of agreement.

Another major handicap was the antiquated philosophy behind
the profession's approach to accounting research. Reliance upon
precedent guaranteed unsystematic results in pursuing the formulation of accounting principles. And accountants were supported in this
approach by the precedent-oriented lawyers on the SEC commission.
As its onetime Chairman Jerome N. Frank phrased it:

> As in law, so in accounting; for not only are many of the rules
> and principles not fixed and certain, but the facts to which they
> are applied, in each particular instance, are often matters about
> which reasonable men can differ. For, frequently, those facts
> rest upon judgment, upon opinion. And judgment and opinion
> are human and therefore fallible (Frank, 1939: 296).

Rather than start fresh and develop sets of accounting rules that had
objectives and assumptions behind them fostering systematic internal
consistency, the accountants relied upon precedent, which perpetuated inconsistent accounting methods justified by different accounting "principles," for identical situations. Their approach to
"principles" was akin to the natural law assumption that one could
"discover" them. It was an approach that resulted in enunciating
"principles" that appeared "natural" to the individual accountant,
which led, understandably enough, to infinite variations.

Practitioner ideology—anti-intellectual and antigovernment—also
placed severe boundaries on the range and depth of accounting research. Practitioner anti-intellectualism preempted the academics
who were thereby placed in ceremonial positions, unable to exercise
significant influence within the AICPA, though the academics, by
and large, accepted their secondary role. Anti-intellectualism resulted

in trivial, but constant, allegations of "impractical" against academics whenever they recommended adoption or consideration of deductively developed and internally consistent accounting systems. Anti-intellectualism also acted as a defense mechanism and helped to insulate themselves from criticism.

Antigovernment feeling caused the accounting practitioners to forgo the only real opportunity they had of achieving independence from their clients. It is highly questionable whether the practitioner was ever strong enough to withstand pressure from a client to use a certain accounting treatment, even when it was against the accountant's judgment. In his dependent employment relationship, the accountant becomes vulnerable when opposing the client's wishes too strenuously. When in the past the client's interest conflicted with the public interest, as in the conglomerate merger movement,[4] the AICPA became paralyzed and incapable of action over an extended period of time, and the public interest suffered. A code of accounting rules developed by the government, or developed by the AICPA and endorsed by the government, which eliminated or seriously restricted alternative treatment for identical transactions, would have provided the accountants with the leverage needed to resist client pressures. The practitioners could then have referred to a higher authority. Practitioner distrust of government in general and of the SEC in particular, however, closed this option. As a result, the practitioners not only have failed to achieve independence, but have had to share the authority for developing accounting rules with the client.

The accounting practitioners were also committed by self-interest to resist the development of comprehensive accounting principles. Reduction of accounting alternatives, each of which could be applied according to the "sound judgment" of the accountant, would also reduce the accountant's ability to serve the client—and, not so incidentally, his fee. Ego and self-esteem needs also work against the likelihood that accountants would create accounting principles limiting discretion.

Finally, the practitioners were isolated by a lack of SEC support at critical times. The failure of the commission to back the APB's February, 1970, exposure draft on business combinations signified the end to possible tight limitations on pooling. Their isolation also made the practitioners vulnerable to the superior political power of their clients, who were able to utilize the legislative and executive branches as sources of pressure upon the SEC. The only possibility for "independence" practitioners had in those instances would have been a pre-existing operating arrangement with the SEC to provide a unified stance.

All of the above factors apply at least as well to the FASB. The ad hoc nature of research is still evident; FASB opinions will still not be binding on the profession; and "principles," rather than a comprehensive code are still being sought. Anti-intellectual and antigovernment perspectives are still in evidence and likely to continue. Accountant self-interest and client orientation, so characteristic of the CAP and APB, has been replaced by a more powerful and more blatant accountant-client combination. Under these circumstances, practitioner allegations of independence are for the very credulous only.

Why Did the SEC Fail to Control the Development of Accounting Principles?

One of the main reasons behind the failure of the SEC to control the development of accounting principles was that the general power of the financial-industrial sector was too great for the new regulatory agency to withstand. Continuing harassment by the nation's financial sector forced the SEC to abrogate its authority to the practitioners. To be sure, several characteristics of the SEC facilitated passage of this authority: the legalistic orientation of the commissioners, their reliance on precedent, their conviction that they were administering a disclosure rather than a regulatory statute, and their preference for minimal government regulation and maximum self-regulation by the private sector. Lack of accounting sophistication in the thirties made it doubtful that *any* group could have devised an effective set of accounting principles. Nevertheless, the commission could have undertaken research leading *toward* the development of accounting principles, rather than abandoning the responsibility to the accounting practitioners.

Another continuing problem for the SEC was the absence of support for it from Congress and the White House, though it was dependent on both. Partly as a result, some have made the claim, and it is a credible one, that the SEC never had the funds and the resources to undertake an extensive accounting research program. It is also true, however, that it never contemplated or requested the funds or resources to do so. Furthermore, the commission's budget was more than $23 million for fiscal 1972, and it did engage in extensive studies of other subjects—of the institutional investor, for example (*Business Week,* April 3, 1971: 19).

Later SEC commissioners were quick to adopt the philosophy of their predecessors regarding financial standards development. The authority transfer saved the SEC from having to deal with the difficult problem of dictating reporting procedures to the politically resourceful financial-industrial sector. And short of a national financial crisis of the magnitude of the 1929 crash, there was, so far as the SEC was concerned, no real need or desire to take back its abrogated authority. As long as accounting principles responsibility could be located with a private group that it was "regulating," the SEC could claim it was being cooperative and that accounting principles were being developed by an authorized, qualified organization. Because the authority had not been legally transferred, the SEC could invoke "the threat" when things went wrong in order to give the semblance of concern and activism. The total effect of this interrelationship was the creation of an arrangement between the SEC and the accounting practitioners that served the needs of each—though it contributed subtantially, of course, to the failure of the SEC to control the development of accounting principles.

The arangement worked well for both groups. The SEC avoided major conflicts while still being able to perform its duties in a reasonably unobtrusive manner without being accused of complete irresponsibility. The accounting practitioners avoided developing accounting systems that would have reduced their own flexibility and remuneration while preserving for their clients a significant number of accounting, hence financial, options. In its failure to see to it that accounting principles were promulgated, the SEC became fully integrated into the financial-industrial system, without ever having deliberately planned it that way.

The SEC and the Financial-Industrial System

Was it an accident that the SEC adopted a cooperative relationship with the accounting profession rather than an adversary role? The allegation of co-optation by the regulated group of an IRA is common in the political science literature. As mentioned earlier, co-optation is most often seen as the result of a game plan of the regulated to capture the regulator. The relation between the Securities and Exchange Commission and the accountants superficially appears to have resulted in co-optation, but the "capture" explanation is too lean, and it ignores some of the more dynamic elements in the events that took place in the 1933–1973 period.

The control of financial accounting in the United States has passed through a four-step cycle since 1887, a somewhat arbitrary date, but the year in which the first national organization of accountants was formed. In this nearly 90-year period, the control of financial accounting began and ended in the corporate and financial sectors. The four-step cycle is as follows:

1887–1932   Financial-industrial system control
1933–1936   FTC-SEC control
1937–1972   Accountant control with increasing corporate influence and decreasing SEC influence
1973–   Financial-Industrial system control shared by accounting practitioners and the corporate sector.

The specific events that took place during these four cycles have been described in this study, and there is no need to repeat them other than to emphasize that the formation of the FASB marked the official return of the control over acounting principles to the corporate and financial sectors for the first time since 1933. During the sequence of events since 1887, major institutional changes occurred that saw the decline in importance of the investment bankers and the stock exchanges, the increase in power of the financial executives and the financial analysts, and the growth and then decline—from about the mid-fifties—in the influence of the accounting practitioners. In 1934 a completely new institution, the SEC, was injected into the financial-industrial system. It had the option of adopting either a cooperative or adversary stance toward those under its administration. It followed the cooperative mode, after the usual fashion of independent regulatory agencies in the United States, and in so doing restored to a very disturbed financial community a considerable degree of stability that had been lacking since the crash. The restoration of structural stability was not an accident.

The SEC's Mission

The purpose of the Securities and Exchange Commission was *not* to perpetuate the unsettled situation in the stock market. It was to restore confidence in the market, to provide investor protection against fraud, and to restore the flow of investment funds into industry. In short, its mission was to restore equilibrium to a disturbed system. It did this successfully, but the price it paid was its potency. The SEC restored equilibrium by following the path of least resistance on the development of accounting principles. Though its abandonment of this authority over principles in the late thirties reconciled the accountants to the SEC, it also provided the basis for the future disruption of the stock market during the conglomerate merger movement, and for the frantic concentration of industrial firms at the same time. It further provided the subsequent return of control over financial reporting conventions to the corporate sector.

In the process of restoring equilibrium to the financial-industrial system, the SEC also became an integral part of that system. The results of that integration process generated observations of "cozy" relations between the SEC and the accountants, of a "partnership" between the two groups, of "joint activity" in the formation of accounting principles and rules. The transfer of authority was the key factor in the SEC's integration into the financial-industrial system. Institutionalizing that responsibility in the private sector cemented the relationship. The resentment directed at the SEC when it initiated action on accounting rules without first consulting the AICPA demonstrates how thoroughly, and rapidly, the transfer of authority had become institutionalized.

GOAL SHARING

At the outset of the SEC's operation, in fact even during the administration of the 1933 act by the FTC, the regulating agency took pains to point out that it shared the goals of the regulated institutions. Statements by Landis and Kennedy manifest this harmony, and they are to be taken seriously. The SEC approach to regulation was gentle, and permitted a considerable amount of self-regulation. The congruence of objectives was supported by other factors, including a high level of personnel interchange between the SEC and the financial community. The mutual dependence of the two institutions also underscores this goal sharing: the accountants were dependent upon the SEC for authority and continued flexibility, the SEC was dependent upon the accountants for information, auditing, and whatever efforts were made at accounting research. Manpower selection came from common pools. Chief accountants and SEC Commissioners frequently eyed and secured financially attractive positions in the private sector, as noted previously. Two recent examples of this interchange occurred when ex-SEC Chairman Budge took a position as head of a large mutual fund; ex-Commissioner Needham became head of the New York Stock Exchange. The practice of selecting chief accountants and commissioners acceptable to the regulated has also helped assure goal congruence, guaranteeing as much as possible that actual and potential conflicts will be smoothed over without any permanent changes in authority allocations.

Conflict avoidance between the SEC and the financial sector is based upon mutual dependency and reliance, increasing familiarity, the political pressure brought to bear upon the SEC, and the institutionalization of authority allocations at an early date. After 1938, the SEC never regained, or tried to regain, its lost authority. Serious conflicts have been limited to three incidents—the 1950 rule-making affair, the investment tax credit encounters, and the 1973–1974 treasury stock for pooling battle. During the conglomerate merger movement, accountants seemed more in conflict with the FTC and FEI than with the SEC. Cooperation and coalition with the FASB is now a popular theme with the SEC (Burton, 1973c: 3; 1973d: 8; Sommer, 1974a: 7–9).

The entire event can be looked at as the "socialization of the SEC" in the sense that the commission adjusted its role within a social system regarding the limits of its authority and *the extent to which the private sector would regard SEC regulatory efforts as legitimate*. The result was that the SEC never used anywhere near the full range of its power over the formulation of rules and procedures for financial reporting, even to the extent of making itself vulnerable to the accusation of having abrogated its powers unlawfully.

The SEC and Public Policy

Independent regulatory agencies in the United States have been under fire for a long time. This study of one aspect of the operations of one IRA provides information about the dynamics of interaction between regulator and regulatee when the stakes involved are high. Whether the results of this study apply to all the operations of the Securities and Exchange Commission, and to other independent regulatory agencies, will have to await further research. The central theme of this study, the transfer of authority for the development of regulatory rules from the public regulator to the private regulatee, would be mainly of administrative and political interest, except for what happened afterward as the result of that transfer of authority.

The conglomerate merger movement and the increased concentration of industrial assets in the United States were, as a matter of fact, the direct consequences of the transfer of authority for the development of financial reporting rules from the SEC to the accounting profession. That transfer constituted, as a matter of opinion, an abrogation of the SEC's statutory responsibility. The conglomerate merger movement and the rise in the concentration of industrial assets were secondary consequences of the interaction between the commission and the accountants. These secondary consequences, however, were far more important than the primary consequences—namely, the return of control over financial reporting conventions to the private sector and the narrow administrative scope of the SEC in the area of financial reporting.[5] There were tertiary consequences as well, in very diverse areas. A considerable number of families were uprooted, many careers were changed, the geographic locus of corporate control to large population centers was accelerated, and many family-controlled enterprises passed into the hands of conglomerators. In terms whether it was all worth it, there is also, of course, the consequence of the conglomerates' performance, which was dismal. Many conglomerates had to be dissolved because of their inability to meet the heavy debts incurred. By carrying through only part of its assignment—and on a minimal level—by assigning its really crucial function to develop GAAPs to a private group in whose interest it was that the assignment not be fulfilled, the SEC set the stage for one of the wildest speculative experiences in American history, one that will have continuing and critically important economic, political, and social consequences.

Part of the reason for the poor performance of the SEC lay with the limited perspective of its commissioners. Not only their narrow view of the agency's assignment, but their inadequate understanding of the importance of controlling the rules of financial reporting by specifying reporting objectives contributed to its dereliction. The SEC failure was related to the commissioners not appreciating what George O. May had seen very clearly: that the type of accounting adopted depended on what it was that one wanted to show. No one in the SEC ever took the responsibility for making that decision on a direct, conscious basis. Instead, the SEC pursued the will-o'-the wisp of disclosure by footnote, and left the choices of accounting alternatives up to the practitioners and corporate management. The SEC's failure to decide what ought to be shown on a corporation's financial statement, and why, made it possible for the private sector to continue its "flexible" use of alternative accounting principles, made it possible to defeat any attempt at achieving comparability of corporate financial statements, and made it impossible to develop uniform systems of accounts. It also guaranteed that any research undertaken in the field of accounting would be fortuitous, and dependent upon what was of interest at the time. Systematic accounting research leading to a comprehensive, internally consistent code was impossible without the SEC having first answered the question, "What should be shown?" Instead, the SEC said in effect "Show everything you think is important, and exercise your discretion about how you are going to show it."

On a political, economic, and social level, the nation today simply has no effective mechanism to deal with incidents like the conglomerate merger movement. Events such as these are allowed to run their course, and the nation picks up the pieces afterward. Split responsibilities can be an asset in insuring jealous surveillance of a private-interest group by government institutions that have matching or overlapping jurisdictions. During the conglomerate merger movement, for example, several governmental institutions had an interest in the event besides the SEC, including the FTC, the Justice Department, the Council of Economic Advisers, the Department of Commerce, and the Federal Reserve System. But none of these functional groups had what might be called the prime responsibility for *determining* the structure of American industry. Nevertheless, was the SEC's mandate the one that gave it the clearest duty to act? The question does not permit a ready answer. In the absence of a clear, national objective regarding the industrial structure of the United States, how, we may ask, could the SEC be expected to administer an undefined policy? Within limits, the argument has merit. Without a policy on the national industrial structure, coordination among the interested institutions becomes impossible; government policy becomes a matter of the art of the moment, based on the political alliances of the time, and the economic philosophy of the Supreme Court.

But the absence of a broad public policy does not absolve any governmental unit that has a specific set of responsibilities and fails to carry them through. The nonfeasance of the Securities and Exchange Commission during the conglomerate merger phase was particularly serious because the pooling abuses of the period were, in effect, sanctioned by the government through the SEC's inaction. The legal adage that one is presumed to intend the natural consequences of one's acts is applicable to the SEC.

The Effectiveness of Disclosure

For 40 years SEC operations in the area of corporate financial standards have been based on the theory that disclosure of relevant corporate information enables investors to make intelligent decisions. Has the disclosed information aided investors? It is a disputed issue, and the advocates pro and con are adamant in their convictions.

The SEC, as one would expect, claims its disclosure policy is a success, and asserts that new requirements for information, like product line sales and forecasts, will make that policy even more effective (Burton, 1973b: 1; 1973c: 4–6). Still, the essence of the pooling controversy during the conglomerate merger movement was that disclosure gave imperfect information, and, after all, the APB did collapse over the point. There are numerous ways in which financial statements can seriously mislead investors, which also underscores the failure of the SEC with respect to requiring crucial information. Its case-by-case approach to the problem of disclosure is an indictment of the SEC's guiding philosophy. Specific studies have been made on the usefulness of disclosure, with some mathematical rigor applied to the question.

Professor George J. Benston of the University of Rochester has analyzed the problem, looking at stock-price behavior of exchange-listed firms before and after the 1934 act. Benston divided the firms into those revealing sales information before passage of the act from those that did not. Using sales disclosure as an indication of a firm's disclosure posture, he concludes that investors were not benefited by the availability of the new data (Benston, 1973: 152–153). Substantially the same conclusion was reached when the information contained in corporate annual reports was directly measured both before and after the regulation and standardization of bank reporting (Hagerman, 1972).

Benston made an initial attempt at the analysis earlier (Benston, 1969a; 1969b) but encountered some skepticism (Backer, 1969). Lawyers challenged whether the effect of disclosure can be measured on the grounds that the information tested was "stale" (Sommer, 1969: 97) or that what the market shows cannot be evaluated and

the impact of the SEC is more properly measured in management behavior and investor psychology (Manning, 1969: 85). Insider information has also been seen as critical (Rooney, 1969: 113); there
is some support for Benston's argument (Stigler, 1964), as well as
more evidence on the other side. Some feel that investor risks were
greater before the SEC than afterward (Henshaw et al.: 1964). The
assertion has also been made that economic performance of markets
for stocks has been improved by the presence of the SEC (Friend,
1969: 186).

It is difficult to gauge the value of these disclosure studies. Certain assumptions, such as the selection of key variables, must be
made, and if they are false the research is invalid. The information
across firms, before and after the SEC, was so noncomparable that
disclosure may not have been critical. Furthermore, the really important information about a corporation's finances or its financial
plans may be disseminated and discounted through other channels—
insider disclosures to others or insider trading. But what is apparent
in these studies is that it cannot be demonstrated conclusively that
SEC disclosure policies have been of material benefit to investors,
a point that may be less important today than it was forty years ago
inasmuch as the bulk of corporate investment now involves the re-
investment of internally generated funds as opposed to funds obtained on the capital market. In any event, the efficacy of the SEC
disclosure policy for investors remains unvalidated.

THE SEC AS AN ADVERSARY

The multiple functions of the SEC, like most administrative
agencies, cover a combination of administrative and judicial operations. The two functions are hard to combine; the complicated Administrative Procedure Act attests to the legal precautions taken to
see that independent regulatory agencies do not abuse their authority.
But this is not the main reason why the SEC was never able to achieve
a truly adversary position with respect to the financial community
over financial standards development. More important was the socialization of the SEC within the financial-industrial system. Once the
SEC was *part* of the system, it became difficult for it, given its
divided functions, to assume a meaningful adversary position. The
ability of the SEC to identify and prosecute individual wrongdoers
is a policing role, by the way, and ought not to be confused with the
SEC as an adversary to the financial community.[6]

Its multiple functions, therefore, suggest that because the SEC has the authority to both develop standards and then administer them, it is structurally incapable of fulfilling its responsibility to develop financial reporting standards. Landis, a superb legal talent, was aware of the problem of combining administrative and judicial functions, and he may have had that problem intuitively in mind when he agreed that the accountants should be given the opportunity to establish financial reporting rules.

Accountants and Corporate Development

The accounting profession in the United States avoids acknowledging sufficiently its dependence for professional existence upon the corporations. It is that relationship, however, that has made it impossible for practitioners to achieve the ideal of independence.

The development of financial accounting was subsidiary to the process of industrialization, and in that sense was similar to the development of U.S. corporation law. The growth of corporate law followed the growth of the corporation, and served its needs. Corporate law largely reflected the desires and requirements of businessmen. Competition among states, such as New Jersey and Delaware, to provide the most generous rules of incorporation established corporation law along permissive lines (Hurst, 1970: 58–111). Hurst's idea is that the modern corporate form grew from the desires of businessmen who wanted permission to do a variety of things, and so prevailed upon states for enabling legislation. The result expanded corporation powers as legal entities and as operating groups. Hurst dates the mature stage of this process from about 1890, and it is no accident that the development of the accounting profession also dates from this point.

The development of modern accounting in America began when the corporate form had become fixed and there were few future legal innovations to take place, aside from the introduction of the holding company form in the late nineteenth century and its extensive use during the twenties. Accounting was first a function within the corporation, then an external function when the corporation required specialized assistance, and finally a social function providing corporate audits for public use.

Inadequate research orientation was a major impediment to full specialization within the accounting profession. With the recent, partial transfer of research power to the financial-industrial sector through the Financial Accounting Standards Board, the accounting practitioners may have lost any real opportunity for meaningful achievement. Perhaps this loss is just as well. Accounting firms have recently diversified into consulting work, wherein the potential for conflict with their accounting and auditing functions is enormous. Sooner or later, the appropriateness of their administration of financial standards would have been challenged because of that conflict in business operations. The road toward wealth is not necessarily the road toward disinterested scholarship.

Both the SEC and the accountants were relative newcomers to the financial-industrial system in the 1930s. The accountants had become prominent after the corporation matured, and their influence expanded quickly in the first decades of the century with the government's growing need for corporate reports. For about two and a half years the SEC managed to retain its power to prescribe accounting principles before transferring it to the accountants in December, 1936. The accountants then held this power, perhaps somewhat conjunctively with the SEC, with the industrial sector heavily represented in the background, from 1937 through 1972, a period of some 35 years, with their power peaking in the mid-1950s. After 1972 the power to determine financial rules began to gravitate back to the corporations where it had resided prior to the 1933 Securities Act. In the forty years between 1933 and 1973, the power to prescribe financial standards went almost full circle. Residual powers remained with both the SEC and the accountants, but pivotal power over standards was back in the hands of the corporate sector. The cycle illustrates that if fundamental productive sectors of the American community are to be regulated and controlled, it will not be accomplished by dependent professional groups or by relatively isolated regulatory agencies possessing incompatible functions and abandoned to work out a cooperative mode of existence in the same social system as the regulated groups.

What, then, ought to be done?

Notes

1.   425 F.2d 796 (2nd Cir. 1970), cert. den'd Mar. 30, 1970.

2.   Attorney Sommer thought the SEC, historically quiescent regarding delineation of accounting principles, had been increasingly restless in the

late 1960s and commented on its greater activity (Sommer, 1970: 210; see also, Isbell, 1970: 33–40).

3.   Some recent cases where plaintiffs were permitted to recover against accountants on a negligence theory, where the plaintiff was held to fall within a class of those known to be likely to rely on the accountant's statement, are *Ryan* v. *Kanne* (1969, Iowa) 170 NW2d 395; *Rusch Factors, Inc.* v. *Levin* (1968, DCRI) 284 F Supp 85; *Shatterproof Glass Corp.* v. *James* (1971, Tex Civ App) 466 SW 2d 873, 46 ALR3d 968. There are several good discussions of the liability of accountants. See, for example, "Public Accountants-Liability" 46 ALR3d/980–1012; "Auditors' Responsibility for Misrepresentation: Inadequate Protection for Users of Financial Statements," *Washington Law Review,* vol. 44: 91968, pp. 139–199; "Auditors' Third Party Liability: An Ill-Considered Extension of the Law," *Washington Law Review,* Vol. 46 (1971), 675–707; "Misrepresentation and Third Persons," William L. Prosser, *Vanderbilt Law Review,* March, 1966, Vol. 19, Number 2, pp. 231–255.

4.   For reasons stated elsewhere in the book, I consider the conglomerate merger movement to have had undesirable effects in industrial-asset concentration, creating unnecessary industrial-financial turmoil through the successive acquisition and divestment of firms by eager conglomerators. The movement, measured against questionable economic benefits, caused a considerable amount of social upheaval. It was not in the public interest that financial manipulations, undecipherable to the investor, were encouraged by the financial sector and effected through the techniques of accounting.

5.   The terms "manifest effects" and "latent effects" are roughly equivalent to primary "consequences" and "secondary consequences" and could be used as well.

6.   "Adversary" as a word has a hostile sound, and it is not meant in that context in this book. By "adversary" I mean "to oppose," "to test," and "to present with vigor opposing views and alternatives."

18

What can be done?

The Need for Certainty

Financial standards involve many aspects of the nation's economic activity, from taxation, to investment, to political and social programs. Determination of financial standards ought not to be an intramural event among those groups who stand to be the prime beneficiaries of those rules. That carries temptation too far.

The flexibility of financial standards is constantly brought to the public's attention in the press, directly and by implication. One firm changes its inventory accounting system and profits fall 19 percent for the first quarter (*Wall Street Journal*, April 16, 1974: 18). An Associated Press report is headlined EXXON ACCUSED OF HIDING PROFITS BY JUGGLING BOOKS (*Buffalo Evening News*, April 26, 1974: 1). The close of the article says "Reacting to news reports of Exxon's profit position, J. K. Jamieson, chairman of the board, branded the reports as 'absolutely wrong' and said the earnings 'have been prepared in accordance with accepted accounting principles.'" Perhaps a happy combination, such as "Exxon hides profits by juggling books in accordance with accepted accounting principles" would have been closer to the truth. The General Accounting Office is reported close to approving the proposal by the Federal Trade Commission to require the nation's 500 largest businesses to disclose sales and profits by line-of-business rather than by company-wide totals (*Wall Street Journal*, May 13, 1974: 7). The stage is thereby set for a confrontation between SEC and FTC, with the not unlikely possibility that the SEC will represent the corporate view. And what will happen when the FTC cleverly realizes that corporate profit data thus gathered—if it is gathered—is noncomparable and aggregates thereof are probably useless? A week of reading the *Wall Street Journal* or *Barrons* will provide anyone with his or her own list of financial or political subjects dependent upon accounting. As confused as the situation is now, it will become immeasurably worse because of the advent of multinational corporations as a major international financial force.

The Multinationals and Corporate Financial Reporting Standards

Riding on international capital markets, the development of rapid communication and transport, and the spread of business techniques, the multinationals have been moving toward a dominant position in world economic affairs. In its most advanced form, a firm like IBM, General Motors, or Phillips will have "multinationalized" foreign manufacturing facilities, management, and stock ownership (Jacoby, 1973: 95). How important are the multinationals? In 1973 the *Wall Street Journal* reported that "large international companies currently do about $500 billion of annual business in each other's territories, or about one-sixth of the world's gross product. That's more than the entire gross national product of Japan" (April, 18: 1). The drive to multinationalize is probably irresistible in a free market situation. Increasingly, greater portions of the world's GNP will be represented by multinationals. The multinationals have generated some lively discussion over such vital issues as whether they are the political agents of the home country and may subvert the host country, whether they have any loyalty at all to the home country, whether they are a force for political stability or strife, whether they assume illegitimate political functions, whether they exploit the host country by using its resources at less than competitive prices (see Woodroofe, 1973: 62–74 for an executive's viewpoint of the problem). All these issues are interesting, and all are related to this central question: What is the relation of multinationals to corporate financial reporting standards in the United States?

The large American accounting firms have become very knowledgeable about the intricacies of different accounting practices and government requirements in nations outside the United States. For those who carry on business in a foreign country, these firms have noted the differences in accounting conventions and prepared guides for the reader of foreign financial statements.[1] U.S. accounting practices and those of other countries vary greatly on significant points such as inventory valuation, supplemental information, leasing, and capital relationships with subsidiaries (Schoenfeld, 1969: 3–6; Morgan, 1967: 21–24).

It is a highly complicated process for the multinational to consolidate its accounts each year, reconciling the techniques used in perhaps twenty different countries and preparing different books that must be used for alternate purposes. One nation may have a specific set of accounting standards covering tax liability, for which the multinational must keep a set of books, while for its own use it must prepare its corporate books in a completely different manner. Problems of accounting reconciliation and of diversity of accounting standards have precipitated international conferences among practitioners. Objectives of uniformity and international accounting standards have been related to the growth of multinational business (Stamp, 1972: 64–67). Centralizing cash liquidity flows and the selection of the proper unit of account are major concerns (Row, 1971: 157; Smith, St. E., 1967: 422–423; McKinneley, 1970a: 300). On the problem of uniformity, foreign writers note that accountants in the United States possess a greater amount of autonomy than European accountants (McKinneley, 1970b: 220). The prime concerns appear to be whether a common denominator can be established for accounting principles, how accounting results in currency values can be translated, and how various enterprises can be consolidated (AAA, 1973: 144). Some believe it is possible to abolish minimum disclosure levels for multinationals (Choi, 1974: 14). The immense difficulty of establishing common, or even compatible, international accounting standards can be understood by considering the problem of accounting principles in the United States.

Basically the same problem prevails in accounting for the multinational as for the U.S. corporation, except that perhaps the stakes are even higher for the multinational. There ought to be no question that it is in the interest of the multinational to have the "flexibility" to prepare accounts in a manner to best suit the corporate purpose. A corporation operating solely in the United States has one disadvantage compared wih its multinational counterpart: revenues and costs may not be easily hidden elsewhere. The multinational *can* obscure and hide some accounts. For example, the profit-embarrassed multinational oil companies ran into trouble with the Federal Energy Office in 1974 because of questionable costs used to justify U.S. price increases. "In explaining why existing rules need . . . clarification, the FEO said they were vulnerable to circumvention by 'sophisticated accounting techniques'" (*Wall Street Journal*, May, 17, 1974: 16). Apparently the difficulties lay in intra-company transfer pricing, because an FEO proposed rule was for a "preferred transfer-price accounting method based on 'sales to or purchased from unrelated parties'. . . ." From a public-policy viewpoint, it is obvious that determining whether the 1973–1974 oil crisis in the United States was real or induced depended as much on a careful cost accounting investigation than on anything else.

U.S. multinationals will oppose any attempt to do on an international basis what they have been unwilling to accept domestically. U. S. firms have an enormous presence in the multinational sphere: direct foreign investment in 1970 by American companies was estimated at more than $70 billion, while foreign investment in the United States was about $12 billion. During 1970 the production value of all foreign affiliates of U.S. corporations was $200 billion, compared with total U.S. exports of $40 billion (Jacoby, 1973: 97; 99). Of the twenty largest multinational firms, thirteen are based in the United States (*Newsweek*, November, 20, 1972: 96). Many are represented on the FASB and its associated groups, a fact that provides a hint of the likely operation of the FASB regarding financial standards as they apply to multinationals. The presence of large multinationals in the United States will undoubtedly make it even more difficult to achieve definitive, comprehensive financial standards in the United States, because the multinationals may now argue that unilateral U.S. action on tightening accounting standards may place domestic firms at a disadvantage in foreign markets. U.S. multinationals argue precisely that point in resisting proposed Treasury Department changes in foreign tax credits that would increase their tax liabilities to the U.S. Government (*Wall Street Journal*, September 13, 1974: 1). It could be argued that foreign governments require *their* domestic firms to reveal far fewer details on sales and cost data, no less being required to reveal their profits or sales on a product breakdown basis. Yet it ought to be kept in mind that U.S. firms operating abroad are subject to U.S. antitrust laws, and they have competed well in spite of those laws—or perhaps *because* of them as they require competition. Because it is not to the advantage of the multinationals to have financial standards formulated in any way other than to maximize their "flexibility," it confirms the conclusion that the FASB will operate as the CAP and APB did before it. Obviously, a new approach is needed to tighten financial standards in the United States, one that ought to have been taken a long time ago.

Codes and Courts

There is no need to repeat, in any except the briefest manner, my skepticism about the future prospects for the formulation of generally accepted accounting principles by the FASB tied as the board is to the financial interests of those who would be directly affected by the financial standards. No guarantee can be made that the FASB's interests are congruent with those of the nation at large, although neither can it be asserted that they are inevitably at cross-purposes. Nor should it be taken for granted that those representing the corporate and financial sectors are inflexible. Even so, as it was pointed out at the beginning of this study, the attempt to develop GAAPs was undertaken in an area removed from the attention and knowledge of the average citizen and his elected representatives. Granting the technical, complex nature of accounting, it can still be argued that the creation of corporate financial reporting standards and their profit and economic impacts ought to more closely approach a systematic process of development and understanding. The establishment of these standards ought to be a public sector function rather than a private sector event. Which is not to suggest that corporate financial standards development as a public function could not conceivably result in an even worse situation than the one that now exists with the function in the hands of the FASB and its supporting groups.

The SEC's policy of disclosure without comparability is a substantially meaningless exercise. Comparability cannot be obtained without uniformity, which in turn must be imposed by a single authority. As long as that single, administering authority is made up of private sector units whose interests are antithetic to both comparability and uniformity, those objectives will remain unattainable. The genesis of corporate financial reporting standards should be in the public sector where the security acts intended it to be. The transfer of this responsibility to the private sector by the SEC in 1936–1937 was unwise, and probably improper. SEC acquiescence to the perpetuation of this arrangement with the creation of the FASB was unfortunate, though understandable in view of SEC's status in the financial-industrial sector. The SEC specifically issued ASR No. 150 as an official endorsement of "a body of the private sector as the source of authoritative pronouncements" (Burton, 1974: 3). The commisison's feeling persists that accounting principles development belongs in the private sector, with government only overseeing the project (Sommer, 1974a: 6). This detachment confirms that the SEC is *not* the institution to be responsible for developing, administering, and judging corporate financial reporting standards. Furthermore, its vulnerability to political pressure is too great, perhaps even greater than the APB's. The SEC, after all, failed to support the APB in the controversies over investment credit and pooling standards. Nevertheless, the SEC could have an important statutory and operating role in the formulation and administration of an accounting code.

An Accounting Code

Accounting is significant in the process of economic development. It should, therefore, be a function of public policy, not corporate policy.

A comprehensive accounting code is needed by the United States. Not the type of code developed by codifying the infinite varities of present practice made hallow by precedent, but the type of code created after conscious decision about the objectives of the accounting system. Once objectives are carefully formulated, accounting rules with minimum internal conflict ought to be possible. The objectives should focus on the needs of macro economic and social public policy.

THE MACRO-USES OF ACCOUNTING SYSTEMS

A good argument can be made that the present method in the United States of developing corporate financial accounting standards is an anachronism that eventually will have to be abandoned, though to those who would rush to create straw men, *premature* abandonment of the present system is not recommended. The economic functions of accounting have recently begun to attract the attention they deserve. The nineteenth century saw a transition from bookkeeping to accounting and auditing. Management accounting for financial decision making was a product of the first half of the twentieth century. Government accounting developed on a separate path in the

United States, as it did in most countries; the government, expanding to supply public needs, required systems of accounting necessary for fiscal policy, budget preparation and execution, tax administration, and control and accountability of public funds. A good government accounting system facilitates budget formulation and control relative to policy objectives.

The objectives of government policy in their turn are related to the socioeconomic objectives of the nation, and is a matter for macro-economic analysis. Prof. Adolf J. H. Enthoven of the Netherlands contrasts the government macro-accounting system with the micro-accounting system of the enterprise. The latter is more tangible and straightforward, and based more on empirical evidence. But it is not concerned with abstractions and little worried about national aggregates or their cumulative meaning (Enthoven, 1973: 67–68). The government's macro-accounts and the enterprise's micro-accounts are not coordinated and represent gaps in thinking, says Enthoven, but they could be made to complement each other. The United Nations model of social accounting tries to integrate and aggregate national economic stocks, accounts, and input-output flows into a coherent system. Enthoven agrees that a parent accounting framework is needed to link economics and accounting to result in a systematically cohesive accounting theory (Ibid., pp. 93, 132).

A meaningful national accounting system must be based upon standardized, published accounting records of individual firms. These in turn would be relatable to the government's budgeting system, a necessary requirement for effective planning and decision making (Ibid., p. 156).

> The basic aim of uniform or standardized accounting, which has to be utilitarian, is the systematic accumulation, measurement, processing and reporting—i.e., uniform treatment—of accounting information for entities in a society in accordance with uniform criteria for micro and macro economic objectives. The standards, which are not necessarily to be rigid, are to be based on a systematically coherent and logical accounting structure (including measurements), having a sound, theoretical and empirical content. They have to be acceptable and enforceable, nationally, regionally, and preferably internationally (Ibid., p. 219).

Measured against this standard, it is clear that in the United States the corporate micro-accounting system is little related to the government macro-accounting system, except perhaps at the tax interchange level, and badly, even then. To reorganize the U.S. corporate accounting system to make it compatible with a government macro-accounting system is a difficult order. One can hear the wolves gathering in the background, growling "impractical." And so it is, in the present context, given the FASB's authority for financial standards development. Happily, it does not have to be done with breakneck speed; it could be accomplished with deliberate, careful effort. It is a project that ought not to be pushed so hard that it collapses. Or as James Thurber puts the moral, "You may as well fall flat on your face as lean over too far backwards." [2] That, to say the least, would be counterproductive.

A comprehensive accounting code devised to meet the needs of government and the requirements of the corporate structure would necessitate a considerable tightening of corporate accounting rules—and a loss of corporate accounting "flexibility," something the corporate sector would obviously resist. But an accounting system of this order might also afford desirable certainty in account keeping, and could have attractions for corporations also. There are models available for such a code.

The French General Accounting Plan is probably the most comprehensive accounting system in operation. Its history traces back to the 1920s. It was formulated in 1944, adopted in 1947; revised in 1950 and 1957, and made mandatory in 1965 on all large firms (Enthoven, 1973: 226). It is estimated that about 90 percent of all firms have adopted the plan (McKinneley, 1970a: 220). The system is uniform in terminology and classification of accounts, and has standardized registration and general valuation rules. It is geared to the entire economic sphere, particularly to the French system of national planning. The objectives of the French system are "improvement in fiscal control; systematic information for the social accounts; and standardization of company rules for financial statement presentation" (Enthoven, 1973: 226).

Other European nations also employ uniform systems. Belgium uses one similar to the French model. Germany has a uniform model, oriented more toward the micro-system. The Soviet Union has a standardized system, of course, because there is no free market to guide investment and output.[3] Practices vary from nation to nation, and there is room for differences of opinion on what particular system would be appropriate for the United States. Nonetheless, serious debate should be encouraged to determine the type of system to be adopted by the United States. Two good reasons supporting adoption of a comprehensive accounting system: it would further the objectives of the securities acts by providing reliable information and discourage financial speculations, and it would integrate private and public accounting systems to assist public policy analysis.

Code Development Implementation

The FASB is not the group to develop a national accounting code; neither is the SEC. The SEC, however, is the logical agent to supervise the funding of a research group assigned to develop such a code. If it takes twenty years to come up with a workable code, twenty years ought to be devoted to it. Code development is a scholarly undertaking, and it cannot be rushed if satisfactory results are the objective. The European legal codes took considerably longer than ten years to devise and, of course, they require periodic revision. A United States accounting code would also require perodic revision, which would prevent its becoming stagnant. Members of the code development group ought to be appointed from the American Accounting Association, the American Economic Association, and the American Law Institute, with *minority* representation from private sector groups. Membership should be small to prevent the group from becoming unwieldy. The authority to make the final decisions on disputed questions should be given to the head of the group in order to provide conceptual continuity; this provision has been the lesson of European law code development. The head of the group ought to be an academic scholar, not a practitioner or corporate representative, and, of course, one sympathetic with the objective of the code. Major segments of existing practice could find their way into the code, but whether existing practice would be the starting point is a matter for debate. Congress's sanction of the code development group and, ultimately, its adoption of the code itself would provide the necessary legitimacy. The corporate and financial sectors would have ample opportunity to register their views with sympathetic congressmen, who may usually be found. The code development group would relieve the SEC of the impossible task of formulating a comprehensive accounting code which it would then have to implement while at the same time being responsible for revising it. If the commission's failure to develop financial standards *is* causally related to its stuctural characteristics, then more effective SEC operations will result if its judicial functions are assigned to a specialized court. Such a court would permit the SEC to assume an adversary role regarding compliance with the code.

The first step toward the establishment of an accounting code may have already been taken, inadvertently. In 1970 Congress established the Cost Accounting Standards Board (CASB) to develop and promulgate uniform cost accounting standards for contractors and subcontractors doing business with the Department of Defense, and whose activities could have a substantial impact on the account keeping of industrial firms (Mautz, 1974: 56). Its scope now extends to contracts negotiated with the Atomic Energy Commission, NASA, and the General Services Administration. There are five board members, one to represent industry, two representing the accounting profession, and one government representative, plus the chairman of the board who is to be the Comptroller General of the United States, presently Elmer B. Staats. Other members are:

Charles A. Dana, director of government accounting controls, Raytheon Corp.

Herman W. Bevis, formerly senior partner, Price Waterhouse & Co.

Robert K. Mautz, former professor of accounting at Illinois, presently a partner at Ernst & Ernst, public accountants

Robert C. Moot, vice president, finance, of Amtrak

The board's operating budget is about $1.5 million; its thirty-five members include twenty-two professionals and thirteen staff. CASB standards have the force of law, and six had been issued by April, 1974. The board tries to let those who will be affected by the rules participate in their formulation. Draft standards are submitted to accounting associations for their review, and the standards may be altered on a basis of the comments received. A proposed standard is then published in the *Federal Register* for the second time, becoming effective unless Congress within 60 days passes a resolution against the standard. A stated "desirable" objective of the CASB is uniformity among all government agencies in cost accounting (Randall, 1974b). Consistency and comparability of cost accounting standards among government contractors are also crucial objectives of the Act creating the CASB (Li, 1973: 11).

All board members are part-timers; they rely upon the staff, but reportedly make all the key decisions. Monthly meetings are held that last from one to three days.

There is potential for conflict between the FASB and the CASB, inasmuch as rules issued by both may affect the same firm. Coordination between the two groups is necessary and is, at the moment, taking place. Considering the range of firms coming under CASB jurisdiction, it is inevitable the CASB will have considerable impact upon corporations by reducing their accounting flexibility. The Financial Executives Institute accordingly opposed formation of the CASB, but quickly established close liason with it after the CASB was created over FEI objections (Schoenhaut, 1973: 29; Heuser, 1969; Mulligan, 1970). Some within the private sector remain unreconciled to the need for uniform accounting standards (Herman, 1972). But so far the CASB's approach to accounting problems is ad hoc, and any attempt to develop an accounting system is not apparent. Yet it is conceivable that the development of a uniform system of accounting for the United States could generate from the formation of the CASB, whose objectives thus far have been limited. If cost is the essence of accounting, the CASB will standardize a major part of accounting technique. The CASB might be a reasonable group to initiate the development of an accounting code, but of course considerable alterations in the organization of the board and its operations would have to be made.

Code development is practicable if supported. Compared with the alternatives, to let things go on as they are with predictable, unsatisfactory results, or to fix the responsibility for code development with the SEC, with equally predictable, unsatisfactory results, code development by a special group has appealing merits. In the American political sphere, any kind of government planning is subject to accusations of communism or authoritarianism, hence the idea of a code would be likely to receive more than its due of ideological opposition. And accounting codes, like any other set of government requirements, *may* be potentially oppressive. It is well to keep this in mind. But if the power of the corporate sector is what it is reputed to be, corporations have little to fear from adoption of a program leading to the development of an American accounting code. And a democratic society has the right to debate whether an accounting code is preferable to the existing ad hocism and "flexibility" in accounting.

Code Administration: An Accounting Court System

Conflicting functions of prosecutor, judge, and rule maker have placed the independent regulatory agencies under the provisions of the debilitating Administrative Procedure Act to prevent them from abusing their authority, and to permit regulatees to keep the IRAs from getting too far out of control. If a comprehensive accounting code is adopted, it would be inappropriate for it to be administered by the Securities and Exchange Commission. The SEC could function as the enforcing agency, however, and bring actions for violation or noncompliance. It would also be the appropriate agent to maintain the code development group and see that it undertook reviews and revisions of the code. But a separate court system to resolve interpretations under the code, and to adjudicate disputes between SEC and defendants, would be in the best traditions of American common law. It would provide the fairest arena for settling disputes over accounting. Judges could be selected and trained in accounting as well as law. The court system could be expanded as necessary. Decisions would provide an open body of information on acceptable practices, thus satisfying the misgivings of Berle about SEC decisions being made in closed session, with the reasoning behind some of them never becoming common knowledge.

Courts consider many cases which at their core revolve around interpretation of accounting issues and liabilities. A specialized accounting court would be an advantage, if expertise counts for anything, considering the increasing technical complexity of accounting and its applications. To set the jurisdiction of such a court would be complicated, but feasible. Special courts are common in the United States.

Forty years of financial-industrial sector administration of accounting rule making have left a legacy of increased concentration of the nation's industrial assets, noncomparable accounting data, and the basis for ruinous stock market speculation. Moreover, little advance has been made in providing the investor with useful information. The presence of the SEC has produced mainly the appearance, rather than the substance, of change in the administration of corporate financial reporting. Meaningful alterations have not occurred in the identity or attitudes of the principal participants. The accounting practitioners and their corporate clients have dominated all financial standards groups, aided and abetted by other financial sector units and the accounting academics. Throughout, the SEC has performed primarily a ceremonial function. Neither have there been any substantial changes in the characteristics of the successive organizations charged with developing financial reporting standards. Structurally, the differences between the CAP, APB, and

FASB have been without real significance; each organization has been larger than the one before it, but to be bigger has not proved to be better.

If a meaningful improvement is to be made in the system for developing corporate financial reporting, it is inescapable that the present institutional structure must be significantly altered. There are only three ways to alter the present system: change the attitudes of the present participants, introduce new participants with attitudes different from those held by the incumbents, or change the entire structure for developing corporate financial standards. The first two alternatives are fruitless endeavors. There is no hope of changing the attitudes of those in control of the present system. The participants within the financial-industrial sector will behave as they always have. They will try to keep power for themselves, and it is only reasonable to anticipate that they will continue in that way. The process of self-selection forecloses the second possible path of change; those in control will continue to exclude others with incompatible viewpoints.

The only potentially effective alternative is to alter the institutional structure of the present system, which would force a change. But not all institutional innovations will change a system. Introduction of the SEC, after all, merely solidified, and gave semi-official sanction to, the private sector control of financial reporting standards as the SEC became firmly integrated within the financial-industrial sector. Institutional devices selected to achieve specific objectives must have potential for inducing behavior along desired lines. It is for that reason that an alteration in the present way of developing financial reporting rules must involve withdrawing some of the SEC's adjudicating functions and assigning those functions to the courts. For the same reason, it is necessary to remove from the private sector the authority to develop financial reporting rules, and restore that authority to the public sector by creating a government sanctioned body charged with the responsibility of developing a comprehensive, uniform accounting code suitable for the purposes of both private and public sectors.

The alternative is clear. Failure to adopt a code and its administration by special federal courts will perpetuate the conditions now inhibiting development of satisfactory corporate reporting standards. The private sector will, of course, resist any major changes in the present arrangement, in which they play the dominant role. The path toward change will therefore be difficult, perhaps impossible. Nevertheless, an attempt should be made to revise the existing system. As in 1933, for the financial-industrial sector and for the public at large, the stakes remain very high.

NOTES

1.   Price Waterhouse & Co. has available an excellent short pamphlet called *Guide for the Reader of Foreign Financial Statements* that lists "differences in Accounting Principles and Practices between the United States and 24 foreign countries."

2.   James Thurber, *Fables for Our Time* (New York: Harper & Brothers, 1939). This particular moral comes from the tale of "The Bear Who Let It Alone," pp. 33–34.

3.   See Enthoven Chapter 12 for details.

appendix A

Financial Accounting Foundation Board of Trustees, 1972

Member	*Affiliation*
Biegler, John C.*	Senior Partner, Price Waterhouse & Co., Public Accountants.
Bull, Ivan O.	Managing Partner, McGladrey, Hansen, Dunn & Co.
Derieux, Samuel A.	Partner, Derieux & Watson.
Edwards, James Don	Professor of Accounting, University of Georgia.
Franklin, William H.	Chairman of the Board, Caterpillar Tractor Co.
Kent, Ralph E.	Senior Partner, Arthur Young & Co., Public Accountants.
Layton, LeRoy*	Senior Partner, Main Lafrentz & Co., Public Accountants.
Murphy, Thomas A.	Vice Chairman of the Board, General Motors Corp.
Pryor, Thomas C.	Senior Vice-President and Chairman of the Investment Policy Committee of White Weld & Co., Inc.

* Original incorporators of the Financial Accounting Foundation. Other incorporators were Marshall S. Armstrong, Winston Brooke, and Walter J. Oliphant. Date of incorporation: June 27, 1972.

Financial Accounting Standards Board: Original Members, 1973

Member	*Previous Affiliation*
Armstrong, Marshall, S., Chairman	Managing Partner, George S. Olive, Public Accountants (Indianapolis); President, AICPA, 1970–1971; former member of Accounting Principles Board.
Kirk, Donald J.	Partner, Price Waterhouse & Co., Public Accountants.
Litke, Arthur L.	Chief of the Office of Accounting and Finance, Federal Power Commission; President of the Federal Government Accountants Association.
Mays, Robert E.	Controller, Exxon Corp.
Queenan, John W.	Managing Partner, Haskins & Sells, Public Accountants, retired, 1970; member, President's Price Commission, October, 1971–January, 1973. President, AICPA, 1961; member, APB for six years; member of CAP prior to formation of the APB.
Schuetze, Walter P.	Partner, Peat, Marwick, Mitchell & Co., Public Accountants.
Sprouse, Robert T.	Professor of Accounting, Stanford University Graduate School of Business; past President of the American Accounting Asscoiation.

Source: Press Release, Financial Accounting Foundation, March 1, 1973.

Financial Accounting Standards Advisory Council: Original Members, 1973

Member	Affiliation
Barr, Andrew	Former Chief Accountant, SEC.
Catlett, George R.	Partner, Arthur Andersen & Co., Public Accountants.
Cook, Donald C.	Chairman and Chief Executive Officer, American Electric Power Co., Inc.
Davidson, Sidney	Dean, Graduate School of Business, University of Chicago.
Defliese, Philip L.	Managing Partner, Lybrand, Ross Bros. & Montgomery, Public Accountants; former Chairman, APB.
Forester, Frank, Jr.	Executive Vice-President, Morgan Guaranty Trust Co.
Hornbostel, Charles C.	President, Financial Executives Institute.
Kocour, Herman J.	Partner, Elmer Fox & Co. (Wichita).
Langenderfer, Harold Q.	Professor of Accounting, University of North Carolina.
Lordan, John J.	Chief, Financial Management Branch, Office of Management and Budget.
Malin, Robert	Vice-President, Reynolds Securities, Inc.
Mautz, Robert K.	Partner, Ernst & Ernst, Public Accountants.
McGaraugh, Charles T.	Senior Vice President, Northwestern National Bank of Minneapolis.
Morgan, Robert A.	Controller, Caterpillar Tractor Co.
Morse, Ellsworth H., Jr.	Assistant Comptroller General of the United States.
Needham, James J.	Chairman, New York Stock Exchange.

Norr, David	Partner, First Manhattan Co.
Parker, Reed C.	Vice-President, Duff, Anderson & Clark, Inc.
Rohatyn, Felix B.	Partner, Lazard Freres & Co., Investment Bankers.
Scott, Stanley J.	Managing Partner, Alford, Meroney & Co.
Sommer, Alphonse A.	Partner, Calfee, Halter, Calfee, Griswold & Sommer, Attorneys. (Sommer was subsequently appointed to the Securities and Exchange Commission in 1973.)
Stone, Frances G.	Research Analyst, Merrill Lynch, Pierce, Fenner & Smith, Inc., Stock Brokers.
Tang, E. Palmer	Partner, Touche Ross & Co., Public Accountants.
Wear, Allan	Assistant Controller, Ford Motor Co.
Wheat, Francis M.	Partner, Gibson, Dunn & Crutcher, Attorneys; former SEC Commissioner.
Willis, John A.	Controller, Union Carbide Corp.
Zlatkovich, Charles T.	Professor of Accounting, University of Texas at Austin.

Source: Press Release, Financial Accounting Foundation, March 1, 1973, announcing the completion of the membership of the FASB and the composition of a 27 member Financial Accounting Standards Advisory Council.

appendix B

Excerpts from the Securities Act of 1933
(as in Effect December 1, 1972)

AN ACT

To provide full and fair disclosure of the character of securities sold in interstate and foreign commerce and through the mails, and to prevent frauds in the sale thereof, and for other purposes.

CIVIL LIABILITIES ON ACCOUNT OF FALSE
REGISTRATION STATEMENT

SEC. 11. (a) In case any part of the registration statement, when such part became effective, contained an untrue statement of a material fact or omitted to state a material fact required to be stated therein or necessary to make the statements therein not misleading, any person acquiring such security (unless it is proved that at the time of such acquisition he knew of such untruth or omission) may, either at law or in equity, in any court of competent jurisdiction, sue—

(1) every person who signed the registration statement;

(2) every person who was a director of (or person performing similar functions) or partner in, the issuer at the time of the filing of the part of the registration statement with respect to which his liability is asserted;

(3) every person who, with his consent, is named in the registration statement as being or about to become a director, person performing similar functions, or partner;

(4) every accountant, engineer, or appraiser, or any person whose profession gives authority to a statement made by him, who has with his consent been named as having prepared or certified any part of the registration statement, or as having prepared or certified any report or valuation which is used in connection with the registration statement, with respect to the statement in such registration statement, report, or valuation, which purports to have been prepared or certified by him;

(5) every underwriter with respect to such security.

If such person acquired the security after the issuer has made generally available to its security holders an earning statement covering a period of at least twelve months beginning after the effective date of the registration statement, then the right of recovery under this subsection shall be conditioned on proof that such person acquired the security relying upon such untrue statement in the registration statement or relying upon the registration statement and not knowing of such omission, but such reliance may be established without proof of the reading of the registration statement by such person.[1]

(b) Notwithstanding the provisions of subsection (a) no person, other than the issuer, shall be liable as provided therein who shall sustain the burden of proof—

(1) that before the effective date of the part of the registration statement with respect to which his liability is asserted (A) he had resigned from or had taken such steps as are permitted by law to resign from, or ceased or refused to act in, every office, capacity, or relationship in which he was described in the registration statement as acting or agreeing to act, and (B) he had advised the Commission and the issuer in writing that he had taken such action and that he would not be responsible for such part of the registration statement; or

(2) that if such part of the registration statement became effective without his knowledge, upon becoming aware of such fact he forthwith acted and advised the Commission, in accordance with paragraph (1), and, in addition, gave reasonable public notice that such part of the registration statement had become effective without his knowledge; or

(3) that (A) as regards any part of the registration statements not purporting to be made on the authority of an expert, and not purporting to be a copy of or extract from a report or valuation of an expert, and not purporting to be made on the authority of a public official document or statement, he had, after reasonable investigation, reasonable ground to believe and did believe, at the time such part of the registration statement became effective, that the statements therein were true and that there was no omission to state a material fact required to be stated therein or necessary to make the statements therein not misleading; and (B) as regards any part of the registration statement purporting to be made upon his authority as an expert or purporting to be a copy of or extract from a report or valuation of himself as an expert, (i) he had, after reasonable investigation, reasonable ground to believe and did believe, at the time such

part of the registration satement became effective, that the statements therein were true and that there was no omission to state a material fact required to be stated therein or necessary to make the statements therein not misleading, or (ii) such part of the registration statement did not fairly represent his statement as an expert or was not a fair copy of or extract from his report or valuation as an expert; and (C) as regards any part of the registration statement purporting to be made on the authority of an expert (other than himself) or purporting to be a copy of or extract from a report or valuation of an expert (other than himself), he had no reasonable ground to believe and did not believe, at the time such part of the registration statement became effective, that the statements therein were untrue or that there was an omission to state a material fact required to be stated therein or necessary to make the statements therein not misleading, or that such part of the registration statement did not fairly represent the statement of the expert or was not a fair copy of or extract from the report or valuation of the expert; and (D) as regards any part of the registration statement purporting to be a statement made by an official person or purporting to be a copy of or extract from a public official document, he had no reasonable ground to believe and did not believe, at the time such part of the registration statement became effective, that the statements therein were untrue, or that there was an omission to state a material fact required to be stated therein or necessary to make the statements therein not misleading, or that such part of the registration statement did not fairly represent the statement made by the official person or was not a fair copy of or extract from the public official document.[2]

(c) In determining, for the purpose of paragraph (3) of subsection (b) of this section, what constitutes reasonable investigation and reasonable ground for belief, the standard of reasonableness shall be that required of a prudent man in the management of his own property.[3]

(d) If any person becomes an underwriter with respect to the security after the part of the registration statement with respect to which his liability is asserted has become effective, then for the purposes of paragraph (3) of subsection (b) of this section such part of the registration statement shall be considered as having become effective with respect to such person as of the time when he became an underwriter.

(e) The suit authorized under subsection (a) may be to recover such damages as shall represent the difference between the amount paid for the security (not exceeding the price at which the security was offered to the public) and (1) the value thereof as of the time such suit was brought, or (2) the price at which such security shall have been disposed of in the market before suit, or (3) the price at which such security shall have been disposed of after suit but before judgment if such damages shall be less than the damages representing the difference between the amount paid for the security (not exceeding the price at which the security was offered to the public) and the value thereof as of the time such suit was brought: Provided, that if the defendant proves that any portion or all of such damages represents other than the depreciation in value of such security resulting from such part of the registration statement, with respect to which his liability is asserted, not being true or omitting to state a material fact required to be stated therein or necessary to make the statements therein not misleading, such portion of or all such damages shall not be recoverable. In no event shall any underwriter (unless such underwriter shall have knowingly received from the issuer for acting as an underwriter some benefit, directly or indirectly, in which all other underwriters similarly situated did not share in proportion to their respective interests in the underwriting) be liable in any suit or as a consequence of suits authorized under subsection (a) for damages in excess of the total price at which the securities underwritten by him and distributed to the public were offered to the public. In any suit under this or any other section of this title the court may, in its discretion, require an undertaking for the payment of the costs of such suit, including reasonable attorney's fees, and if judgment shall be rendered against a party litigant, upon the motion of the other party litigant, such costs may be assessed in favor of such party litigant (whether or not such undertaking has been required) if the court believes the suit or the defense to have been without merit, in an amount sufficient to reimburse him for the reasonable expenses incurred by him, in connection with such suit, such costs to be taxed in the manner usually provided for taxing of costs in the court in which the suit was heard.[4]

(f) All or any one or more of the persons specified in subsection (a) shall be jointly and severally liable, and every person who becomes liable to make any payment under this section may recover contribution as in cases of contract from any person who, if sued separately, would have been liable to make the same payment, unless the person who has become liable was, and the other was not, guilty of fraudulent misrepresentation.

(g) In no case shall the amount recoverable under this section exceed the price at which the security was offered to the public.

Special Powers of Commission

Sec. 19. (a) The Commission shall have authority from time to time to make, amend, and rescind such rules and regulations as may be necessary to carry out the provisions of this title, including rules and regulations governing registration statements and prospectuses for various classes of securities and issuers, and defining accounting, technical, and trade terms used in this title. Among other things, the Commission shall have authority, for the purposes of this title, to prescribe the form or forms in which required information shall be set forth, the items or details to be shown in the balance sheet and earning statement, and the methods to be followed in the preparation of accounts, in the appraisal or valuation of assets and liabilities, in the determination of depreciation and depletion, in the differentiation of recurring and nonrecurring income, in the differentiation of investment and operating income, and in the preparation, where the Commission deems it necessary or desirable, of consolidated balance sheets or income accounts of any person directly or indirectly controlling or controlled by the issuer, or any person under direct or indirect common control with the issuer; but insofar as they relate to any common carrier subject to the provisions of section 20 of the Interstate Commerce Act, as amended, the rules and regulations of the Commission with respect to accounts shall not be inconsistent with the requirements imposed by the Interstate Commerce Commission under authority of such section 20. The rules and regulations of the Commission shall be effective upon publication in the manner which the Commission shall prescribe. No provision of this title imposing any liability shall apply to any act done or omitted in good faith in conformity with any rule or regulation of the Commission, notwithstanding that such rule or regulation may, after such act or omission, be amended or rescinded or be determined by judicial or other authority to be invalid for any reason.[5]

(b) For the purpose of all investigations which, in the opinion of the Commission, are necessary and proper for the enforcement of this title, any member of the Commission or any officer or officers designated by it are empowered to administer oaths and affirmations, subpena witnesses, take evidence, and require the production of any books, papers, or other documents which the Commission deems relevant or material to the inquiry. Such attendance of witnesses and the production of such documentary evidence may be required from any place in the United States or any Territory at any designated place of hearing.

Excerpts from the Securities Exchange Act of 1934 (as Amended to December 30, 1970)

NECESSITY FOR REGULATION AS PROVIDED IN THIS TITLE

SECTION 2. For the reasons hereinafter enumerated, transactions in securities as commonly conducted upon securities exchanges and over-the-counter markets are affected with a national public interest which makes it necessary to provide for regulation and control of such transactions and of practices and matters related thereto, including transactions by officers, directors, and principal security holders, to require appropriate reports, and to impose requirements necessary to make such regulation and control reasonably complete and effective, in order to protect interstate commerce, the national credit, the Federal taxing power, to protect and make more effective the national banking system and Federal Reserve System, and to insure the maintenance of fair and honest markets in such transactions:

(1) Such transactions (a) are carried on in large volume by the public generally and in large part originate outside the States in which the exchanges and over-the-counter markets are located and/or are effected by means of the mails and instrumentalities of interstate commerce; (b) constitute an important part of the current of interstate commerce; (c) involve in large part the securities of issuers engaged in interstate commerce; (d) involve the use of credit, directly affect the financing of trade, industry, and transportation in interstate commerce, and directly affect and influence the volume of interstate commerce; and affect the national credit.

(2) The prices established and offered in such transactions are generally disseminated and quoted throughout the United States and foreign countries and constitute a basis for determining and establishing the prices at which securities are bought and sold, the amount of certain taxes owing to the United States and to the several States by owners, buyers, and sellers of securities, and the value of collateral for bank loans.

(3) Frequently the prices of securities on such exchanges and markets are susceptible to manipulation and control, and the dissemination of such prices gives rise to excessive speculation, resulting in sudden and unreasonable fluctuations in the prices of securities which (a) cause alternately unreasonable expansion and unreasonable contraction of the volume of credit available for trade, transportation, and industry in interstate commerce, (b) hinder the proper appraisal of the value of securities and thus prevent a fair calculation of taxes owing to the United States and to the several States by owners, buyers, and sellers of securities, and (c) prevent the fair valuation of collateral for bank loans and/or obstruct the effective operation of the national banking system and Federal Reserve System.

(4) National emergencies, which produce widespread unemployment and the dislocation of trade, transportation, and industry, and which burden interstate commerce and adversely affect the general welfare, are precipitated, intensified, and prolonged by manipulation and sudden and unreasonable fluctuations of security prices and by excessive speculation on such exchanges and markets, and to meet such emergencies the Federal Government is put to such great expense as to burden the national credit.

PERIODICAL AND OTHER REPORTS

Section 13. (a) Every issuer of a security registered pursuant to section 12 of this title shall file with the Commission, in accordance with such rules and regulations as the Commission may prescribe as necessary or appropriate for the proper protection of investors and to insure fair dealing in the security—

(1) such information and documents (and such copies thereof) as the Commission shall require to keep reasonably current the information and documents required to be included in or filed with an application or registration statement filed pursuant to section 12, except that the Commission may not require the filing of any material contract wholly executed before July 1, 1962.

(2) such annual reports (and such copies thereof), certified if required by the rules and regulations of the Commission by independent public accountants, and such quarterly reports (and such copies thereof), as the Commission may prescribe.

Every issuer of a security registered on a national securities exchange shall also file a duplicate original of such information, documents, and reports with the exchange.[6]

(b) The Commission may prescribe, in regard to reports made pursuant to this title, the form or forms in which the required information shall be set forth, the items or details to be shown in the balance sheet and the earning statement, and the methods to be followed in the preparation of reports, in the appraisal or valuation of assets and liabilities, in the determination of depreciation and depletion, in the differentiation of recurring and nonrecurring income, in the differentiation of investment and operating income, and in the preparation, where the Commission deems it necessary or desirable, of separate and/or consolidated balance sheets or income accounts of any person directly or indirectly controlling or controlled by the issuer, or any person under direct or indirect common control with the issuer; but in the case of the reports of any person whose methods of accounting are prescribed under the provisions of any law of the United States, or any rule or regulation thereunder, the rules and regulations of the Commission with respect to reports shall not be inconsistent with the requirements imposed by such law or rule or regulation in respect of the same subject matter, and, in the case of carriers subject to the provisions of section 20 of the Interstate Commerce Act, as amended, or carriers required pursuant to any other Act of Congress to make reports of the same general character as those required under such section 20, shall permit such carriers to file with the Commission and the exchange duplicate copies of the reports and other documents filed with the Interstate Commerce Commission, or with the governmental authority administering such other Act of Congress, in lieu of the reports, information and documents required under this section and section 12 in respect of the same subject matter.

(c) If in the judgment of the Commission any report required under subsection (a) is inapplicable to any specified class or classes of issuers, the Commission shall require in lieu thereof of the submission of such reports of comparable character as it may deem applicable to such class or classes of issuers.

NOTES

1. This paragraph was added by Public No. 291, 73d Cong.
2. Clause (C) and (D) of subsection (b)(3) were amended by Public No. 291, 73d Cong. Prior to amendment the clause read as follows:

"(C) as regards any part of the registration statement purporting to be made on the authority of an expert (other than himself) or purporting to be a copy of or extract from a report or valuation of an expert (other than himself), he had reasonable ground to believe and did believe, at the time such part of the registration statement became effective, that the statements therein were true and that there was no omission to state a material fact required to be stated therein or necessary to make the statements therein not misleading, and that such part of the registration statement fairly represented the statement of the expert or was a fair copy or extract from the report or valuation of the expert; and (D) as regards any part of the registration statement purporting to be a statement made by an official person or purporting to be a copy of or extract from a public official document, he had reasonable ground to believe and did believe, at the time such part of the registration statement became effective, that the statements therein were true, and that there was no omission to state a material fact required to be stated therein or necessary to make the statements therein not misleading, and that such part of the registration statement fairly represented the statement made by the official person or was a fair copy or extract from the public official document."

3.   Amended by Public No. 291, 73d Cong. Prior to amendment subsection (c) read as follows:

"(c) In determining for the purpose of paragraph (3) of subsection (b) of this section, what constitutes reasonable investigation and reasonable ground for belief, the standard of reasonableness shall be that required of a person occupying a fiduciary relationship."

4.   Amended by Public No. 291, 73d Cong. Prior to amendment subsection (e) read as follows:

"(e) The suit authorized under subsection (a) may be either (1) to recover the consideration paid for such security with interest thereon, less the amount of any income received thereon, upon the tender of such security or (2) for damages if the person suing no longer owns the security."

5.   This sentence was added by Public No. 291, 73d Cong.

6.   Public No. 88–467, approved Aug. 20, 1964 (78 Stat. 565), amended section 13(a).

appendix C

Commissioners of the Securities and Exchange Commission, 1934–1941

	1934	1935	1936	1937	1938	1939	1940	1941
Kennedy, Joseph P. (C)	Kennedy, Joseph P. (C)	Kennedy (C) r—Sept.						
Healy, Robert E.	Healy	Healy	Healy	Healy	Healy	Healy	Healy	Healy
Landis, James M.	Landis (C)	Landis (C) Chmn—Sept.	Landis (C)	Landis (C) r—Sept.				
Mathews, George C.	Mathews	Mathews	Mathews	Mathews	Mathews	Mathews	Mathews r—Mar.	
Pecora, Ferdinand	Pecora	Pecora r—Jan.						
Ross, James D.		Ross n—Aug.	Ross	Ross r—Oct.				
Douglas, William O.			Douglas (C) n—Jan.	Douglas (C) Chmn—Sept.	Douglas (C)	Douglas (C) r—Apr.		
Frank, Jerome N.				Frank n—Dec.	Frank	Frank (C) Chmn—May	Frank (C)	Frank r—Apr.
Hanes, John W.					Hanes n—Jan. r—July			
Eicher, Edward C.					Eicher n—Dec.	Eicher	Eicher	Eicher (C) Chmn—April
Henderson, Leon						Henderson n—Apr.	Henderson	Henderson r—July
Pike, Sumner T.							Pike n—May	Pike
Purcell, Ganson								n—May
Burke, Edmund Jr.								n—July

(C)—Chairman
n—Nominated
r—Resigned

bibliography

AAA
    1973   "Report of the Committee on International Accounting." *AR* 48 October supplement: 121–167.

AICPA
    1971   *APB Accounting Principles: Original Pronouncements as of December 1, 1971,* vol. 2, pp. 6001–9720. New York: AICPA. (Vol. 1 shows Curent Text of APB Pronouncements as of December, 1971.)
    1972   *Establishing Financial Accounting Standards.* Report of the Study on Establishment of Accounting Principles. New York: AICPA.

Allen, Frederick Lewis
    1931   *Only Yesterday.* Reprint. New York: Bantam Books, 1959.

Andersen, Arthur
    1935   "Present-day Problems Affecting the Presentation and Interpretation of Financial Statements." *JA* 60 (November): 330–344.

Andersen, Arthur & Co.
    1960   "Pooling of Interests." In *Accounting and Reporting Problems in the Accounting Profession.* Chicago: Arthur Andersen & Co.
    1962   *Accounting and Reporting Problems of the Accounting Profession.* Chicago: Arthur Andersen & Co.
    1965   *Establishing Accounting Principles—A Crisis in Decision Making.* Chicago: Arthur Andersen & Co.
    1972   *AICPA Study on Establishment of Accounting Principles.* Chicago: Arthur Andersen & Co.

Andrews, Frederick B.
    1934   "The Public Accountant and the Investing Public." *JA* 57 (January): 55–65.

Anthony, Robert N.
    1963   "Showdown on Accounting Principles." *Harvard Business Review* 41 (May–June): 99–106.

Armstrong, Marshall S.
    1970   "Public Image of the APB: The Philosophers of Accounting." *JA* 130 (September): 67–70.
    1974   "Will Washington Listen to the Private Sector?" *Financial Executive* (March): XLII No. 3 52–58.

Auld, George P.
1929   "Accounting Aspects of Investment Trusts." *CPA* 9 (December): 363–368.

Backer, Morton
1969   "Comments on 'The Value of the SEC's Accounting Disclosure Requirements.'" *AR* 44 (July): 533–538.

Bailey, George D.
1940   "The Research Work of the American Institute of Accountants." *JA* 70 (July): 50–57.

Bane, Baldwin B.
1933   "The Securities Act of 1933." *CPA* 13 (October): 587–593.

Barnett, George E.
1934   "The Securities Act of 1933 and the British Companies Act." *Harvard Business Review* 13 (October): 1–18.

Barr, Andrew
1938   "Comments on 'A Statement of Accounting Principles.'" *JA* 65 (April): 318–323.

1940   "Accounting Research in the Securities and Exchange Commission." *AR* 15 (March): 89–94.

1959   "Accounting Aspects of Business Combinations." *AR* 34 (April): 175–181.

1963   "The Influence of Government Agencies on Accounting Principles with Particular Reference to the Securities and Exchange Commission." Address before the Thirty-seventh Annual Michigan Accounting Conference, October 18, at Ann Arbor. From SEC files.

1964   "Consolidated Financial Statements—Questions of Valuation." A discussion prepared for the "Arbeitskreis der Wirtschaftsprufungs—Aktiengesellchaften," June 29, at Frankfurt. From SEC files.

1965   "Trends in Financial Reporting." Address before the Nineteenth Annual Conference of Accountants, April 29, at University of Tulsa. From SEC files.

1967a   "Corporate Financial Reporting: The Developing Debate on 'Line of Business' Disclosure—Establishing Criteria for Line of Business Reporting." Address given at the Annual Conference National Association of Accountants, June 27, at Denver. From SEC files

1967b   "The International Harmonization of Accounting Principles." Report representing the Federal Government Accountants Association given in September at the Ninth

International Congress of Accountants in Paris. From SEC files.

1967c   "Need for Product-Line Reporting." Address presented at Symposium on Financial Reporting for Conglomerates, November 13, at Tulane University, New Orleans. From SEC files.

1968   "Changing Financial Reporting—Yesterday, Today and Tomorrow—As Seen from the Standpoint of the Investor." Paper read at the Accounting Educators Conference, February 17, at California State College, Long Beach. From SEC files.

1969a   "An Assessment of the Conglomerate Idea." Panel discussion at the Second Annual Institutional Investor Conference, January 24, in New York. From SEC files.

1969b   "Financial Reporting by Conglomerates." Address before the Twenty-third Annual Conference of Accountants, April 23, at the University of Tulsa. From SEC files.

1969c   "The United States Securities and Exchange Commission and the Accounting Profession." *The Accountant's Magazine* (Edinburgh) (April): 209–215.

1970a   "The SEC's Role in Changing Patterns in Financial Reporting." Address before the Hankamer School of Business Alumni Conference, April 24, at Baylor University, Waco. From SEC files.

1970b   "Financial Reporting under the Securities Acts." Address at the First Annual Conference of the British Accounting and Finance Association, September 14 and 15, at Edinburgh University. From SEC files.

1970c   "When Clients Go Public: The Place of the Local Firms; Topic: Who is Qualified to Practice?" Remarks at the Eighty-third Annual Meeting of the AICPA, September 22, in New York. From SEC files.

1970d   "The Significance of Recent and Pending Opinions of the Accounting Principles Board." Remarks at the Conference Institute on Public Disclosure and the Corporation, November 19, in New York. From SEC files.

Barr, Andrew, and Koch, Elmer C.
1959   "Accounting and the SEC." *The George Washington Law Review* 28 (October): 176–193.

Bell, William H.
1940   "Recent Pronouncements of the Securities and Exchange Commission on Accounting Subjects." *JA* 69 (June): 431–437.

Beman, Lewis
1973   "What We Learned from the Great Merger Frenzy." *Fortune* 87 (April): 70–73; 144; 148–150.

Benston, George J.
1969a   "The Value of the SEC's Accounting Disclosure Requirements." *AR* 44 (July): 515–532.
1969b   "The Effectiveness and Effects of the SEC's Accounting Disclosure Requirements." In *Economic Policy and the Regulation of Corporate Securities,* edited by Henry G. Manne, pp. 23–80. Washington, D.C.: American Enterprise Institute for Public Policy Research.
1973   "Required Disclosure and the Stock Market: An Evaluation of the Securities Exchange Act of 1934." *The American Economic Review* 63 (March): 132–155.

Berle, Adolf A., Jr.
1933   "Public Interest in Principles of Accounting." Paper presented before the AIA annual meeting, October, in New Orleans. From AICPA files.
1938   "Accounting and the Law." *JA* 65 (May): 368–378.

Berle, Adolph A., Jr., and Fisher, Frederick S., Jr.
1932   "Elements of the Law of Business Accounting." *Columbia Law Review* 33 (April): 573–622.

Berman, Daniel S., and Cooper, Bernard S.
1963   "How the Tax Laws Encourage Corporate Acquisitions." *JA* 116 (November): 61–64.

Bevis, Herman W.
1961   "Riding Herd on Accounting Standards." *AR* 36 (January): 9–16.
1966   "Progress and Poverty in Accounting Thought." *JA* 122 (July): 34–40.

Beyer, Robert
1969   "Goodwill and Pooling of Interests: A Re-assessment." *Management Accounting* 6 (February): 9–15.

Blass, Andrew H.
1933   "A New Unholy Alliance." *CPA* 13 (January): 37–39.

Blough, Carman G.
1937a   "The Relationship of the Securities and Exchange Commission to the Accountant." *JA* 63 (January): 23–39.
1937b   "The Need for Accounting Principles." *AR* 7 (March): 30–37.
1938   "Accountants' Certificates." *JA* 65 (February): 106–118.
1939   "Accounting Reports and Their Meaning to the Public." *JA* 68 (September): 162–168.

1961　　　　　"Principles and Procedures." *JA* 111 (April): 51–53.

1967　　　　　"Development of Accounting Principles in the United States." Paper read at Symposium on *Foundations of Financial Accounting*, January 13 and 14, at University of California at Berkeley. 1–25.

Boyd, Orton W.
1934　　　　　"Uniform Cost Accounting Systems under the N.R.A." *CPA* 14 (November): 671–676.

Briloff, Abraham J.
1964　　　　　"Needed: A Revolution in the the Determination and Aplication of Accounting Principles." *AR* 39 (January): 12–15.

1967　　　　　"Dirty Pooling." *AR* 42 (July): 489–496.

1968　　　　　"Distortions Arising from Pooling-of-Interests Accounting." *Financial Analysts Journal* 24 (March–April): 71–80.

1969　　　　　"Much-Abused Goodwill." *Barron's* (April 28): 3, 14, 16, 18, 20, 24.

　　　　　　　"The Funny-Money Game." *Financial Analysts Journal* 25 (May–June): 73–80.

1972　　　　　*Unaccountable Accounting.* New York: Harper & Row.

Broad, Samuel J.
1935　　　　　"Examination of Financial Statements by Independent Public Accountants." *The New York Certified Public Accountant* 6 (October): 23–26.

1938　　　　　"Cooperation with the Securities and Exchange Commission." *JA* 66 (August): 78–89.

Brown, Edith-Adelyn
1932　　　　　"The Evolution of Accounting Procedures through the Middle Ages." *CPA* 12 (July): 411–415.

Bryan, Lyman
1970　　　　　"Washington Background." *JA* 130 (July): 28.

Burck, Gilbert
1969　　　　　"The Merger Movement Rides High." *Fortune* 79 (February): 78–82, 158, 161.

Burton, John C.
1969　　　　　*Corporate Financial Reporting: Conflicts and Challenges,* edited by Burton. New York: AICPA.

1971　　　　　"An Educator Views the Public Accounting Professions." *JA* 132 (September): 47–53.

1973a　　　　"Paper Shuffling and Economic Reality." *JA* 134 (January): 20; 26; 28.

1973b　　　　"Forecasts: A Changing View from the Securities and Exchange Commission." Speech before the Conference on

Public Reporting of Corporate Financial Forecasts, April 2, at Northwestern University, Evanston, Ill. From SEC files.

1973c　"General Thoughts on the Accounting Environment and Specific Thoughts on Accounting for Lease Financing." Speech before the AGA-EEI Accounting Conference, May 7, in San Francisco. From SEC files.

1973d　"The SEC and the Accounting Profession: Responsibility, Authority and Progress." Speech delivered at Accounting Colloquium 3, May 10–11, at the University of Kansas. From SEC files.

1973e　"Some General and Specific Thoughts on the Accounting Environment." *JA* 136 (October): 40–46.

1974　"The SEC and the Changing World of Accounting." Speech before the Dean's Forum, Graduate School of Management, UCLA, January 17, in Los Angeles. From SEC files.

Business Week

1969　"Accountants Turn Tougher." (October 18): 124–125.

1970　"CPA's Finally Agree on a Merger Rule." (July 4): 23.

1971　"A New Man to Guide the Troubled SEC." (February 6): p. 18.
"The SEC's Own Money Problems." (April 3): 19.
"Casey: An SEC Chairman Wall Street Loves." (October 16): 70–73.

1972　"The Man behind the CPA Study." (April 1): 73–74.
"SEC Finds a Gadfly to Watch Accountants." (April 8): 21.

1973　"Accountants Set Targets for Reform." (April 14): 31.

Byerly, F. P.

1937　"Formulation of Accounting Principles or Conventions." *JA* 64 (August): 93–99.

1938　"Relationship between the Practice of Law and of Accounting." *JA* 66 (September): 154–160.

Byrne, Gilbert R.

1937　"To What Extent Can the Practice of Accounting be Reduced to Rules and Standards?" *JA* 64 (November): 364–379.

Carey, John L.

1969　*The Rise of the Accounting Profession.* Vol. 1, *From Technician to Professional, 1896–1936.* New York: AICPA.

1970　*The Rise of the Accounting Profession.* Vol. 2, *To Responsibility and Authority, 1937–1969.* New York: AICPA.

Carter, A. H.
    1933   Testimony at the hearings before the Senate Committee on Banking and Currency, Seventy-third Congress, March 31 to April 8.

Cary, William L.
    1963   Statement before the Subcommittee on Commerce and Finance, Committee on Interstate and Foreign Commerce, House of Representatives, November 19. Quoted in Andersen & Co., *Establishing Accounting Principles—A Crisis In Decision Making*. Chicago, 1965.

Casey, William J.
    1971a   "Evolution in the Capital Markets." Address given to the Society of American Business Writers, May 5, in Washington, D.C. From NEWS-SEC.

    1971b   "The Public Interest in our Securities Markets." Address given at the Institutional Trading Conference, June 17, in New York. From NEWS-SEC.

    1971c   "Responsibility for and Questions on the Structure of the American Securities Markets." Address given to the Association of Stock Exchange Firms, September 8, in New York. From NEWS-SEC.

    1971d   "A Sense of Confidence, Direction and Movement." Address given to the Investment Bankers Association of America, December 1, in Boca Raton, Fla. From NEWS-SEC.

    1972a   "Keystone for 'The SEC Speaks.'" Address given to the Practicing Law Institute February 18, at Washington, D.C. From NEWS-SEC.

    1972b   "The Future of the American Equity Market." An Address given to the Economic Club of New York, March 8, at New York. From NEWS-SEC.

    1972c   "The Search for Clarity and Certainties in Securities Transactions with More and More Realistic Information for Investors." Address given to the New York Law Journal Association of the Bar of the City of New York, April 21, at New York. From NEWS-SEC.

    1972d   "Toward Common Accounting Standards." Address given at the Conference on Financial Reporting—Commission des Opérations des Bourse, May 19, Paris. From NEWS-SEC.

    1972e   Speech to the American Bar Association Section of Corporation, Banking and Business Law, August 15, at San Francisco. From NEWS-SEC.

    1972f   "The Enforcement Activities of the SEC: An Interim Report." Address to the North American Securities Administrators Association, September 11, at Quebec. From NEWS-SEC.

1972g   "Ruminations and Action on Enforcement" Address given to the New York Law Journal Enforcement Conference, September 29, at New York. From NEWS-SEC.

1972h   "Investor Relations and Corporate Credibility." Address given to the National Investor Relations Institute, October 3, in Washington, D.C. NEWS-SEC.

1972i   "The Annual Report as Part of a Comprehensive Disclosure System." Address given at the Financial World 1972 Annual Report Awards Banquet, October 25, at New York. From NEWS-SEC.

1973   Remarks before the New York Stock Exchange Board of Directors, January 4, in New York. From NEWS-SEC.

Catlett, George R.
1960   "Relation of Acceptance to Accounting Principles." *JA* 109 (March): 33–38.

Catlet, George R., and Olsen, Norman O.
1968   *Accounting for Goodwill.* Accounting Research Study 10. New York: AICPA.

Chamberlain, John
1963   *The Enterprising Americans.* New York: Harper Colophon Books.

Chambers, Raymond J.
1966   *Accounting Evaluation and Economic Behavior.* Englewood Cliffs, N.J.: Prentice-Hall, Inc.

Chatov, Robert
1973   "The Role of Ideology in the American Corporation." In *The Corporate Dilemma,* edited by Dow Votaw and S. Prakash Sethi. Englewood Cliffs, N.J.: Prentice-Hall, Inc.

Chori, Frederick D. S.
1974   "Multinational Financing and Accounting Harmony." *Management Accounting* 56 (March): 14–17.

Cleveland, F. A.
1905   "The Scope of the Profession of Accountancy." *JA* 1 (November): 40–56.

Cohen, Manuel F.
1965   "Current Developments at the SEC." *AR* 40 (January): 1–8.

1966a   "Analysts, Accountants and the SEC—Necessary Joint Efforts." *JA* 122 (August): 57–62.

1966b   "The SEC and Accountants: Cooperative Efforts to Improve Financial Reporting." *JA* 12 (December): 56–60.

Cohen, Milton H.
1966 " 'Truth in Securities' Revisited." *Harvard Law Review* 79
(May): 1340–1408.

Cohen, Sheldon S.
1969 "Conglomerate Mergers and Taxation." *American Bar Association Journal* 55 (January): 40–44.

Cole, Ralph, W. E.
1933 "The Securities Act." *CPA* 13 (July): 385–388.

Collins, Clem W.
1939 "Report of the President." *JA* 68 (October): 223–226.

Conn, Robert L.
1973 "Performance of Conglomerate Firms: Comment." *Journal of Finance* 28 (June): 754–759.

Cook, G. Bradford
1973a "Keynote for 'The SEC Speaks Again.' " Address given to the PLI Conference, February 23, at Washington, D.C. From NEWS-SEC.
1973b "The Role of the Analyst in the Evolving Market System." Address given to the New York Society of Security Analysts, March 27, at New York. From NEWS-SEC.
1973c "The Director's Dilemma." Address given to the SMU School of Business Administration, April 6, at Dallas. From NEWS-SEC.
1973d "Disclosure and the Changing Business Environment." Address given to the American Society of Corporate Secretaries, April 19, New York. From NEWS-SEC.
1973e "Democracy in the Markets." Address given to the Economic Club of Chicago, April 25, at Chicago. From NEWS-SEC.

Couchman, Charles B.
1934 "Uniform Accounting for Industry." *JA* 58 (November): 333-357.

Crane, Ralph T.
1935 "Practical Effects of the Securities Act." *JA* 60 (November): 370–374.

Daines, H. C.
1929 "The Changing Objectives of Accounting." *AR* 4 (March): 94–110.

Davidson, Sidney
1963 "The Day of Reckoning—Managerial Analysis and Accounting Theory." *Journal of Accounting Research* 1 (Autumn): 117–126.
1969 "Accountancy and Financial Reporting in the Seventies." *JA* 128 (December): 29–37.

Dawson, Joseph P.
1971   "Auditor's Third Party Liability: An Ill-Considered Extension of the Law." *Washington Law Review* 46 (July): 675–707.

Dean, Arthur H.
1934   "As Amended: The Federal Securities Act." *Fortune* 10 (September): 80–152.

de Bedts, Ralph F.
1964   *The New Deal's SEC: The Formative Years.* New York: Columbia University Press.

DeMond, C. W.
1951   *Price Waterhouse & Co. in America.* New York: Price Waterhouse & Co.

Demski, Joel S.
1973   "The General Impossibility of Normative Accounting Standards." *AR* 48 (October): 718–723.

Dewing, Arthur S.
1953   *The Financial Policy of Corporations.* 5th ed. 2 vols. New York: The Ronald Press Co.

Dickinson, Arthur Lowes
1905   "Duties and Responsibilties of the Public Accountant with Regard to New Isues of Stocks and Bonds." *JA* 1 (November): 16–27.

Dominiak, Geraldine F., and Louderback, Joseph G., III
1972   "'Present Fairly' and Generally Accepted Accounting Principles." *The CPA Journal* 42 (January): 45–49.

Dun's Review
1970   "Accounting and the SEC." (Interview with Commissioner Needham) (October): 10–11.
1970a   "It's Up to the SEC: What's a Poor Accountant to Do?" (Interview with Savoie) (June): 64; 66.
1972   "Accounting: New Numbers, Same Game." (August): 38–40; 84.

Edey, H. C., and Panitpakdi, P.
1956   "British Company Accounting and the Law 1844–1900." In *Studies in the History of Accounting,* edited by A. C. Littleton and B. S. Yamey. Homewood, Ill.: R. D. Irwin, Inc.

Edwards, D. E., and Salmonson, R. F., editors
1961   *Contributions of Four Accounting Pioneers,* East Lansing: Michigan State University.

Edwards, James Don
1960   *History of Public Accounting in the United States.* East Lansing: Michigan State University.

Eigen, Martin
  1965   "Is Pooling Really Necessary?" *AR* 40 (July): 536–540.

Eis, Carl
  1969   "The 1919 Merger Movement in American Industry." *The
            Journal of Law and Economics* 12 (October): 267–296.

Ellis, George Price
  1934a   "Acountancy: Profession and Business." *CPA* 14 (August):
            451–453.
  1934b   "Upbuilding the Profession." *CPA* 14 (September): 513–
            515.

Enthoven, Adolf J. H.
  1973   *Accountancy and Economic Development Policy.* Amster-
            dam, North-Holland Publishing Company; American El-
            sevier Publishing Company, Inc. New York.

Federal Trade Commission
  1969   *Economic Report on Corporate Mergers.* Staff report to
            the Federal Trade Commission and the Subcommittee on
            Antitrust and Monopoly, U.S. Senate, Ninety-first Con-
            gress, Washington, D.C.

Fernald, Henry B.
  1929   "Accountants' Certificates." *JA* 47 (January): 1–19.

Financial Accounting Foundation
  1972   *Exposure Draft: Certificate of Incorporation; By-Laws;
            Proposed Rules of Procedure of the Financial Accounting
            Standards Board.* New York: FAF.
  1973   *Certificate of Incorporation and By-Laws.* Stamford,
            Conn.: FAF.

Financial Accounting Standards Board
  1973   *Rules of Procedure.* Stamford, Conn.: FASB.

Fisch, Jack H., and Mellman, Martin
  1968   "Poolings of Interests: The Status of The Criteria." *JA*
            126 (August): 42–48.

Fiske, Wyman P.
  1938   "A Statement of Accounting Principles." *JA* 65 (April):
            308–316.

Flexner, Bernard
  1934   "The Fight on the Securities Act." *Atlantic Monthly* 153
            (February): 232–250.

Flink, Julius E.
  1934   "Co-operation between Bench and Bar and the Account-
            ancy Profession." *CPA* 14 (November): 659–670.

Foster, William C.

1974a   "Setting Standards for Treasury Shares." *Financial Executive* XLII No. 2 (February): 48–52.

1974b   "The Current Financial Reporting Environment." *The CPA Journal* 44 (March): 31–35.

Frank, Jerome N.

1939   "Accounting for Investors." *JA* 68 (November): 295–304.

Frankfurter, Felix

Felix Frankfurter Papers, Library of Congress (FFPLC).

1934   "The Securities Exchange Act of 1934." *Fortune* 10 (September): 55–111.

Friedman, Milton, and Schwartz, Anna Jacobson

1963   *A Monetary History of the United States.* A study by the National Bureau of Economic Research. Princeton: Princeton University Press.

Friend, Irwin

1969   "The SEC and the Economic Performance of the Securities Markets." In *Economic Policy and the Regulation of Corporate Securities,* edited by Henry G. Manne, pp. 185–216. Washington, D.C.: American Enterprise Institute for Public Policy Research.

Gaa, Charles J.

1961   "Uniformity in Accounting Principles." *JA* 111 (April): 47–51.

Galbraith, John K.

1954   *The Great Crash.* Boston: Houghton Mifflin Co.

Gale, Frank A.

1937   "Professional Accounting Has 'A Story to Tell.'" *CPA* 17 (April): 2–5.

Gerboth, Dale L.

1972   "Muddling Through with the APB." *JA* 133 (May): 42–49.

Gilman, Stephen

1944   "Accounting Principles and the Current Classification." *AR* 19 (April): 109–116.

Goldberg, L. G.

1973   "The Effect of Conglomerate Mergers on Competition." *The Journal of Law and Economics* 16 (April): 137–158.

Gordon, Spencer

1933   "Accountants and the Securities Act." *JA* 56 (December): 438–451.

1934   "Liability of Accountants under the Securities Exchange Act of 1934." *JA* 58 (October): 251–257.

Gort, Michael, and Hogarty, Thomas F.
1970   "New Evidence on Mergers." *The Journal of Law and Economics* 13 (April): 167–184.

Grady, Paul, editor
1962   *Memoirs and Accounting Thoughts of George O. May.* New York: Ronald Press Co.

Greer, Howard C.
1932   "A Council on Accounting Research." *AR* 7 (September): 176–181. See also "The Council of Accounting Research." *CPA* 12 (October): 592–593; 626.
1938   "To What Extent Can the Practice of Accounting Be Reduced to Rules and Standards?" *JA* 65 (March): 213–223.

Hacker, Louis M.
1970   *The Course of American Economic Growth and Development.* New York: John Wiley & Sons.

Hagerman, Robert L.
1972   "The Value of Regulation F: An Empirical Test." *Journal of Bank Research* 3 (Autumn): 178–185.

Hagerman, Robert L.; Keller, Thomas F.; and Petersen, Russell J.
1973   "Accounting Research and Accounting Principles." *JA* 135 (March): 51–55.

Hall, James
1933   "Problems of Accountants under the Securities Act of 1933." *JA* 56 (December): 452–461.

Hamel, Charles D.
1930   "The Accountant's Responsibility for Negligent Misrepresentations in Certified Statements." *CPA* 10 (November): 335–342.
1933   "The Securities Act and the Responsibility of the Accountant." *CPA* 13 (October): 594–604.

Harmon, Jr., David Perry
1968   "Pooling of Interests: A Case Study." *Financial Analysts Journal* 24 (March–April): 82–88.

Haskell, John
1936   "Objectives and Activities of the Committee on Stock List of the New York Stock Exchange under Present-Day Conditions." *JA* 62 (October): 271–281.
1938   "The Securities and Exchange Commission, the Accountant, and the Stock Exchange." *JA* 65 (April): 293–302.

Hatfield, Henry Rand
1927   "What Is the Matter with Accounting?" *JA* 44 (October): 267–279.

Hays, Samuel P.
  1957   *The Response to Industrialism, 1885–1914.* Chicago: University of Chicago Press.

Healy, Robert E.
  1938   "The Next Step in Accounting." *AR* 13 (March): 1–9.

Henderson, A. I.
  1934   "Practice under the Securities Act of 1933 and the Securities Exchange Act of 1934—From the Viewpoint of the Lawyer." *JA* 58 (December): 448–458.

Henshaw, Richard D.; Olson, Olden C.; and O'Donell, John L.
  1964   "The Case for Public Regulation of the Securities Market." *Business Topics* 12 (Autumn): 69–77.

Herman, Michael P.
  1972   "Uniform Cost Accounting Standards: Are They Necessary?" *Managment Accounting* 53 (April): 15–19.

Herwood, Herman
  1933   "The Status of the Certified Public Accountant under the Securities Act." *CPA* 13 (December): 746–748.
  1934   "Regulation of Corporate Practices." *CPA* 14 (September): 544–546.

Heuser, Forrest L.
  1969   "The Question of Uniform Accounting Standards." *Management Accounting* 51 (July): 20–23.

Hicks, Ernest L.
  1969   "APB: The First 3600 Days." *JA* 128 (September): 56–60.

Hofstadter, Richard
  1955   *The Age of Reform.* Vintage Book ed. New York: Random House.
  1962   *Anti-intellectualism in American Life.* New York: Alfred A. Knopf.

Horngren, Charles T.
  1962   "Choosing Accounting Practices for Reporting to Management." *NAA Bulletin* 44 (September): 3–15.
  1971   "The Accounting Discipline in 1999." *AR* 46 (January): 1–11.
  1972   "Accounting Principles: Private or Public Sector?" *JA* 133 (May): 37–41.

Hunt, Bishop C.
  1935   "Auditor Independence." *JA* 59 (June): 453–459.

Hurst, James Willard
  1970   *The Legitimacy of the Business Corporation.* Charlottesville: University Press of Virginia.

Institute of Chartered Accountants in England and Wales

1966   *The History of the Institute of Chartered Accountants in England and Wales 1800–1965, and of Its Founder Accountancy Bodies 1870–1880.* London: Heineman Ltd.

Isbell, David B.
 1970   "The Continental Vending Case: Lessons for the Profession." *JA* 130 (August): 33–40.

Jacoby, Neil H.
 1973   *Corporate Power and Social Responsibility.* New York: Macmillan Co.

Jaenicke, Henry R.
 1962a "Management's Choice to Purchase or Pool." *AR* 37 (October): 758–765.
 1962b "Ownership Continuity and ARB No. 48." *JA* 114 (December): 57–65.

Jennings, Alvin R.
 1958   "Accounting Research." *AR* 33 (October): 547–554.

Johns, Gordon M.
 1972   "Reflections on the Wheat Committee Recommendations." *The CPA Journal* 42 (July): 533–539.

Kaplan, Maurice C., and Reaugh, Daniel M.
 1939   "Accounting Reports to Stockholders, and the SEC." *AR* 14 (September): 203–236.

Kapnick, Harvey E., Jr.
 1970   "The Time for Decision Is Now." Paper submitted to the Estate Planning Council of Cleveland, June 16. Arthur Andersen & Co.

Kaysen, Carl, and Turner, Donald F.
 1959   *Antitrust Policy: An Economic Analysis.* Cambridge, Mass.: Harvard University Press.

Kennedy, Joseph P.
 1934a "Securities and Exchange Commission." *CPA* 14 (August): 454–456.
 1934b "Securities and Exchange Commission." *CPA* 14 (December): 722–728; 736.

King, Earle C.
 1948   "Presentation of Pertinent Data in Financial Statements." *AR* 23 (October): 345–354.

Knollmuller, August L.
 1934a "German Legislation Bearing upon Public Accounting," Part 1. *CPA* 14 (January): 16–20; 48.
 1934b "German Legislation Bearing upon Public Accounting," Part 2. *CPA* 14 (February): 72–77; 106.

1934c   "German Legislation Bearing Upon Public Accounting,"
           Part 3. *CPA* 14 (March): 150–155.

Knortz, Herbert C.
1971   "The Credibility of Accounting Principles." *Conference
           Board Record* (April): 33–38.

Kolko, Gabriel
1963   *The Triumph of Conservatism.* Glencoe, Ill.: The Free
           Press.

Kripke, Homer
1961   "A Good Look at Goodwill in Corporate Acquisitions."
           Banking Law Journal 78 (December): 1028–1040.
1968   "Accounting for Corporate Acquisitions and the Treat-
           ment of Goodwill: An Alert Signal to All Business Law-
           yers." *The Business Lawyer* 24 (November): 89–114.
1970a   "Is Fair Value Accounting the Solution?" *The Business
           Lawyer* 26 (November): 289–295.
1970b   "Accounting Choices and Related Techniques Which Are
           Claimed to Have Been Used to Facilitate Conglomerate
           Growth." *The Business Lawyer* 25 (January): 593–598.
1970c   "The SEC, the Accountants, Some Myths and Some Reali-
           ties." *New York University Law Review* 45 (December):
           1151–1205.
1972   "The Objective of Financial Accounting Should Be to
           Provide Information for the Serious Investor." *CPA* 42
           (May): 389–397.

Krooss, Herman E., and Gilbert, Charles
1972   *American Business History.* Englewood Cliffs, N.J.: Pren-
           tice-Hall.

Landis, James M.
           James M. Landis Papers, Harvard Law Library (JMLP-
           HLL) and Library of Congress (JMLPLC).
1933   "The Securities Act of 1933." CPA 13 (November): 656–
           662.
1934a   "The Securities and Exchange Commission: Its Origin,
           Personnel and Objectives." *The World Today* 2 (Decem-
           ber): 40–42.
1935a   "Interpretations of Rules for Listing and Issuance of
           Securities." *The New York Certified Public Accountant* 5
           (January): 18–31.
1935b   "The Federal Securities Act of 1933." American Manage-
           ment Association, Financial Management Series, *FM* 46
           (October): 99.3–8. JMLPHLL.
1935c   Address to the Fourteenth Annual Dinner of the New
           York Stock Exchange Institute, June 19, at New York.
           JMLHLL.

1959   "The Legislative History of the Securities Act of 1933." *George Washington Law Review* 28 (October): 29–49.

Lane, Chester T.
1938   "Cooperation with the S.E.C." *The New York Certified Public Accountant* 8 (April): pp. 5–11.

Lauver, R. C.
1966   "The Case for Poolings." *AR* 41 (January): 65–74.

Lamden, Charles William
1949   "The Securities and Exchange Commission: A Case Study in the Use of Accounting as an Instrument of Public Policy." Ph.D. dissertation, University of California, Berkeley.

Li, David H.
1973   "Cost Accounting Standards Board: A Progress Report." *Management Accounting* 54 (June): 11–14.

Littleton, A. C.
1933   *Accounting Evolution to 1900.* New York: American Institute Publishing Co.
1935a "Auditor Independence." *JA* 59 (April): 283–291.
1935b "An Inevitably Mediocre Bureaucracy." *JA* 60 (October): 264–269.
1938   "Tests for Principles." *AR* 13 (March): 16–24.

Lorie, James H., and Halpern, Paul
1970   "Conglomerates: The Rhetoric and the Evidence." *The Journal of Law and Economics* 13 (April): 149–166.

Louis, Arthur M.
1968   "The Accountants are Changing the Rules." *Fortune* 77 (June): 177–179, 330, 336, 339, 346.

Manning, Bayless A.
1969   "Discussion and Comments on Papers by Demsetz and Benston." In *Economic Policy and the Regulation of Corporate Securities,* edited by Henry G. Manne, pp. 81–88. Washington, D.C.: American Enterprise Institute for Public Policy Research.

Markham, Jesse W.
1973   *Conglomerate Enterprise and Public Policy.* Division of Research, Graduate School of Business Administration, Harvard University, Boston.

Mason, Perry
1933   "Frankenstein, Incorporated." *CPA* 13 (August): 465–472. See July, 1933, issue for part 1.

Mathews, George C.
1938   "Accounting in the Regulation of Security Sales." *AR* 13 (September): 225–233.

Mathieson, John K.
    1940   "Report of the President." *JA* 70 (November): 391–395.

Mautz, Robert K.
    1965   "Challenges to the Accounting Profession." *AR* 40 (April):
                299–311.
    1974   "The Other Accounting Standards Board." *JA* 136 (Feb-
                ruary): 56–60.

Mautz, R. K., and Gray, Jack
    1970   "Some Thoughts on Research Needs in Accounting." *JA*
                130 (September): 54–62.

May, George O.
    1934   "The Position of Accountants under the Securities Act."
                JA 57 (January): 9–23.
    1936a   "The Influence of Accounting on the Development of an
                Economy," part 1. *JA* 61 (January): 11–22.
    1936b   "The Influence of Accounting on the Development of an
                Economy," part 2. *JA* 61 (February): 92–105.
    1936c   "The Influence of Accounting on the Development of an
                Economy," part 3. *JA* 61 (March): 171–184.
    1936d   *Twenty Five Years of Accounting Responsibility*, vol. 1.
                New York: American Institute Publishing Co.
    1937a   "Improvement in Financial Accounts." *JA* 63 (May): 333–
                369.
    1937b   "Principles of Accounting." *JA* 64 (November): 423–425.
    1937c   "Eating Peas with Your Knife." *JA* 63 (January): 15–22.
    1938   "Uniformity in Accounting." *Harvard Business Review* 17
                (Autumn): 1–8.
    1940   "Fundamentals of Accounting Procedures." *The New York
                Certified Public Accountant* 11 (November): 73–83.
    1941   "Some Implications of Original Cost." *The New York
                Certified Public Accountant* 11 (May): 481–485.
    1943   "The Nature of the Financial Accounting Process." *AR*
                18 (July): 189–193.
    1957   "Business Combinations—An Alternate View." *JA* 103
                (April): 33–36.
    1961   "Retrospect and Prospect." *JA* 112 (July): 31–36.
    1962   *Memoirs and Accounting Thoughts of George O. May*,
                edited by Paul Grady. New York: Ronald Press Co.

McAlister, W. M.
    1932   "Famous Failures and Infamous Swindles." *CPA* 12 (Sep-
                tember): 521–525.

McKinneley, I. I.
    1970a   "Patterns of International Accounting." *Management Ac-
                counting* 48 (June): 219–222.

1970b   "Accounting Problems for the International Enterprise." *Management Accounting* 48 (August): 299–301.

McLaren, Norman
1937   "The Influence of Federal Taxation upon Accountancy." *JA* 64 (December): 426–439.

Montgomery, Robert H.
1905   "Professional Standards—A Plea for Co-operation among Accountants." *JA* 1 (November): 28–39.
1906   Letter to the editor, *JA* 1 (January): 246–247.
1936   "Accounting Methods Must be Revised to Meet the Increasing Burden of Taxation." *JA* 62 (August): 90–102.
1937   "What Have We Done, and How?" *JA* 64 (November): 333–349.
1939   *Fifty Years of Accountancy.* New York: Ronald Press. Privately printed.

Moonitz, Maurice
1942   "The Entity Approach to Consolidated Statements." *AR* 17 (July): 236–242.
1961   *The Basic Postulates of Accounting.* Accounting Research Study 1. New York: AICPA.
1963   "Why Do We Need Postulates and Principles?" *JA* 116 (December): 42–46.
1970   "Three Contributions to the Development of Accounting Principles Prior to 1930." *Journal of Accounting Research* 8 (Spring): 145–155.

Moonitz, Maurice, and Littleton, A. C., editors
1965   *Significant Accountant Essays.* Englewood Cliffs, N.J.: Prentice-Hall, Inc.

Moonitz, Maurice, and Sprouse, Robert T.
1962   *A Tentative Set of Broad Accounting Principles for Business Enterprises.* Accounting Research Study 3. New York: AICPA.

Morgan, Robert A.
1967   "The Multinational Enterprise and Its Accounting Needs." *International Journal of Accounting Education and Research* 3 (Fall): 21–28.

Morrison, William D.
1935   "One National Organization." *CPA* 15 (October): 579–580.

Mosich, A. N.
1965   "Impact of Merger Accounting on Post-Merger Financial Reports." *Management Accounting* 47 (December): 21–28.

Mulligan, Richard G.
    1970   "An Alternative to Uniform Cost Accounting Standards."
                Management Accounting 51 (April): 18–20; 23.

Murphy, Mary E.
    1961   "The British Accounting Tradition In America," *JA* 111,
                April, 54–63.

National Association of Accountants
                50 Years, 1919–1969. New York: National Association of
                Accountants.

Needham, James J.
    1971a   "Remarks" before the Illinois Society of Certified Public
                Accountants, April 1, at Chicago. From the SEC files.
    1971b   "Financial Imperatives for the 70's: Restructuring the
                Securities Industry." Speech before the annual AMA Fi-
                nance Conference, May 17, at New York. From NEWS-
                SEC.
    1972   "Temporizing, the Major Cause of Uncertainty in the
                Financial Community." Speech before the New York
                Chamber of Commerce, March 2, at New York. From
                NEWS-SEC.

Nelson, Ralph Lowell
    1959   *Merger Movements in American Industry, 1895–1956.*
                Study by National Board of Economic Research. Princeton:
                Princeton University Press.

Nerlove, S. H.
    1930   "Insiders and Corporate Income Streams." *AR* 5 (June):
                153–156.

New York Times
    1961   "Mergers Create Financial Magic." (April, 30): sec. 3:
                1–13.

Nissley, Warren W.
    1935   "Education for Professional Accountants." *JA* 59 (Jan-
                uary): 12–27.
    1937   "The Future of Professional Accountancy." *JA* 63 (Feb-
                ruary): 99–115.

Owens, Hugh F.
    1971   "The SEC and the Accounting Profession." Address be-
                fore Accounting and Auditing Symposium of the Texas
                Society of CPAs, May 25, at Houston. From the SEC files
    1972   "The Securities Industry and the Changing Regulatory
                Scene." Address given to the Mid-Atlantic District Securi-
                ties Industry Association, October 27, at Hot Springs, Va.
                From NEWS-SEC.

Parrish, Michael E.
    1970   *Securities Regulation and the New Deal.* New Haven: Yale University Press.

Parsons, Talcott
    1954   "The Professions and Social Structure." In *Essays in Sociological Theory,* rev. ed. Glencoe, Ill.: The Free Press.
            "A Sociologist Looks at the Legal Profession." In *Essays in Sociological Theory,* rev. ed. Glencoe, Ill.: The Free Press.
    1971   *The System of Modern Societies.* Englewod Cliffs, N.J.: Prentice-Hall, Inc.

Parsons, Talcott, and Smesler, Neil J.
    1956   *Economy and Society.* Paperback ed. New York: The Free Press, 1965.

Paton, William A.
    1934   "Shortcomings of Present-Day Financial Statements." *JA* 57 (February): 108–132.
    1938   "Comments on 'A Statement of Accounting Principles.'" *JA* 65 (March): 196–207.
    1971   "Earmarks of a Profession—and the APB." *JA* 131 (January): 37–45.

Payne, Robert E.
    1935   "The Effect of Recent Laws on Accountancy." *AR* 10 (March): 84–95.

Peisch, Herman, C. J.
    1932   "Accountancy on Trial." *CPA* 12 (December): 706–707.

Peloubet, Maurice
    1961   "Is Further Uniformity Desirable or Possible?" *JA* 111 (April): 35–41.

Phillips, Lawrence C.
    1965   "Accounting for Business Combinations." *AR* 40 (April): 377–381.

Pilcher, Dalton J.
    1935   "Certain Historic Accounting Facts and Trends." *CPA* 15 (March): 134–142.

Pines, J. Arnold
    1965   "The Securities and Exchange Commission and Accounting Principles." *Law and Contemporary Problems* (Autumn): 727–751.

Powell, Weldon
    1964   "The Development of Accounting Principles." *JA* 118 (September): 37–43.
    1969   "Generally Accepted Accounting Principles in the United

States." In *Readings in Inernational Accounting*, edited
by Berg, Kenneth B., Mueller, Gerhard G., and Walker,
Lauren M., Boston: Houghton Mifflin Co. First printed in
1963.

Preinreich, Gabriel A. D.
1937   "Goodwill in Accountancy." *JA* 64 (July): 28–50.

Preston, Lee E.
1970   "A Probabilistic Approach to Conglomerate Mergers." *St.
John's Law Review* 44 (special ed., spring): 341–355.
1973   "Giant Firms, Large Mergers and Concentration: Patterns
and Policy Alternatives, 1954–68." *Industrial Organization
Review* 1 (November): 35–46.

Prosser, William L.
1964   *Handbook of the Law of Torts*, 3rd. ed. St. Paul, Minn.:
West Publishing Co.

Randall, Robert F.
1974a   "FASB: The Year For Decisions." *Management Accounting* 57 (January): 55–59.
1974b   "CASB: Developing Standards for Cost Accounting."
Management Accounting 57 (April): 46–49.

Reid, Samuel R.
1971   "A Reply to the Weston/Mansinghka Criticisms Dealing
with Conglomerate Mergers." *Journal of Finance* 26 (September): 937–946.

Reiling, Henry B., and Burton, John C.
1972   "Financial Statements: Signposts As Well As Milestones."
Harvard Business Review 50 (November–December): 45–
54.

Reiling, Henry B., and Taussig, Russell A.
1970   "Recent Liability Cases—Implications for Accountants."
JA 130 (September): 39–53.

Ripley, William Z.
1926   "From Main Street to Wall Street." *The Atlantic Monthly*
137 (January): 94–112.
          "Stop, Look, Listen! The Shareholder's Right to Adequate
Information." *The Atlantic Monthly* 138 (September):
389–399.
          "More Light!—And Power Too." *The Atlantic Monthly* 138
(November): 667–687.
1927   *Main Street and Wall Street*. Boston: Little, Brown and
Co.

Rooney, Robert F.
1969   "Discussion and Comments on Papers by Demsetz and
Benston." In *Economic Policy and the Regulation of Corporate Securities*, edited by Henry G. Manne, Washington,

D.C., American Enterprice Institute for Public Policy Research, pp. 106–115.

Roosevelt, Franklin D.
1933 Message to Congress, March 29. *Congressional Record* 77, part 1.

Rorem, Rufus C.
1928 "Social Control through Accounts." *AR* 3 (September): 261–268.

Ross, Howard
1966 *The Elusive Art of Accounting.* New York: Ronald Press Co.

Rowe, D. A.
1971 "Features of Accounting for International Operations." *The Accountant* 165 (London) (July 29): 156–160.

Salmonson, R. F.
1964 "Reporting Earnings after an Acquisition." *JA* 117 (March): 51–54.

Sanders, Thomas H.
1934 "Reports to Stockholders." *AR* 9 (September): 201–219.

1935a "The Development of Accounting Principles." *AR* 10 (March): 100–106.

1935b "Corporate Information Required by Federal Security Legislation." *The New York Certified Public Accountant* 5 (April): 9–22.

1936a "Influence of the Securities and Exchange Commission upon Accounting Principles." *AR* 11 (March): 66–74.

1936b "Review of *Twenty-Five Years of Accounting Responsibility,* by G. O. May." AR 11 (December): 390–392.

1937 "Accounting Aspects of the Securities Act." *Law and Contemporary Problems* 4 (April): 191–217.

Sapienza, Samuel R.
1961 "Distinguishing Between Purchase and Pooling." *JA* 3 (June): 35–40.

1962 "Pooling Theory and Practice in Business Combinations." *AR* 37 (April): 263–278.

1963 "Business Combinations—A Case Study." *AR* 38 (January): 91–101.

1964 "Business Combinations and Enterprise Evaluation." *Journal of Accounting Research* 2 (Spring): 50–66.

Savoie, Leonard M.
1968 "Controversy over Accounting Principles Board Opinions." *JA* 125 (January): 37–41.

1974 "The Destruction of the Accounting Principles Board." *The CPA Journal* 44 (February): 11–12.

Schlesinger, Arthur M., Jr.
   1958   *The Coming of the New Deal.* Boston: Houghton Mifflin Co.

Schlesinger, Hymen
   1931   "The Liability of Accountants." *CPA* 11 (March): 73–75.

Schoenfeld, Hans-Martin
   1969   "Some Special Accounting Problems of Multinational Enterprises." *Management International Review* 9 (Germany): 3–11.

Schoenhaut, Arthur
   1973   "CASB—Past, Present and Future." *Financial Executive* XLI (September): pp. 28–37.

Scott, Donald A.
   1970   "The Corporate Lawyer and Generally Accepted Accounting Principles." *The Business Lawyer* 26 (November): 199–206.

Scott, DR
   1939a   "Accounting Principles and Cost Accounting." *JA* 67 (January): 70–76.
   1939b   "Responsibilties of Accountants in a Changing Economy." *AR* 14 (December): 396–401.

Scovill, H. T.
   1941   "Reflection of Twenty-Five Years in the American Accounting Association." *AR* 16 (June): 167–175.

Securities and Exchange Commission
   1939   Accounting Series Release 19. *In the Matter of McKesson & Robbins, Inc.* Summary of Findings and Conclusions.

Seidman, J. S.
   1959   "What is the Future of the Accounting Profession?" *JA* 107 (March): 29–36.

Shank, John K.
   1974   "The Pursuit of Accounting Standards—Whither and Whence." *California CPA Quarterly* 41 (April): 59–62.

Shank, John K., and Calfee, John B. Jr.
   1973   "Case of the Fuqua Forecast." *Harvard Business Review* 51 (November–December): 1–9.

Smelser, Neil J.
   1968   *Essays in Sociological Explanation.* Englewood Cliffs, N.J.: Prentice-Hall, Inc.
   1962   *Theory of Collective Behavior.* New York: The Free Press.

Smith, C. Aubrey
   1935   "Accounting Practice under the Securities and Exchange Commission." *AR* 10 (December): 325–332.

Smith, Frank P.
    1936   "Stock Exchange Listing Requirements and Publicity." *AR* 11 (March): 35–42.
    1937   "Accounting Requirements of Stock Exchanges." *AR* 12 (June): 145–153.

Smith, St. Elmo V.
    1967   "Accounting Problems Peculiar to Multinational Businesses." *Canadian Chartered Accountant* 91 (Toronto) (December): 420–424.

Sommer, A. A., Jr.
    1969   "Discussion and Comments on Papers by Demsetz and Benston." In *Economic Policy and the Regulation of Corporate Securities*, edited by Henry G. Manne, pp. 88–106. Washington, D.C.: American Enterprise Institute for Public Research.
    1970   "Survey of Accounting Developments in the '60's: What's Ahead in the '70's." *The Business Lawyer* 26 (November): 207–214.
    1974a   "The SEC and the FASB: Their Roles." Speech prepared for Accounting Day, University of Washington, January 21, at Seattle. From NEWS-SEC.
    1974b   "The Emerging Responsibilities of the Securities Lawyer." Speech before the Banking Corporation and Business Law Section, New York State Bar Association, January 24, at New York. From NEWS-SEC.
    1974c   "Directors and the Federal Securities Laws." Speech before the Colorado Association of Corporate Counsel, February 21, at Denver. From NEWS-SEC.
    1974d   "Differential Disclosure: To Each His Own." Speech delivered at Second Emanuel Saxe Distinguished Accounting Lecture, Baruch College, March 19, at New York. From NEWS-SEC.
    1974e   "Professional Responsibility: The Public Client." Speech before the Columbus Chapter of Certified Public Accountants and Columbus Bar Association, March 20, at Columbus, Ohio. From NEWS-SEC.

Sorg, H. Theodore
    1934   "The Legal Relationship of the Accountant to the Investor." *CPA* 14 (June): 345–352.

Spacek, Leonard
    1958   "The Need For An Accounting Court." *AR* 33 (July): 368–379.
    1961   "Are Accounting Principles Generally Accepted?" *JA* 111 (April): 41–46.

1964a   "A Suggested Solution to the Principles Dilemma." *AR* 39 (April): 275–284.

1964b   "The Treatment of Goodwill in the Corporate Balance Sheet." *JA* 117 (February): 35–40.

1969   "Umpiring the Earnings Per Share Results." *Management Accounting* 50 (March): 9–27.

1973   *A Search for Fairness in Financial Reporting to the Public,* vol. 1, 1969; vol. 2, 1973. Chicago: Arthur Andersen and Co.

Springer, Durand W.

1929   "Why Regulatory Legislation?" *CPA* 9 (May): 137–139.

1932   "Reconstruction Finance Corporation." *CPA* 12 (March): 132–133.

1934   "The Securities Act of 1933." *CPA* 14 (February): 69–71.

1936   "Regulatory Legislation." *CPA* 16 (September): 522–531.

Sprouse, Robert T.

1969   "Diversified Views about Diversified Companies." *Journal of Accounting Research* 7 (Spring): 137–159.

Stamp, Edward

1972   "Uniformity in International Accounting Standards." *JA* 133 (April): 64–67.

Starkey, Rodney F.

1934   "Practice under the Securities Act of 1933 and the Securities Exchange Act of 1934—From the Viewpoint of the Accountants." *JA* 58 (December): 431–447.

1936   "Importance of Flexibility in Accounting Principles and Procedures." *New York Certified Public Accountant* 6 (October): 27–31.

1937   "Cooperation with the SEC." *JA* 63 (June): 434–443. A report, dated April 12, 1937, of the AIA Special Committee on Cooperation with SEC.

Stegman, Walter A.

1929   "Accounting—Its Relation to the Stock Exchange." *CPA* 9 (December): 361–362.

Stempf, Victor H.

1937   "How the SEC Affects Your Pocketbook." *CPA* 17 (December): 2–6.

1938   "The SEC and the Accountant." *The New York Certified Public Accountant* 8 (April): 12–16.

1939   "Accounting in the Public Interest." *JA* 68 (July): 23–28.

1940   "Published Financial Statements." *The New York Certified Public Accountant* 10 (June): 523–531.

Sterrett, J. E.
    1905   "Education and Training of a Certified Public Account-ant." *JA* 1 (November): 1–15.

Stewart, Andrew
    1938   "Accountancy and Regulatory Bodies in the United States." *JA* 65 (January): 33–60.
    1941   "The Work of the Professional Accountant under the Securities Act of 1933." *The New York Certified Public Accountant* 11 (May): 459–466.

Stigler, George J.
    1964   "Public Regulation of the Securities Market." *The Journal of Business* 37 (April): 117–142.

Storey, Reed K.
    1964   "Accounting Principles: AAA and AICPA." *JA* 117 (June): 47–55.

Study Group on Business Income, Report of
    1952   *Changing Concepts of Business Income.* New York: The MacMillan Co.

Suton, Francis X.; Harris, Seymour E.; Kaysen, Carl; and Tobin, James
    1956   *The American Business Creed.* Paperback ed. New York: Schocken Boks, 1962.

Sweet, Homer N.
    1940   "Amended Requirements for Financial Statements Pre-scribed by the Securities and Exchange Commission on Regulation S-X." *JA* 69 (March): 167–174.

Taylor, J. R.
    1941   "Some Antecedents of the Securities and Exchange Com-mission." *AR* 16 (June): 188–196.

Thurber, James
    1939   *Fables for Our Time.* Reprint ed. New York: Blue Rib-bon Books, 1943.

Turner, Donald F.
    1965   "Conglomerate Mergers and Section 7 of the Clayton Act." *Harvard Law Review* 78 (May): 1313–1395.
    1969   "The Scope of Antitrust and Other Economic Regulatory Policies." *Harvard Law Review* 82 (April): 1207–1244.

van Pelt, John V. III
    1972a   "A Management Reaction to the Wheat Report on Ac-counting Principles." *The CPA Journal* 42 (October): 819–822.

1972b   "The Future of Accepted Accounting Principles." *Management Accounting* 53 (March): 15–20.

Wagner, Edwin H.
1937   "A United Profession and Its Current Problems." *CPA* 17 (June): 15–20.

Wall Street Journal
1971   "Former SEC Chairman Budge Is Named President, Chief of 6 IDS Mutual Funds." (January 15): 5.
"Nixon as Anticipated, Nominates Casey, A New York Lawyer, to be SEC Chairman." (February 3): 4.
"Nominee to Head SEC Was Sued for Breach of Securities Laws." (February 12): 1.
"Hearings on Casey's Qualifications to Head SEC to Be Reopened by Senate Committee." (March 3): 2.
"SEC Commissioner Backs an Agency Run by One Administrator; Needham Agrees with Nixon That Move Should Help Effectiveness and Efficiency." (April 2): 2.
"Casey at the Bat: SEC Chief Surprises Many by Taking Tough Stand on Wall Street; He Budges Sluggish Agency to Require Added Data, Cut Costs for Investors; 'Now Let's Go Give 'em Hell.'" (April 12): 1.
"Casey Says SEC Must Improve Methods to Keep Investing Public Better Informed." (May 6): 2.

1972   "Casey Warns Accountants of SEC Action If Industry Doesn't Upgrade Standards." (October 3): 3.
"SEC Aide Tells Auditors Not to Let Fear of Suits Curb Review of Firms' Reports." (December 20): 9.

1973   "New Accounting Board's Last 2 Seats Filled by Rivals on Key Issue; 27 Advisers Named." (March 1): 6.
"New Accounting Board Selects 7 Topics For Initial Agenda, Shunning Oil-Gas Issue." (April 5): 7.
"Fiscal Standards Board Fills 4 of 6 Seats by Naming 3 Accountants and a Professor." (January 23): 7.
"Panel Aims to Unify Accounting Methods Across Globe, Sees Strong Effect by '83." (July 2): 10.
"Accounting Panel Votes to Approve New Rules for Land Developers—Board Formally Adopts by 15 to 3 the Controversial Standards; SEC to Reserve Its Decision." (January 10): 12.

1974   "Multinational Firms Resist the Treasury in Major Tax Battle." (September 13): 1.
"Ernst & Ernst Case Is Ordered to Trial Over Accountants' Duty to Detect Fraud.' (September 19): 4.

Watson, Albert J.
1933   "Compulsory Audits by Public Accountants." *JA* 56 (October): 250–260.
1935   "Practice under the Securities Exchange Act." *JA* 59 (June): 434–445.

Watson, Deneen A.
1933   "The Securities Act of 1933 from the Viewpoint of the State Securities Commissioner." *CPA* 13 (October): 599–604.

Watt, George C.
1970   "Pooling of Interest Concept Validated." *The Business Lawyer* 26 (November): 215–219.

Weidenhammer, Robert
1933   "The Accountant and the Securities Act." *AR* 8 (December): 272–278.

Wellington, C. Oliver
1934   "Accountants and the Recovery Act." *JA* 57 (January): 43–54.

Werntz, William W.
1940   "The Government's Responsibility for the Regulation of Accounting Reports." Paper delivered before Bicentennial Conference of the University of Pennsylvania, September 17. In *Studies in Economics and Industrial Relations*. Philadelphia: University of Pennsylvania, 1941.

Weston, J. Fred, and Mansinghka, Surenda K.
1971   "Tests of the Efficiency Performance of Conglomerate Firms." *Journal of Finance* 26 (September): 919–936.

Wheat Report
1968   *Disclosure to Investors—A Reappraisal of Federal Administrative Policies Under the '33 and '34 Acts.* New York: Commerce Clearing House, Inc. See also "The Disclosure Policy Study of the SEC." *The Business Lawyer* 24 (November): 33–42.

Wiebe, Robert H.
1967   *The Search for Order, 1877–1920.* New York: Hill & Wang.

Wildman, John R.
1931   "The Accountant's Liability for Failure to Discover Fraud." *CPA* 11 (January): 3–4; 26–27.

Wilkinson, George
1928a   "The Genesis of the C.P.A. Movement," part 1. *CPA* 8 (September): 261–285.

1928b   "The Genesis of the C.P.A. Movement," part 2. *CPA* 8 (November): 297–301.

Woodroofe, Ernest
1973   "The Multinational Company: Solving Social Problems." *Financial Executive* 41 (December): 62–70.

Wyatt, Arthur R.
1963   *Accounting for Business Combinations.* Accounting Research Study 5. New York: American Institute of Certified Public Accountants.
1965   "Accounting for Business Combinations: What Next?" *AR* 40 (July): 527–535.
1970   "Accounting Principles and Conglomerate Growth." Arthur Andersen & Co., Subject File AD 7221—Item 9.

Yamey, Basil S.
1964   "Accounting and the Rise of Capitalism: Further Notes on a Theme by Sombart." *Journal of Accounting Research* 2 (Autumn): 117–136.

Zeff, Stephen A.
1966   *The American Accounting Association: Its First 50 Years.* New York: American Accounting Association.
1971   *Forging Accounting Principles in Five Countries: A History and an Analysis of Trends.* Champaign, Ill.: Stipes Publishing Co.

Index